The market does not spontaneously generate democratic or participatory economic institutions. This book asks whether a modern, efficient economy can be rendered democratically accountable and, if so, what strategic changes might be required to regulate the market-mediated interaction of economic agents. The contributors bring contemporary microeconomic theory to bear on a range of related issues, including the relationship between democratic firms and efficiency in market economies; incentives and the relative merits of various forms of internal democratic decision-making; and the effects of democratically accountable firms on innovation, saving, investment, and on the informational and disciplining aspects of markets. Various approaches to the study of economic interaction (game theory, transactions' cost analysis, social choice theory, rent-seeking, etc.) are considered in an attempt to understand the relationship between power and efficiency in market economies.

Markets and democracy: participation, accountability and efficiency

Markets and democracy: participation, accountability and efficiency

Edited by

SAMUEL BOWLES

Department of Economics,
University of Massachusetts, Amherst

HERBERT GINTIS

Department of Economics,
University of Massachusetts, Amherst

and

BO GUSTAFSSON

Department of Economic History, University of Uppsala
and Director, Swedish Collegium for Advanced Studies in Social Sciences

CAMBRIDGE
UNIVERSITY PRESS

Published by the Press Syndicate of the University of Cambridge
The Pitt Building, Trumpington Street, Cambridge CB2 1RP
40 West 20th Street, New York, NY 10011-4211, USA
10 Stamford Road, Oakleigh, Melbourne 3166, Australia

First published 1993
Reprinted 1994

Transferred to digital printing 1998

Printed in Great Britain by Biddles Short Run Books

A catalogue record of this book is available from the British Library

Library of Congress cataloguing-in-publication data

Markets and democracy: participation, accountability, and efficiency
edited by Samuel Bowles, Herbert Gintis, and Bo Gustafsson.
    p.   cm.
Includes bibliographical references and index.
ISBN 0 521 43223 5
1. Economic policy. I. Bowles, Samuel. II. Gintis, Herbert.
III. Gustafsson, Bo, 1931–
HD87.M2747 1993
338.9 – dc20 92–30242 CIP

ISBN 0 521 43223 5 hardback

Contents

Figures

Tables

Preface

If it were not for the hope that a scientific study of men's social actions may lead, not necessarily directly or immediately, but at some time and in some way, to practical results in social improvement, not a few students of these actions would regard the time devoted to their study as time misspent. (A. C. Pigou, *The Economics of Welfare*, 1932)

The contributions to this volume encompass a wide range of subjects pertaining to the analysis, understanding and evaluation of economic systems in regard to their structural as well as to their behavioral and evolutionary aspects: capitalism, socialism, institutions, rules, ownership, power, participation, agency, incentives, conflict, cooperation, productivity, and investment behavior. But it seems to me that the underlying common denominator is somehow related to the quest for an economic régime that is able to bring about an acceptable trade-off between efficiency and participation (democracy) in modern society. It may be held that this quest has seemingly been removed from the agenda as a consequence of the decline and fall of socialism in the world. But such a conclusion would certainly be premature, and for several reasons. In the first place, it is debatable whether the socioeconomic system in Eastern Europe had anything more in common with traditional images of socialism than collective ownership of the means of production and planning. Even these two attributes were very peculiarly designed in so far as the collective ownership implied, on the one hand, an almost total absence of links between individual effort and individual reward and, on the other, the rewards of collective effort were, to a great extent, appropriated by a totalitarian élite; while planning in effect had abolished all horizontal (market) relations between economic agents and was excessively centralized. Secondly, the historical conditions (economic development level, political culture, etc.) were so unfavorable for success that the attempt to skip capitalism and democracy was doomed to fail from the very start, a point which was made abundantly clear by prominent critics of Bolshevism even before the Revolution (by Plekhanov and others). Still, the demise of dictatorial state socialism in Eastern Europe has exposed socialist ambitions in general, and certain Marxist tenets in particular, to a rough test that hopefully has prepared the ground for a thorough reconsideration of the conditions for a viable modern economic system. One of those conditions is certainly the existence of markets for labor as well as for means of production and consumption, not only because of the information carrying capacity of markets but also, and more important, because of markets' capacity to structure incentives and cater for social needs (two points which were underestimated or even neglected in the early market-socialist tradition). Another condition is the existence of well-functioning property rights (private, cooperative and social) that permit economic agents to capture rewards from their efforts and thus give them incentives to make rational decisions and permit long-run time horizons in economic action. A third condition is that a viable modern economic system needs not only enterprises but also entrepreneurs, who are willing, capable and motivated to create new combinations (innovations) and not just react "correctly" to given information; without such entrepreneurs any economic system will at best remain stationary. A fourth condition is that a collectivism that goes too far and encroaches on fundamental individual interests is self-defeating and gives rise to extreme ego-centered behavior; from which it seems to follow that there must always be some appropriate mix of individual and collective decision-making in an efficient economic system. A final condition is that if collectivism (socialism) has a future, it must have some tangible positive importance in the everyday life of the individual members of society.

These considerations, as well as other, more far-reaching ones, have motivated some people to conclude that modern capitalism does after all represent the best possible option, particularly with regard to efficiency and participation. Since capitalism is outcompeting alternative economic régimes it must, so one argument goes, surely meet fundamental human requirements better than those alternative régimes. In this social-Darwinist argument, existence is taken as an indication of superiority. This may be true as far as it goes, but it does not go very far. It does not demonstrate any necessary and sufficient conditions for the assumed superiority; it implicitly assumes that capitalism as an economic system represents not only an *optimum optimorum* but also the final stage of human economic performance; and it sidesteps those problematic aspects of the capitalist system which now and again give rise to criticism as well as plans to reform it: first and foremost persistent unemployment; inequalities of wealth, income and power; a deficient supply of basic social services; and promotion of competitive as opposed to cooperative motives in the operation of society. If the argument includes a plea for some form of far-reaching welfare capitalism, which modifies negative effects and supplements what is missing, it carries much more force and cannot easily be disposed of. Still, even the most advanced cases of welfare capitalism, such as the Scandinavian varieties, have not solved the problems generated by ownership and control of firms leading to differences in capacities and opportunities for participating in those firms as well as in society (wealth, status, control over information, etc.). Furthermore, the experiences of the 1980s seem to show that the achievements of the welfare society are not permanent.

If we take a very long view, it may be maintained that modern history has been characterized by the parallel growth of democracy and efficient capitalism and this observation is not entirely wrong. In comparison with earlier modes of production capitalism did indeed foster a mobilization of initiative and participation on a mass scale and notwithstanding setbacks, democracy has increasingly gained ground since it was ushered in by the French and the American Revolutions. From this some people have concluded that democracy is caused by capitalism and that democracy cannot exist without a capitalist economic system. But correlation is not causation. It may well be that democracy has been victorious not because of but in spite of capitalism (defined as a market economy combined with wage labor) and that democracy and capitalism in fact are essentially incompatible. This was the traditional conservative view as expressed by Justice Story in the early nineteenth-century and almost echoed verbatim in the twentieth-century by the socialist Wigforss, Minister of Finance and architect of the Swedish welfare state, who wrote:

General suffrage is incompatible with a society divided into a small class of property owners and a large class of non-owners. Either the rich and the property owners will abolish the general suffrage; or the poor, by means of the suffrage, will appropriate a share of the wealth.

The fact that capitalist economic régimes have coexisted with very many different kinds of non-democratic political régimes should also make us careful in hypothesizing any necessary link between capitalism and democracy.

Ideally we are in search of an economic system, which combines the flexibility and vitality of modern capitalism with full employment, extensive participation in decision-making, a more egalitarian distribution of income and wealth in firms, and promotion of values oriented toward cooperation and solidarity between people. It may be argued that it is impossible to devise an economic system capable of meeting these requirements simultaneously, either because the goals are inherently contradictory (competition and innovative activity versus cooperation and solidarity, flexibility and change versus full employment, etc.); because some of them are contrary to "human nature as we know it" (Frank Knight, 1921); or because self-interest is the only reliable motivation in mass cooperation (Mandeville's dichotomy of "private vices–public benefits"). At the same time it is clear that different sub-sets of the social system do interact and that, in this interaction, the economic system occupies a crucial role. A society based on big private corporations owned by an élite fosters sets of behavior and values that differ from those found in a society based on some kind of generalized and collective property ownership. With this in mind, the task of devising an economic system capable of meeting several contradictory requirements remains. But at the same time it reduces itself to more manageable proportions and opens up a possibility of alternative solutions depending upon what precisely we want to achieve and what we want to take as constraints on the solution. It may well be, as suggested by several contributions to this volume, that labor-managed firms could become the core structure in the search for a superior solution to the trade-off between democracy and efficiency in the economic system. At the same time these contributions make abundantly clear that this institution does not represent a "magic wand" capable of solving all problems. On the one hand such firms may transform the relationship between labor and capital to the benefit of labor; they may extend democracy to one of the most important spheres of human existence – the working life; they may make income and wealth more egalitarian; they may foster values of cooperation and solidarity; and they may even be more productive than capitalist firms. On the other hand, they may be more reluctant to innovate and more resistant to structural change; they may be less inclined to make risky and long-term investments; and they may be less flexible in their reactions to market signals than capitalist firms. Other aspects of a labor-managed economy are still not much discussed. Will there be big differences in income and wealth levels between firms? Can we take for granted that the transformation of large sections of the working population into competitive entrepreneurs will not extend rather than diminish values focused on competition? And we know next to nothing about the stability properties of such a system.

Nonetheless, the contributions to this volume shed new and important light on many key aspects of labor-managed firms. Other contributions provide frames of reference for analyzing not only such firms but also economic systems in general. On the basis of this, Samuel Bowles and Herbert Gintis have made a bold attempt to outline the elements of a post-Walrasian political economy, which not only represents a challenge to the substance of the standard neoclassical model but also "appears likely to foster some fundamental rethinking about the structure of economic theory itself and its relationship to empirical studies and to neighboring disciplines."

It is up to the readers of this volume to judge if, how and to what extent its contributors have succeeded in this attempt. For my part it is quite clear that the thrust of argument in this volume is wholly in line with the objective of SCASSS, namely to promote advanced interdisciplinary study in new and progressing areas of social science research.

This volume has been made possible thanks to the generous financial support afforded the SCASSS research program, "Property Rights, Organizational Forms and Economic Behavior," by the Tercenary Fund of the National Bank of Sweden.

BO GUSTAFSSON
*Director of the Swedish Collegium for
Advanced Study in Social Sciences (SCASSS)*

1   Post-Walrasian political economy

SAMUEL BOWLES
HERBERT GINTIS

1   Introduction: new light on an old debate

What rules of the game render an economy participatory, fair, and democratically accountable without compromising efficiency and other valued social goals? The chapters in this volume explore this question from the vantage point of the revolution currently under way in microeconomic theory constituted by the abandonment of the simple world of Walrasian general equilibrium in favor of a richer world of imperfect information, incomplete markets, unenforceable contracts, costly transactions, and strategic interaction. In this new world people do not always do what they are supposed to do, nor do they always know all that they would like to know.[1]

By the "Walrasian model" we mean the strand of neoclassical economics that proceeds from the assumptions that preferences are exogenously determined, contracts are exogenously enforced, and economic agents have infinite information-processing capacity (Arrow and Debreu, 1954). Post-Walrasian economics, as we will see in this Introduction, departs from one or more of these assumptions, asserting instead the implications of bounded rationality (Heiner, Chapter 5 in this volume), the importance of incomplete or incompletely-enforceable contracts and the social origin of tastes, values, and commitments.

These new developments in microeconomic theory provide the basis for a rethinking of the old debate that pits economic planning against the market. Post-Walrasian microeconomic theory also allows us to add an essential missing term to the economists' "socialism versus capitalism" debate: namely, democracy (Weitzman, Chapter 18 in this volume). The last great round of this debate took place during the 1930s, with Oscar Lange and other advocates of socialist planning contesting the claims of Friedrich Hayek and other advocates of capitalist market allocations (Hayek, 1935; Lange and Taylor, 1938). The upshot of that debate, at least with the hindsight made possible by modern general equilibrium economics (Ortuño-Ortin, Roemer and Silvestre, Chapter 17 in this volume), was that in a world of fully informed and well-motivated agents a socialist planner could allocate resources as well as the market in the absence of market failures, and could do better in the presence of market failures arising from externalities and increasing returns to scale.

The socialist's victory in that round was ironic, for the debate was waged and won entirely on the terrain of the then-standard Walrasian model, often thought to be little more than an apologia for capitalism. Not surprisingly, the victory was short-lived. The advocates of capitalism quickly challenged the Walrasian model in favor of more plausible assumptions about information and motivation. Starting with Hayek's essay on information (Hayek, 1945) and extending through contemporary developments in the theory of public choice, mechanism design, and rent-seeking, the critics of socialism forged a compelling counter-argument: in a world of imperfect information and opportunistic agents, markets and private property provide advantageous if second-best solutions to problems of allocation.

But this conservative counter-attack has been only partly successful. For one thing, the problems of externalities and non-convexities raised in criticism of unregulated market allocations half a century ago are if anything even more pressing today, as environmental problems and global income inequality command increasing attention. For another, the new theoretical tools deployed in the defense of the free market reveal with microanalytic clarity what non-neoclassical economists have long maintained: pervasive market failures operate in the labor and financial markets of capitalist economies. The possibilities for a new economic order lie in understanding, exploiting, and correcting these market failures.

2   Post-Walrasian democratic theory

Just as the Walrasian model proved to be an inadequate framework for analysis of problems of allocation and distribution in the 1930s and subsequent decades, it is increasingly recognized as an impoverished approach to the questions of liberty and democratic accountability, especially as these are now raised in the context of economic organizations.

To see why this is true it is well to note the chasm that separates democratic concerns from the assumptions of the Walrasian model. First, the most influential advocates of economic democracy, from J. S. Mill to C. B. Mac-Pherson and Robert Dahl, have seen democracy not only as a decision-making process but as a type of society fostering particular paths of human development. In *Representative Government*, Mill asserted that:

The most important point of excellence which any form of government can possess is to promote the virtue and intelligence of the people themselves. The first question in respect to any political institutions is how far they tend to foster in the members of the community the various desirable qualities, moral and intellectual. (Mill, 1958:25)

Yet the Walrasian assumption of exogenous preferences, and indeed the limited concept of human agents captured in the notion of the utility function, precludes any such inquiry. A viable theory of democratic governance must encompass, or at least not exclude, questions surrounding the process of human development.

A second major concern in democratic theory is the legitimacy of institutions and the obedience to laws. Indeed it seemed obvious to nineteenth- and early twentieth-century democratic thinkers that adherence to law in a society of autonomous citizens was problematic and that democratic participation in the making of laws might enhance voluntary compliance and reduce enforcement costs. In what is perhaps the most frequently cited nineteenth-century text on democracy, *Democracy in America*, Alexis de Tocqueville wrote:

The American man of the people has conceived a high idea of political rights because he has some ... Whereas the corresponding man in Europe would be prejudiced against all authority, even the highest, the American uncomplainingly obeys the lowest of his officials. (Tocqueville, 1969:238)

While Tocqueville's description of the law-abiding citizen may be overdrawn, his conclusion is difficult to fault:

In a country with universal suffrage ... the moral strength of the government is greatly increased. (Tocqueville, 1969:238)

Tocqueville is not alone in asserting the superiority of democratic rule from the standpoint of *voluntary compliance to* and *enforcement of* laws and regulations. But the Walrasian paradigm provides no tools for the analysis of enforcement when compliance is contingent. Indeed, even the standard theoretical treatments of the democratic firm are flawed in this respect, taking no account of the possibly superior ability of a democratic system of firm governance to foster voluntary compliance and to reduce enforcement costs in the face of such common problems as free-riding. The underlying issue here is one of agency: what contribution can democracy make to the solution of problems that arise in social interactions in the presence of incentive incompatibilities that generate market failures or their analogues in the realm of governance?

A third concern of democratic theory that escapes scrutiny within the Walrasian paradigm is the stability and evolutionary viability of systems of democratic governance in a competitive environment. It has long been recognized that democratic organizations or states might be superior in a number of respects, but yet be unable to survive in military or economic competition with despotic organizations. Tocqueville, for example, thought that

For a democratic republic to survive without trouble in a European nation, it would be necessary for republics to be established in all the others at the same time. (Tocqueville, 1969:224)

Issues of evolutionary viability and stability are essential to the analysis not only of states but also of democratic firms in a competitive environment (Levine, Chapter 10 in this volume). But on these and related questions, the Walrasian paradigm is silent, for adequate treatment requires the analysis of multiple equilibria, the resulting path dependency of social outcomes and the evolutionary consequences of strong environmental effects (Dow; Moene and Wallerstein, Chapters 11 and 9 in this volume). These are excluded from the Walrasian paradigm, by practice if not by logic.

These deficiencies of the Walrasian approach have not, of course, deterred political scientists and economists from constructing what might be called a neoclassical economic theory of democracy. But if we are correct, it is precisely the abstraction from issues of human development, agency, and evolutionary dynamics – shortcomings endemic to the Walrasian model – that has sharply limited the major contributions in this area by Mancur Olson (1965), Anthony Downs (1957), and others. The same might be said of the neoclassical theory of economic democracy developed by Evsey Domar (1966), Benjamin Ward (1958), Jaroslav Vanek (1970), James Meade (1972a, 1972b, 1979), and subsequent writers.

In the remainder of this Introduction we will survey some of the central characteristics of the Walrasian model that have been challenged by the emerging post-Walrasian approach.

3   Walras' fiction

The Walrasian general equilibrium model is based on an artificially truncated concept of self-interested behavior, depicting a charming but utopian world in which conflicts abound but a promise is a promise. Abandoning this world will redirect economists to an older conception of our profession: political economy. Adam Smith and Karl Marx alike knew that a promise is not always a promise. The broad compass of their political economy embraced not only the analysis of simple acts of exchange, but issues of opportunism, changes in tastes and sentiments, collusion among agents, reciprocity, and altruism as well.

The formal codification of Smith's "invisible hand" in the economics of Leon Walras, and later of Kenneth Arrow and Gerard Debreu, was the result of a progressive paring away of what seemed extraneous or excessively complex. During the process, political economy became economics, and the analysis of the evolution of economic institutions fell to those operating on the periphery of the discipline.

The resulting model achieved a rigor that is at once its greatest appeal and the basis of the doubts now being raised concerning its adequacy. Indeed, not a decade after the Arrow–Debreu analysis swept the profession it had become clear that human actors with capacities and opportunities for strategic action were unrecognizable in the model. The *Homo economicus* of classical political economy had all but disappeared.

Adam Smith had exemplified the liberal philosophical tradition in his lively concern with human agency and its ramifications in economic theory. Walras, by contrast, had defined the pure science to which he aspired as the study of relationships among things, not people, and sought, with notable success, to eliminate the problem of agency from his purview. His device for accomplishing this – Walras' fiction – was the notion that human relationships in economics might be represented as if they were relationships among inputs and outputs:

Assuming equilibrium, we may even go so far as to abstract from entrepreneurs and simply consider the productive services as being, in a certain sense, exchanged directly for one another ... (Walras, 1954:225)

Beginning in the 1970s, with some notable precursors, economists in a variety of fields introduced a new *Homo economicus* to the profession. The new economic man is uncompromisingly thorough, and often less benign, in pursuing his objectives, although he may not conform to the classical axioms of choice under uncertainty, his objectives need not be purely self-regarding, and he may lack infinite information-processing ability. Not satisfied with calculating marginal rates of substitution while shopping for groceries, he now optimizes while deciding how hard to work for his employer, how truthfully to transmit information to others, and whether the benefits exceed the costs of defaulting on a loan. These troublesome activities of the new *Homo economicus* that, Oliver Williamson notes, include "the full set of *ex ante* and *ex post* efforts to lie, cheat, steal, mislead, disguise, obfuscate, feign, distort and confuse," (Williamson, 1985:51) are no less examples of sophisticated self-interest than buying cheap and selling dear, the bedrock behaviors of neoclassical economics.

Post-Walrasian approaches, including several chapters in this book, often deploy the tools of constrained optimization. This apparent continuity with the past has allowed the new models to be assimilated into the discipline with only token resistance. But in the process it has become clear that the Walrasian model is not premised on the informed fully rational optimizer that we had imagined, but rather on a stripped-down version of the rational agent. By taking optimizing more seriously, post-Walrasian approaches have inspired a revolution in economic thought fostering both new theoretical departures and alternative visions of capitalism.

The post-Walrasian approach differs from previous critiques of neoclassical economics by being an inside job. Earlier critics have largely questioned either its methodological precepts, such as the concept of instrumental action or of competitive equilibrium, or the empirical relevance of its standard assumptions concerning convexities and the absence of externalities. By contrast the post-Walrasian revival of political economy is based not on a rejection of neoclassical methodological precepts but rather on the systematic unravelling of their implications, and particularly on a relentless exploration of the concept of instrumental action.

4   Walrasian economics and post-Walrasian political economy

Let us review the representation of exchange relationships and economic institutions in the textbook neoclassical model. James Buchanan describes the *anonymity* of the market and the *uncontested nature of claims* by reference to "a roadside stand outside Blacksburg":

I do not know the fruit salesman personally, and I have no particular interest in his well-being. He reciprocates this attitude ... Yet the two of us are able to ... transact exchanges efficiently because both parties agree on the property rights relevant to them. (Buchanan, 1975:17)

Armen Alchian and Harold Demsetz capture the *absence of substantive hierarchy* in their provocative observation that the firm

has no power of fiat, no authority, no disciplinary action any different in the slightest degree from ordinary market contracting between any two people ... [The firm] can fire or sue, just as I can fire my grocer by stopping purchases from him, or sue him for delivering faulty products. (Alchian and Demsetz, 1972a:777)

Indeed, there is nothing in a Walrasian model suggesting that capital has even *formal* power over labor. As Paul Samuelson (1957:894) has noted, "in a perfectly competitive market it really doesn't matter who hires whom; so let labor hire capital." The result, noted long ago by Joseph Schumpeter, is a *decentralization of effective power to consumers*:

The people who direct business firms only execute what is prescribed for them by wants . . . Individuals have influence only in so far as they are consumers. (Schumpeter, 1911, 1942:21)

These views taken together imply an *apolitical conception of the economy*, as noted by Abba Lerner:

An economic transaction is a solved political problem. Economics has gained the title of queen of the social sciences by choosing *solved* political problems as its domain. (Lerner, 1972:259)

Through the post-Walrasian lens the economy looks considerably different.

4.1   Markets are disciplining mechanisms

Markets are both allocative, promoting movements to and along an exogenously defined production possibility frontier, and disciplinary, providing mechanisms for altering the supplies of inputs and production functions alike and thus shifting the production possibility frontier. Thus the labor market not only allocates workers to jobs, it also provides an environment governing the extraction of work from workers (Marglin, 1974; Gintis, 1976; Shapiro and Stiglitz, 1984; Bowles, 1985). Credit markets also exhibit non-Walrasian features: money is borrowed against a promise to repay that is not third-party-enforceable. Thus capital markets provide analogous disciplinary effects on the provision of risk-taking and other non-contractible behavior by borrowers (Stiglitz and Weiss, 1981; Gintis, 1989a , 1989b). Similar observations apply to goods markets (Telser, 1980; Klein and Leffler, 1981; Holmstrom, 1982; Gintis, 1989c). Just as allocative efficiency is a sensible normative standard for economic institutions, we may ask under what conditions markets will provide effective disciplining mechanisms.

4.2   Enforcement capacities are a determinant of institutional evolution

Like markets, all institutions of economic importance have consequences for the enforcement of claims arising from exchange. The evolution of institutions responds to the changing tasks and techniques of enforcement no less than to the changing techniques of production and demographic shifts stressed in standard neoclassical economic history.[2] Economic institutions may likewise have a substantial impact on endogenous enforcement environments (Skillman and Ryder, Chapter 13 in this volume). The effect of the welfare state on the distribution of income, for example, operates in part on the way in which it alters the functioning of the labor market as a worker-disciplining mechanism and not simply through the direct tax and transfer effects generally studied (Bowles and Gintis, 1982). These causal relations suggest that a major task of post-Walrasian theory is to develop a theory of institutional stability (Pagano, Chapter 6 in this volume) and institutional change (Hurwicz, Chapter 4 in this volume) where all outcomes diverge systematically from the Pareto-efficiency frontier of Walrasian economics.

4.3   Enforcement rents persist in competitive equilibrium

Non-Walrasian markets do not generally clear in equilibrium, since it is not generally optimal for an agent facing an endogenous enforcement problem to make an offer equivalent to a trading partner's next-best alternative. Should such an offer be accepted the partner will be indifferent to the continuation of the exchange, and there will be no means of using the threat of contract termination to enforce the *de facto* terms of exchange. As a result, some agents receive competitively determined rents that are not dissipated through the rent-seeking behavior of identical agents.

These rents include the cost of job loss in a non-clearing labor market. The cost of job loss is a rent, as it expresses the excess of the value of the worker's position over that of his or her next-best alternative. This rent is an enforcement rent, since the fear of losing it ensures the level of work intensity desired by the employer. Even where collateral is required as a condition of borrowing, credit markets may also exhibit enforcement rents: some agents would like to borrow at the going interest rate but cannot secure a loan. Identical agents who have secured loans enjoy enforcement rents, which generally afford the lender a credible threat, the termination of the loan, sufficient to induce borrower compliance with lender wishes.

4.4   Exchange is a strategic non-anonymous relationship

In a post-Walrasian exchange, it is often cost-minimizing to forgo the flexibility of spot contracting and to make and secure from one's trading partners long-term commitments (Goldberg, 1980; Lazear, 1981; Rebitzer, 1987). The durability of exchange relationships generally lends them a face-to-face quality involving sufficiently few actors to allow the reciprocal effects of one's actions to be taken into account in selecting a strategy. The paradigmatic form of economic action is not an agent intervening in a given external world (e.g., the behavior of a price-taking firm) but rather an interaction among two or more agents, mutually aware of the reciprocal effects of their actions.

4.5   *Exchanges are constitutive of economic agents*

Because exchanges are durable and personal each agent has an interest in altering the capacities and preferences of the other, and at least one has the possibility of so doing, given the long-term and non-anonymous nature of the exchange. Agents are not "endowed" with preferences that they then take to market. Rather, the transactions are constitutive of economic agents: agents make exchanges, but exchanges also make agents.[3] As a result exchanges have an evolutionary component, involving learning on the part of both agents. In this sense they are path-dependent.

These results are of course far from exhaustive. But they are suggestive of the radical shift in focus fostered by the post-Walrasian approach. Many of the contributions to this volume reflect just such a shift.

Conspicuously absent from the chapters in this volume is the traditional preoccupation with central planning versus the free market. With the unravelling of the economic systems of Eastern Europe and the Soviet Union, centrally planned non-market economies have joined unregulated laissez-faire economies as existing only in the realm of academic textbooks, and the theory of comparative economic systems must be reconceptualized accordingly (Meurs, Chapter 7 in this volume). The question, as Robert Dahl and Charles Lindblom (1953) have argued, is *how* and *when*, not *whether*, to regulate the market interactions of autonomous agents. Conspicuously present, by contrast, is the concern for participatory economic institutions, reflecting a heightened global awareness of the centrality of popular representation and civil liberties to social welfare, and the pressure to extend these from political to economic institutions.

Several chapters in this volume reflect this concern with participatory institutions by studying democracy at the lowest level of the economy: the democratic, worker-controlled, or worker-owned enterprise. The theory of enterprise democracy has been significantly deepened by the application of post-Walrasian concepts, but some of the fundamental problems remain open (Putterman, Chapter 8 in this volume). Ben-Ner (Chapter 12 in this volume) develops a general theory of cooperation and conflict in the enterprise that can be used to assess distinct distributions of control and rewards in capitalist and democratic firms. Nuti (Chapter 3 in this volume) argues that the form of worker compensation is central to the size and distribution of the firm's net revenues. Our own Chapter 2 in this volume suggests that a key to the viability of worker ownership and control of firms in a competitive economy is the design of credit institutions and rules of ownership that overcome the failures of capitalist credit markets. Ognedal (Chapter 15 in this volume) argues that a capitalist-style stock market with extensive worker ownership is generally infeasible and unstable. Fehr (Chapter 16 in this volume) suggests that under certain conditions a membership market for labor-managed firms, with appropriate legal structures, can produce efficient outcomes. Aoki (Chapter 14 in this volume) argues that a bank-centered financial system, in which worker control in the firm is balanced by the participation of an external creditor (the bank) in the firm's decision-making process can produce outcomes superior to either the pure capitalist or worker-controlled firm.

5   Varieties of post-Walrasian economics

To speak of a post-Walrasian "school" would, of course, be misleading. We may clarify some common dimensions and distinct variants of the approach by pinpointing the two most critical abstractions of the Walrasian paradigm: the exogenous enforcement axiom and the assumption that agents are exogenously determined. We can then generate three variants of post-Walrasian economics by selectively dropping the exogenous enforcement and exogenous agent assumptions (see Figure 1.1).

Economists dropping the external enforcement axiom alone model what may be termed *instrumental contested exchange*, as the activities of the agents are explained as instruments towards pre-formed objectives. Yet the exchange is "contested" in the sense that the contract is not third-party-enforceable at zero cost to the parties to the exchange. Efficiency wage theory (Solow, 1980; Akerlof and Yellen, 1986) and principal–agent analysis (Ross, 1973; Shavell, 1979), as well as transactions cost analysis (Williamson, 1985) are generally of this type.

Conversely, economists who retain the external enforcement axiom but reject the exogeneity of preferences – one thinks of Sen (1977), for example – work with a model of *constitutive contractual exchange*. Here the exchange process constitutes the parties to the exchange, but the claims arising from the exchange need not be endogenously enforced. Lastly, those who drop both Walrasian assumptions, taking both the agents' behavioral rules and the enforcement of claims as endogenous model a *constitutive contested exchange*.

It may be thought that the issue of the constitution of the actors in economic theory is independent of that of endogenous enforcement. As we have stressed, by accepting the Walrasian model's methodological individualism and objecting only to its artificially truncated notion of self-interest, much of the post-Walrasian critique is indeed an "inside job." Nonetheless the contested nature of social relations among economic agents in post-Walrasian approaches undermines the traditional asocial conception of the economic agent. Thus the

Enforcement of Claims

Constitution of Agents	Exogenous	Endogenous
Exogenous	Walrasian Exchange	Instrumental Contested Exchange
Endogenous	Constitutive–Contractual Exchange	Constitutive–Contested Exchange

Figure 1.1   Enforcement of claims

introduction of action dependent on custom, commitment, conformity, collusion, fairness, regret, and a host of additional complex human behaviors, into economic calculation is permitted, indeed encouraged, by such a deepening of the concept of self-interest. We have suggested that such behaviors can often be modeled through a constitutive conception of individual action (Bowles and Gintis, 1986). But however they are conceptualized, the stress on the explanatory power of such behaviors for economic theory (notably in Akerlof, 1984; Jones, 1984) may well be the beginning of a series of successful incursions of sociological issues into microeconomic theory. Douglass North's (1981) treatment of transactions' cost economics with endogenous ideology is another example, as is the emerging game-theoretic literature on cooperation (Taylor, 1987).

Whether in its transactions' cost, contested exchange, efficiency wage, or some other version, the post-Walrasian approach does more than challenge the substance of the standard neoclassical model; it appears likely to foster some fundamental rethinking about the structure of economic theory itself and its relationship to empirical studies and to neighboring disciplines. The new approach endows economic theory with a degree of open-endedness and path-dependency more characteristic of biology and geology than of physics, to which economists of the Walrasian persuasion have turned for a model of their intellectual pursuits. Faced with this open-endedness, and the proliferation of theoretically coherent results and multiplicity of equilibria generated by complex exchanges, economic theory may restore a more symbiotic relationship with economic history, experimental studies, and econometric testing, these latter being essential to the choice of correct postulates incapable of derivation from any plausible set of axiomatic first principles. The interdisciplinary focus of the research of some of the leading contributors to post-Walrasian economics is suggestive in this respect. No less important, the post-Walrasian paradigm is likely to expand the disciplinary boundaries of economics to include, as in the nineteenth-century, the selective study of law, history, sociology, psychology, and politics.

Notes

1. Varieties of what we term post-Walrasian microeconomics are surveyed in Stiglitz (1987), Akerlof and Yellen (1986) and Bowles and Gintis (1990).
2. Here Douglass North's work (1990b) represents the post-Walrasian approach to the theory of economic evolution, while his earlier work with Thomas (1973) exemplifies the Walrasian tradition.
3. See Gintis (1972, 1974), Bowles and Gintis (1986: Chs.5. 6). In an earlier work (Bowles and Gintis, 1976) we analyzed the structural determinants of the constitution of agents.

Part I

Agency, incentives, and democratic accountability

2 The democratic firms: an agency-theoretic evaluation

SAMUEL BOWLES
HERBERT GINTIS

1 Introduction

Two fundamental reasons why firms should be owned and run democratically by their workers may be given. (1) *Accountability*: because the employment relationship involves the exercise of power, its governance ought on democratic grounds to be accountable to those most directly affected. (2) *Efficiency*: the democratic firm uses a lower level of inputs per unit of output than the analogous capitalist firm.[1]

Neither claim is obvious. If wage labor is a voluntary exchange in a competitive market, how can it exhibit a well-defined power relationship? If the democratic firm is more efficient, what prevents the capitalist from replicating it and reaping the profits? And if capitalist firms cannot capture the efficiencies of democratic firms, why do democratic firms not simply outcompete capitalist firms? In this chapter we will substantiate these claims through a comparative analysis of a capitalist and a democratic firm facing incentive incompatibilities concerning worker effort, managerial performance, and risk-taking.

Our approach differs from much of the literature on economic democracy in two ways. First, our focus on the agency problems associated with the regulation of the intensity of labor allows us to define precisely the exercise of power of employers over workers in a competitive capitalist economy, to advance specifically democratic criteria for the evaluation of the organization of the firm, and to demonstrate the superior efficiency characteristics of the democratic firm. Neither the political nor the efficiency argument, we think, can be sustained in a framework that ignores agency problems. Indeed, the elimination of agency problems by assumption, typical of much of the literature on worker self-management, reduces the case for the democratic firm to the curious claim that it would mimic the capitalist firm.

Second, by providing a unified treatment of agency problems arising in labor and capital markets, we can assess the strengths and weaknesses of the democratic firm more adequately than when labor and capital markets are treated in isolation. In particular, we can offer a coherent explanation of the failure of the democratic firm to outcompete its capitalist counterparts despite its efficiency advantages, and we can formally analyze what we believe to be the major weakness of the democratic firm: its tendency to engage in socially sub-optimal levels of risk-taking and innovation.

The basic model of the capitalist enterprise, presented in section 2, is based on the need for endogenous enforcement in the exchange of labor for a wage. Competitive labor and capital markets are assumed throughout. Faced with a non-contractible input, labor effort, the capitalist designs a monitoring system and wage offer to maximize profits, taking the workers' best response function as given.

In section 3 we use this model to substantiate our claim that in the capitalist–employment relationship the employer exercises power over the worker. We use the following conception of power: Agent A has power over agent B if, by imposing or threatening to impose sanctions on B, A is capable of affecting B's actions in ways that further A's interests, while B lacks this capacity with respect to A. Our model has the property that even under conditions of competitive equilibrium, the threat of dismissal will be used to induce the worker to act in ways favorable to the firm's interests. This power exists by virtue of the employer's location on the short side of a non-clearing market. We term this form of power *short-side power*.

The standard Walrasian model of competitive equilibrium not only eliminates power, but obliterates any efficiency differences between a capitalist and a democratic firm as well. As Dow (1986a), Drèze (1976, 1989) and others have pointed out, where market failures are absent and agents are unconstrained in their contracting, the two institutional forms are indistinguishable on efficiency grounds. Dow's conclusion is instructive:

The debate over labor management proposals should accordingly be refocused around the actual prevalence of various market failures and the relative strength and weakness of LMFs (labor-managed firms) and CMFs (capital-managed firms) in coping with them. (Dow, 1986:52)

Following Dow's suggestion, we begin our efficiency evaluation in section 4 by identifying agency problems that arise when markets are competitive but exogenous enforcement of claims cannot be assumed. Barring self-employment and self-finance, the firm is a team of producers facing two intrinsic agency problems: the regulation of work intensity and the treatment of risk, neither of which can generally be specified in a third-party-enforceable contract. We then ask how different firm types handle the market failures arising from the absence of exogenous enforcement in capital and labor markets.[2]

In section 5 we demonstrate that a redistribution of residual claimancy status over firm decision-making and control to a team of homogeneous risk-neutral workers results in efficiency gains for a firm facing a single agency problem: the determination of work intensity. This efficiency gain is an instance of a general agency principle: where the contribution of one party to an exchange is difficult to monitor, residual claimancy and control should *ceteris paribus* reside with this party. Where the transaction involves the exchange of an easy-to-monitor claim (e.g., money) for a difficult-to-monitor service (e.g., labor) the party supplying labor effort should, on efficiency grounds, be the residual claimant.

This rule extends to the case where the suppliers of labor are a team. In this case the argument entails that the design and control of the enforcement system should also reside with the team. Labor services in team production are typically more difficult to monitor than other inputs, including the task of monitoring itself. Because monitoring is generally not performed by teams it is far simpler to design incentive compatible contracts for monitors than for worker team members.

The capitalist firm allocates residual claimancy to the supplier of financial capital, the most easily monitored input of all. Yet this arrangement is clearly inferior to a firm in which residual claimancy is allocated in some degree to those performing the difficult-to-monitor services of risk-taking and work.

In section 6 we show that despite their enhanced capacity to handle the agency problems surrounding labor, democratic firms operate at a competitive disadvantage in a capitalist economy, facing higher capital costs than their capitalist counterparts because of the agency problems arising in capital markets and the limited wealth of workers. In section 7 we address the issue of sub-optimal risk-taking by the democratic firm. We conclude that the optimal ownership structure of the democratic firm, taking account of the tendency of external ownership to promote innovation and risk-taking, and of worker ownership to promote productive efficiency, involves a balance of internal and external ownership.

We have made a number of simplifying assumptions, two of which deserve comment as they favor the democratic firm. First, we have assumed that workers are identical, thus skirting a number of serious problems concerning the costs of democratic decision-making and even the possibility of a democratic aggregation of diverse preferences. Second, we have assumed the absence of agency problems concerning the task of monitoring itself. Effectively we assume either that monitoring uses only non-labor inputs or that contracts may be designed to eliminate the incentive incompatibilities associated with the performance of the work of monitoring. Thus there are, by assumption, no grounds for making the monitor a residual claimant.[3] Third, by abstracting from the democratic firm's decision concerning the quantity of labor hired, we avoid the issue much emphasized in the literature on the democratic firm (Ward, 1958; Domar, 1966). We do not consider this a serious deficiency in view of the fact that perverse labor hiring behavior of the worker-run firm in these models results from a poorly designed ownership structure of the firm (Drèze, 1989; Dow, 1986).

2   The employment relationship and contested exchange

Where third-party-enforcement of claims arising from an exchange is infeasible or excessively costly, the exchanging agents must themselves enforce their agreements. In this situation exchange becomes a strategic, non-anonymous relationship, in the sense that the terms of exchange depend on the power of the exchanging parties to enforce favorable outcomes, and are continually subject to *de facto* respecification.

Consider agent A who purchases a good or service from agent B. We call the exchange *contested* when B's good or service possesses an attribute that is valuable to A, is costly for B to provide, yet is not adequately specified in a costlessly enforceable contract. Where claim enforcement is costless to the exchanging parties we say that enforcement is *exogenous*. Exogenous enforcement fails when there is no relevant third party (as when A and B are sovereign states), when the contested attribute can be measured only imperfectly and at considerable cost (work effort, for example, or the degree of risk assumed by a firm's management), when the relevant evidence is not admissible in a court of law (such as an agent's eye-witness but unsubstantiated experience) when there is no possible means of redress (e.g., when the liable party is bankrupt), or when the nature of the contingencies concerning future states of the world relevant to the exchange precludes writing a fully specified contract. In such cases enforcement is *endogenous*: the *ex post* terms of exchange are determined by the monitoring and sanctioning mechanisms instituted by A to induce B to provide the desired level of the contested attribute.[4]

We shall here analyze only one, but an extremely important, endogenous enforcement mechanism: *contingent renewal*. Contingent renewal obtains when A elicits performance from B by promising to renew the contract in future periods if satisfied, and to terminate the contract if not. For instance a manager may promise an employee re-employment contingent upon satisfactory performance, or a lender may offer a borrower a short-term loan, with the promise of rolling over the loan contingent upon the borrower's prudent business behavior. The labor market is a case in point.

An employment relationship is established when, in return for a wage, the worker agrees to submit to the authority of the employer.[5] The worker's promise to bestow an adequate level of effort and care upon the tasks assigned, even if offered, is legally unenforceable. At the level of effort expected by management, work is subjectively costly for the worker to provide, valuable to the employer, and difficult to measure. The manager–worker relationship is thus a contested exchange. The endogenous enforcement mechanisms of the enterprise, not the state, are thus responsible for ensuring the delivery of any particular level of labor services per hour of labor time supplied.[6]

Let e represent the level of work effort provided by employee B, a member of a team of identical employees. B's employer, A, uses production $q = q(e)$, where q is output per worker hour. We assume effort is costly for B to provide above some minimal level $\bar{e}$. A knows that B will choose e in response to both the cost of supplying effort and the penalty that employer A imposes if dissatisfied with B's performance. For simplicity we assume the penalty A will impose is the non-renewal of the employment relationship – i.e., dismissing the worker.

We define the *value of employment* $v(w)$ as the discounted present value of the worker's future utility taking account of the probability that the worker will be dismissed. For obvious reasons it is an increasing function of the current wage rate w. We define the employee's *fallback position* z as the present value of future utility for a person not now holding a job – perhaps including the present value of a future stream of unemployment benefits, or the value of employment in some other job, or more likely a sequence of the two.

A's threat of dismissal is effective only if $v(w) > z$. We call $v(w) - z$, the difference between the value of employment and the fallback position z, the *employment rent*, or the *cost of job loss*.[7] Employment rents accorded to workers in labor markets are a particularly important case of the more general category – *enforcement rents* – that arise in all cases of competitively determined contested exchange under conditions of contingent renewal. We measure v and z in common units (utils or dollars).

Let $\bar{w}$ be the wage that equates $v(w)$ and z. This wage rate implies a zero employment rent, and hence induces the worker's freely-chosen effort level $\bar{e}$. We term $\bar{w}$ the *reservation wage* corresponding to the fallback position z. We assume A uses monitoring equipment to identify inadequate work performance. Thus B's performance will be found inadequate with a probability f that depends inversely on B's level of effort and positively on the amount m of resources per hour of labor employed devoted to monitoring: $f = f(e, m)$ with $f_e < 0$ for $m > 0$ and $f_m > 0$ for e less than the effort level desired by the employer. If the worker's effort level is found to be inadequate, B is dismissed; it is the link between effort and the likelihood of job retention that induces the B to provide effort above $\bar{e}$.[8]

To elicit greater effort than $\bar{e}$, A is obliged to offer a wage greater than $\bar{w}$, balancing the cost of paying the larger wage against profits associated with B's greater effort induced by a higher cost of job loss. Noting that the fallback position z is exogenous to the exchange, we may write B's *best response function*, which may also be called the *labor extraction function*, simply as $e = e(w, m)$. As depicted in Figure 2.1, the labor extraction function is the level of effort that maximizes B's present value of employment for each wage and level of monitoring, and is thus defined by $v_e = 0$, the first order condition for the worker's maximum problem.[9]

The iso-v function $\bar{v}^c$ in Figure 2.1 represents wage/effort combinations yielding the same present value of employment, taking account of the implied level of the employment rent and the relationship between the level of effort and the probability of job loss. By construction the iso-v functions are vertical where they intersect the worker's best response function (since the latter is defined by $v_e = 0$ and the slope of the iso-v function is $-v_w/v_e$). In the neighborhood of the competitive equilibrium, e increases with w at a diminishing rate ($e_w > 0, e_{ww} < 0$).

The comparative statics of the best response function are as follows. An increase in the disutility of labor shifts the best response function downward. An increase in the fallback position z (e.g., through a decline in the expected duration of unemployment) increases $\bar{w}$, and hence shifts $v(w)$ to the right. An increase in ease of monitoring will generally shift the best response function upwards, as will any other change that increases the probability that sub-standard work will be detected.[10]

For expositional purposes we abstract from the employer's choice of the level

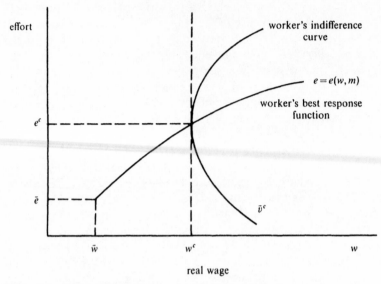

Figure 2.1   The worker's choice of optimal work effort

of monitoring. The equilibrium wage and effort level are then determined as follows. Agent A knows B's best response function $e(w, m)$. Once A selects the wage, the level of effort that will be performed is known with certainty. The profit-maximizing employer thus chooses the wage w to maximize $e/(w + m)$ (i.e., work done per unit of labor cost, where labor cost equals wage plus hourly monitoring expenses), subject to the worker's best response schedule $e = e(w, m)$. The solution to A's optimum problem is to set w such that $e_w = e/(w + m)$, or the marginal effect of a wage increase on effort equals the average effort provided per unit of labor cost. This solution yields the equilibrium effort level e^c and wage w^c, shown in Figure 2.2. The ray emanating from $-m$ on the w-axis is an employer iso-labor cost locus, with slope $e^c/(w^c + m)$. Steeper rays are obviously preferred, while the employer is indifferent to any point on a given ray, as each entails an identical labor cost.

The equilibrium effort/wage configuration (w^c, e^c) in this contested exchange results from A optimizing *given the best response function of B*. Two important results are apparent. First $e^c > \bar{e}$, so B provides a level of effort greater than would have been the case in the absence of the enforcement rent and the employer's monitoring systems; and second, $w^c > \bar{w}$, so B receives a wage greater than the reservation. The first result indicates that A's enforcement strategy is effective; the second indicates that the labor market does not clear in competitive equilibrium: workers holding jobs are not indifferent to losing them (because $v > z$), and there are identical workers who are involuntarily unemployed.

The existence of involuntarily unemployed workers may be inferred from the fact that were this not the case, the expected duration of unemployment would be zero and hence the fallback position z would equal the value of employment v,

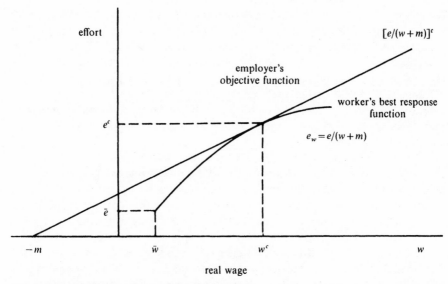

Figure 2.2 Optimal wages and labor intensity

since identical workers receive identical pay in equilibrium. That this unemployment persists in equilibrium follows from the fact that if B enjoys an employment rent, there must be another otherwise identical agent, C, who would be willing to fill B's position at the going, or even a lower, wage.[11] Moreover, should C promise A to work as hard as B for a lower wage, the offer will rightly be disbelieved and hence rejected by A. The reason is that other than their employment status, B and C are identical, A knows exactly how much effort is forthcoming for a given employment rent, and has already selected a cost-minimizing wage.[12]

As this argument hinges critically on the fact that the capitalist will choose a wage rate yielding a positive cost of job loss, and indeed that such a wage will also be the competitive equilibrium wage, we should explore whether this might not be the case. In making a wage offer the capitalist balances two effects working in opposite directions; an increase in the wage will enhance worker effort, raising output and firm revenues; but at the same time a wage increase is costly. The rule allowing the employer to find the wage which maximizes the firm's profits is: "start with the reservation wage and then increase the wage as long as the gains from increased effort are greater than the cost of the wage increase itself." As long as the gains to a wage increase exceed the direct costs of the increase when the capitalist is offering the reservation wage, a higher wage rate will be offered, and the cost of job loss will be positive, sustaining our argument.

If counter to our argument the capitalist were to offer the reservation wage the worker would do exactly as she pleases at work, putting in what we call the "whistle while you work" level of effort (or on-the-job leisure as the case may be). Under what conditions could this be optimal for the capitalist? Two suggest themselves. First, the worker could be *income-satiated*, so that increases or losses in income have little or no effect on her behavior; in this case the cost of job loss would be ineffective as a sanction. The result would be to flatten the worker's best response function $e(w)$, yielding an equilibrium at point $(\bar{w}, \bar{e})$ with the employer's first order condition taking the form of an inequality $e'(\bar{w}) < \bar{e}/\bar{w}$. Second, the worker could be *unalienated*, wishing voluntarily to work at such a high pace that little increase in the intensity of labor could be induced, even by powerful incentives. As in the case of income satiation, $e'(\bar{w}) < \bar{e}/\bar{w}$ so $(\bar{w}, \bar{e})$ is the equilibrium outcome.

While these two conditions leading to a zero cost of job loss and hence a clearing labor market are imaginable, they are not plausible as a general rule, and in any case the suggestion that the labor market clears is empirically contradicted not only by data on the unemployed but by evidence that the cost of job loss is indeed substantial for most workers. Further less direct confirmation is suggested by the fact that employers regularly hire supervisors to monitor the labor process; yet this expenditure would be irrational if the employer had already conceded that there existed no means of affecting the behavior of the employee, as would be the case for either the income-satiated or unalienated worker.

3   Short-side power and democratic accountability

Our first claim is that in a capitalist economy the employment relationship gives the employer power over the worker, that on democratic grounds this power should be democratically accountable, and that a workplace democracy is a means towards securing this democratic accountability.[13] We will focus on demonstrating the first part of the claim. But the second and third part deserve comment as well. We take it as axiomatic that the unaccountable exercise of power (in our sense, the ability to further one's interests by the asymmetric capacity to impose costly sanctions on others) is undemocratic and that a democratic society should implement institutional means of rendering the exercise of power accountable, to the extent that this is not precluded by other valued social objectives.[14] As the firm's decisions affect non-members, and because all feasible democratic decision rules (such as majority-voting) have shortcomings, the issue of accountability is difficult. We will here simply assume that the periodic democratic election of management by workers, coupled with the firm's regulation by a democratic state, provide serviceable, if flawed, mechanisms of accountability.

Consider our model of the employment relationship: does A (the employer) have power over B (the worker)? First, A may dismiss B, reducing B's present value to z. Hence A can apply sanctions to B.[15] Second, A can use sanctions to elicit a preferred level of effort from B, and thus to further A's interests. Finally, while B may be capable of applying sanctions to A (e.g., B may be able to burn down A's factory), B cannot use this capacity to induce A to choose a different wage, or to refrain from dismissing B should A desire to do so. Should B make A a take-it-or-leave-it offer to work at a higher than equilibrium wage, or should B

threaten to apply sanctions unless *A* offers a higher wage, *A* would simply reject the offer and hire another worker. *B* would have nothing to gain by carrying out her threat, so *B*'s threat is not credible. Thus *A* has power over *B*.

But is *A*'s threat to dismiss *B* credible? Would it be reasonable for *A* to carry it out, once having caught *B* not working hard enough? If all workers are identical, it might be objected that *A* will have no reason to replace *B* with *C*, who will behave no differently than *B*, and hence will not carry out the threat. But this reasoning is false, for given the team nature of production, inflicting the cost on *B* is essential to persuading other workers that they, too, will be fired if caught not working up to standard. Thus the only way to support the expectation by other workers that on-the-job leisure will be punished by job termination is by replacing *B* with an identical *C*. Thus the employer has reason to carry out the threat, which is therefore credible.

The manager's power is thus based on her favorable position in a non-clearing market. We say that the employer *A*, who can hire any number of workers and hence is not quantity-constrained, is on the *short side* of the market. Where excess supply exists – as in the labor market – the demand side is the short side, and conversely.[16] Suppliers of labor are on the *long side* of the market.

When contingent renewal is operative, the principle of *short-side power* holds: agents on the short side of the market have power over agents on the long side with whom they transact. Long-side agents are of two types: those such as *B* who succeed in finding an employer and receive a rent that constrains them to accept the employer's authority, and those such as *C* who fail to make a transaction and hence are rationed out of the market.

4   Market failures arising from contested exchange

Our efficiency evaluation of the democratic and capitalist firm will focus upon the ability of each to address the market failures associated with the two agency problems arising from the non-contractible aspects of work effort and risk-taking. We begin by identifying social optima with respect to work effort and risk-taking. Ideally, economic institutions would generate a structure of incentives such that potential investments would be evaluated on a risk-neutral basis and work intensity would be set such that the marginal productivity of a unit of labor effort would be equated to the marginal rate of substitution between effort and goods.[17]

Figure 2.3 illustrates these implied social optima. In Figure 2.3a, the output of goods per hour of labor is represented as a function of labor effort per hour, or $y = y(e)$, while utility of a representative worker depends on both effort and goods, or $u = u(y, e)$, giving rise to a set of indifference contours with slope u_e/u_y. Setting aside the determination of hours or labor, the optimal choice of an effort level is e^*, that is the level which implements the optimality condition mentioned above. Figure 2.3b represents the present value of the flow of future goods (for $e = e^*$) as a function of the level of risk taken in selecting investment projects or $Y = Y(f, e^*)$. Where the risk associated with distinct projects is uncorrelated,

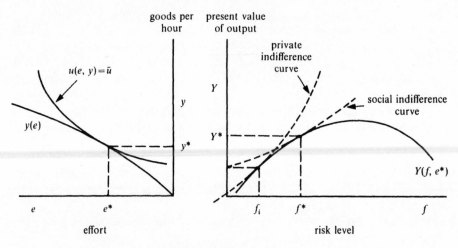

Figure 2.3   Socially optimal effort and risk-taking

and where the economy is large relative to the size of projects, the social optimum will simply be to maximize Y, yielding an optimal level of risk f^*.

Feasible institutions – democratic, capitalist, or other – generally fail to achieve these optima. With team production in virtually any institutional setting, feasible pay schemes insufficiently reward the contribution of individual team members. Whether residual claimants or not, team members have an incentive to free-ride by reducing effort.[18] On the other hand where contingent renewal is operative, workers have an individually compelling but socially irrational reason to work hard: they would rather somebody else be unemployed. The level of risk-taking may differ from the social optimum. Where risk-taking is assumed by borrowers who are limited liability residual claimants, the level of risk will generally exceed the social optimum, as they benefit from high payoffs and face limited losses in the case of failure. Conversely where risk-taking is assumed by agents who are not residual claimants but who must bear the costs in case of project failure (e.g., managers), the level of risk will generally be sub-optimal.

One's intuition is that in coping with the effort determination problem the democratic firm has significant advantages stemming from the residual claimancy status of workers, but that the inability of workers to diversify the labor and non-labor assets they have invested in worker ownership will tend to render the democratic firm unduly conservative in the face of risks. By contrast, the classic equity-financed capitalist firm insulates the risk-taking decision from workers, who hold the most concentrated assets, placing authority in the hands of managers who may be responsive to the more nearly risk-neutral objectives of residual claimant owners. But by assigning residual claimancy to the owners of capital, the capitalist firm is deprived of the superior work incentives available to the worker-owned democratic firm.

To make these intuitions precise, we shall formally identify the market failures resulting from the two agency problems under consideration. We first treat the wage and effort level, abstracting from the question of risk and assuming an exogenously determined level of monitoring. Where the capitalist firm chooses a profit-maximizing wage given the worker's reaction function, the resulting equilibrium wage and effort levels (w^c and e^c in Figure 2.2) are readily shown to be Pareto-inferior to some combination of a higher wage and a greater level of work effort. However the implied Pareto-improvements are infeasible for the capitalist firm as the superior outcomes lie above the worker's best response function.

This market failure is illustrated in Figure 2.4. We know that the capitalist is indifferent to points along the function $[e/(w + m)]^c$ while the worker is indifferent to points along the iso-present value function $\bar{v}^c$. These two functions must intersect at the equilibrium point, as the iso-present value function is (by the worker's first order conditions) vertical where it intersects the worker's best response function. There must necessarily exist, then, a lens of combinations of wage rates and effort levels superior to (w^c, e^c) from the standpoint of both the capitalist and the worker. These combinations are the shaded lens in Figure 2.4. While these Pareto-superior points are unattainable for the capitalist firm, we will see presently that at least some are feasible for the democratic firm.

A second market failure arises in the determination of the level of monitoring. The enforcement structure of the firm consists of two instruments, the monitoring system and the employment rent. Both are costly to the firm, but only monitoring entails the use of socially costly resources. Variations in the employment rent (effected by varying the wage rate) represent a redistribution of claims on output, but do not imply variations in the use of resources with positive social

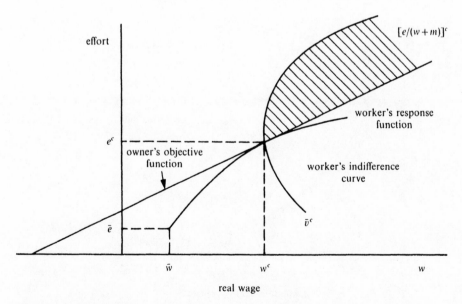

Figure 2.4   The lens of opportunity for efficiency gains

opportunity costs. Thus the selection of the cost-minimizing enforcement structure gives rise to a market failure based upon the divergence of private and social costs.

An analogy will make this reasoning clear. Imagine a trucking company choosing between a shorter route over a toll road or a somewhat longer route without tolls. The two prices in question are the operating cost per mile and the road tolls. The trucking company would treat the two prices as equivalent, perhaps avoiding use of the shorter toll road. But the toll does not represent a real social cost, while the operating costs on the truck (fuel, wear and tear) do. The choice of the longer road, like the choice of lower wages and more intense monitoring, is cost-minimizing but socially inefficient.[19]

This market failure may be illustrated in a model identical to that developed in section 2 except that the level of monitoring m is selected along with the wage w to maximize profits subject to the worker's best response function $e(m, w)$. In Figure 2.5, we represent the equilibrium enforcement structure of the firm (w^c, m^c) as a tangency between an iso-cost function and an iso-effort function derived from $e(w, m)$. The optimum lies along an expansion path defined by the first order condition $e_w = e_m$, assuming that monitoring inputs are measured in the same units as the wage, so that a unit change in each implies the same change in costs. Starting from the capitalist equilibrium (w^c, m^c) at point a, we can move up the iso-effort curve $e(w, m) = e^c$ to point a', at which efficiency has unambiguously increased: production is the same, while monitoring inputs have been reduced by $m^c - m'$, and could be reallocated to productive purposes. In addition, worker welfare has risen $(\bar{v}^{w+} > \bar{v}^w)$ because effort is unchanged, monitoring and hence dismissal probability is reduced, and wages are higher.

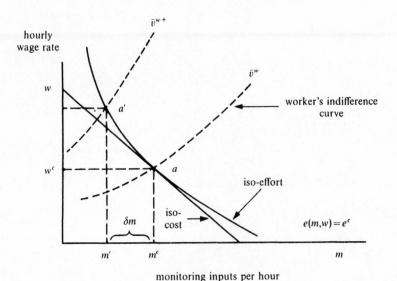

Figure 2.5 The inefficient trade-off of monitoring and wages

We can confirm this result by inspection of the worker's value of employment functions in Figure 2.5. These must be upward-rising near the capitalist equilibrium, as the slope of the iso-v function is $-v_m/v_w$, and v_m must be negative, since increased monitoring raises the probability of dismissal, while v_w is obviously positive. Hence a reduction in monitoring and an increase in the wage along a given iso-effort function must be welfare enhancing for the worker.[20]

Turning to the problem of risk-taking, we will identify two additional market failures. For simplicity we have taken effort levels as given. The first and most obvious market failure occurs when a residual claimant owner, highly diversified and hence risk-neutral, employs a manager to make decisions concerning the level of risk. The manager's assets (an income stream with the firm, a reputation) are highly concentrated in the firm and tied to its survival. The manager may thus prefer a lower level of risk-taking than the more diversified owner. To address this conflict of interest, the owner may offer the manager, in addition to a fixed salary, a share of firm profits, setting both such that the manager may expect to receive an income y_m in excess of her next-best alternative, thus giving the owner short-side power over the manager (other means of influencing the manager may of course be used, but we ignore them here).

The manager will thus choose the level of risk to maximize her present value of utility, taking account of the income on the job and the likelihood that overly conservative risk choices will result in the loss of the position. The manager's best response function is depicted in Figure 2.6, along with one of the manager's iso-value of employment functions, which like the analogous worker's iso-value

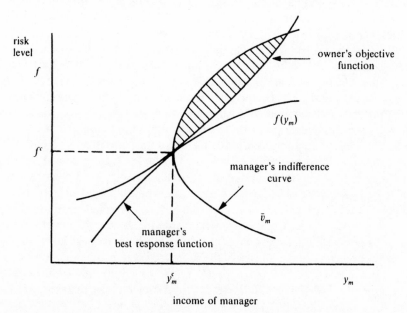

Figure 2.6   The owner–manager relationship and the choice of risk

of employment function is by construction vertical where it intersects the best response function.

The owner will offer a payment scheme for the manager designed to maximize expected profits, which will vary (over the relevant range) positively with the level of risk and negatively with the manager's income. At the resulting optimum, (f^c, y_m^c), the iso-expected profit function of the owner and the iso-present value function of the manager necessarily intersect, yielding a lens of superior combinations of the failure rate and the manager's income, indicated by the shaded lens in Figure 2.6. The owner would be willing to pay the manager more if a higher level of risk-taking could be secured, but given the manager's best response function, these Pareto-improving increases in both y_m and f are not feasible.

Our final market failure arises when a borrower is residual claimant on a variable income stream, the level of which depends on the borrower's choice of risk level. An obvious conflict of interest arises because the borrower (as residual claimant) stands to gain from high return but risky projects, while the lender gains nothing from the enhanced returns of these projects, and stands to lose should the projects fail.

It will simplify our argument if we assume for the moment that collateral cannot be posted (collateral will play an important role in subsequent arguments). Thus the lender must rely solely on a contingent renewal enforcement strategy: the borrower would like to continue the relationship with the lender insofar as the lender offers a greater amount of credit or a lower rate of interest than the borrower's next-best alternative. But the lender may terminate the relationship should the borrower engage in business practices considered by the lender to be overly risky. For any interest rate offered by the lender, the borrower thus maximizes her present value v^b by choosing a risk level (denoted f, for the probability that the project will fail) to balance the expected gains from high risk projects against the probability that risky strategies will be detected by the lender and the loan not be renewed in subsequent periods. The borrower's best response function, like the manager's, is constructed analogously to the worker's effort function: Figure 2.7 depicts one of a family of the borrower's iso-present value functions $\bar{v}^b$, which yields a point on the best response function, $f(i)$.

The lender seeks to maximize the expected return $\hat{\imath}$ which depends on both the interest rate and the probability of failure. The lender's iso-expected return function appears in Figure 2.7, labeled $\hat{\imath}$. The lender sets an interest rate to maximize $\hat{\imath}(i, f)$ subject to $f(i)$, yielding the equilibrium (i^c, f^c). The borrower's iso-present value function must intersect the lender's iso-expected return function at this point, as the borrower's iso-present value function is by construction vertical at its point of intersection with the borrower's best response function. As the borrower prefers points to the left of the iso-present value function, and as the lender prefers points below the iso-expected return function, Pareto-improving combinations of i and f exist, characterized by lower interest rates and lower levels of risk-taking, indicated by the shaded lens in Figure 2.7.

The four market failures we have identified in Figure 2.4–2.7 suggest that even

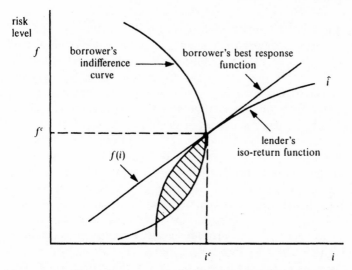

Figure 2.7   The borrower–lender relationship and the choice of risk

under highly competitive conditions democratic firms might allocate resources differently than capitalist firms. We turn first to the possible advantages of the democratic firm in regulating the pace of work.

5   The efficiency of the democratic firm in regulating work

Consider two firms, one owned and governed by its workers, the other owned and governed by profit-maximizing owner.[21] We assume that workers direct the managers of the democratic firm to select a payment scheme and monitoring structure to maximize v, the workers' value of employment, subject to a budget constraint. We assume that both firms employ identical workers, produce with identical technologies, and make use of a dismissal-based system of labor discipline. There are three reasons to think that the democratic firm will be more efficient than the capitalist firm in the sense that it uses less of at least one input to produce the same output.

First it is reasonable that workers, being integrated into the democratic firm by both property and political rights, will treat work as a more rewarding experience, and will therefore offer more effort than in the capitalist firm, when facing a given wage and monitoring structure. The improved motivational incentives may be positive, as when the worker identifies more strongly with the firm, or negative, as when the worker fears dismissal more because the work is more rewarding. We refer to both the carrot and stick aspects as the *participation effect.*

The participation effect, which operates through changes in the worker's utility function, is easily confused with what might be termed the *direct residual claimancy effect*, which does not. This effect arises because the worker, as a residual claimant, will take account of the effect of working harder on total firm income, thereby reducing the incentive incompatibility in the employment relation. Though it may be an important consideration in small work teams, the direct residual claimancy effect seems simply too small to provide a major motivational basis for increased work intensity in work teams of reasonable size. As we will see, however, it may be sufficiently large to provide a motivation for reporting information to management even in the largest firms.

Our second reason for the superior efficiency of the democratic firm is that the residual claimancy status of workers provides such a firm with monitoring mechanisms unavailable or prohibitively costly for the capitalist firm. Abstracting from the participation and direct residual claimancy effects, one might think that the worker would have no less incentive to free-ride on the democratic firm than on the capitalist firm by pursuing on-the-job-leisure. But this view is mistaken. Workers frequently have virtually costless access to information concerning the work activities of fellow workers, and in the democratic firm each has an interest in the effort levels of other workers. The residual claimancy status of workers thus provides a motive for mutual monitoring.[22] The democratic firm could thus deploy a more effective monitoring structure than the capitalist firm. We refer to this as the *mutual monitoring effect*.[23]

To see that the mutual monitoring and participation effects do indeed generate gains in technical efficiency, consider Figure 2.8, which compares the worker's best response functions in a democratic and a capitalist firm. Let the "wage" paid by the democratic firm be the worker's share of the firm's net output. Termination of employment with the democratic firm results in the loss of this income stream. We assume that the worker's fallback position is unaffected by the form of firm organization and ownership. We also assume the monitoring levels for the two firms are identical.

The worker's best response function in the democratic firm lies above the corresponding function in the capitalist firm. The enhanced utility of work shifts the best response function upward and the increased efficacy of monitoring both shifts the function upward and renders it steeper. By comparison with the capitalist equilibrium at point *a*, we cannot say that point *b* on the democratic firm's best response function represents an efficiency gain, as workers are exerting more effort at *b* (namely $e^d > e^c$). But we clearly could hypothetically reduce the level of monitoring to m_1, thereby lowering e^d sufficiently so that point *a* (the equilibrium of the capitalist firm) now lay on the democratic best response function. In this case the democratic firm would extract the same amount of effort as the capitalist firm, but using fewer monitoring resources, with a reduced (or at worst unchanged) disutility of labor for the employees. Analogous demonstrations are possible for any initial capitalist equilibrium, of course. The democratic firm is thus technically more efficient.

It can also be shown that converting the capitalist firm to a democratic firm would be Pareto-improving. By reducing monitoring costs the democratic firm could produce at point *a*. But at point *a* output net of wages was for the capitalist

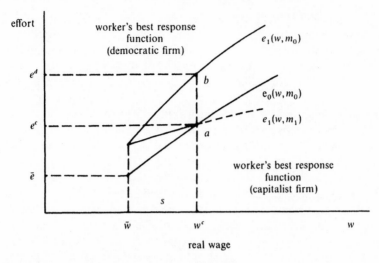

Figure 2.8   The gains from mutual monitoring

firm sufficient to pay both the return to the capitalist and the prior (higher) level of monitoring costs.[24] Thus it would be possible to compensate the former owners at the level of their previous claim on the surplus, and pay out the reduced monitoring input costs to members of the firm. The former owners would be no worse off and the worker-members would be doubly better off: they would experience less disutility of labor and would receive a payment corresponding to the reduced monitoring expenditures.[25]

However this efficiency gain associated with the democratic firm does not implement the social optimality condition introduced in section 4 (Figure 2.3), since, even apart from the free-riding problem, workers in the democratic firm maximize the present value of their utility, which takes account of the probability that they will lose their jobs. The social optimality criterion, by contrast, is indifferent to which workers will hold jobs. Workers in a democratic firm, like those in a capitalist firm, thus have a job retention incentive to work hard corresponding to a private distribution claim on output but no social benefits.

Our third reason for the technical efficiency of the democratic firm is that the wage offered in the capitalist equilibrium is too low (in a sense to be made clear presently), and the range of possible ownership structures and payment schemes of the democratic firm allows it to overcome this source of inefficiency. As we have seen in the previous section, the capitalist firm faces two prices in selecting its enforcement structure: one, the price of monitoring, under real conditions correctly measures a social marginal cost, while the other, the wage, does not measure it under *any* condition. Not surprisingly the capitalist firm uses too little wage incentive and too much monitoring relative to an efficient alternative. We refer to these efficiency gains as the *wage incentive effect* favoring the superiority of the democratic firm.

A simple example will make this clear. Consider a firm whose capital stock is jointly owned by the members employed by the firm. Workers joining the firm contribute an amount k_0 per hour of labor time for the duration of their employment with the firm. The sum of all worker contributions equal the value of the capital stock of the firm. This is certainly a feasible, if extreme, form of ownership (we will see presently that in the presence of agency problems concerning risk-taking, and for other reasons, it is generally sub-optimal).

Figure 2.9 contrasts this firm's extraction opportunities with that of the capitalist firm, whose equilibrium as before is point a. For simplicity, we assume that the best response function is not favorably altered by the participation effect, but that the mutual monitoring effect shifts up the effort level for a given wage. The equilibrium for the democratic firm is determined by the effort function and a constraint on feasible payment schemes. We have drawn the new effort function $e^d(\tilde{y}, m)$ as the capitalist effort function $e(w, m)$ shifted upward for $w > \bar{w}$, holding the monitoring level m constant, and replacing the capitalist wage w by the democratic firm's equivalent: the income $\tilde{y}$ the worker receives contingent on employment with the firm. Income per hour equals the net income $y = q(e) - m$ of the firm; however, should the worker be dismissed, the worker would regain the capital contribution to the firm with its hourly return rk_0. Hence the worker's contingent income satisfies

$$\tilde{y} = q(e) - m - rk_0. \tag{2}$$

We call (2) the *feasible payments constraint*.

Assuming for the moment that the democratic firm does not alter the level of monitoring inputs, it will produce at point b, the intersection of the feasible

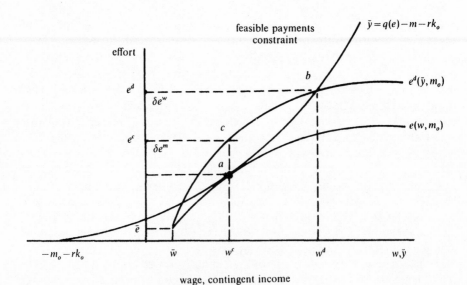

Figure 2.9   Efficiency gains in the democratic firm

payments constraint and the effort function. Since under the terms described the firm could have come into existence by buying out the capitalist at the market value of the firm, the shift to the democratic firm is Pareto-improving.[26] Indeed, Figure 2.9 shows that the mutual monitoring effect δe^m on effort is augmented by the wage incentive effect δe^w, entailing increased effort $\delta e^m + \delta e^w$. Indeed, if we then lower the level of monitoring, simultaneously shifting the worker's best response function downward and the feasible payments constraint to the right, we eventually reach a point of increased technical efficiency, at which equilibrium effort equals e^c, the wage exceeds the capitalist wage w^c, and since the dismissal rate cannot have increased at this point, the workers are unambiguously better off.

6   Impediments to the success of the democratic firm in a competitive capitalist economy

Why do democratic firms, while more efficient in regulating work than their capitalist counterparts, nonetheless operate at a competitive disadvantage and hence not flourish in a capitalist economy? Furthermore, why can the efficiency gains associated with workplace democracy not be reaped by a capitalist firm?

We assume without argument that the participation and mutual monitoring effects are positive so, in the absence of optimal bonding, the wage incentive effect is an efficiency advantage of the democratic firm as well.

If the capitalist firm cannot reap the advantages of the democratic firm, why do capitalist firms nonetheless prevail? Three general answers may be considered. First, learning to govern a firm effectively through democratic means takes time, and requires a work force schooled in common deliberation and decision-making. Unless the efficiency gains associated with the democratic firm are considerable, the costs of learning and the lack of a pool of workers experienced in democratic management may be prohibitive. We call this the *democratic capacities' constraint.* This constraint is reinforced to the extent that the experience of work in capitalist firms and formal schooling foster personal capacities that are more functional in the context of hierarchical rather than reciprocal relationships and that discourage the development of cognitive capacities necessary for the governance of production (Bowles and Gintis, 1976).

Second, conditions favoring the democratic firm may be more likely to obtain in an economy with many such firms, and similarly for the capitalist firm. Thus an economy composed primarily of capitalist firms might sustain and foster general economic conditions precluding the viability of the democratic firm, and vice-versa. We call this the *economic environment constraint.* For instance, Levine and Tyson (1990) argue that the variability of demand, the level of unemployment, and the general inequality of income differentially favor the capitalist over the democratic firm in a capitalist economy, but would change in a direction favorable to the democratic firm in an economy composed primarily of democratic firms.

Third, the capital requirements of the democratic firm are generally not within the means of workers, nor would risk-averse workers rationally choose to concentrate their wealth in a single asset. Unable to finance the democratic firm directly, and lacking even the collateral required for borrowing the necessary funds, workers may find the democratic firm an unattractive option despite its superior efficiency. We refer to this as the *wealth inequality constraint*.

To formalize these considerations, we define conditions for the viability of the democratic firm in a competitive capitalist environment, namely that it be able to recruit members, taking account of the opportunities available to those currently employed in capitalist firms and those unemployed. We will thus define the following *viability condition*: given the structure of financial markets and the wealth position of potential worker-members, joining a democratic firm must result in an increase in the wealth position of the worker by comparison with that of a currently unemployed person.

Of course were capital markets as depicted by Walrasian economic theory, worker wealth limitations would pose no impediment, for workers could borrow on terms no more costly than the wealth-holding capitalist, and this would allow financing of the democratic firm at competitive rates of interest, as long as the democratic firm were indeed efficient. But capital markets are as much arenas of contested exchange as are labor markets: the promise to repay a loan is enforceable only if the borrower is solvent at the time repayment is due, and the borrower's promise to repay is not amenable to third-party-enforcement (Stiglitz and Weiss, 1981).

Of course the lender can devise contracts that induce more favorable performance than borrowers would spontaneously exhibit. Among the most effective is that of requiring the borrower to post collateral.[27] Since this collateral is forfeited in case of borrower insolvency, the incentive incompatibility between borrower and lender is attenuated: a highly collateralized borrower has objectives closer to the lender's. But collateral must involve the borrower's own wealth, and cannot (except through subterfuge) itself be borrowed without undermining the collateral's enforcement effect.

We can illustrate with a simple model our point that, since workers tend to lack assets, they have only limited ability to post collateral, and hence are in a disadvantageous position *vis-à-vis* the capital market.

Let k_0 be the required capital per worker for the firm analyzed in the previous section. We assume that this capital requirement is fixed, that there is a positive probability of bankruptcy, and that the salvage value of the capital goods is zero. Suppose a group of workers attempts to form a firm using the same techniques of production as existing capitalist firms. The hours of work per year are identical for each worker, and are normalized at unity. We may assume workers each contribute an amount k_w of equity to the firm, which then borrows an amount k_f per worker sufficient to finance the firm's capital investment. We thus have

$$k_0 = k_f + k_w. \tag{3}$$

We take workers to be risk-averse, so the larger the proportion of wealth devoted to a risky project, the less the subjective value of the portfolio of which it is an element. Suppose each worker has, in addition to a value of employment v, a portfolio W of non-labor-related wealth which, for simplicity, we assume is earning the risk-free interest rate ρ, which in turn is identical to the worker's rate of time preference. To join the firm, the workers must thus transfer an amount k_w from the portfolio W to purchase a risky asset: firm membership. Let us write the opportunity cost period to workers of transferring k_w to the democratic firm as $k_w r_w$, where r_w is the risk-free interest rate the worker regards as equivalent to the distribution of expected returns in the risky portfolio when proportion k_w/W of the worker's wealth is transferred. Risk-aversion then implies that r_w is an increasing function of k_w/W and $r_w(0) = \rho$.[28]

The efficacy of collateral as an enforcement mechanism is captured by the assumption that the lender will provide funds at lower rates, the greater is the worker's own equity stake with the firm. Thus the interest rate r_f on the firm's external debt k_f is an increasing function of the debt ratio k_f/k_0:

$$r_f = r_f(k_f/k_0) \quad r_f', r_f'' > 0, r_f(0) = \rho. \tag{4}$$

Then since workers in the democratic firm are residual claimants, and writing $\tilde{y}$ for the worker's income contingent on employment, we have[29]

$$\tilde{y} = q(e(\tilde{y})) - r_f(k_f/k_0)k_f - r_w(k_w/W)k_w. \tag{5}$$

If we rewrite (5) as

$$q(e(\tilde{y})) - \tilde{y} = r(k_w, W)k_0 \tag{5'}$$

where $r(k_w, W)$, the weighted cost of capital funds, is defined as $r(k_w, W) = [r_f(k_f/k_0)k_f + r_w(k_w/W)k_w]/k_0$, it is clear if a solution to (5) exists, it can be attained by first choosing k_w to minimize $r(k_w, W)$, and then (assuming that both the production function $q(e)$ and the effort function $e(\tilde{y})$ are convex) choosing the larger of the two resulting values of $\tilde{y}$. This situation is shown in Figure 2.10 which in the first quadrant plots $r(k_w, W)$ as a function of k_w at various levels of W, the locus of optimal k_w as W varies being labeled $r^*(k_0/W)$.

The second quadrant of Figure 2.10 plots $q(e(\tilde{y})) - \tilde{y}$ as a function of $\tilde{y}$, where $q(e)$ is output per worker hour, $e^d(\tilde{y})$ is the effort level in the democratic firm when contingent income per hour is $\tilde{u}$, and $e^c(w)$ is the effort per hour in the capitalist firm at wage w. The superior labor productivity of the democratic firm is depicted by $q(e^d(\tilde{y}))$ lying above $q(e^c(w))$.[30] It is clear that the democratic firm is viable only if worker wealth W is sufficiently high that the minimum of $r(k_w, W)$ in the first quadrant is not greater than the maximum of $q(e(\tilde{y})) - \tilde{y}$ in the second quadrant. The minimum wealth at which this occurs is labeled W^{min}, and corresponds to a contingent income $\tilde{y}(W^{min})$ at point A in the second quadrant. It follows that if worker wealth is less than W^{min}, despite the superior labor productivity of the democratic firm, only capitalist firms will exist. Indeed, if capitalists are risk-neutral (equivalent in this model to being infinitely wealthy) the market equilibrium will be at B, where only capitalist firms are financially viable, but each operates at lower efficiency than its democratic counterpart.

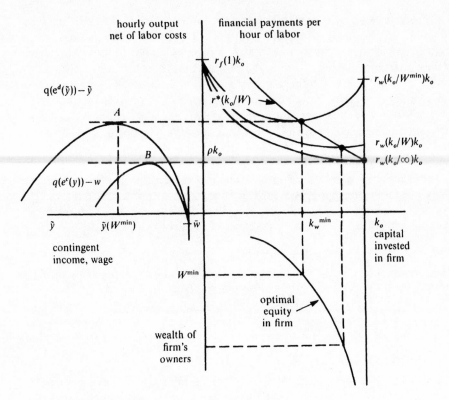

Figure 2.10   Internal finance of the democratic firm

7   Conclusion

We have argued that capital market imperfections account for the competitive disadvantage of the democratic firm, despite its superior ability to deal with the labor agency problem. There is thus a *prima facie* case for considering some form of subsidy for the democratic firm. Suppose credit were made available to the democratic firm on the same terms as its capitalist counterpart, thus eliminating its competitive disadvantage. How would we then assess the democratic firm's ability to handle the twin agency problems surrounding labor and risk-taking?

Concerning the labor agency problem, we expect the democratic firm to benefit from the participation, mutual monitoring and wage incentive effects, plus possibly for small teams the direct residual claimancy effect. Is there any reason, however, to believe that democratic firms would provide an adequate solution to the choice of risk and innovation? As we have seen, it is socially optimal that agents controlling the firm act in as risk-neutral manner as possible whereas, assuming decreasing absolute risk-aversion, economic agents are not only risk-averse, but are more so the less their wealth and the larger the portion of their wealth involved in a particular project. The property rights of capitalist firms mitigate this problem in two ways: they vest control in relatively wealthy and hence less risk-averse agents, and they imply financing through institutions, such as banks and stock markets, capable of inducing firms to innovate and take risks.

The capitalist solution is probably too conservative. But the internally financed democratic firm can be expected to act in an even more risk-avoiding manner on both counts: its members are not wealthy and are not compelled by outside interests to take risks. Indeed, members of the democratic firm, even were they risk-neutral, would have an additional reason to shun high-risk high-return projects: since workers earn employment rents, they incur additional bankruptcy costs (the loss of job rents) not imposed on their capitalist counterparts (Gintis, 1989b).

From the democratic perspective this insight raises the following dilemma: some degree of external ownership of the firm by those who are not worker-members is justified by its contribution to a socially optimal level of risk-taking; but external control of the firm would compromise the principle of democratic accountability.[31] Moreover the democratic argument for workers controlling their conditions of employment does not extend to creditors controlling the conditions under which their assets are used, since creditors are not generally long-side agents facing short-siders who wield power over them.

This tension can be seen in Figure 2.11, which portrays in highly simplified form the positive effect of an increase in the degree of external ownership on risk-taking and its negative effect on effort, giving rise to the "risk–effort frontier" $\gamma(e, f)$, which shows the feasible trade-offs as the degree of external ownership moves from the purely democratic (e^d, f^d) to the purely capitalist (e^c, f^c). The combination (f^*, e^*) of effort and risk-taking that is optimal in the

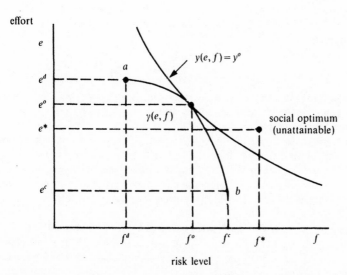

Figure 2.11   The optimal choice of effort and risk

absence of agency problems is clearly unattainable in our model. To find the degree of external ownership that maximizes social welfare, we posit a present value of future production function of the form $y = y(e, f)$. The present value maximum is then given by the tangency at (e^0, f^0) of an iso-y schedule with the production frontier $y(e, f)$. Note that neither the purely capitalist nor the purely democratic solution is optimal, but that if we add democratic accountability as an independently desired social value, the socially preferred trade-off will move toward the democratic alternative.

Notes

We would like to thank George Akerlof, Pranab Bardhan, Greg Dow, Philippe van Parijs, Louis Putterman, John Roemer, and Peter Skott for helpful remarks in the preparation of this chapter.

1. See Elster and Moene (1989) for a broader set of criteria.
2. The study of market failures stemming from other sources (externalities concerning environmental effects, employment stability, or on-the-job learning, for example) also reveal efficiency differences between the democratic and the capitalist firm. On the superior efficiency of the democratic firm in choosing levels of public "bads" (such as pollution), see Roemer (1990).
3. This monitoring assumption is the opposite of that adopted by Alchian and Demsetz (1972a). We defend our assumption by noting that monitoring (unlike productive labor) is not generally performed in teams. The range of effective incentive mechanisms available to attenuate the incentive incompatibilities arising when non-residual claimants are assigned monitoring tasks is thus considerably greater than in the case of a production team.
4. Our analysis is limited to the case where enforcement problems are present on only *one side* of the exchange. We thus set aside the more general problem of "bilateral endogenous enforcement."
5. This definition conforms to neoclassical (Coase, 1937), as well as to Marxian (Marx, 1976), neo-Marxian (Gintis, 1976) and organization-theoretic (Simon, 1951) approaches.
6. The analysis presented in this section is developed in Gintis (1976), Bowles (1985), and Gintis and Ishikawa (1987). Related models have been developed by Calvo (1979), and Shapiro and Stiglitz (1984).
7. We term this a "rent" as it represents a payment above and beyond the income of an identical employee without the job. It is distanced from the rents in the theory of rent-seeking behavior (Buchanan, Tollison, and Tullock, 1980; Krueger, 1974), in that contested exchange rents arise through the *lack* of effective state intervention in contract enforcement, while the rent-seeking literature focuses on state intervention as the source of rents.
8. More complete models allow an endogenous selection by A of an optimal schedule $f(e, m)$, an optimal choice of the level of surveillance (Bowles, 1985; Gintis and Ishikawa, 1987), and the choice of production technologies as an aspect of endogenous enforcement (Bowles, 1989).
9. Such a best response function can be derived as follows. Let $u = u(w, e)$ be B's utility

function, and assume $u_w > 0$, $u_e < 0$ for $(w, e) > (\bar{w}, \bar{e})$. B's value of employment is then

$$v = \{u(w, e) + [1 - f(e, m)]v + f(e, m)z\}/(1 + \rho),$$

where ρ is the employee's rate of time preference: B receives $u(w, e)$ this period plus the present value v if retained, that occurs with probability $1 - f(e, m)$, and plus the present value z if dismissed, that occurs with probability $f(e, m)$. Assuming for simplicity that income and the disutility of effort are both evaluated at the end of the period, the whole expression is discounted to the present by the factor $1/(1 + \rho)$. Solving for v, we obtain

$$v = [u(w, e) - \rho z]/[\rho + f(e, m)] + z, \tag{1}$$

where the first term on the right-hand side is obviously the employment rent, $v - z$; or *value of employment = employment rent + fallback position*. The $e(w, m)$ schedule then results from B's choosing e to maximize v for given w and m.

10. To see this, suppose no monitoring implies no information concerning effort, and perfect monitoring implies that effort can be measured perfectly and costlessly. Then if the disutility of effort is independent of the wage, no monitoring implies that the effort curve is horizontal, given by $e(w) = \bar{e}$. The reason is that greater effort, not being detectible, does not alter the probability of dismissal. Similarly with perfect monitoring, for any wage $w \geq \bar{w}$, the employer can induce the worker to choose effort e such that $u(w, e) = z$; i.e., the best response function coincides with the iso-v curve through $(\bar{w}, \bar{e})$, which must lie above the best response function with imperfect monitoring.

11. Such agents, rather than being unemployed, may simply prefer B's position to their own at the going wage. The point is that they are quantity-constrained: they would prefer to sell more of their services at the going rate but are unable to (unless B is diminished).

12. Does A have power over C? The negative sanction that A may impose on B (withdrawal of the employment rent) is exactly equal to a positive sanction that A might offer or refuse to extend to C. If A refuses to hire C in order to maintain a racially homogeneous workplace, for instance, we might say that A has furthered her interests (gratification of racial prejudice) and has sanctioned C (refused to offer the employment rent). Thus A has power over C in the sense defined here. However by contrast to the relationship of A to B, the sanction is not imposed to affect C's behavior and thus is incidental to the furthering of A's interests.

13. We do not refer here to the *administrative*, but rather to the *political* structure of the enterprise. The former refers roughly to its organizational chart while the latter refers to the locus of final accountability. We might envisage, for example, a bureaucratic administrative structure combined with a democratic political structure, all members of the firm electing the chief executive officer who then enjoys broad organizational authority.

14. In a related paper (Bowles and Gintis, 1993) we argue that the grounds on which democratic governance of the state have been advocated entail democratic governance of the enterprise as well. See also Dahl (1985).

15. In the theory of contested exchange, non-clearing market equilibria play the same role as transaction-specific investments in transactions' cost economics: both generate rents in competitive equilibrium and give one or both parties to exchange something to lose should the relationship be terminated.

16. More generally: the short side of an exchange is located where the total amount of desired transactions is least; the demand side if there is excess supply and the supply side if there is excess demand (Benassy, 1982).

17. The social optimality of risk-neutrality follows only if the covariance among investment projects is zero, which we assume is approximately the case. More important, it assumes the existence of perfect insurance markets, an assumption incompatible with the agency problems stressed in this chapter. Nevertheless it is reasonable to take the socially optimal level of risk in individual projects to exceed the private.

18. One can imagine pay schemes which avoid this problem: paying each worker the total output of the team minus a constant would generate the right first order conditions for the worker's determination of the effort level assuming that workers acted non-cooperatively. But collusion among workers would then be a highly remunerative strategy and would lead to overwork (because the reward to collectively-agreed-upon levels of effort would be n times the marginal product of effort, where n is the number of members of the team); and variations in total output due to unobservable stochastic influences would preclude the scheme if workers were credit-constrained.

19. This market failure is endemic to any contested exchange in which endogenous enforcement instruments include some which are resource-using and others which are purely distributive.

20. Of course the capitalist's costs have risen: we have defined an efficiency improvement brought about by a redistribution of income. Can an arbitrary wage increase of this type be shown to be a Pareto-improvement? Because the capitalist has chosen m and w to minimize costs, at the capitalist optimum (w^c, m^c) a small variation in w and m yields variations of second order magnitude in labor costs and hence in profits. But, as we have just seen, a small increase in w and decrease in m effect a first order gain in worker welfare. Thus there exists some small increase in wages and decrease in monitoring which will yield sufficient benefits to workers so that a lump-sum tax could be levied on the currently employed sufficient to compensate the capitalist for the cost increase while leaving the workers better off.

21. We assume that workers are homogeneous and risk-neutral, and that in the democratic firm they are the sole and equal residual claimants. We relax these assumptions later.

22. In the early nineteenth-century Owenite community at Orbiston, England each of the over 300 members was assigned responsibility to be the "personal monitor" of another member (Taylor, 1983). While mutual monitoring could introduce sufficient discord among workers to undermine the positive effect of participation on worker productivity, we believe that mutual monitoring in a democratic setting should strengthen the participation effect, in part by enhancing the perception of equal contribution among members, and hence of reducing the incentive to free-ride.

23. Our claim here is not that the democratic firm exhibits an optimal solution to the monitoring problem. One could imagine a structure of incentives for mutual monitoring that under suitable conditions would be more effective than residual claimancy at less cost; e.g., identifying workers whose jobs give them convenient access to information concerning the performance of other workers, and offering such workers "bounties" for information leading to the detection and dismissal of fellow workers. The fact that such schemes are not widely employed in capitalist firms, however, suggests to us that their implementation may be infeasible in the absence of the residual claimancy structure of the democratic firm.

24. We are assuming that the monitoring equipment was purchased in competitive clearing markets, so that the reduced purchases would inflict no cost on the margin to the producers of the equipment.
25. If the capital stock per worker hour is k_0, the rate of return in the capitalist equilibrium is r, and q is the average output per unit of effort, then $rk_0 = qe^c - m_0 - w^c$, so clearly $qe^d - m_1 - w^c > rk_0$.
26. The position, curvature of the feasible payments' constraint, as well as its tangency with the capitalist effort function at point a, follow from the assumption that the production function $q(e)$ is convex.
27. Contingent renewal, in which the lender promises a perpetual "line of credit" provided the borrower behaves prudently, is also available as an enforcement strategy, but for a variety of reasons is less potent, and hence less widely employed, than in the case of the labor market (Bowles and Gintis, 1990).
28. Since $k_w r_w/\rho$ is the certainty equivalent of investing k_w in the firm, we are implicitly assuming that workers obey constant relative risk-aversion.
29. For simplicity we assume in (5) that monitoring costs are zero and that W does not directly affect the worker's best response function $e(\tilde{y})$.
30. The democratic and capitalist net output curves intersect at $w = \bar{w}$, since both use contingent renewal-based incentive systems, and the cost of termination for both types of firm is zero at $w = \bar{w}$.
31. To complicate the picture, it is likely that a democratic firm would require a considerably *greater* degree of external influence to achieve the same level of risk-taking as a managerially-controlled enterprise, since the external owners and creditors of a capitalist firm can focus their risk-enhancing incentives (e.g., bonuses and stock options) on a small group of agents (the managers), while to induce a majority of workers to act in the same manner would generally require that such incentives extended to a majority of the firm members (Gintis, 1989c).

3 Alternative employment and payment systems

D. M. NUTI

1 Wage employment: fixed rate, subjection, and job insecurity

The standard employment contract has three main features:

(i) A fixed rate (whether in money or in indexed contracts, targeted in real terms) per unit of time at a monitored effort supply above a minimum level.

(ii) Subjection to the employer's authority in the workplace.

(iii) Job insecurity (i.e., exposure to unemployment risk), depending among other things on the enterprise's success or failure.

Alternative employment and payment systems involve modifications of these three features, introducing:

(i) Profit-sharing or payments related to other indicators of enterprise performance (e.g., group productivity in physical terms, sales, value added); this includes collective participation in enterprise capital (Employee Stock Ownership Schemes or Trusts, ESOPs and ESOTs). Personal share ownership (PEPs in the UK) and wage-earners' funds at national or regional level (such as the Meidner Plan or its blander implementation in Sweden) do not alter the fixed nature of earnings with respect to the performance of the employee's enterprise.

(ii) Workers' participation in enterprise decision-making, which we could call power-sharing (as in the German-style Mitbestimmung).

(iii) Job security.

2 Permutations of the employment contract

There are only eight possible combinations and permutations demonstrating the presence or absence of profit-sharing, power-sharing and job security; all are actually observed or have been proposed, and their main types are illustrated in Table 3.1. Of course each combination contains any number of alternative degrees of intensity of any of the three features actually present.[1]

3 Lowering the marginal cost of labor

The first argument for profit-sharing is that it can lower the marginal cost of labor, thus raising employment, without necessarily lowering workers' average

Table 3.1. *The employment contract*

	Profit-sharing	Power-sharing	Job security
1. Wage employment	No	No	No
2. Public sector employment	No	No	Yes
3. German-type Mitbestimmung	No	Yes	No
4. Weitzman's share economy	Yes	No	No
5. Vanek's participatory economy	Yes	Yes	No
Capital-sharing (ESOPs)	Yes	Yes	No
6. University teachers	No	Yes	Yes
7. Japanese model	Yes	No	Yes
8. Coops and Yugoslav firms	Yes/limited	Yes 100%	Yes
Meade Capital – Labor partnerships	Yes/pro rata + social dividend	Yes/pro rata	Yes/or compen-sation

Workers' participation in enterprise results and decision-making are discussed in Hill, McGrath and Reyes, 1981; Bartlett and Uvalic, 1986. See also Vanek, 1965; Ward, 1958 and Vanek, 1970; Weitzman, 1984; Meade, 1986a and 1986b, 1989; Nuti, 1991a, 1991b; Uvalic, 1991a.

earnings (Vanek, 1965). A share of profits paid to workers can be seen as a labor subsidy paid out over and above a lower fixed wage, and financed out of a neutral profit tax (neutral in the sense that the same resource allocation and price policy maximize pre- and after-tax profits), leading enterprises to behave as they would if there was no sharing and wages were fixed at that lower level. For example, consider three otherwise identical enterprises A, B, and C. Enterprise A paying a wage of $100 will employ fewer workers than enterprise B paying a wage of $40; but enterprise B will employ as many workers as enterprise C which pays a fixed rate of $40 plus a share of profit amounting to $60 per man; a shift from wage contract A to participatory contract C will raise employment.

However, the additional employment will have been subsidised either out of the firm's profits or out of the wages of those already employed. Out of the firm's profits if average earnings after employment expansion are maintained at an unchanged level; out of the wages of previously employed workers if initially the participatory formula is equivalent to the fixed wage, but the profit share component then is diluted by subsequent employment expansion. There are no miracles; taxation and subsidies could achieve the same result in a more transparent manner. It should be noted that this effect of profit-sharing (unlike subsidies on additional employment financed out of taxation) requires that workers should have no say on employment decisions, or they would be tempted to restrict employment to raise profit per man and therefore their share, instead of generating additional employment (Ward, 1958; Vanek, 1970). Since all important decisions affect employment, directly or indirectly, this formula must necessarily exclude power-sharing other than over minor details of enterprise activity.

4   Cyclical flexibility of earnings

The second benefit expected from profit-sharing is that it will make labor earnings more flexible over the cycle; this greater variability of earnings will not appeal to traditionally risk-averse workers, and for the same average earnings it may or may not be overcompensated by the higher probability of employment associated with profit-sharing. This flexibility is expected to stabilize employment (Weitzman, 1984) but, if employment is governed (as is implicit in profit-maximization) by the marginal cost of labor, i.e., by the fixed component of labor earnings, enterprise profits will be stabilized instead of employment. Capitalists, traditionally risk-lovers, will not necessarily appreciate greater profit stability accompanied by a flattening of their profitability distribution; they will appreciate that stability only if it is obtained more cheaply (in terms of average expected return) than with other methods of reducing risk (for instance, through diversification) and if their actual attitude to risk is such that they wish to take advantage of the profit stabilization opportunity offered by profit-sharing. For employment to be stabilized instead over the cycle the fixed component of earnings would also have to vary anti-cyclically, i.e., we would be back to the standard argument for wage flexibility under standard wage contracts.

5   Productivity enhancement

Productivity is expected to be higher under profit-sharing not because of the workers' fractional participation in the extra output produced by extra effort (on the contrary, from this viewpoint they would be encouraged to reduce effort, being exposed only fractionally to the consequences of their reduced effort), but because of the incentive to use their own labor intelligently and cooperatively at no extra cost to themselves, and to monitor everybody else's intelligent and cooperative use of their labor (at the cost of turning everybody into an invigilator).

6   Overclaims

In addition to these positive effects, profit-sharing has been claimed to lead to full employment, indeed to overfull employment, non-inflationary and resilient to deflationary shocks (Weitzman, 1984). These claims rest on a number of unspoken assumptions:

    (i)   that unemployment is neither classical (i.e., due to lack of capital equipment) nor Keynesian (i.e., due to lack of effective demand, when the marginal revenue product of labor is non-positive);

(ii)   that the fixed element of participatory earnings is downward flexible, right down to the level of the marginal revenue product of labor at full employment;

(iii) that managers would continue to regard the fixed element of participatory earnings as the marginal cost of labor also at full employment, instead of realizing that they always have to offer the going rate of average earnings in order to attract and retain employees.

These claims are therefore unwarranted overclaims (see Nuti, 1987a, 1987b and 1987c).

More generally, a strong and little appreciated limitation of the effects of profit-sharing comes from the unavoidable periodic renegotiation of all employment contracts, including profit-sharing contracts. At renegotiation, new parameters will be fixed which will bring back average earnings in any enterprise in line with the going rate of earnings in new employment everywhere else. The beneficial effects of profit-sharing will thus be short-lived and totally eroded by renegotiations.

7   Profit, capital gains, and capital-sharing

The definition of profit as a cash flow excludes workers from participation in a most important element of entrepreneurial reward (penalty), namely the likely increase (decrease) in the value of the enterprise as a going concern. For full participation in entrepreneurial profit workers ought to share also in such a change in value which is due to a market reassessment of future profits' prospects. This full net profit can be easily calculated as the sum of distributed profits plus the increment in the value of the enterprise during the period (whether due to reinvestment of profits or to a revaluation of future profits expected from older capital).[2]

This argument leads to workers' capital-sharing, both as a way to make workers share also in enterprise success, and as a way to pay out – in the form of free shares – their claim to an increment in the value of enterprise capital.

This fuller form of profit-sharing would have to apply to capital losses as well as gains, if necessary through withdrawals of shares and bonds or transfers of debt to workers; their earnings in cash and capital issues (or withdrawals) would be markedly more variable than if they shared profit as a cash flow (and, moreover, if they did not share losses). Because of workers' inability to diversify their labor employment to any meaningful extent, they would be bound to accept this kind of exposure only if it were to be partial, i.e., affect only part of workers' earnings – a part which could be collectively or individually negotiated – and preferably if it was compensated by economy-wide forms of income support.

8   Power-sharing

Participation in decision-making, like German-style Mitbestimmung, is a natural consequence of workers' exposure to unemployment risk; the argument for participation is strengthed by profit-sharing, because it involves also exposure to income risk. Moreover, the very presence of profit-sharing necessarily involves access to information and therefore discussion of past performance and current plans; this formal or informal consultation is only a small step from decisional participation. Participation in both enterprise decisions and performance is expected to defuse conflicts, and facilitate restructuring and redeployment, by eliminating, or at any rate reducing, internal antagonism between labor and capital.

9   Job security

This is not a necessary complement of participation but is expected to strengthen workers' identification with the interests of the enterprise, reduce risk from participation and amplify the effects of profit participation when this excludes increases in the capital value of the firm, by lengthening the workers' time horizon. What really matters is income security, so that job security could be replaced by compensatory payments topping up the income of dismissed workers (i.e., their unemployment benefits or their income in new employment if lower than in their former employment in the enterprise) to the level enjoyed prior to dismissal.

10   Cooperatives

Cooperatives embody the potential transformation of workers into entre-preneurs, given the combination of up to 100 percent self-management (though sometimes they also use wage labor) and the residual nature of cooperative members' income; members also have tenure. However the classical cooperative has statutory limits to income levels and/or to the distribution of the increment in the value of enterprise assets (either on a member's exit, or at the point of enterprise liquidation when the residual value of the cooperative has usually to be transferred to other cooperatives). The same is true of the classical Yugoslav-type enterprise, which in addition has the obligation to maintain the real capital entrusted to it by the state (Uvalic, 1991b).

These limitations, and the exclusion of possible capital members with voting rights, are the cause of cooperatives being concentrated in labor-intensive, low-risk and small-scale activities, such as construction, agriculture, food processing, handicraft, transport and other services. These limitations are also responsible for the alleged inefficiencies and instabilities investigated in the vast literature on self-management.[3] The current trend, both in the reforming East European countries (Nuti, 1989) and in the West, is to extend worker-members' capital rights (as is already done in the Mondragon group, see Thomas and Logan, 1982; Wiener and Oakeshott, 1986) and to open membership to suppliers of risk capital (Nuti, 1991b). These developments would bring the cooperative closer to the kind of labor–capital partnerships envisaged by James Meade (1989).

11   Meade's labor–capital partnerships

The simplest way of illustrating Meade's scheme – or at any rate my own interpretation[4] of one of its versions – is by imagining the transformation of an already existing capitalist firm. At the point of transition the level of enterprise value added (net of amortization) in the last period and the number of existing shares are considered; workers and all other recipients of contractual incomes (rents, interest, patents, etc.) are given a number of free shares – let us call them contractual shares – which have the same duration of the underlying contractual relation but otherwise are paid a full dividend like ordinary shares; all value added and capital gains are distributed as cash dividends or as issues of free ordinary shares or bonds. Initially contractual income recipients receive the same income they would have obtained contractually; from then on they obtain a yield on their temporary shares. Workers can choose to continue to be employed at a fixed wage, wholly or partially (say, 75 percent of their work time as partners and 25 percent as wage workers). Workers are entitled not to job security as such, but to a continuous income at a guaranteed level even if they are dismissed (as indicated in section 9 above).

In order to alleviate the riskiness of variable incomes Meade envisages a social dividend paid out of state revenue on state assets, which are presumed to have been accumulated out of a sequence of budget surpluses and to be managed through state holding companies. This last feature makes Meade's model unattainable for the time being by most countries except those with a large state capital net of national debt. At present these are the UK (which has almost entirely repaid public debt and has net public capital assets) and the reforming East European countries, (where a large state capital stock is now being or is about to be privatized); unfortunately these are also the countries least inclined to introduce such a scheme.

Moreover capitalist enterprises would be unlikely to support a transfer of power to workers and a dilution of enterprise rewards to their advantage, unless they were subjected to very considerable political pressure and workers' contractual power. However Meade's partnership scheme could be much more easily introduced by existing cooperatives if they were to open their membership to capital shares and to pay out their entire entrepreneurial revenue including net capital gains/losses. Cooperatives, unlike capitalist enterprises, do have an incentive to introduce such changes in order to eliminate all their traditional drawbacks (mentioned in section 10 above). Such developments are being proposed in Italy, and in the former Soviet Union have been made possible by legislation (passed since May 1988, see reference in section 10 above).

Meade's model is attractive because it gives labor an entrepreneurial role on a scale which is voluntarily determined by workers themselves; this entrepreneurial option alters the nature of the entire labor relation even if part of workers' labor is paid at a contractual fixed wage and even for the laborers who are wholly fixed wage-earners, because their position is determined by choice and not by default.

12   From dependent workers to part-time co-entrepreneurs

It is tempting to suggest, on the basis of the reflections developed in this chapter, that there is an evolution of the labor contract away from dependent labor – with money income security, subjection to authority and job insecurity – to entrepreneurial labor – with higher income risk tempered by partial fixed earnings and by fiscal support, with participation in decision-making and with job-related income security which is as good as job security. If this is not a convincing actual trend in positive economics, it is certainly a feasible and desirable evolution path worthy of consideration – whether by normative economics or by political action – in all market economies, not only in the West but also in the transformation of Central Eastern European economies.

Notes

1. The classification refers to a capitalist economy. In traditional centrally planned economies (CPEs) employment in state enterprises is usually of type 2 (see Table 3.1); wage employment is restricted to a small private sector; cooperatives are similar to type 8. However central planning and administrative methods of resource allocation, together with enterprise-specific subsidies and taxes, prevent the exercise of entrepreneurship and therefore any possibility of effective participation.
2. Let us call

FNP = Full net profits
P = cash flow profits (gross of depreciation)
D = depreciation
DV = change in the value of the enterprise
DP = distributed cash flow profits
RP = reinvested cash flow profits
NI = net investment
DVR = change in the value of the enterprise due to other than net investment, i.e., revaluation of profit prospects from already existing capital plus quasi-rents from net investment.

By definition,

$$FNP = P - D + DVR, \tag{1}$$
$$P = DP + RP, \tag{2}$$
$$RP = NI + D, \tag{3}$$
$$DVR = DV - RP. \tag{4}$$

Therefore using (2)–(4) we can rewrite (1) as:

$$FNP = DP + NI + D + DV - NI - D = DP + DV. \tag{1'}$$

Thus, although D is a purely arbitrary accounting convention and DVR is not directly observable, full profits can be expressed as the sum of distributed profits and the total increment in the value of the enterprise due to both revaluation of profit prospects and new investment.

The workers' share of full profits can be paid out of distributed profits or, necessarily,

if their claims jointly with those of shareholders add up to more than distributive profits, in enterprise bonds/or and shares.
3. Classical cooperatives have seven major drawbacks: a bias against undertaking activities with above-average capital intensity; a bias against risky ventures; a tendency to restrict employment, and to behave monopolistically, with respect to an otherwise similar capitalist firm; a rigid and possibly perverse response to changes in the prices of output and capital inputs; a bias against profit reinvestment; a bias in favor of labor-saving investment (see Nuti, 1991a).
4. Strictly speaking Meade's original scheme involves inequality among workers in the form of a different number of shares held *qua* workers; this creates difficulties such as unequal pay for equal work, and continuous renegotiation of everybody's shares when new members are hired (see Nuti, 1991a). My version of Meade's scheme would eliminate these difficulties, all workers receiving the same current income for the same current work but obtaining unequal additional income from ordinary shares.

Part II
Institutions and institutional change

4 Toward a framework for analyzing institutions and institutional change

LEONID HURWICZ

1 Introduction

In an era of major changes across the globe in economic as well as political institutions, there should be little argument about the need for an analytical framework to help us understand the observed phenomena. In the past, the development of such a framework was obstructed by imperfect communication between "theorists" and "institutionalists." Our objective here is to facilitate communication by integrating institutional phenomena into models that have been developed for the study of economies, voting systems, and organizations. Primarily, we are interested in economic institutions, but certain aspects of the model are general enough to be applicable to political and other social institutions as well. Indeed, these non-economic aspects cannot be ignored, since introduction, implementation, and enforcement of the rules are essential features of the model.

Our point of departure will be the theory of economic mechanisms (formalized, for example, as adjustment processes or game forms). Although this theory has had a normative orientation, we intend our framework to be usable for descriptive and explanatory analysis as well. We do not share the view that at the present stage formalization is premature. It seems important to make institutional phenomena amenable to analysis with tools that have resulted in progress in many areas of economics and other social sciences.

Before proceeding with details, let us clarify the intended meaning of the term "institution." In common parlance, this term has two distinct meanings. To illustrate by example, we refer to such organizational entities as a university, a central bank, an ombudsman's office, or a state as institutions. On the other hand we also call institutions certain arrangements, rules, or behavior patterns such as private property, marriage, representative democracy, anti-monopoly laws, or markets. In this chapter the term "institution" is intended to refer to the latter meaning, i.e., an *institutional arrangement*, rather than the former (which can be called an *institutional entity*). Although some writers find the distinction unnecessary, it is useful in the present context.

Institutions (in the sense of institutional arrangements) do play an important role in models of economies or voting systems. The latter often presuppose a representative democracy, while the former, implicitly at least, postulate the existence of certain forms of ownership, markets, or central planning processes. But when it comes to formal treatment, the typical models contain only implications or consequences of the existence of an institution but do not formalize the institution itself. Thus neoclassical models presuppose the existence of markets, and the Arrow–Debreu model, with its profit shares going to consumers, presupposes private ownership of the means of production. (Indeed, Debreu uses the label "private ownership economy.") A study by Grossman and Hart (1986) explores the implications of ownership for vertical and lateral integration. But the institution of ownership itself is, in my view at least, not formalized in any of these models. However, there are contributions where specific institutions are modeled. An important example is Stiglitz's work (1974) providing a basis for distinguishing such institutions as share-cropping, renting, and wage labor.

We shall approach the concept of an institution by stages, through two intermediate concepts: an adjustment process and a mechanism.[1] This approach takes advantage of our familiarity with an example of an adjustment process, the Walrasian (perfectly competitive)[2] tâtonnement process.[3] Similarly, examples such as second price auctions and procedures proposed for making decisions concerning public goods (e.g., Groves and Ledyard, pivotal, Groves mechanisms) can be helpful in gaining an insight into the notion of a mechanism.

More fundamentally, we shall be proposing a concept of institution based on that of a mechanism, namely as a particular type of a class of mechanisms. Hence it is essential that a foundation be laid by clarifying the notion of a "mechanism" and of the closely related (but not identical) concept of an "adjustment process." This will be attempted in the next section.

Our indirect approach to theorizing about institutions may seem cumbersome, but it enables us to build on an analytical framework whose many properties are already known in considerable detail, and to integrate the theory of institutions with the existing body of theory.

2   Mechanisms and adjustment processes

First, a few words about the need for "embedding" the notion of a competitive process in a more comprehensive concept. From the *descriptive* point of view, at least since Cournot's time, economics has modeled various *market* phenomena other than perfect competition – including monopoly (single and bilateral), oligopoly, oligopsony, monopolistic competition (with product differentiation and discriminatory pricing), etc. But both in the present-day world and in earlier epochs a variety of *non-market* systems, including government regulation, central planning, and feudalism, have been observed. Hence just for descriptive purposes we need a concept capable of covering these varied structures, and having enough flexibility and generality to accommodate various mixtures as well as new structures that might be observed in the future.

2.1   Normative aspects

The need for such a general concept is at least equally evident from a *normative* point of view. Clearly, for normative purposes we want to be able to cover known candidates (in particular, perfect competition) for some notion of optimality, as well as to cover alternative systems (such as central planning) that have been advocated as desirable. But more important, one wants to have a concept that can accommodate economic processes or structures that are potentially superior to those already tried or known. This need becomes especially obvious when we consider some of the well-known normative deficiencies of perfectly competitive equilibria, not to mention dynamic instability.

First, accepting for a moment Pareto-optimality as the "evaluation criterion," competitive equilibria are guaranteed to exist and be optimal only in a class of *environments* that excludes externalities, indivisibilities, infinite horizons, and increasing returns to scale, i.e., only in *"classical"* environments. (A standard interpretation of "environment" includes the structure of the commodity space, initial endowments, technology, and preferences. The general idea covers those aspects of the economy that cannot be affected by policy or institutional changes.) Yet one wishes to consider whether there might be economic processes that yield optimal outcomes even in these "non-classical" environments. (Indivisibilities and increasing returns seem particularly important for economies developing their infrastructures. That detrimental externalities are universally important needs hardly to be pointed out in an era of major concerns with global warming, integrity of the ozone layer, and various forms of pollution. Education and health are among important examples of positive externalities.)

Second, the Pareto-criterion is neither sufficiently specific nor universally accepted as having priority over egalitarian and minimum standards criteria. Greater specificity can be achieved by a social welfare function compatible with Pareto-optimality, but we are then faced with the dilemma implied by Arrow's impossibility result. It is at least partly for this reason that a more general vehicle for formulating social desiderata has been developed, here to be called a *goal correspondence*. (We use this term in preference to the more usual "social choice correspondence," in order to avoid terminological ambiguities associated with the term "choice." A *correspondence* is simply a multi-valued, i.e., set-valued, function. A single-valued function is viewed as a special case of a correspondence.) This set of normative considerations also argues in favor of broadening one's horizon beyond that of the Walrasian process.

Third, the behavior of economic agents implicit in the definition of Walrasian equilibrium is not "natural" for any agent that is not infinitesimal as compared with the market as a whole, hence not plausible in economies with few agents. While profit and utility-maximization may create an impression that perfectly competitive equilibrium is consistent with selfish motivations, the requirement that prices be treated parametrically means that agents are supposed to ignore, and refrain from using, their "market power." Indeed, models of monopoly and oligopoly have been developed to deal more realistically with such situations. It follows that even if perfectly competitive outcomes are desired it is necessary to introduce additional incentive structures to attain such results. The latter point also applies to proposals for marginal cost pricing in economies with increasing returns (Hotelling, Lange, Lerner) where parametric treatment of prices is postulated.

The preceding observations should not be interpreted as detracting from the important, indeed central, role played in economic theory by the Walrasian and Arrow–Debreu models of a perfectly competitive economy. Our point is rather that a broader framework is necessary and that there is a need for a general concept of the economic process. Obviously, this concept must include the market structures (in particular, perfect competition) as well as forms of central planning. It is also clear that there is a great deal of arbitrariness in formulating such a concept.

2.2   Formulating a generalized concept

In constructing a generalized concept, we start by distinguishing two aspects of the economic process: the *rules* governing the process and the *behavior* induced by (or at least compatible with) those rules.

There are two elements typically involved in the specification of the rules: the class of *admissible choices* and an outcome function specifying the outcome produced by the choices made. These choices may be actions or messages (e.g., proposals, bids, production plans, preference revelations), or – in the language of game theory – moves or strategies. The rules may also impose restrictions on the agent's choices given the agent's characteristic. (Typically, the agent's *character-istic* is described by its admissible consumption set, its preferences, its initial endowment, and its production possibility set. The *environment*[4] is the configuration of all the agents' characteristics.) To complete the description of the economic process we must specify the relation defining agents' choices given the agents' characteristics. (In static models, this relation is called the *equilibrium correspondence*.) This relation is affected by the behavioral properties of the agents and is here called "behavior" for short. It includes, in particular, the game-theoretic solution concepts such as Nash, dominance, or maximin.

To illustrate: in a typical Walrasian market tâtonnement model, the admissible choices are messages consisting of price and/or quantity proposals; the outcome function accepts the equilibrium quantities proposed; behavior involves maxi-mization (of profit or utility) with prices treated parametrically. (The consumer's preferences and endowments, as well as a firm's production function, i.e., their characteristics, enter into the maximization process.) But in a Hotelling–Lange–Lerner model profit-maximization (or, more generally, marginal cost pricing) is prescribed by the rules, hence is not to be viewed as "behavior" in the sense of our definition, but rather as a restriction on permissible strategies.

In a revelation model of public choice with preferences assumed transferable (so that the Pareto-optimal level of the public good is uniquely defined by the valuation functions), an agent's admissible choices are statements (claims) about valuation functions; the outcome function picks the level of public good that is Pareto-optimal for the claimed (not necessarily true) valuations, and monetary payments defined by the transfer rules (e.g., a Groves mechanism such as the pivotal mechanism). The agent's behavior consists in its choice of the statement (i.e., claimed preferences) given the truth. It is known that, for a Groves mechanism, the agent will in fact choose to tell the truth.

2.3   Formalization

At this point it seems desirable to introduce some notation and formalize to some extent the concepts just introduced, confining ourselves to economies with a finite number n of agents. The set of agents is denoted by N. Thus $N = (1, \ldots, n)$. With each agent we associate its characteristic; the characteristic of agent i is denoted by e^i. Typically, e^i is defined by the commodity space, the initial endowment, admissible consumption, set, preferences, and the production possibility correspondence.[5] The environment, denoted by e, is defined as the configuration of the individual characteristics, i.e., $e = (e^1, \ldots, e^n)$. The class of *a priori* admissible environments is denoted by E. We assume (as is customary, though unrealistic) that it is the Cartesian product of *a priori* admissible sets of individual characteristics denoted by E^i. That is, $E = E^i \times \cdots \times E^n$. This means that whether a particular individual characteristic is admissible for a given agent is independent of the characteristics of other agents.

We shall denote by C the space of possible choices and by Z the space of conceivable outcomes. In economic models the space Z typically consists of conceivable (not necessarily feasible) resource allocations, including consumption, input–output vectors, and public goods levels. In political models, the space Z may consist of potential candidates for office or alternative answers in a referendum. The importance of the outcome space lies in the fact that, in normative models, social goals are formulated in terms of what happens in it. For instance, in Arrow's model, the social welfare function has as its domain the environment space[6] E and its value is a social ordering on the outcome space Z. A more general normative concept is that of a (*social*) *goal correspondence* (often called social choice correspondence[7]) denoted by F, which associates with a given environment e a sub-set $F(e)$ of the outcome space Z. The outcomes belonging to the sub-set $F(e)$ are thought of as F-optimal given the environment e. For example, if $F(\cdot)$ is the Pareto-correspondence then $F(e)$ is the set of Pareto-optimal outcomes given the feasibility conditions and preferences implicit in e.

An Arrow welfare function f generates a goal correspondence as follows. Let $R^S = f(e)$ be the social ordering for the environment (preference profile implicit in) e. Then the goal correspondence, say F_f, is defined by the relation $F_f(e) =$ the set of feasible outcomes in Z that maximize R^S. Thus a normative approach based on an Arrovian social welfare function can be subsumed under the social goal formulation. The converse, however, is not true because it may be impossible to rationalize the F correspondence in terms of any social choice function f. Hence the social goal correspondence formulation has greater generality. In particular, it can embody various egalitarian and minimum standards criteria, and it need not be compatible with the Pareto-criterion.

There are various possible interpretations of what we have called the *choice space C*. In tâtonnement-type (not necessarily Walrasian) models, *C* may be interpreted as the *message space M*. In game-theoretic models *C* may be interpreted as the *strategy space S* or (for games in extensive form) the space of histories of all agents' moves. In any case, the outcome function is defined as a function, denoted by *h*, from *C* into *Z*. That is, it associates a specified outcome with choices made by agents. In the terminology of game theory, the strategy space together with the outcome function, i.e., the pair (S, h), is called a *game form*. (In everyday language, this might be called a "game." But in game theory the term "game" is reserved for the pair consisting of *S* and the *n* "payoff functions" that are being maximized by the players. To obtain the *i*th payoff function, it is necessary to apply the *i*th utility function to the outcome function *h*.) In other literature the game form is usually identified with the notion of a *mechanism*.

To complete the picture, we must describe the transition from the environment to choices. We do so by introducing the concept of an *equilibrium correspondence* μ, which is a correspondence from the space of environments *E* into the choice space *C*. That is, $\mu(e)$ is the set of equilibrium choices that can prevail in the environment *e*. But what determines the nature of the correspondence μ? The answer depends on the model.

For example, in a game-theoretic model it depends on the solution concept, which we view as a behavioral postulate. Thus if we postulate Nash-behavior of the players then the set $\mu(e)$ consists of Nash-equilibrium strategies given the players' preference profile implicit in *e*. But with alternative behavioral assumptions this set might represent various Nash-refinements or the dominant strategies, or maximin strategies.

It may, however, be the case that the equilibrium correspondence is constrained by restrictions on strategies. For example, in a Hotelling–Lange–Lerner economy, the enterprise is required to choose an input–output vector resulting in the equalization of output prices and marginal costs (with prices treated parametrically). In an extreme case, the equilibrium correspondence may be totally prescribed by the rules; furthermore, it may be singleton-valued (i.e., equivalent to a function). In the latter case choice is completely determined by the rules.

We are now in a position to introduce formally the notion of an *adjustment process* as defined by the three entities: the choice space *C*, the outcome function *h*, and the equilibrium correspondence μ, i.e., the triple (μ, C, h). Of course, this presupposes the specification of the two underlying spaces, the environment space *E* and the outcome space *Z*.[8]

2.4   *Performance, realization, and implementation*

We now proceed to define the value of the *performance correspondence* Ψ_π of an adjustment process $\pi = (\mu, C, h)$ as the set of equilibrium outcomes associated with an environment e. In set notation, $\Psi_\pi(e) = \{z \in Z : z = h(c)$ for some c satisfying $c = \mu(e)\}$.

The situation can be represented diagrammatically by the Mount–Reiter triangle shown in Figure 4.1.

Clearly, the performance correspondence specifies the possible equilibrium outcomes given the environment. But in addition to its descriptive value it is of central importance in the normative context. Given the environment e, it enables us to compare the outcomes generated by an adjustment process with the desired outcomes defined by a goal correspondence. We say that an adjustment process π *realizes* the goal correspondence F on the class of environments E if the following two conditions are satisfied: (i) an equilibrium exists for every environment in E; and (ii) the outcomes generated by π at e are among those defined as desirable by F. That is: (i) $\mu(e)$ is nonempty for all e in E; (ii) $\Psi_\pi(e)$ is a sub-set of $F(e)$ for all e in E.[9] Informally, this means that the equilibrium outcomes generated by the process satisfy the F-optimality criterion, and that the existence of equilibrium is guaranteed whenever the environment is within the specified class E, so that the guarantee is nonvacuous.

A case of special interest is that of the Nash-equilibrium correspondence $v(\cdot)$. This correspondence is completely determined by the mechanism, i.e., by the game form (S, h). (Note the equilibrium strategy s^* depends on the environment, i.e., $s^* = v(e)$, since strategies chosen are determined by the players' preferences as well as the game rules represented by S and h. But, of course, the equilibrium correspondence $v(\cdot)$ itself does not depend on e.) Therefore, the adjustment process is completely determined by the mechanism and one could ask whether a particular mechanism (rather than the adjustment process it defines) Nash-realizes a given goal correspondence. Following the terminology introduced by

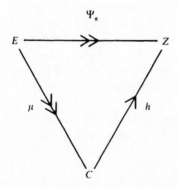

Figure 4.1   Performance, realization, and implementation

Maskin, it is now customary to speak of *Nash-implementation*, rather than Nash-realization. That is, we shall say that a mechanism (S, h) Nash-implements a goal function F over the class E of environments if, for every e in E: (i) there is a Nash-equilibrium strategy; and (ii) every Nash-equilibrium outcome in an environment e is an element of $F(e)$.[10] An analogous terminology is used for other game-solution concepts.[11]

3   Institutions

In the literature there are various approaches to the theory of institutions. For our purposes there are two important, and related, distinctions: (a) endogenously developed versus consciously created (designed), and (b) viewing institutions (in the sense of institutional arrangements rather than entities) as stable behavior patterns versus seeing them as sets of rules governing behavior. There is no doubt that there are many instances of endogenous development of institutions, and ideas such as those of Hayami and Ruttan concerning demand for institutional change throw light on an important aspect of such phenomena. My own interest is focused to a greater extent on the design of new or modified institutions, but there is no conflict between the two aspects of the process of institutional change. Indeed, when underlying conditions (e.g., technology, tastes, or attitudes) change, this may create a need, and demand, for institutional innovation, and the process of satisfying this demand may involve conscious design activities. Legislation is one example of such a process.

As for the distinction between the rules and behavior pattern interpretations, again, it need not be regarded as implying a contradiction, since behavior is affected, and in certain situations determined, by rules and so likely to remain stable as long as the rules are unchanged. As for semantics, the term "institution" may be applied either to the rules or to the resulting behavior, the (institution of the) market is an example. But from the point of view of policy choices and design it seems clear that it is the rules that are susceptible to conscious change, with the behavior changes as a consequence. It is for this reason that we opt for a concept of an institution involving rules rather than behavior patterns.[12]

Within the framework discussed in the earlier sections of this chapter it is tempting to identify a set of rules defining an institution with a mechanism, specifying the set C of admissible choices and the outcome function h associating outcomes z with choices c.[13] In some cases this formulation might be adequate, but in general it is too narrow for the following reason. Suppose we adopt as our model of interactions that of a non-cooperative game with Nash-equilibrium as the solution concept. Suppose we identify an institutional arrangement with a game form (S, h). Then, given the environment (i.e., specifying individual characteristics such as preferences, production functions, initial endowments), the set of equilibrium strategies is uniquely determined. But in many examples of institutional arrangements behavior patterns are not uniquely determined by these arrangements.

To illustrate the point: it seems reasonable to think of price controls as an example of an economic institution. But to determine the behavior of economic agents it is not enough to know that there are some price ceilings; one must know their numerical levels. Once such levels have been specified, we may consider that the ith seller's choice domain C^i has been defined, say as the numerical interval $[0, k]$ where k is the ceiling price the seller is permitted to charge. Assuming that the other agents' choice domains have also been specified and the outcome function h defined to represent the rules governing market transactions, the Nash-equilibrium set is uniquely determined. But a different Nash-equilibrium set would be obtained if the price ceiling k were chosen at a different level. Yet we would not say that changing the value of k changes the institutional setup: we have price controls regardless of the ceiling level. This leads to the idea that, in this example, the institutional arrangement (price controls) does not involve a particular choice domain but rather a *type of choice domain*, namely a choice domain for sellers which is an interval bounded from above.[14] Now we note that when only the *type* of choice domain is specified, we wind up not with a single mechanism but a whole *family of mechanisms*.[15]

While the price control example identifies an economic institution with a family of choice domains, there are also examples of economic institutions that can be identified with a *type of outcome function*. As an illustration we borrow a model from Stiglitz (1974); this paper considers the reward of a person working the land belonging to someone else. The reward (which we interpret as the outcome for the worker) is given by the formula

$$r = ay + b$$

where r is the reward, y the worker's output (or, perhaps, value added), while a and b are real numbers. Three institutional arrangements are defined by selecting certain sets of values for the parameters a and b. Thus the worker is a share-cropper if $b = 0$ while a is a number between zero and one. The worker is on wages if $a = 0$ while b is some positive number; he/she is a renter if $a = 1$ while b is some negative number. Now to specify uniquely, it is necessary to specify the outcome function,[16] i.e., the numerical values of the two parameters. But we note that each of the three economic institutions (share-cropping, wage labor, renting) is identified with a range of values for one of the two parameters, i.e., with a set of points in the (a, b) plane, not a single such point. This means that each institution is identified not with a single outcome function but with a family of outcome functions, hence – as in the price control example – with a *family of mechanisms*. It is important to note that other sets of points in the (a, b) plane might define either entirely new institutions or mixtures of the three ones previously described.

It is not difficult to think of other examples of institutions which are identified with a type of choice domain and a type of outcome function, where neither the choice domains nor the outcome function are uniquely defined. This, then, leads to the concept of an *institution as a family of mechanisms*, rather than a single mechanism.[17] But, of course, not every family of mechanisms is an institution.

We have seen in the preceding examples that a convenient way of identifying an institution with a family of mechanisms is to consider it as restricting the type of mechanism that is admissible. It is a rule about rules. This means specifying which type of choice domain or of outcome function is admissible. But there are various possible sources of inadmissibility. The most obvious is physical impossibility. Obviously, restrictions due to the laws of physics would not be viewed as institutional. Only those restrictions that are due to human actions or behavior patterns are candidates for institutional interpretation, but not even all of these.[18]

It was mentioned earlier that the legislative process is a source of new or modified institutions. An example would be a law introducing price controls. Here the institution introduced is a system of price controls, and the human action generating it is the legislative process culminating in the price control law being passed. This pattern suggests a paradigm for modeling institutional change as a two-phase phenomenon. In the first phase, the institution is formed (in our example, by legislative act). But this does not uniquely specify the mechanism. For that to occur, the specific price ceilings (as well as a variety of regulatory details) must be decreed.[19] Typically, that will be done by an agency – either an existing one or one created for this special purpose, such as the US Second World War Office of Price Administration (OPA).[20]

Such process of institutional change can be modeled in various ways. Indeed, there are several possibilities even within the framework of game theory. The route adopted in a pioneering paper by Reiter and Hughes (1981) is that of a sequence of two games, the first corresponding to the legislative stage and the second to the regulatory stage.[21] But there is an alternative, so far not yet explored in detail, of regarding the phases as stages in a single game in extensive form. Here, again, the early stages of such a game would result in restrictions on the nature of the mechanism to be crystallized in the later stages.[22]

A different view, in the nature of a generalization of the Reiter–Hughes approach, is to view the process of institutional change as a (finite) sequence of games, say $1, 2, \ldots, T$, where for $t = 1, \ldots, T - 1$ the outcome function specifies, in increasing detail, the rules for game $t + 1$. Then the T-game determines the "substantive" outcome, e.g., resource allocation, or who gets elected (while the earlier games only determine the electoral rules). As an illustration, game 1 might result in formulating the country's constitution, games $2, \ldots, t - 2$ legislation, and $t - 1$ the rules specified by a regulatory agency. We may think of such a sequence as a *cascade* of games.

Suppose that we have designed a mechanism that Nash-implements (in the sense of the above technical definition) a given goal correspondence, and that the mechanism has been adopted. This implies that any Nash-equilibrium outcome is consistent with the stated goals and, furthermore, that equilibria do exist. Leaving aside the problem of dynamics, are we now entitled to expect the desired equilibria to prevail? Clearly, this depends on what is meant by the mechanism being "adopted." In the most favorable circumstances, one could imagine that all players are willing to stay within the prescribed choice (strategy) domains and that there is a procedure for making the outcome function effective. It is then correct to say (as is often said) that a Nash-equilibrium is "self-enforcing." The meaning of "self-enforcing" in this context is interpreted as implying that there is no need for external policing because (by definition of a Nash-equilibrium) no player has an incentive to depart from his/her equilibrium strategy given the others' choices.[23]

But rules implicit in an institutional arrangement are not necessarily internalized by the player. Also, there are problems with putting an outcome function into effect, unless one can expect players to volunteer monetary transfers, paying fines, etc. Taking these problems into account, Schotter (1981:11) proposes the following definition of a social institution:

A social institution is a regularity in social behavior that is agreed to by all members of society, specifies behavior in recurrent situations, and is either self-policed or policed by some external authority.

Although not all elements of this definition are in agreement with ours,[24] Schotter's concept is valuable for its stress on the enforcement (policing) aspect.

The problem of modeling the enforcement aspect of an institutional arrangement presents some conceptual difficulties. Elsewhere (Hurwicz, 1988) we have suggested a possible approach, involving an *"augmented game form."* To enforce a given (not self-policing) mechanism we introduce additional players, whose mission is to perform the policing functions. These additional players may be either physical persons or institutional entities (courts, police, ombudsmen, etc.). These additional players must be given appropriate incentives to perform their mission. Thus we have designed a game including both the original players (e.g., the traders or other economic agents) and the additional ones, and the situation thus created is viewed as the augmented game. This game must have a game form (i.e., a governing mechanism) which, *inter alia*, prescribes the choice domains and outcomes for the additional players. The hope, of course, is that the equilibrium outcomes of the augmented game agree with the goal function which was being Nash-implemented by the mechanism designed for the original players (e.g., the traders).

But two problems arise. First, even if the new players abide by the rules of the augmented mechanism, the enforcement system calls for the use of social resources. This limits resources remaining for the satisfaction of the original goal function, e.g., production of food. Consequently, the resulting outcome cannot be Pareto-optimal with regard to the total endowment.[25] Hence it becomes necessary to reformulate the goal criteria taking into account the costs of "operating the system." Some ideas along these lines were introduced in Hurwicz (1972a, 1972b).

But, again, why should one expect that the enforcers will be carrying out their missions rather than, say, trying to enrich themselves through corrupt activities? There is no more reason to expect the augmented mechanism to be self-enforcing than the original one. One way to view the problem is to think of the "natural" game form which includes not only the permitted choices but all those that are physically or psychologically possible for the participants, and where the "natural" outcome function simply reflects the necessary effects of actions taken.

Thus one does not postulate an outcome function which automatically results in a fine being paid by a transgressor but rather describes the actions of all the participants (including the police, courts, etc.) that would have to be taken in order that the transgressor actually be made to pay the fine, or a lottery winner to collect his/her prize.

Needless to say, conceiving or announcing institutional modifications will not necessarily result in the desired behavior. The difficulties encountered in criminal law enforcement (e.g., drug interdiction) in various parts of the world is one obvious example. The obstacle to economic reform in various communist countries is another. How can analysis deal with this issue?

One possible approach is to consider in some detail the first phase of the institutional change process discussed above. If we view this phase as a game (whether cooperative or not), it seems appropriate that the outcomes of this game (i.e., what the players care about) be the institutional rules to be adopted. For a given institutional change to be adopted it is necessary that there be players who desire that particular institutional change, and secondly that they have the means to prevail. We may refer to these means as "assets." An example might be the role played by the international institutions (e.g., IMF or World Bank) desiring changes away from command centralized planning systems and subsidies, and which possess financial assets helping them prevail. But our interpretation of the term "assets" in this context is broader: it may involve political power or even personal charisma. It is convenient to have a term referring to players with both a desire and assets for effecting institutional change; they may be called "intervenors." An intervenor may be an individual, an institutional entity, an organization, a social class, or even an unorganized human mass. Recent events provide examples of all these types. When the intervenors' assets are strong enough as compared with those of the opponents, institutional change is likely to occur. The existence of a "demand" for institutional innovation will, of course, increase the probability of the intervenors' success.

The intervenors' role is not confined to the first phase, that of effecting institutional change. We have noted that in the augmented game there is a possibility that, due to the failure of the enforcement system, the equilibrium outcome will not be the intended one. By joining the augmented game and using their assets the intervenors may be able to see to it that the enforcement system works as intended.[26]

A few further remarks concerning the role of the intervenor in my model may be helpful here. First, although there may be some relationship between the role of an intervenor and of what some have called a "political entrepreneur," I do not identify the two. This is especially clear when we think of the intervenor as participating in the enforcement (as distinct from the institutional innovation) process.

Second, why introduce the intervenor into the model at all? One possible answer that it seems to be a realistic element of many observed phenomena of institutional change and of enforcement. It may also help explain why certain reform efforts change – either through lack of adequate "assets" on the part of would-be reformers, or due to lack of clarity or intensity in their preferences for the relevant institutions.

It seems less controversial that a presence of successful intervenors is helpful in effecting change and/or maintaining institutions. The question is whether it is necessary to have such intervenors. On preference side, the issue is whether in the cascade of games suggested above it is necessary to have players in game t whose preferences are defined on the space of rules for game $t + 1$ and/or subsequent games (rather than some discounted expected payoffs in the substantive game T). The presence of such preferences may be characterized as ideology, extended sympathy, or by treating rule outcomes as proxy variables for the final expected substantive outcomes. Whether, or under what circumstances, such phenomena are essential in models of institutional innovation and maintenance seems to me still an open question.

Finally, a comment concerning the possible application of existing results from the theory of adjustment processes and mechanisms to the institution formation problems discussed here.

First, the relevance of adjustment process results for mechanism theory. These results are mostly to be viewed as informational possibility and impossibility findings. In particular there are interesting results showing that finite-dimensional spaces are inadequate in economies with non-convexities (e.g., increasing returns) and infinite horizons (Hurwicz, 1972a; Calsamiglia, 1977; Hurwicz and Weinberger, 1990). If no finite-dimensional adjustment process of the required type exists, it follows that no such mechanism exists. In general, negative results in adjustment process theory carry over to mechanism theory, and indirectly also apply to institutions. On the other hand, the fact that a certain type of adjustment process is possible does not imply the feasibility of a corresponding mechanism, since the adjustment process may be postulating behavior inconsistent with the agents' incentives. However, such positive results are not without value for mechanism design in that they suggest directions in which appropriate mechanisms can be sought.

A similar relationship exists between results in mechanism design and those in institutional theory. Negative results in mechanism theory carry over into institutional theory, positive results are suggestive but inconclusive. This may be so because a desirable mechanism may be either impossible to put into operation, or so costly in resources for enforcement and implementation that its net efficiency is lower than that of alternative mechanisms whose "gross" efficiency is higher. Aside from these purely economic considerations, even efficient operation may be undesirable in terms of ethics, human rights, or other social and political consequences.

Notes

The author wishes to express his appreciation for insightful comments to his discussant Gil Skillman, as well as to Samuel Bowles and Herbert Gintis.

1. A warning to the reader: even though the term "process" is used, we shall largely confine ourselves to its static, i.e., equilibrium, properties.
2. From now on "competitive" will be understood to mean perfectly competitive, i.e., where prices are treated parametrically.
3. Whose equilibrium is, of course, the perfectly competitive equilibrium configuration of prices and quantities.
4. A word of explanation for what may seem somewhat artificial terminology used here. Informally, the term "economy" is used in two meanings that it is important to distinguish. On the one hand we speak of an economy as defined by properties such as preferences, technology, etc.; for example, we speak of a "regular" or "convex" economy. In this sense, the term "economy" refers to those properties that are to be taken as given in the context of institutional or structural change. To avoid confusion, we use the term "environment" (originally suggested by Jacob Marschak) as a synonym for this meaning of "economy". The other sense in which "economy" is used is that of the economic system, e.g., a capitalist or a socialist economy, more generally those aspects that are subject to deliberate change. For this meaning of "economy," we shall use "mechanism" as a substitute. Finally, the term "adjustment process" is meant to encompass the mechanism together with behavior. The observed phenomena are viewed as determined by the three elements: environment, mechanism, and behavior. (Equivalently, by the environment and the adjustment process.) Conventional treatments, in listing their postulates, often fail to distinguish these categories, but for our purposes the distinctions are essential and this explains the terminological devices adopted here.
5. In the absence of externalities on production side, we need only a production possibility set. But when productivity of a unit is affected by the activities of others, the more general concept of a correspondence (suggested by Antonio Camacho) is appropriate. A similar correspondence might also be required in the presence of certain types of externalities on consumption side, or between production and consumption.
6. More precisely Arrow's SWF is defined on the space of possible preference profiles, which may be viewed as a sub-space of E.
7. To repeat an earlier comment, we prefer the term "goal" to "choice" as the name of this correspondence because of its clear normative connotation. The term "choice" might be misinterpreted as referring to actions or decisions.
8. What we call an "adjustment process" here is the stationary solution of the dynamic (tâtonnement) version of such a process. (It should be stressed that the term "tâtonnement" as here used has a much broader scope than Walrasian tâtonnement: it refers to the fact that physical actions such as production or consumption do not take place until the "dialogue" phase of the process has been terminated – either by a deadline or because equilibrium has been achieved.) Dynamically, the process consists of two phases: the dialogue and transition from dialogue to outcomes. The choices are messages. The ith agent chooses a message m^i from its *language* M^i. The process constitutes a system of first order temporally homogeneous difference equations. (This, of course, is a special case, chosen for the sake of simplifying

exposition.) The message emitted by agent i at time t is denoted by m_t^i. Each agent has a *response function* f^i which determines the ith agent's message emitted at time $t + 1$ given the n-tuple, m_t of messages emitted by the n agents at time t and the environment e, i.e.,

$$m_{t+1}^i = f^i(m_{t;e}) \quad i = 1,\ldots,n \quad \text{and} \quad t = 0,1,\ldots$$

where $m_t = (m_t^1,\ldots,m_t^n)$.

The process is called *privacy-preserving* if the ith response function depends on e^i only; that is, if in the above equation the symbol e can be replaced by e^i. *Informational decentralization* can be defined as requiring the privacy-preserving property together with certain other features.

The n-tuple $m = (m^1,\ldots,m^n)$ constitutes a *stationary* (or *equilibrium*) value of the above difference equation system if

$$m^i = f^i(m;e) \quad i = 1,\ldots,n.$$

(When messages belong to an additive group, the preceding equation can also be written as

$$g^i(m;e) = 0^i,$$

where 0^i is the null element of the ith language M^i.)

Let $m(e)$ denote the set of stationary values compatible with environment e. Then the correspondence associating with each e in E the set $m(e)$ is the *equilibrium correspondence* (elsewhere denoted by μ). The choice space, elsewhere denoted by C, here is the joint *message space*, i.e., the Cartesian product $M = M^1 \times \cdots \times M^n$. The outcome function h then associates an element z of the outcome space with an equilibrium message m; i.e., $z = h(m)$ where m is a stationary n-tuple.

9. Condition (i) is the requirement of existence of equilibrium, familiar from the theory of competitive equilibrium. The second condition can be illustrated by taking the goal correspondence to be Pareto. In that case condition (ii) requires that all equilibrium outcomes be Pareto-optimal, i.e., that the conclusion of the first theorem of welfare economics hold for the given adjustment process. (Occasionally, a stronger requirement is proposed, that $\Psi_\pi(e) = F(e)$ for all e in E. This requirement is so strong that it is not satisfied by the Walrasian adjustment process when F is the Pareto-criterion. On the other hand, requirements (i) and (ii) are satisfied by the Walrasian adjustment process over the set of "classical" environments, i.e., environments satisfying the familiar assumptions of absence of externalities, of convexity, continuity, etc., as formulated by one of the well-known existence theorems together with a version of the first welfare economics theorem.)

10. Some writers refer to this concept as "weak" implementation. The corresponding "strong" concept requires that the set of equilibrium outcomes possible for a given environment e be equal to $F(e)$.

11. As we shall see, there might be an advantage in reserving the term "implementation" for a somewhat different concept.

12. To the extent that the two can be clearly distinguished. There may be cases where the dividing line is quite ambiguous.

13. We recall that a mechanism (also called a game form) is defined as the pair (C, h) where C is the space of choices and h a function from C into the outcome space Z, so that $z = h(c)$. In the game context, $C = S = S^i \times \cdots \times S^n$; here S is the ("joint") strategy space, assumed to be the Cartesian product of (independent) individual strategy spaces S^i.

14. While in the absence of price ceilings that choice domain may be thought of as the infinite half-line $(0, \infty)$.
15. This would be true even if the institutional arrangement were characterized by a unique outcome function.
16. As well as the choice domains.
17. The term "family" is used here as a synonym for "set." A one-element set (a singleton) is a legitimate special case. Hence we are not saying that an institution can never be identified with a single mechanism, but rather than in general it is more natural to identify it with a set consisting of many (perhaps an infinity of) mechanisms.
18. There may be restrictions other than physical (or physiological) on the admissibility of mechanisms that would not qualify for institutional interpretation. Instinctive aversions or inclinations to certain actions as well as psychological factors may play a role analogous to physics in excluding or compelling certain choices.
19. The term "implementation" would seem appropriate for this phase of the process.
    The economic process (trading, production, etc.) might be a third game in this sequence, but neither it nor the second stage (the transition to a unique mechanism) would constitute a part of institution formation process.
20. This example illustrates an important phenomenon, namely that in order that an institutional arrangement (here price control) become effective it may be necessary to create an institutional entity (here the OPA) whose mission is to implement (in the ordinary, not game-theoretic, sense of this word) the institutional rules. Thus there is an intimate relationship between institutions in the "arrangements" and "entity" senses.
21. The two stages in the Reiter–Hughes model do not correspond precisely to the two phases of our example. It may also be noted that in their model the first game is cooperative, the second non-cooperative.
22. Some aspects of the extensive form approach are discussed in Hurwicz (1987). The extensive form approach provides a natural framework for introducing the informational aspects of the institution formation process. The extensive game model involves a sequence of moves some of which are actions producing outcomes (e.g., transaction costs) before the game is completed, while others are in the nature of messages (e.g., proposals). From the economist's viewpoint, this is a mixture of tâtonnement and non-tâtonnement. (In another context, a suggestion for such a mixed model was put forward some years ago by Tom Marschak.)
    Interim outcomes (i.e., outcomes produced before the completion of the game), especially transaction costs, play an important role in modern "institutionalist" theory (see Williamson, 1985). They are also implicit in the informational theory of message exchange adjustment processes, where requirements such as the privacy-preserving property or limits on complexity may be attributed, in part at least, to communication or computation costs.
23. This may sound like a tautology, but I prefer to interpret it as a behavioral assumption (that players do not unilaterally depart from their Nash-equilibrium strategies).
24. In particular, our concept is formulated in terms of rules governing behavior rather than the behavior itself. Also, to require the agreement on the part of *all* members of society seems too strong.
    The requirement that an institutional arrangement apply to specific recurrent situations can perhaps be put in a more general form, namely that the institutional rules apply to a category of situations rather than to a particular one. (This excludes a

"bill of attainder" type of rule.) We shall call this property of rules "categoricity," and regard recurrence as a special case.

25. The same issue arises with regard to costs of communication, other information processing, or other "transaction costs." This includes the costs of operating markets as well as those of a central planning bureaucracy.

26. An interesting example of an intervenor is an experimenter testing, e.g., alternative hypotheses concerning the likely behavior of economic agents in game situations. The experimenter prescribes rules of the game. It is important for the experimenter that the human subjects abide by the rules of the game (otherwise the experimental results lose validity) and he/she presumably has the means ("assets") to make certain that they do – for instance, by being able to control their communications and actions, as well as motivating them by monetary rewards or other methods.

5　Imperfect choice and rule-governed behavior

RONALD A. HEINER

1　Introduction

Economics has traditionally assumed that agents always make best decisions based on available information. The latter may itself be inaccurate or incomplete, but no further imperfection enters into the analysis about agents' ability to decide optimally. Not surprisingly, perfect decisions have been criticized by many investigators including Simon (1983), Elster (1984), Tversky and Kahneman (1974), Slovic and Lichtenstein (1983), as well as by decision theorists such as Arrow (1982, 1986), Nelson and Winter (1982). Despite the plausibility of these criticisms, it has still proven difficult to develop useful analytical tools that do not depend on assuming perfect choice. I shall thus describe a conceptual framework and related theoretical tools for studying the behavioral implications of imperfect choice that may not always react optimally to information. The resulting analysis implies that imperfect agents will benefit from following rules adapted only to recurrent situations rather than allowing complete freedom to decide independently on a case-by-case basis, thereby producing a tendency to ignore relevant and even costlessly available information.

2　From imperfect choice to predictable behavior

I begin by suggesting a conceptual basis for analyzing imperfect choice. Figure 5.1 depicts a flow chart beginning with imperfect decisions and ending with systematic behavior patterns. Two guiding intuitions on how to model behavior are shown. Standard analysis combines the first two steps leading to conclusion *A*: that modeling systematic features of behavior requires exclusive focus on perfect choice. Despite many helpful ways of modifying standard theory, like adding search and transaction costs (Williamson, 1979; McCall, 1965; Stigler, 1961), decision errors still ultimately represent unpredictable tendencies which cannot in and of themselves contribute to systematic regularities in behavior.

The other conceptual pathway to conclusion *B* in Figure 5.1 also recognizes that decision errors by themselves cannot explain systematic behavioral tendencies. However, it continues beyond steps one and two to recognize further that decision errors create systematic incentives to regulate choice with rules and procedures, thereby producing relatively more predictable behavior than freely deciding without such constraints. Consequently, the incentives toward rule-governed behavior created by imperfect choice expands the analytical basis for studying behavior beyond that attainable from assuming perfect decisions. I next

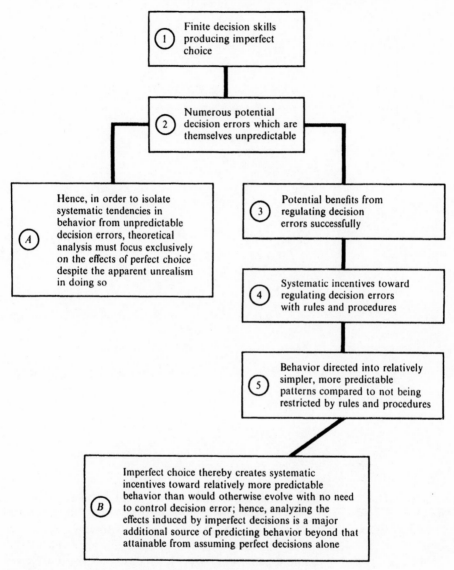

Figure 5.1   Two conceptual pathways for analyzing behavior

describe certain modeling tools for exploring the behavioral implications of this expanded analytical framework.

3   Analytical tools for studying imperfect choice

Figure 5.2(a) is modified from Levy (1988) to provide a familiar economic setting to motivate certain concepts. However, these concepts apply well beyond this

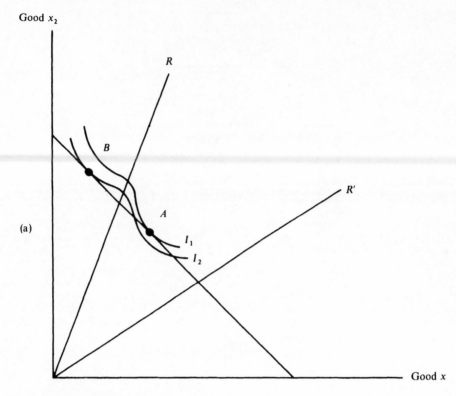

Figure 5.2   The global optimum
(a) Global optimum lies at point A inside the R-zone

example (Heiner, 1983:1985b). Lines I_1 and I_2 represent an agent's utility indifference curves, and the negatively sloped line represents the agent's consumption possibility boundary. Points A and B represent two local optimizing points for a given consumption possibility boundary, of which only point A is a global optimum for that boundary. In this example, I_1 and I_2 are nonconvex, so that shifting in locally more preferred directions may converge to only local instead of global optima. Another boundary or "rule-zone" or R-zone is formed by the two rays R and R'. It contains those choices permitted under a set of behavioral rules restricting an agent's decision flexibility or freedom of choice beyond the unavoidable restrictions due to resource scarcity represented by the consumption possibility boundary. For example, staying within a restrictive R-zone that contains only those choices over which agents have relatively full understanding of their preferences may enable them to overcome the problem of distinguishing local from global optima. R-zones can also represent a variety of other possibilities such as instinctive constraints in animal behavior, ethical

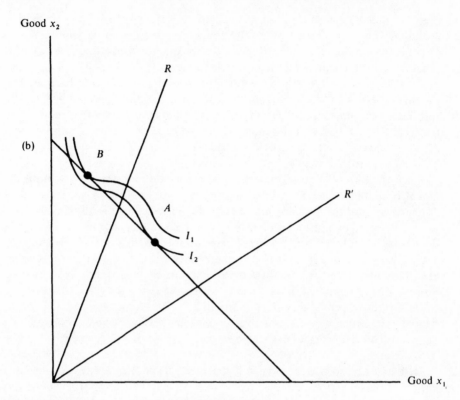

(b) Global optimum lies at point *B* outside the R-zone

norms for human conduct, sexual taboos and ritual in tribal cultures, psychological fear prompting retreat from potential danger, or legal restrictions on transferring property. Standard economics sometimes incorporates factors like instinctive, ethical, cultural, or psychological constraints into an agent's indifference curves. In contrast, the present analysis seeks a deeper explanation of why such constraining factors arise in the first place, instead of only assuming them in the form of preferences.

Figure 5.2(b) is identical to Figure 5.2(a) except that point *B* rather than point *A* is now the global maximum for the same consumption possibility boundary. Thus, in Figure 5.2(a) the global maximum is within the R-zone while in Figure 5.2(b) it is not. The likelihood of these two cases depends in part on how different decisions affect the local curvature of an agent's indifference curves (and thereby which of the two local optima *A* or *B* is relatively more preferred).

Whether a global optimum lies within an R-zone also depends on its restrictiveness, as shown by the area between rays *R* and *R'*. Totally restrictive rules result from converging *R* and *R'* into a single ray. A global optimum will then "almost always" lie outside the resulting degenerate R-zone with zero area;

meaning that a degenerate R-zone has zero probability of containing a global optimum. The other extreme of totally nonrestrictive rules means shifting R and R' apart so that they coincide with the vertical and horizontal decision axes. All potential decisions can then be freely made. Hence, any potential global optimum such as A or B is automatically within the resulting unrestricted R-zone. The intermediate case corresponds to behavioral rules that are neither totally restrictive nor unrestrictive, thereby allowing a limited range of free choice. The resulting R-zone is neither degenerate nor all-inclusive. A global optimum will thus sometimes lie outside as well as inside the R-zone, as illustrated in Figures 5.2(a) and 5.2(b).

When the former situation arises, an agent would be better off selecting the global optimum rather than choosing in the R-zone. This situation is called "preferred exception" to following rules by staying in the R-zone. Failing to make such a preferred exception represents a Type 1 error, meaning failing to deviate from rules when there exist preferred exceptions to them. On the other hand, a Type 2 error means mistakenly to violate rules when there exist no preferred exceptions (because the global optimum lies within the R-zone). Note that so long as some potential choices are inconsistent with a set of rules, there always exists a positive probability of encountering preferred exceptions. Thus, let π_d denote the probability of preferred exceptions arising, where appropriately deviating from a set of rules (indicated by the subscript d) is preferred to following them.

Mistaken decisions (resulting in Type 1 and Type 2 errors) can arise for a variety of reasons. For example, agents may have imperfect information about the nature of nonconvexities in their preferences, so that local "hill-climbing" search methods become unreliable in arriving at global instead of local consumption optima. Other possibilities may involve incomplete or inconsistent preferences in valuing different consumption points, separate from imperfect knowledge about such imperfectly structured preferences. In addition, they might be psychologically affected by several partially conflicting motivations and criteria about what is more or less desirable (rather than being guided by a single comprehensive and self-consistent value system; see for example Elster, 1985). Agents may also be imperfect at deciphering complex causal patterns, including both cooperative and competitive behavior of other interacting agents. The latter also depends on internal (possibly genetic) factors affecting agents' cognitive and perceptual abilities, along with numerous external factors affecting the complexity of their environment.

These imperfections can be understood as arising from a gap between agents' decision-making competence and the difficulty of their decision problems (called a C–D gap). Standard choice theory implicitly assumes that no C–D gap exists. Consequently, it has never investigated the behavioral implications of widening the gap, that is, of varying agents' decision-making competence *relative to* the difficulty of their decision problems. The objective is to extend existing theory so that optimal decision rules become limiting cases within a larger set of behavioral possibilities which now opens up for analysis. The theory thus ceases to be at odds with imperfect decisions due to the existence of C–D gaps, but can now itself focus directly on the behavioral implications arising from them (see Heiner, 1983, 1988a, 1988b for more discussion of this issue).

One way to accomplish this objective is to use probability concepts related to the earlier definition of π_d (as the likelihood of encountering preferred deviations from a set of rules). We can similarly consider the likelihood of imperfect agents correctly or incorrectly deciding when to deviate from or follow a set of rules. In particular, let r_d be the conditional probability of rightly deciding to deviate from a set of rules when it is genuinely preferred to do so (i.e., when preferred exceptions exist because the consumption optimum lies outside the R-zone). As before with π_d, the subscript d refers to deviating from rules. Alternatively, let w_d be the conditional probability of wrongly deciding to deviate from a set of rules when doing so is actually less preferred than following them (i.e., when no preferred exceptions exist because the consumption optimum lies inside the R-zone).

By introducing the conditional probabilities r_d and w_d we can explicitly model the behavioral effects of C–D gaps as discussed above, rather than analyzing only the limiting case where no C–D gaps exist. In particular, r_d and w_d can be used formally to represent an agent's reliability at deciding when to follow or deviate from a set of rules by defining the ratio $\rho_d = r_d/w_d$; meaning the relative likelihood of rightly instead of wrongly deciding to deviate if given the freedom to do so. A perfect agent with no C–D gap in solving any decision problem would always rightly deviate and never wrongly deviate from a set of rules; so that $r_d = 1$, $w_d = 0$, and $\rho_d = r_d/w_d = \infty$. Perfect agents who always maximize utility are thus infinitely reliable at having the freedom to decide for themselves when to follow or deviate from any partially restrictive set of rules.

On the other hand, imperfect agents correspond to $r_d < 1$ and $w_d > 0$, meaning that they will sometimes fail to deviate when preferred exceptions exist, and sometimes mistakenly deviate when this is not the case (if given the freedom to decide for themselves when to deviate or not). Consequently, imperfect agents are only finitely reliable ($\rho_d < \infty$) at deciding when to deviate from partially restrictive rules.

Note that any of the above-mentioned sources of imperfect decisions may contribute to lowering r_d below one or raising w_d above zero, thereby determining the particular finite size of ρ_d. Thus r_d and w_d are not introduced as exogenous factors outside of subsequent analysis. They instead depend on a number of potentially endogenous variables affecting peoples' perceptual ability to interpret incoming information, to formulate internally consistent value systems for evaluating different decisions, to understand possibly complex interaction patterns of other agents, and so on.

As one example, it is possible to analytically distinguish imperfect information from imperfect decisions about using information, and thereby study the interrelationships between errors arising from *both* sources of imperfection. In order to do so, r_d and w_d can be separated into sub-components. Let I denote information for which deviating from rules raises expected utility compared to not doing so (Fishburn, 1952); representing the "right information" for choosing to deviate. In this context, expected utility is a weighted average of utility depending on the likelihood of global optima being within an R-zone or not; where information I might arise under either case (Heiner, 1988b). For example, I could represent barometer readings for which carrying an umbrella is on average the best choice even though it may or may not rain after recording these readings. Let r_d^I denote the conditional probability of observing information I when a preferred exception truly arises (the chance of observing information I when a global optimum actually lies outside the R-zone). Similarly, let w_d^I denote the conditional probability of still observing information I when no preferred exception arises. Likewise, let w_d^B and r_d^B denote the conditional probabilities of agents deviating from rules when they observe information I or other messages besides I respectively, where the latter messages are the "wrong information" for choosing to deviate (because doing so reduces expected utility when messages besides I are observed). The superscript B signifies their behavior in responding to information.

The ratio $\rho_d^B = r_d^B/w_d^B$ measures the reliability of agents' behavior in reacting to information. Similarly $\rho_d^I = r_d^I/w_d^I$ measures the reliability of messages I in revealing when preferred deviations to rules arise (because deviating when messages I are observed will raise expected utility). Perfect information or decisions means being infinitely reliable at either revealing when to deviate from rules or reacting to the right messages for doing so ($\rho_d^I = \infty$ or $\rho_d^B = \infty$). Standard choice theory analyzes the effects of imperfect information ($\rho_d^I < \infty$), but implicitly assumes perfect response to information ($\rho_d^B = \infty$). Using the above concepts, we can now analyze the effects of both sources of imperfection. In particular, the ratio $\rho_d = r_d/w_d$ defined earlier can now be understood as measuring agents' relative likelihood of rightly instead of wrongly deviating from rules as *jointly* affected by imperfect information and imperfect decisions. Its general structure is the following (shown in Heiner, 1988b):

$$\rho_d = \frac{r_d^I(\rho_d^B - 1) + 1}{w_d^I(\rho_d^B - 1) + 1}. \tag{1}$$

Note that $\rho_d^B < \infty$ implies $\rho_d < \rho_d^I = r_d^I/w_d^I$ whenever $\rho_d^I > 1$, and $\rho_d^B \to 1$, implies $\rho_d \to 1$ no matter how high ρ_d^I might be (where $\rho_d = 1$ implies a 50–50 chance of deviating from rules when preferred rather than mistaken to do so). Thus, (1) implies that less reliable use of information reduces agents' joint reliability ρ_d in response to any partially-informative information source for which $\rho_d^I > 1$ (no matter how reliable the information itself might be), eventually to the point of only a 50–50 chance of deviating when appropriate to do so. Moreover, this gives rise to an *information–complexity* trade-off whereby agents become less reliable at using increasingly complex information, thereby causing ρ_d^B to drop as ρ_d^I rises (Heiner, 1988b). The Shannon–Weaver information measure (Shannon and Weaver, 1963) can be used to quantify this trade-off; showing that a finite error threshold exists beyond which decision-reliability ρ_d^B is necessarily finite, and there always exists a positive marginal incentive to use information beyond this threshold, where perfect decisions are no longer possible (Heiner, 1988b).

Let g_d denote the expected gain from "rightly deviating" when preferred exceptions exist (the expected gain from moving toward a global optimum when it lies outside the R-zone). Similarly, let I_d denote the expected loss from "wrongly deviating" when no preferred exceptions exist (because the true global optimum lies inside the R-zone).

4   Rule-governed plus information-ignoring behavior

With the above concepts, we can determine whether imperfect agents will benefit from continually following a set of rules, or from the freedom to decide independently in each specific case whether or not to do so. The answer is given by an inequality called the reliability condition, which I have developed elsewhere (see Heiner, 1985a, 1986, which formalize the original argument in Heiner, 1983). In this context, the condition implies that agents will benefit from the freedom to choose when to follow or deviate from a set of rules if and only if the following inequality holds,[1]

$$\rho_d > T_d$$

where

$$\rho_d = \frac{r_d^I(\rho_d^B - 1) + 1}{w_d^I(\rho_d^B - 1) + 1} \quad \text{and} \quad T_d = \frac{l_d}{g_d} \cdot \frac{1 - \pi_d}{\pi_d}. \tag{2}$$

Inequality (2) means that agents' joint reliability at deciding when to deviate, ρd, must exceed a minimum reliability, or tolerance limit given by T_d. The minimum tolerance T_d rises as the expected loss from mistakenly deviating grows relative to the expected gain from correctly deviating (so that l_d/g_d rises), or as preferred deviations become less likely relative to no preferred deviations arising (so that $(1 - \pi_d)/\pi_d$ rises). If $\rho_d > T_d$ is violated, agents would benefit from following a set of rules instead of freely deciding with no choice constraints. Otherwise such rules are not evolutionarily stable, since agents would be better off without them (Heiner, 1989b).

Now consider imperfect agents with finite decision reliability $\rho_d^B < \infty$, which in turn implies that their joint reliability ρ_d is also finite ($\rho_d < \infty$) no matter how high ρ_d^I may be. So long as the expected gain from making preferred deviations to rules, g_d, is not infinitely larger than the expected loss from mistakenly deviating when no preferred exceptions arise, l_d (so that l_d/g_d stays above some positive $K > 0$), then the minimum tolerance T_d rises to infinity as the likelihood of preferred exceptions π_d goes to zero. Thus, $\infty > \rho_d > T_d$ is necessarily *violated* by imperfect agents for sufficiently small π_d (meaning that preferred exceptions are rare rather than typical or recurrent). Hence, imperfect agents in general will benefit from following partially restrictive rules allowing adjustment only to recurrent situations, rather than freely adjusting to all potential conditions or information. That is, *imperfect agents necessarily benefit from rule-governed behavior adapted only to typical or recurrent situations.*

Next assume π_d is small enough to imply $T_d > 1$, so that more than a 50–50 chance of deviating correctly is required for $\rho_d > T_d$. As information becomes more reliable (ρ_d^I rises) the information–complexity trade-off noted earlier, and Ashby's law of variety (1963) together imply that agents' decision reliability ρ_d^B drops toward one (also reducing their joint reliability ρ_d toward one, as implied by (1), so that $\rho_d > T_d > 1$ is violated. Thus, *imperfect agents eventually benefit from ignoring more reliable information, regardless of whether there are any costs of observing such information or not.*

We thus have two basic principles: imperfect agents benefit from being governed by rules adapted only to recurrent situations, and from ignoring more reliable, perhaps even *costlessly* available, information.

Before continuing, the preceding analysis is applied to four basic topics in decision theory.

(1) Standard game theory also provides an explanation of why agents might agree to rules that restrict their social interactions (such as a social convention to drive on a certain side of the street, or to follow other traffic regulations). However, such agreements are not necessarily optimal under all circumstances affecting the initial conditions that define a game-theory problem. For example, the relative amounts in a payoff matrix may vary considerably under different conditions (such as changes in weather or traffic density that alter the likelihood or severity of a collision while passing through an intersection). If agents were infinitely reliable at adjusting to information about such changes ($\rho_d^B = \infty$) then they would not benefit from rules that would sometimes restrict their social interactions from adjusting optimally to changing information about traffic conditions. On the other hand, the above analysis implies that imperfect agents (who cannot always respond optimally to information about particular circumstances) will at some point benefit from continually obeying social rules that are adapted only to typical or recurrent situations (for which the probability of preferred exceptions π_d is relatively small but still positive). Applied to standard game theory, this implication means that such analysis implicitly assumes what are in effect recurrent or typical situations as part of the initial conditions (such as a certain pattern of relative outcomes in a payoff matrix), and then deduces an optimal social rule for those implicitly assumed typical conditions.

The preceding imperfect choice analysis thus explains why such social rules will tend to be stable even across changing circumstances that sometimes vary beyond the range where following such rules is still optimal. The latter conclusion also means that standard game theory ceases to provide a truly independent explanation of social rules, but rather itself presupposes one of the key implications of imperfect choice analysis, namely, that rule-governed behavior is adapted only to typical or recurrent situations.

(2) As noted earlier, standard choice theory represents the limiting case where agents are infinitely reliable at responding to information, and thus will never benefit from being constrained always to obey any partially-restrictive set of rules (for which the probability of preferred deviations π_d is still positive). This implies that such agents will necessarily benefit from loosening any partially-restrictive choice constraints and would thus always choose to loosen them if given the freedom to do so. Consequently, there is no endogenous reason arising from standard choice theory to account for agents imposing constraints on their behavior that would sometimes prevent them from making most preferred choices. On the other hand, the preceding analysis necessarily implies the opposite conclusions for imperfect agents; namely, that they will at some point be worse off from ignoring sufficiently loose constraints (since $\infty > \rho_d > T_d$ is necessarily violated as $\pi_d \to 0$), even though there still remains a positive probability of preferred deviations from them.

The above analysis thus establishes an intrinsic theoretical reason for analyzing constraints that limit an agent's reaction to changing information or circumstances at all levels of analysis where decision-theoretic principles might be applied. That is, a focus on rules that constrain freedom of choice (through social institutions, cultural norms, internal psychological mechanisms, and so on) arises directly from the basic principles of imperfect choice.

(3) Recall again that the above analysis derives from an explicit recognition of imperfect agents who lack the ability always to make optimal decisions. From a conventional standpoint it is thus tempting to view the present analysis as reflecting a "non-rational" or "irrational" approach to behavior (because it is no longer built on the postulate of optimal decisions). Nevertheless, such a viewpoint is mistaken, because essentially the *opposite* is true, namely, the preceding analysis instead investigates the theoretically implied meaning of rationality for imperfect agents (in the form of rule-governed behavior with limited sensitivity to potentially available information). The traditional link of rationality to optimal decisions is valid only at the limiting extreme where agents have infinite decision reliability ($\rho_d^B = \infty$), because only in this case would agents not benefit from always following any partially restrictive set of rules. The analysis thus enables one to broaden the meaning of rationality concepts to encompass a whole range of behavioral possibilities previously thought incompatible with them. In so doing, the analysis also shows how traditional modeling tools can be modified with reliability concepts in order explicitly to investigate imperfect choice, even though such tools were originally motivated from the assumption of optimal decisions.

(4) As just discussed, the above analysis represents a theoretical characteriz-ation of rational behavior for imperfect agents. However, providing such a characterization does not mean that any kind of rule-following behavior is necessarily rational. As noted earlier, partially restrictive rules imply a positive probability of Type 1 errors in failing to deviate from rules when it is genuinely preferred to do so. Agents may thereby fail even to consider the best course of action for certain situations. Appropriate rules thus involve a balancing between avoiding a mistaken response to information associated with Type 2 errors, and avoiding an unnecessary recurrence of Type 1 errors associated with overly-restrictive rules.

Acknowledging such a potential balance, however, does not imply that appropriate or "optimally balanced" rules will necessarily evolve. The reason is that the very imperfections giving rise to decision errors will also hinder agents' ability fully to comprehend the pattern of Type 1 and Type 2 mistakes associated with different rules (otherwise, agents able perfectly to forecast both types of errors could foresee how to avoid them, and thereby eliminate any need to follow partially-restrictive rules in the first place). This problem applies with particular force to institutional rules involving government and other social organizations; because the intelligence needed to understand complex social interdependencies may far exceed that needed to understand why rules affecting mostly private conduct are beneficial (i.e., the C–D gap discussed earlier will rise as agents' decisions involve increasingly complex social relationships). Imperfect choice theory thus implies that appropriate government and other social institutions are *not* necessarily likely to evolve. This implication contrasts with the tendency of standard neo-classical theory simply to extend the assumption of optimal choice from individual to collective decisions (i.e., from individual actions to the behavior of collective institutions).

These issues are further developed in the latter part of this chapter concerning the stability properties of rules as agents become more intelligent. Before doing so, I first illustrate how the preceding analysis can be applied across a number of areas, involving both human and non-human behavior.

5   Instinctive rules in non-human behavior

Recall that imperfect agents benefit from being governed by rules adapted only to recurrent situations and from ignoring relevant, even costlessly available, information. In relation to this, note that instinctive constraints limiting behavioral sensitivity to relatively simple signals (even when more reliable and complicated information is costlessly observable) is a wisely documented feature across many animal species, including "releasing mechanisms," "imprinting," "fixed communication" patterns (like the waggle-dance of honey bees, Keeton, 1980), and so on.

Two common examples are displayed by European robins who will attack a simple tuft of red feathers much more often than a realistically mounted young robin with a dull brown breast; and by farm hens who will vigorously react to distress calls of a chick, yet still ignore clearly visible distress movements if they cannot also hear the chick's distress calls (for these and several other examples, see Keeton, 1980:498–505).

Still another example involves Tinbergen's studies of male stickleback fish, which illustrate a striking pattern:

The male fish attacked the red-bellied models, despite their unfishlike appearance, much more vigorously than they did the fishlike ones that lacked red. Surely the sticklebacks could see the other characteristics of the models, but they reacted essentially only to the releasing stimuli from the red belly. (Keeton, 1980:504)

Note also that in many cases animals have more accurate sensory mechanisms (thereby lowering observation costs) and quicker reflexes (allowing potentially more flexible reaction) than humans, yet they still exhibit noticeably more rigid responses to simpler information than typical for human behavior.

Now broaden the analysis to different species. Recall that as rules become more flexible (analogous to larger R-zones) the likelihood of preferred exceptions π_d drops toward zero, thereby raising the minimum tolerance T_d toward infinity for any l_d/g_d ratio bounded above zero. Consider a thought experiment where conditions affecting two agents 1 and 2 are the same, so that T_d rises in the same manner for both agents as rules become more flexible. However, agent 2 is more reliable at using potential information than 1 (say, due to better mental equipment). The information–complexity trade off from (1) thus implies that using more complex information will reduce both agents' joint reliability, denoted ρ_d^1 and ρ_d^2; yet ρ_d^2 still remains above ρ_d^1. Consequently, as shown in Figure 5.3, $\rho_d > T_d$ is violated *later* for agent 2 than for agent 1 as rules become more flexible. Agent 2 will thus benefit from flexibility to use more information than agent 1. When extended beyond two agents, this means that successively more reliable agents will benefit from increasingly flexible rules allowing greater sensitivity to potential information. It is noteworthy that a similar pattern has evolved biologically. At one extreme are rigid self-replication rules embodied in the DNA structure that virtually eliminate sensitivity to potential chemical messages (whose correct interpretation would allow flexible changes in its genetic sequence to improve its long-run viability or to produce better adapted phenotypes). Then proceeds a long evolutionary sequence of instinctively programmed behavior that gradually allows more flexible decisions as superior perceptual and cognitive mechanisms develop. For example, a relatively simple organism like a sow bug (often found under wooden logs) is governed by "forced movement" mechanisms allowing almost no learning plasticity to new information. Much later in evolutionary development are numerous animals and birds, whose behavior is noticeably more flexible, yet still governed by various instinctive guidance mechanisms (including releasing and imprinting mechanisms, as mentioned earlier). Still later in evolution are the higher primates (chimpanzees, gorillas, etc.) which display noticeable behavior plasticity to new

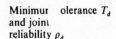

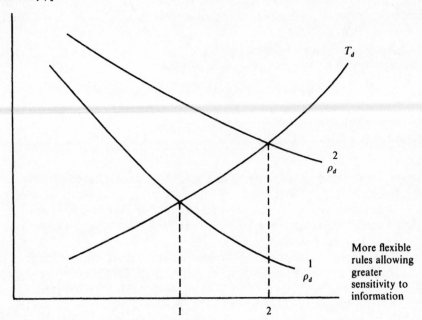

Figure 5.3   Rule flexibility
Points 1 and 2 on the lower axis show where the inequality $\rho_d > T_d$ is violated for the more reliable agent 2 compared to agent 1, thereby allowing agent 2 to benefit from more flexible decision rules and greater sensitivity to information than agent 1. Rule flexibility can be measured by the ratio of area within an R-zone divided by the total area for all potential choices (see Figure 5.2a)

information, including adaptive learning to situations not encountered in their natural environment. Finally, we have the largely non-instinctive, sometimes highly creative behavior of human decision-makers, thereby allowing self-generated beliefs, subjective preferences plus conscious goal-seeking behavior, strategic planning, entrepreneurial discovery, and so on.

By comparison with animal instinct, human behavior is much more flexible and sensitive to potentially received information. Yet even here, manifestations of rule-governed behavior are evident. I next briefly illustrate the latter specifically in the context of adapting to dynamically changing conditions.

6   Dynamic rules and ethics in human exchange

Two topics are briefly described.

(1)   Recent advances in nonlinear systems theory imply that optimal dynamic behavior often looks like random "chaotic" variation (Ben-

habib and Day, 1981; Day and Shafer, 1985; Li and Yorke, 1975; Jensen, 1987), thereby preventing imperfect agents from following such random target motion without dynamic errors. However, one can show that imperfect agents can still gradually approach the optimal target if and only if they partially adjust toward its perceived location so as to induce their behavior to converge to a stable equilibrium (see Heiner, 1989a). The need to reduce dynamic errors thereby induces a self-organizing or spontaneous tendency toward stable regularity in behavior that otherwise may never evolve. This result further illustrates the basic theme of Figure 5.1 above, namely that imperfect choice creates systematic incentives toward relatively more predictable behavior (i.e., toward stable instead of chaotic dynamics). This result also suggests that equilibrium behavior may be quite different from the disequilibrium (partial adjustment) principles needed for such properties ever to be dynamically realized (see also Heiner, 1985d). When applied to expectation formation, such partial adjustment is equivalent to adaptive expectations. Imperfect agents thus have a generic incentive toward adaptive adjustment as the only means of stabilizing to rational expectations equilibria. This result also agrees with recent asset-trading experiments by Smith, Suchanek and Williams (1988). The rational expectations hypothesis introduced by Muth (REM) explained the data only near the end of a dynamic process characterized by adaptive expectations; as summarized in the concluding sentence of the paper (1988:1150) "the general conclusion [is] that the REM model of asset pricing is supported only as an equilibrium concept underlying an adaptive capital gains adjustment process" (a similar conclusion is given for another experimental study by Williams, 1987:16):

Experimental research ... suggests that rational expectations may be a useful equilibrium concept ... [However], the evidence presented here indicates that the market dynamics leading to a rational expectations equilibrium are likely to be governed by an adaptive process that is inconsistent with Muthian individual rationality.

(2) Imperfect agents in general will benefit from delayed reaction to decision and expectation parameters (Heiner, 1988c). This result holds irrespective of whether there are any information, search, transaction, or other costs of adjusting decisions. For example, it applies even to consumption of perishable goods such as food where the existence of psychological habits has been postulated (Houthakker and Taylor, 1966) to account for delayed reaction to consumer prices. Delayed adjustment to new information is further evidenced in the stock market (Kaen and Rosenman, 1985). The latter may also produce punctuated dynamic behavior (Heiner, 1983, 1985c) as evidenced in persistent tendencies toward "bubbles and crashes" in stock prices (Smith, Suchanek and Williams, 1988; Smith, 1986).

7   Rule instability with sufficient intelligence

The preceding two sections discussed applications of results (1) and (2) to evolutionary biology and human behavior in dynamically changing exchange environments. These applications were selected in part to suggest that rule-governed behavior is a pervasive phenomenon; one that applies both to human and non-human behavior. Think of this also from what might be called a "constitutional perspective" about the need for defining "rules of the game" within which a sequence of ongoing decisions are made. Such rules can be understood not only as constraints on how people may interact under different institutional or cultural settings, but also as biological constraints on the behavioral flexibility of non-human agents. The latter constraints might even be called "instinctive constitutions." Indeed, the progression of agents evolved in nature suggests that such instinctive constitutions were a central factor in biological evolution long before human social institutions began to develop. This in turn suggests the importance of developing appropriate institutional rules to guide the largely non-instinctive social interactions of human agents.

I now briefly pursue this line of thought. In order to do so, it is important first to recognize a key difference in the nature of rule-governed behavior between humans and animals that is also suggested by results (1) and (2) above. Recall that Type 1 errors mean failing to deviate from rules when doing so is truly preferred, and that preferred exceptions arise with positive probability $\pi_d > 0$ except at the limit of totally unrestrictive rules. Type 1 errors thus gradually accumulate from obeying any partially-restrictive set of rules. For example, human observers have often identified conditions where instinctive rigidity is detrimental to an animal's survival. This amounts to recognizing Type 1 errors in obeying instinctive rules. The animals themselves, however, lack the requisite mental equipment to recognize Type 1 errors in following their own instincts. That is, non-human agents have little or no *self-recognition* of Type 1 errors from obeying their instincts.

However, a lack of self-recognition will eventually disappear as the mental capabilities of agents increase, such as for human agents. As mental ability rises sufficiently, self-recognition of Type 1 errors may itself motivate agents toward attempting to realize the net gains from preferred exceptions, producing a tendency to deviate from previously followed rules. The very experience generated by following rules thereby undermines their own continued stability, as agents' ability to self-recognize Type 1 errors increases. Obedience to rules is no longer self-stabilizing, but instead may be self-*de*stabilizing. Note further that self-recognition of past Type 1 errors does not imply that agents can interpret future events and information with sufficient reliability to benefit from greater freedom in making prospective future decisions. As discussed above, following rules necessarily generates Type 1 errors, but also prevents gaining any direct experience with Type 2 errors (since mistaken deviations never arise so long as rules are followed). The ability to recognize Type 1 errors from "hindsight knowledge" may thus be wholly insufficient for avoiding future Type 2 errors, which can arise only after agents begin deviating from rules.

Consequently, agents of sufficient but still imperfect intelligence may find themselves in the uncomfortable situation of still needing guidance from partially-restrictive rules (perhaps allowing considerably greater freedom than instinctive rules), while at the same time also self-recognizing Type 1 errors too often for obeying such rules to be self-stabilizing. Such agents may thus develop a general awareness of the need for certain rules, yet still face recurring psychological tension in following them successfully.

For example, ethical inquiry often involves problems with weakness of will, or lack of self-discipline, moral fiber, fortitude, and so on (Schelling, 1984; Strotz, 1956; Thaler and Sheffrin, 1981; Elster, 1984). Many novels also depict a protagonist under poignant circumstances challenging their allegiance to certain "universally recognized" moral principles. Social norms are also enforced in many societies with various types of sanctions for deviant behavior. In addition, philosophical arguments about morals often stress abstract moral duties, imperatives, and obligations that predispose obedience to moral principles without trying to behave flexibly on a case-by-case basis (Kant, 1985; Ross, 1963). These examples can be understood as indirect symptoms of ethical rules that are not self-stabilizing through the perceived experience generated by following them.

8 Agreement versus stability of social rules

The above analysis also has implications for political and constitutional theory. Consider initially the above issue of self-recognizing Type 1 errors through the experience generated by following rules, but now applied to social rules and institutions designed to promote the collective welfare of a whole society. To the extent that such rules constrain future interactions between individuals, Type 1 errors will accumulate in the process of following them after they are initially agreed upon. Imperfect agents may thus be unable to foresee preferred deviations to institutional rules agreed upon *ex ante* without actually being exposed to the *ex post* experience generated only through applying such rules to future conditions. Social rules agreed on *ex ante* may thus create recurrent future opportunities for preferred deviations, thereby also undermining their own *ex post* stability if such opportunities are eventually self-recognized through the very ongoing experience generated by following them.

Note further that the relative difficulty (compared to agents' decision-making competence) in understanding cost–benefit relationships across a complex network of interacting agents may far exceed that needed to understand an individual's private circumstances. People may thus face the dilemma of still noticing preferred exceptions to social and institutional rules, but with even less reliability at deviating from them than for private decisions affecting only their own private circumstances. Consequently, it may be more difficult to develop stable institutional rules than rules governing only private decisions just when there is an even greater need to do so.

The above discussion suggests a basic trade-off between ignorance and uncertainty that promotes consensus over *ex ante* rules, and the reliability of any such advance agreement in avoiding rules that are eventually destabilizing due to self-recognition of *ex post* Type 1 errors. This trade-off has not been stressed in contractarian political theory (Buchanan, 1977; Rawls, 1971) which has mainly analyzed how uncertainty about people's future conditions will help them mutually agree on social rules before anyone has had any actual experience living under them. Yet maintaining allegiance to previously agreed social rules may be a far more difficult challenge than reaching initial agreement about which rules to begin following (especially if the initial agreement was achieved under a veil of ignorance about the practical consequences of applying rules to future conditions).

As an historical example of the latter possibility, consider the American constitutional convention of 1787. Despite conflicts of interest about states' rights and slavery, there was much uncertainty about how many provisions of the constitution would intermingle with future political, economic, and technological developments. Suppose that as enough (*ex post*) historical experience and new developments unfold, citizens (including legislators, judges, executives, and voters) become increasingly aware of possible Type 1 errors in strictly interpreting the written language and "original intentions" of those present in 1787. On the other hand, they are not sufficiently reliable to develop new law on a more piecemeal basis without some sort of principled link to the written constitution. A persistent conflict may thus develop between judicial interpretation that would hinder or promote a more flexible and open-ended evolution of constitutional doctrine (even with no explicit passages in the written constitution to justify either tendency).

9   Conclusion

Three main areas have been discussed in this chapter. The first topic is a general theoretical perspective that imperfect choice creates systematic incentives for rules directing behavior into relatively simpler and more predictable patterns than otherwise needed for perfect agents who never decide mistakenly. The analysis implies that such rule-governed behavior is adapted only to recurrent situations, tending to ignore relevant and even costlessly available information. Existing theory can also be generalized for analyzing imperfect choice with reliability concepts; thereby expanding its use into previously unexplored areas. The second topic illustrates the pervasiveness of rule-governed behavior in diverse areas ranging from instinctive behavior in non-human biology to partial adjustment dynamic tendencies in human exchange institutions. The objective is also to suggest a constitutional perspective on the importance of developing rules to govern individual conduct and the behavior of social institutions. The third topic concerns a basic difficulty in behavioral rules being self-stabilizing through their ongoing application, once agents' ability to recognize preferred exceptions reaches a certain level. Applied to political constitutions, this means there is an intrinsic trade off between obtaining initial agreement over prospective rules, and avoiding future tendencies toward unraveling compliance once such rules are put into practice (even when maintaining such rules would still be beneficial to most future citizens).

Notes

1. To get a brief intuitive rationale for the condition, compare the expected benefits from either continually obeying a set of rules or having the freedom to deviate from them. The expression $\pi_d r_d g_d$ represents the expected *ex ante* gains from having the latter freedom compared to always obeying (the chance of preferred deviations arising times the chance of agents rightly deviating when this happens times the expected gain achieved by doing so). Similarly, the expected *ex ante* losses from the freedom to deviate compared to not doing so is $((1 - \pi_d)w_d l_d)$. Prospective gains will thus cumulate above prospective losses if $\pi_d r_d g_d > ((1 - \pi_d)w_d l_d)$. Hence, by rearranging terms the latter inequality can be expressed, $r_d/w_d > l_d/g_d \cdot ((1 - \pi_d)/\pi_d)$. See Heiner, 1985a for a general derivation which holds both under standard expected utility axioms as well as the more recent nonexpected utility theories of Machina, Chew, Fishbum, Tversky and Kahneman, etc.

6 Organizational equilibria and institutional stability

UGO PAGANO

1 Introduction

In the New Institutional economics firm ownership or its governance system is endogenously and efficiently determined by the characteristics of the resources which are used in the organization: namely their degree of specificity and their monitoring requirements. Section 2 of this chapter summarizes the New Institutional view.[1] Section 3 inverts the New Institutional view by arguing that the characteristics of the resources, employed in the firm are, in turn, determined by the nature of its ownership and/or governance system. This view supports some of the claims of the Radical economists[2] who have traditionally argued that the technology and the internal organization of the firm are often not due to the need for increasing efficiency and can be better explained as an outcome of given property relations. The two arguments are integrated by introducing the concept of property rights and technological equilibria and, more generally, the concept of organizational equilibria. In section 4 these equilibrium concepts are developed by means of a simple model. There, we argue that institutionally stable property rights' equilibria need not be efficient. In section 5 we consider Williamson's contracting scheme and suggest two ways in which the scheme can be generalized. Finally, in the concluding section 6 we apply briefly the framework developed in this chapter to two issues. The first concerns the diversity of institutions which characterized the major Western capitalist countries after 1945 in spite of their different efficiency. The second is related to the possible inability of democratic institutions to come about in spite of their greater efficiency.

2 The New Institutional view of the firm

New Institutional economics includes transaction costs' literature and property rights' literature. The first stems from Coase (1937) and has found its most complete exposition in Williamson (1985).[3] The second stems from another article by Coase (1960) and has been enriched by the contributions of Alchian and Demsetz (1972b), Alchian (1984, 1987), and Demsetz (1966).

Both streams of literature have concentrated their attention of the economic nature of the firm, the existence of which is explained on the basis of market transaction costs.[4] The first stream has emphasized the role of the firm as a governance system able, under some circumstances, to organize production at costs lower than market transactions. The second has emphasized the ownership of the firm by particular agents as a condition of its efficiency. The differences between these two streams of literature are, however, more a matter of focus and terminology than a matter of substance. Property rights, if interpreted in a general way, imply management rights and governance systems, and the latter are founded on explicit or implicit systems of rights.

Moreover, these two streams of literature come to the common conclusion that the ownership structure of the firm or its governance system can face the asset-specificity and monitoring problems better than the market – this being a relative advantage which explains the very existence of the firm.[5]

The asset-specificity problem arises because, under conditions of bounded rationality, market transactions, supported by specific investments, expose the partners to the hazards of opportunistic behavior. After "the fundamental transformation" (Williamson, 1985, Ch. 2) due to the development of specific assets, the agents cannot move on to trade relations with other partners without suffering substantial losses. Hence, the threat of competition cannot restrain the opportunism of the partners. Market relations fail to support specific investments, even if they are technologically superior.

The monitoring problem arises when it is difficult to write, or to enforce, a market contract specifying the contributions of the agents. Typically, these problems arise with team production when joint inputs are required for the production of a non-separable output, but are by no means limited to this case (Alchian and Demsetz, 1972b; Jensen and Meckling, 1976). In this case firm hierarchies replace market contracts to ease the monitoring problem.

Thus, monitoring and asset-specificity[6] are used to explain the emergence of the firm. Firms exist because they can be more efficient than markets in an environment characterized by the asset-specificity and/or the monitoring problems. They are also used to explain the property or the governance structure of the firm. The property right or the governance structure of the firm will be that which is the most efficient at solving the monitoring and the asset-specificity problems which are the cause of its existence. The rights on or the control of the firm are likely to be acquired by the owners of firm-specific or difficult-to-monitor resources. Owners of general-purpose or easy-to-monitor resources will have no rights on the firm. The former will be more efficient at solving the monitoring and the asset-specificity problems and will be willing to offer a higher price for the control of the firm than the latter.

This is clear if we consider the case of owners of firm-specific resources. The value of their resources will increase or decrease with the success or the failure of the firm, will change with the policies of the firm, and will be lost if they are fired from the organization – a set of circumstances which does not hold for the owners of the general-purpose resources.[7] Thus, rights of the specific factors will be most efficient at solving the asset-specificity problem. Under this structure of rights "insurance" costs which should otherwise be paid for "specificity hazards" can be saved. For this reason, the owners of specific resources will be willing to offer a higher price for the control of the firm.

Consider now the case of the owners of the difficult-to-monitor resources. If they own the firm, they will have an incentive to perform efficiently and the high cost of monitoring their contribution can be saved. Such saving will obviously be much less if the owners of the easy-to-monitor resources own the organization. Thus, if the owners of the difficult-to-monitor resources own the organization they can make it more profitable and efficient. They will therefore be willing to offer a higher price for the control of the organization.

It may be useful to concentrate our attention on some simple cases in which capital and labor are either entirely general-purpose or entirely specific.

Denote general-purpose capital and labor respectively by K_G and L_G and denote firm-specific capital and labor respectively by K_S and L_S. Call M_K spot markets for renting capital and F_K a firm controlled by capital owners. Similarly, denote by M_L spot markets for labor and by F_L a firm controlled by labor.

We can then distinguish four cases:

$$(K_G, L_G) \to (M_K, M_L). \tag{A}$$

Both capital and labor are general-purpose resources. In this case spot markets for labor and capital can efficiently organize production. This is the case considered in orthodox economics where firms do not really exist and "it does not really matter who hires whom" (Samuelson, 1957:894). No factor makes investment specific to an organization of production and therefore no factor is interested in its control. Anyone can move to trade relations with other partners at low costs.

$$(K_S, L_G) \to (F_K, M_L). \tag{B}$$

Capital is specific to a certain organization of production, whereas labor is general-purpose. In this case the organization of production cannot entirely be left to the market and a "capitalist firm" is likely to exist. Capital has an interest in controlling the organization of production because it is specific to this organization and would lose its value if it was separated from it. Capital will thus be interested in the management of the organization and, in particular, in holding firing and hiring rights. Labor is general-purpose and can move to other organizations without losing its value. Capital will offer more than labor for the control of the organization. Thus, a capitalist firm and a labor market, where labor is hired by capital, will be generated. This is also an efficient solution because the control of the organization is given to the factor which is more interested in its efficient management because its value is organizational-specific.

$$(K_G, L_S) \to (F_L, M_K). \tag{C}$$

In a similar way, when capital is the general and labor the specific factor, New Institutional economics explains workers' ownership of the firm and a rental market for capital. This justifies the relationship above.

$$(K_S, L_S) \to (F_K, F_L). \tag{D}$$

In this case, both labor and capital are specific to the organization of production. As a consequence both will be interested in some degree of control of the latter because they are both liable to be expropriated if they are separated from the organization. Many solutions, such as "governance institutions" or "labor–capital partnerships," can satisfy this requirement. In all these cases the efficient solution is achieved by safeguards and joint decision-making which make the expropriation of one specific factor by another specific factor more difficult and costly.[8]

Similar relations hold for the monitoring problem. Denote by a subscript E "the easy-to-monitor resources" and by subscript D "the difficult-to-monitor resources." Then K_E and L_E will stand for easy-to-monitor capital and labor[9] and K_D and L_D will stand for difficult-to-monitor capital and labor. Again, the characteristics of the resources to be employed will determine the efficient set of institutions:

$$(K_E, L_E) \rightarrow (M_K, M_L). \tag{a}$$

The market solution is implied by a situation where both labor and capital are easy-to-monitor resources. Here, standard contracts can easily specify the characteristics of the goods and the services to be exchanged.

$$(K_D, L_E) \rightarrow (F_K, M_L). \tag{b}$$

The capitalist firm solution arises when labor is the easy-to-monitor resource and capital (possibly including not only machinery but also management services) the difficult-to-monitor resource. Under capitalist ownership, the relatively higher costs of monitoring capital can be saved by having it as the residual claimant.

$$(K_E, L_D) \rightarrow (F_L, M_K). \tag{c}$$

Opposite conditions, where labor is the difficult- and capital the easy-to-monitor resource, generate the labor-owned firm.

$$(K_D, L_D) \rightarrow (F_K, F_L). \tag{d}$$

If both labor and capital are difficult to monitor then a system of joint ownership that gives to both capital and labor an incentive to improve the efficiency of the organization is the most preferable solution.

In conclusion, changes in technology affect the degree of specificity and the monitoring characteristics of the assets which it is optimal to employ and, in this way, determine property rights. Transaction costs due either to the specificity or the monitoring characteristics to be employed justify the existence of the variety of institutions which characterize a market economy by their relative efficiency.

3   A "radical" inversion of the New Institutional view

In the New Institutional literature the firm exists because of costs which would otherwise be incurred through market exchanges. At the same time, the efficiency of firms relies on the fact that the property rights on these organizations can be exchanged and acquired by the individuals who can rule them more efficiently and therefore are able to offer a higher price for their ownership. Still, things are not so simple. If transaction costs are admitted these gains may be lower than the costs of exchanging property rights. Moreover, exchange may take time. Because of the costs and the time taken by the transactions, changes in technology may have a weak or slow effect on the reallocation of property rights. This point is important because if property rights are not immediately exchanged according to the dictates of efficient technology, then in the meantime the opposite effect may take place. Property rights may influence the technology used by the firm and, in particular, the degree of specificity and the monitoring characteristics of the resources used by these organizations. A similar conclusion is obtained when one simply observes that, because of time preference and uncertainty the present assets of the firm determine the value of a firm to a much greater extent than the future assets which could be developed under a future system of property rights and that the nature of the existing assets is necessarily influenced by (pre-)existing property rights.

However, the influence of property rights on technology has also to be examined for a more fundamental reason. Technology is not created and adopted in a property rights' and institutional vacuum. The technology adopted by the firm may well determine that some property rights have to be changed following the efficiency drive examined by New Institutional economics. But, in turn, this technology is always shaped within the framework of a certain ownership structure which influences the nature of the technology and the resources employed by the firm.[10] In particular, the specific or general and the difficult- or easy-to-monitor character of the resources employed by the firm cannot only be a factor determining the ownership structure of the firm but must also be influenced by it. In fact, we are going to argue that all the relations considered in the preceding section can be inverted and that the "inverted" causal relationships are as convincing as the ones expressing the New Institutional view:

$$(M_K, M_L) \rightarrow (K_G, L_G). \tag{A'}$$

Only spot market relations, where factors are rented, are possible for both factors and it is not possible to acquire any right which guarantees one factor against the possible opportunism of the other in unforeseen circumstances. In this situation both capital owners and workers will be inhibited in the development of specific resources. The employment of general resources will be strongly preferred. An insurance cost will have to be sustained to employ specific resources to guarantee them against the opportunism of the other factor owners.

$$(M_K, M_L) \rightarrow (K_E, L_E). \tag{a'}$$

If both capital and labor can only rent their services on the market, they have a strong incentive to keep the costs of monitoring these services low. If a factor becomes more difficult to monitor it also becomes more expensive to rent and loses its competitiveness. In this situation, investments which increase productivity but imply an increase in monitoring costs tend to be strongly discouraged and investments characterized by lower productivity and lower monitoring costs tend to be strongly preferred. Thus a system, where sometimes labor hires capital and other times capital hires labor, is characterized by a strong incentive to plan investments that shape capital and labor as "easy-to-monitor" factors. Investments, otherwise yielding high benefits, are sacrificed because the property right system cannot easily deal with "difficult-to-monitor" factors.

$$(F_K, M_L) \rightarrow (K_S, L_G). \tag{B'}$$

In this case, resources are employed in an organization controlled by capital owners. This insures the owners of specific capital against the possible opportunism of the workers at a zero or low insurance cost.[11] By contrast, no similar guarantee exists for the workers who develop firm-specific skills. An insurance cost will therefore be sustained for the employment of these factors, and the technology of the firm will therefore be biased in the direction of the employment of firm-specific capital and against the employment of firm-specific labor. This is a result consistent with the job deskilling hypothesis[12] considered by Braverman (1974). Braverman describes and explains job deskilling on the basis of the property relations which, according to him, characterize capitalism. This job deskilling effect is obtained by (over-)applying the Babbage criterion.[13] A very detailed division of labor is introduced because this organization of the labor process minimizes the insurance costs which would otherwise be sustained in order to develop workers' firm-specific assets. In particular, under capitalist ownership, the development of firm-specific learning and assets specific to the preferences of the workers[14] presently employed in the firm is inhibited. Human resources will tend to be general-purpose (or, better, "generic") instead of firm-specific.

$$(F_K, M_L) \rightarrow (K_D, L_E). \tag{b'}$$

Ownership of capital by its users saves monitoring costs and makes the investment in "difficult-to-monitor capital" cheaper. By contrast any investment in "difficult-to-monitor labor" is relatively expensive under this property right system. The workers have no property rights in the firm and they have little incentive to perform well. Monitoring hired labor is expensive and this cost can be reduced by investing in "easy-to-monitor labor." Thus the classical capitalist firm (F_K, M_L) has investments relatively biased in favor of "difficult-to-monitor capital" (K_D) and "easy-to-monitor labor" (L_E). Again, this analysis provides a rationale for the analysis of the labor process under capitalist relations given by the Radical Economists and, in particular, by Braverman (1974). Whereas in New Institutional economics the workers have no rights in the firms where they work because they are "easy-to-monitor" and/or "general-purpose" factors, in Braverman's book the workers become "easy-to-monitor" and "general-purpose" factors because, under capitalism, they have no rights in the firm where they work. According to Braverman, it is because of capitalist property rights that a detailed division of labor (on the lines suggested by Babbage and Taylor) is implemented and workers perform simple tasks which are easy to control, and require only "generic" skills. Under capitalism, the development of difficult to monitor human resources is inhibited by the fact that the workers have no rights in and attachment to the organization where they work.

$$(F_L, M_K) \rightarrow (K_G, L_S).$$ (C')

Whereas in the previous case capital hires labor, in this case labor hires capital. If labor can hire and fire machines, machine owners will want an insurance cost to cover the risks of premature termination in circumstances, unforeseen in the market contract, where workers may behave in an opportunistic manner.[15] By contrast, firm-specific labor can be employed without paying the insurance costs which are sustained by the capitalist firm. Thus, whereas the capitalist firm will tend to employ firm-specific capital and general-purpose labor, the workers'-managed firm will be biased in the opposite direction. It will be a hospitable environment for the development of firm-specific labor and general-purpose capital.

$$(F_L, M_K) \rightarrow (L_D, K_E).$$ (c')

Under workers' ownership of the firm, each worker has some incentive to work and an incentive to see fellow workers doing their share of work. Under these circumstances cheap horizontal monitoring may be performed, jointly with production activity, by each one of the workers.[16] As long as workers have some knowledge of each others' activities, "difficult-to-monitor labor" is relatively inexpensive for firms characterized by this system of property rights. By contrast, "difficult-to-monitor capital" is costly for these organizations because the agents leasing the equipment know that for any given rent the agents have an incentive to use the equipment with insufficient care if this is cheaper. Hence the workers will have to pay a relatively high rent for "difficult-to-monitor capital" which inhibits their investment in this type of equipment.[17] Thus, a classical workers' cooperative (F_L, M_K) will have investments biased in favor of "difficult-to-monitor labor" (L_D) and easy-to-monitor capital (K_E).

$$(F_K, F_L) \rightarrow (K_S, L_S).$$ (D')

If both workers and capital, or at least some of them, have rights in the firm which guarantees them against the opportunism of the other partners in unforeseen circumstances, then both firm-specific labor and capital will be developed in the organization. Even if rights and safeguards do not have necessarily zero-sum characteristics, some clashes of rights may occur and may make them less effective. In spite of these caveats,[18] the obvious advantages of this solution explains its success among both economists and real-life economies.

$$(F_K, F_L) \rightarrow (K_D, L_D).$$ (d')

If both labor and capital have some property rights on the organization (F_K, F_L), the neither the investment in "difficult-to-monitor capital" (K_D) nor the investment in "difficult-to-monitor labor" (L_D) are inhibited. If a cooperative attitude among the holders of these rights is developed within the organization, then the coexistence of labor and capital rights can favor investments in both types of "difficult-to-monitor resources." However, the same caveats considered in case (d) apply also in this case.

Thus, the arguments developed by New Institutional economics can be inverted by following the suggestions of the Radical Economists. However, in our opinion the arguments, developed by the two streams of literature are far from being incompatible. We believe that the analysis of property rights and technology can progress only by integrating the contributions of these two streams. In order to visualize in the easiest way the meaning of this integration, denote by K_{EG} and L_{EG} easy to monitor and/or general capital and labor and by K_{DS} and L_{DS} difficult-to-monitor and/or specific capital and labor. Let us now join A and A' and a with a', B with B' and b with b', C with C' and c with c', D with D' and d with d'. We obtain the following relations which capture the interaction of property rights and technology and provide the framework for a definition of the notion of "equilibrium property rights and technologies."

$$\rightarrow (M_K, M_L) \rightarrow (K_{EG}, L_{EG}) \rightarrow (M_K, M_L) \rightarrow (K_{EG}, L_{EG}) \rightarrow. \tag{A}$$

$$\rightarrow (F_K, M_L) \rightarrow (K_{DS}, L_{EG}) \rightarrow (F_K, M_L) \rightarrow (K_{DS}, L_{EG}) \rightarrow. \tag{B}$$

$$\rightarrow (F_L, M_K) \rightarrow (K_{EG}, L_{DS}) \rightarrow (F_L, M_K) \rightarrow (K_{EG}, L_{DS}) \rightarrow. \tag{C}$$

$$\rightarrow (F_K, F_L) \rightarrow (K_{DS}, L_{DS}) \rightarrow (F_K, F_L) \rightarrow (K_{DS}, L_{DS}) \rightarrow. \tag{D}$$

We can in fact give the two following definitions which clarify the reasons for which the relations considered above may define equilibrium property rights and technologies.

Definition 3.1
A property-right system (F_i, M_i) $(i = K, L)$ is a property-right equilibrium if it generates a technology (K_j, L_j) $(j = EG, DS)$ which regenerates (F_i, M_i).

Definition 3.2
A technology (K_j, L_j) $(j = EG, DS)$ is an equilibrium technology if it generates a property-right system (F_i, M_i) $(i = K, L)$ which regenerates (K_j, L_j).

The arguments which we have examined so far, provide some good reasons to believe that each one of the four relations considered above may define equilibrium property rights and technologies or, in other words, a self-sustaining *organizational equilibrium*. In other words, joining together the two streams of literature may imply that property rights and technologies have a self-generating capacity which may characterize and define their equilibrium states.

In order to make the argument simpler let us concentrate our attention on cases (B) and (C) which define respectively the "capitalist" and the workers' property-rights' equilibria.

In the first case (B) a system where the capitalists own the firm and hire labor on the market (F_K, M_L) implies that investment is biased in favor of "difficult-to-monitor and specific capital" and "easy-to-monitor and general-purpose labor" (K_{DS}, L_{EG}); but this technology implies that capital can save more than labor on monitoring and insurance costs if it owns the firm. Therefore this technology regenerates the initial system of property rights (F_K, M_L) which, in turn, again brings about the technology (K_{DS}, L_{EG}) and so on.

In the second case (**C**), a system where the workers own the firm and hire capital on the market (F_L, M_K) implies that investment is biased in favor of "difficult-to-monitor labor" and "easy-to-monitor capital" (K_{EG}, L_{DS}); but this technology implies that labor can save more on monitoring costs than capital if it owns the firm. Therefore this technology regenerates the initial system of property rights (F_L, M_K) which in turn again brings about the technology (K_{EG}, L_{DS}), etc.

This argument implies that history matters in the sense that organizational equilibria may depend on initial conditions having self-generating and self-reinforcing properties which cause their institutional stability.[19] Or, in other words, past history rather than ahistorical efficiency may determine which particular organizational equilibrium exists. The purpose of the following section is to make these intuitions a bit more precise. In particular we will concentrate our attention on cases (**B**) and (**C**). These have been chosen only in order to simplify the analysis and not because they are more relevant than the other cases.

4   Property rights/technological equilibria: a simple model

In our simple model there are two agents, capitalists and workers. Capital can be employed either as difficult-to-monitor and/or specific (DS) capital **K** or as easy-to-monitor and/or general (EG) capital K. Similarly, the workers can be employed in either difficult-to-monitor or specific (DS) labor **L** or in easy-to-monitor (EG) labor L. R and **R** are respectively the price of one unit of EG capital and of one unit of DS capital (net of insurance and monitoring costs). W and **W** denote respectively the price of one unit of EG labor and one unit of DS labor (net of insurance and monitoring costs).

We focus our analysis on one representative firm and we assume that ownership of the firm goes to the owners of factors of production, *presently employed in the firm*, which would cost more, because of the DS character of their resources, if employed in other agents' organizations. In other words, these resources are most valuable in organizations controlled by the owners of the resources. These agents will be able to reap a pure rent, because of the DS character of their resources, when they own the organization. This rent is equal to the price which should otherwise be paid by employers of their resources (different from themselves) as insurance and monitoring costs.

We assume that the workers sustain an additional cost Z when they employ a unit of DS capital which is not sustained by the capitalists when they employ this factor. We also assume that the capitalists pay an additional cost H when they employ DS labor. H is not paid by the workers when they employ DS labor. For this reason Z is also the rent which is realized by the owners of capital on each unit of DS capital when they own the organization and H is the rent which is realized by the workers on each unit of DS labor when the workers own the organization. The total capitalists' rent under capitalist ownership will be equal to **ZRK** and the total workers' rent under workers' ownership will be equal to **HWL**. We will call **ZRK** and **HWL** the total ownership rents perceived by the factors.

We can now state the two following assumptions. The first concerns the behavior of the firm for any *given* (*capitalist or workers'*) *ownership*. The second concerns the ownership of the firm for any *given amounts of factors employed in the firm*.

Assumption 4.1
The firm maximizes profits (inclusive of ownership rents). Profits are equal to:

$$R^c = Q(K, \mathbf{K}, L, \mathbf{L}) - [RK + \mathbf{RK} + WL + (1 + \mathrm{H})\mathbf{WL}] \tag{1}$$

under capitalist ownership, and to:

$$R^L = Q(K, \mathbf{K}, L, \mathbf{L}) - [RK + (1 + \mathrm{Z})\mathbf{RK} + WL + \mathbf{WL}] \tag{2}$$

under workers' ownership.[20]

Assumption 4.2
For any given amounts of factors employed in the firm, its ownership will be acquired by the factor which can earn the highest ownership rent.

Assumption 4.2 implies that capitalist property rights will prevail if, given the factors currently employed,

$$\mathbf{ZRK} - \mathbf{HWL} > 0 \tag{3}$$

workers' property rights will prevail if, given the factors currently employed,

$$\mathbf{HWL} - \mathbf{ZRK} > 0. \tag{4}$$

We introduce now the following definition concerning the characteristics of the technology employed in the firm:

Definition 4.1
A technology which satisfies (3) is a "DS capital-intensive technology" and a technology which satisfies (4) is a "DS labor-intensive technology." The ratio **K/L** denotes the degree of DS capital intensity of a technology.

.Conditions (3) and (4), expressing respectively the definitions of a DS capital-intensive and a DS labor-intensive technology, can be written in terms of the degree of DS capital intensity as follows:

$$\mathrm{ZR/HW}\ \mathbf{K/L} > 1. \tag{3'}$$

$$\mathrm{ZR/HW}\ \mathbf{K/L} < 1. \tag{4'}$$

The following proposition follows immediately from Assumption 4.2 and Definition 4.1.

Proposition 4.1
A DS capital- (labor)-intensive technology "causes" the introduction of capitalist (workers') property rights.

We can also state the following "inverse" proposition:

Proposition 4.2
Capitalist (workers') property rights imply the choice of a more DS capital-(labor)-intensive technology than the one implied by workers' (capitalists) property rights.

Given the usual standard assumptions about the shape of the profit function, and assuming that the inputs are sufficiently good substitutes, Proposition 4.2 follows immediately from comparing the values of K and L which maximize (1) and (2). Denote by K^c and L^c the values of K and L which maximize (1) and by K^L and L^L the values of K and L which maximize (2). Then we have:

$$K^c > K^L \quad \text{and} \quad L^L > L^c, \tag{5}$$

or,

$$K^c/L^c > K^L/L^L, \tag{5'}$$

which is a different way of stating Proposition 4.2.

Proposition 4.1 expresses the mechanism by which technology influences property rights and Proposition 4.2 the mechanism by which property rights influence technology. Joining together these two Propositions we obtain cumulative processes by which property rights influence themselves (via technology) and technology influences itself (via property rights). We thus have the following two Propositions 4.3 and 4.4.

Proposition 4.3
Capitalist (workers') property rights are self-reinforcing in that they bias technology in a direction which is favorable to capitalist (workers') property rights.

Suppose, for instance, that we have capitalist property rights. Then, a technology more DS capital-intensive than that prevailing under workers' property rights will be introduced (Proposition 4.2 and condition (5')). This increases the probability that constraint (3'), expressing the conditions of a DS capital-intensive technology, will be satisfied. In turn the satisfaction of this constraint implies the introduction of capitalist property rights (Proposition 4.2).

Proposition 4.4
A DS capital- (labor)-intensive technology is self-reinforcing in that it biases property rights in a direction which is favorable to this technology.

Suppose, for instance, that we have a DS capital-intensive technology. This implies that capitalist property rights will prevail (Proposition 4.1 and condition (3′)). In turn, capitalist property rights will bias the technology towards a higher degree of DS capital intensity which reinforces the DS capital-intensive character of the technology.

We introduce now two new definitions of property rights and DS technological equilibria which specify the meaning of Definitions 3.1 and 3.2 in the context of the present simple model.

Definition 4.2
A given set of property rights are equilibrium property rights when the technology, maximizing the profits of the present owners of the firm, does not upset these property rights.

In particular:
Capitalist property rights are equilibrium property rights if the technology which maximizes (1) satisfies (3), or, if profit maximization under capitalist property rights implies the introduction of a DS capital-intensive technology which, in turn, implies capitalist property rights. Or, capitalist property rights are equilibrium property rights when:

$$ZRK^c - HWL^c \geqslant 0. \tag{6}$$

Workers' property rights are equilibrium property rights if the technology which maximizes (2) satisfies (4), and, therefore, when:

$$HWL^L - ZRK^L \geqslant 0. \tag{7}$$

Definition 4.3
A given (DS capital- or labor-intensive) technology is an equilibrium technology when the profit-maximizing choices, taken under the associated system of property rights, do not upset this technology.

In particular:
A DS capital-intensive technology satisfies (3) by definition and implies capitalist property rights which involve the maximization of (1). A DS capital-intensive technology is an equilibrium technology when the technology resulting from the maximization of (1) also satisfies (3). Or a DS capital-intensive technology is a technological equilibrium when:

$$ZRK^c - HWL^c \geqslant 0. \tag{6'}$$

In the same way it can be argued that a DS labor-intensive technology is a technological equilibrium when:

$$HWL^L - ZRK^L \geqslant 0. \tag{7'}$$

We have seen that a property rights equilibrium defines a technology supporting the initial set of property rights. Could it be that the system is not in a technological equilibrium even if it is in a property right equilibrium? Clearly not, because the technology which is implied by these rights in the first place will again be implied over and over again by them.

Similarly, suppose that the system is in a technological equilibrium. This would mean that the existing technology supports property rights which imply the same technology. This in turn must imply the same property rights. Thus the system must also be in a property right equilibrium.

For this reason it is not surprising that a DS capital-intensive technological equilibrium and a capitalist property right equilibrium occur under the same conditions (6) and (6′) and that a DS labor-intensive equilibrium and a workers' property rights' equilibrium occur under the same conditions (7′) and (7).

Thus, a property right equilibrium is also a DS technological equilibrium and a technological equilibrium is also a property right equilibrium. Referring to one of them simply emphasizes the initial conditions relative to the technology or the property rights on the basis of which the equilibrium is determined.

In what follows we will therefore refer to property rights/DS technological equilibria or simply to *organizational equilibria*.

Proposition 4.5

At least one organizational equilibrium exists.

Supposing that this is not so, then conditions (6) and (7) would simultaneously not be satisfied. This implies that the two following conditions would be simultaneously satisfied

$$ZRK^L - HWL^L \geqslant 0 \tag{8}$$

$$HWL^c - ZRK^c \geqslant 0. \tag{9}$$

But if (8) is satisfied then

$$HWL^L - ZRK^L \leqslant 0$$

and because of (5)

$$HWL^c - ZRK^c \leqslant 0$$

which contradicts the possibility that (9) is also satisfied and proves the existence of at least one organizational equilibrium.

We will now consider three relevant cases of organizational equilibria. In the first two cases the system has a unique equilibrium independent of initial conditions. In the third case, the system has two equilibria which depend on the initial conditions of the system.

(a) $$ZRK^L - HWL^L \geqslant 0 \tag{8}$$

or condition (7) cannot be satisfied. Even under workers' ownership or a initially given DS labor-intensive technology, a workers' property right equilibrium is not sustainable.

Because of Proposition 4.5 a capitalist property right equilibrium

$$ZRK^c - HWL^c \geqslant 0 \qquad (6)$$

is sustainable. The system has a unique capitalist right equilibrium independent of initial conditions. Workers' property rights cannot be equilibrium property rights.

(b) $$HWL^c - ZRK^c \geqslant 0 \qquad (9)$$

or condition (6) cannot be satisfied. Even under capitalist property rights or an initially given DS capital-intensive technology, a capitalist property right equilibrium is not sustainable. Because of Proposition 4.5 a workers' property right equilibrium

$$HWL^L - ZRK^L \geqslant 0 \qquad (7)$$

is sustainable. The system has a unique workers' property right equilibrium independent of initial conditions.

(c) $$ZRK^c - HWL^c \geqslant 0 \qquad (6)$$

and

$$HWL^L - ZRK^L \geqslant 0 \qquad (7)$$

then the system has two property rights' equilibria which depend entirely on the initial conditions. Capitalist and workers' property rights are simultaneously feasible because of (5) and Propositions 4.3 and 4.4.

We can therefore state the following proposition:

Proposition 4.6
Multiple organizational equilibria are possible. These equilibria are historically dependent and self-sustaining in the sense that they reproduce a given set of initial property rights or DS technological conditions. Or, in other words, a given set of initial property rights or DS technological conditions may be an equilibrium because it has first come into existence.

Observe that, even in the case in which we have multiple equilibria, these equilibria are efficient in the sense that they minimize costs and, in particular monitoring and (asset-specificity) insurance costs for an initially given structure of property or technological conditions.

Still, efficiency can be defined as unconstrained by these initial conditions in terms of the property right equilibrium which is characterized by the lowest costs.[21] Or, in other words, we could state which set of initial conditions would have allowed cost minimization.

Observe that, although in a capitalist property right equilibrium $ZRK^c \geqslant HWL^c$, only HWL^c will be effectively paid and will involve the expenditure of useful resources.

Observe also that, although in a workers' property right equilibrium $HWL^L \geqslant ZRK^L$, only ZRK^L will be effectively paid and consume real resources.

We can therefore say that overall efficiency is achieved when these costs, which are effectively paid, are minimized. In other words, capitalist property rights are efficient when:

$$ZRK^L - HWL^c \geqslant 0 \tag{10}$$

and workers' property rights are efficient when

$$HWL^c - ZRK^L \geqslant 0. \tag{11}$$

Proposition 4.7
When only one organizational equilibrium exists, then that equilibrium is efficient.

Suppose that we are in a unique capitalist property right equilibrium defined by:

$$ZRK^L - HWL^L \geqslant 0 \tag{8}$$

then, because of (5), (10) is also satisfied.

The same argument holds for a unique workers' right equilibrium.

In the case of multiple equilibria it follows from conditions (10) and (11) that only one of the two property rights' equilibria defined by conditions

$$ZRK^c - HWL^c \geqslant 0 \tag{6}$$

and

$$HWL^L - ZRK^L \geqslant 0 \tag{7}$$

can be efficient, except for the special case in which conditions (10) and (11) are satisfied as equalities, which implies:

$$ZRK^L = HWL^c.$$

We can therefore state the following proposition:

Proposition 4.8
When multiple organizational equilibria exist, then an equilibrium can be inefficient.

Can inefficient organizational equilibria be institutionally stable?

In order to consider this point, imagine that an inefficient organizational equilibrium is subject to "weak" technological or to property rights shocks.

Let us define a "technological shock" as an exogenous change in the productivity of the factors. A technological shock, such as an innovation, may imply that a given organizational equilibrium becomes inefficient. Suppose, for instance, that we are in a capitalist efficient equilibrium where both conditions:

$$ZRK^c - HWL^c \geqslant 0 \qquad (6)$$

and

$$ZRK^L - HWL^c \geqslant 0 \qquad (10)$$

are satisfied. Suppose now that the technological shock implies that workers' ownership becomes more efficient and (10) is not satisfied because ZRK^L is now smaller than HWL^c.

However, because of (5), ZRK^c is greater than ZRK^L. This implies that (6) could still be satisfied even if (10) is not satisfied. In this case, we would still be in a capitalist property right equilibrium even if, after the technological shock, this equilibrium is now inefficient. In other words, the technological shock may not be strong enough to imply that the capitalist–DS capital-intensive equilibrium is upset and the economy moves to a worker's property right – DS labor-intensive technological equilibrium. Equilibria can thus resist "weak" technological shocks which imply that a different equilibrium is more efficient.

Let us now define a property right shock as an exogenous change of property rights. In our simple model a property right shock can only be a change from capitalist to workers' ownership and vice-versa. Organizational equilibria can be resistant to property rights' shocks even when these shocks would push the system towards more efficient solutions. Suppose that we are in an inefficient capitalist property right equilibrium or that conditions

$$ZRK^c - HWL^c \geqslant 0 \qquad (6)$$

and

$$ZRK^L - HWL^c \leqslant 0 \qquad (11')$$

are satisfied. If a property rights shock occurs and the workers are given by authority (for instance, state intervention) the ownership of the firm, the new owners of the firm will find themselves with a structure of resources given by (6) which is the result of the preceding capitalist property rights' equilibrium. Under these circumstances it may be convenient for both the capitalists and the workers to transfer back ownership to the capitalists because, with the resources employed by the capitalists in the preceding equilibrium, monitoring and insurance costs are higher under workers' ownership. Still, if workers' ownership is protected for some time (i.e., immediate exchange is forbidden) they will then employ a new structure of resources which allows the achievement of the more efficient workers' property rights equilibrium. In other words, inefficient property rights may be resistant to property rights' shocks which do not last long enough to allow the development of a technology consistent with the new property rights.

We can define as "weak technological shocks," shocks which imply that a different equilibrium is more efficient but do not violate condition (6) and as "weak property rights' shocks," shocks which do not last for a sufficiently long time to develop resources consistent with the new property rights. We can then state the following proposition.

Proposition 4.9
Inefficient organizational equilibria are institutionally stable in the sense that there are "weak" property rights and technological shocks to which they are resistant, even if these shocks push the system in the direction of an efficient equilibrium.

We may conclude this section by pointing out some limitations and possible extensions of the simple model which we have considered:

(1)   We have implicitly assumed that the entire human and physical capital can be immediately adjusted according to the profit-maximizing behavior defined by (1) and (2). If we assume that only part of the stock of human and physical capital could be immediately adjusted, then the institutional stability properties of the model would become much stronger. Any change in the technological specification of the resources, bringing about new property rights, would take time. In the meantime, the existing property rights would continue to shape technology and reinforce themselves. Changes which cannot immediately be implemented may never be implemented.

(2)   We have also implicitly assumed that transactions of property rights between firms' members take place at zero transaction costs. If transaction costs are positive then, denoting by T the value of these transaction costs conditions (3) and (4) should be rewritten as follows:

$$ZRK - HWL - T > 0. \tag{3'}$$

$$HWL - ZRK - T > 0. \tag{4'}$$

Clearly, the assumption of positive transaction costs would reinforce the institutional stability characteristics of property rights' equilibria. (Indeed for a sufficiently large value of T property rights' equilibria would become resistance to any shock.) Transaction costs could also be introduced into the analysis by assuming that transactions take time. This would also greatly reinforce the institutional stability characteristics of property rights' equilibria. While transactions could be organized, in the meantime the existing property rights would shape the technological specification of the resources in a self-reinforcing manner. Transactions, which cannot immediately take place may never take place.

(3)   We have simplified the analysis by considering the case of a representative firm. This restricts the generality of the propositions which have been considered in this section. It is the task of further research to state which of these propositions hold under a less aggregate analysis. Indeed, the purpose of these propositions is to stimulate research in this direction rather than to state any definitive conclusion on the subject.

5 Generalization of the argument, drawing an "inverted" Williamson contracting scheme

The analysis carried out in section 4 has been restricted to the particular cases of rights implying either complete workers' or capitalist ownership. The New Institutional economics has concentrated its attention on more complicated cases. Still, even in these other cases and, perhaps, even more in these cases, the set of rights and duties and the governance system characterizing the modern firm must be seen not only as an "efficient" outcome of the technological specification of resources but also as one of its causes.[22] This suggests that the concepts of property rights and technological equilibria and the concept of institutional stability have a wider application. In what follows I will try to argue that the Oliver Williamson contracting scheme, which is the most popular expression of this approach, can be generalized by developing the approach considered in the preceding sections.

Williamson's (1985) contracting scheme is summarized in Figure 6.1. In this figure $k = 0$ denotes the absence of specific investment and $k > 0$ denotes its existence. Williamson argues that, in the case of the adoption of the specific technology, there will be a tendency to develop safeguards ($s > 0$) to protect this specific investment. If these safeguards are not developed ($s = 0$), then specific investments cannot be sustained because the agents will be subject in an uncertain world to the possible opportunism of their partners. For this reason, Williamson argues that node B is unstable and that there is a tendency to move either to node A or to node C. Typically, Williamson explains the existence of the unions as due to the interest of the workers in protecting their specific assets. Thus, the existence of a particular technology explains the rights (such as

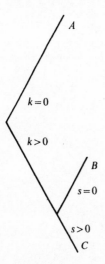

Figure 6.1 Williamson's contracting scheme

safeguards against premature termination or even job tenure) which the workers have in particular organizations.

Still, there is no reason why Williamson's scheme could not be "inverted" on the lines suggested in the preceding sections as it is done in Figure 6.2. For instance, workers may want safeguards in their jobs in particular firms for reasons other than the protection of their specific assets (changing the distribution of income being an obvious one). However, once they have these safeguards ($s > 0$) they may be ready to invest in firm-specific assets without claiming any additional insurance premium. One can argue that if specific investments ($k > 0$) are generated, then workers' rights are particularly stable (node C) because the workers have an additional interest in defending them. Otherwise, these rights or safeguards may be lost ($s = 0$) and the system may turn back to node A'.

The priority given by Williamson to (specific versus general-purpose) technology is due to the fact that he sees the general or specific character of the resources as independent of the property rights or the safeguard systems. However, the specific, general (or, as we will see, "generic") nature of the resources may entirely depend on the property right or the governance system which is adopted.

In order to appreciate this possibility consider the case of two identical firms where four identical tasks t_1, t_2, t_3, t_4 are performed. Suppose that in the first firm there are two jobs

$$J_1 = \{t_1, t_2\} \quad \text{and} \quad J_2 = \{t_3, t_4\}$$

and in the second firm there are two jobs:

$$J_3 = \{t_2, t_3\} \quad \text{and} \quad J_4 = \{t_1, t_4\}.$$

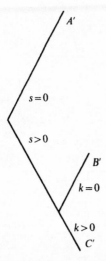

Figure 6.2   An inverted Williamson contracting scheme

Then, in spite of the fact that identical tasks are carried out in each one of the two firms, jobs are firm-specific. This situation is likely to arise if the workers have rights in their jobs in each one of the firms and these safeguards guarantee their firm-specific investments.

Two alternative property rights' systems may push the technology adopted in a different direction. The first relies on a different system of rights and safeguards at industry level which brings about a form of job standardization across firms which eliminates the firm-specific character of the jobs. The second is the likely result of a situation where workers have no rights either at firm or at industry level.

In the first case, otherwise firm-specific skills become general-purpose. The organization of work is the subject of a contractual agreement between unions and employers' association with the possible support of the state and, in particular, public educational institutions. The contractual agreement specifies the definition of jobs and of job training which becomes the same for all the firms operating in a particular industry. In the particular case of our example the structure of the organization of labor will be either

$$J_1 = \{t_1, t_2\} \quad \text{and} \quad J_2 = \{t_3, t_4\}$$

or

$$J_3 = \{t_2, t_3\} \quad \text{and} \quad J_4 = \{t_1, t_4\}$$

for both firms. This implies that jobs cease to be firm-specific. In this way, occupational markets are created and the workers have an incentive to enhance their skills even if they have no right to a job in a particular firm. If fired by a particular organization, the workers can still exploit the skills they have acquired in other organizations. In this system the occupational market which is created is a public good for both employers and employees. Each employer may have an incentive to free-ride on the rules and safeguards which allow a market for skilled labor. Each one of them may find it advantageous to introduce an organization of work which is more specific to the particular needs of their own firm. In this case, the occupational markets for skilled labor may collapse. Then, whereas the free-rider employer takes all the benefit of his free-riding, all the other employers and employees share the damage caused by his misbehavior. However, if everyone misbehaves, then all the agents will be worse off. It will therefore be in the interest of all employers and employees to organize some form of monitoring to prevent each employer from free-riding.[23] Observe that a market for general-purpose skilled labor may require rules, safeguards and rights which are more complex than those required for the development of firm-specific skills.[24] Williamson seems to miss the point when (see Figure 6.3) he suggests that only firm-specific assets imply the creation of safeguards and rights. Occupational markets do also require safeguards. It is ironic that the market which is often regarded by New Institutional economists as some sort of "natural environment," where efficient institutions spontaneously evolve, needs itself to be supported by those institutions which it is supposed to select.

In the second case no general or specific resource is created and no safeguard exists. In this case there will be an incentive to employ "generic" resources. These resources are "generic" in the sense that they can be employed in a wider variety of uses only because they have developed neither general nor specific qualities which could otherwise increase their productivity. Their employment is convenient only because it does not require the existence of those rights and safeguards which would be necessary to employ specific or general resources. In the particular instance of our example we can imagine that the need for specific or general skills is eliminated by introducing a very detailed division of labor. Or, in other words, the organization of work becomes:

$$J_1^* = \{t_1\}, J_2^* = \{t_2\}, J_3^* = \{t_3\} \text{ and } J_4^* = \{t_4\}$$

for both firms, which implies that jobs cease to be either general or firm-specific.

Under this organization of work, workers can move, without the development of any safeguard, from one firm to the other. Thus, "generic" resources are characterized by the same market flexibility of general resources. But, here, market flexibility may be due to a failure of the system of rights and safeguards which inhibits the development of either specific or general qualities and must not be associated with the Pareto-efficiency qualities of competitive markets. The Tayloristic methods of production, where the workers do not develop general or specific skills, may bring about this situation for labor power. Observe that the kind of market flexibility associated with Taylorism is complementary to the existence of rigid hierarchies. Only if bosses tell the workers the detailed task which should be done, how it should be done and the time within which it should be done, can "generic" un-skilled labor be employed. Again, the working of markets needs the support of non-market institutions. Indeed, the more "flexible" the markets are (in the sense that rights and safeguards do not exist for either general or specific resources) the more rigid the hierarchies of the firms operating in these markets may have to be. When workers do not develop general and/or specific skills the hierarchies become rigid in two senses. The first is that only simple orders and simple instructions can be given to workers having these characteristics. The second is that few chances of promotion either within a firm or in an occupation having a recognized status in more firms exist under this system.

Also in the case of general resources, the rights and safeguards associated with them can reinforce these resources and be the cause of their existence. However, the opposite may also be true: the existence of general skills may give an incentive to develop rights and safeguards which can defend the investments sustained in these resources and favor their development. In both cases whatever comes first reinforces the other, and the possible failure of the second to follow the first weakens the first.

The case in which general resources come first is represented in Figure 6.3 which is obtained by generalizing Williamson's contracting scheme. Node A describes the situation in which only "generic" resources are employed. No rights or safeguards are necessary for the use of this technology. Nodes D and E

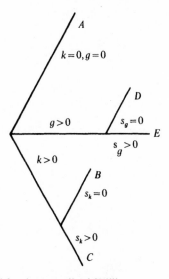

Figure 6.3   A generalized Williamson contracting scheme

describe the use of general-purpose technology ($g > 0$). But, unlike the case of Williamson's scheme the use of this technology requires the development of safeguards which defend the agents who have invested in general resources against the possible opportunism of employers of general resources which could in an uncertain world deviate from the common standards which guarantee a market for these resources. In the case that these safeguards are developed by unions, professional organizations and state intervention, then the investment in general resources can be sustained. This is the case of node E where $s_g > 0$ denotes that these rights and safeguards are developed. Failure to develop these safeguards ($s_g = 0$) pushes the system to node D which is unstable. The system may either move to a "generic" technology, which requires no safeguard, or to a firm-specific technology ($k > 0$) sustained by safeguards developed only at firm level ($s_k > 0$). In fact the collapse of safeguards at industry level implies that former general resources become firm-specific and may give an incentive to develop safeguards and rights at firm level. This latter case is described by node C which represents a situation identical to that considered by Williamson. Moreover here too, as in Williamson's contracting scheme, node B denotes the failure to create safeguards ($s_k = 0$) for the investment in firm-specific resources. However, in the case of Figure 6.4, this failure can push the system either to node A or to node E. In the first instance, no safeguard replaces the safeguard at firm level and the resources tend to become generic. In the second instance, the workers may try to make more general-purpose previously firm-specific resources and, later, succeed in developing a system of safeguards which guarantees the generality of these resources. This may happen under pressure from unions, which organize workers doing similar jobs in different firms. The absence of

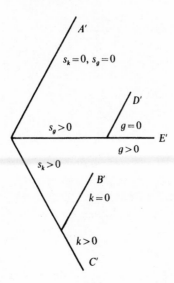

Figure 6.4   An inverted generalized Williamson contracting scheme

rights at firm level may give workers an incentive to organize collective bargaining and obtain these type of safeguards.

However, Figure 6.3 can be inverted in a way similar to Figure 6.1. This is done in Figure 6.4. Rights and safeguards for jobs in different firms can logically and/or temporally come before the development of general resources. For instance, collective bargaining can come in the first place for political or distributional reasons and may include the negotiation of a uniform job specification which is seen as a necessary condition for the negotiation of a uniform wage. Safeguards and rights concerning job definition can thus come before standardization and be the cause of the development of general resources instead of being only one possible effect of it. Still, one may wish to distinguish between those cases in which, after the institution of these safeguards, there is a development of general resources and those cases in which this does not happen. In the first case, (node E' of Figure 6.4, where $g > 0$), the development of general resources reinforces the initial system of rights and safeguards. The workers (as well as the employers) will have a vested interest in their defense because they protect the general type of investments that they have sustained. In the second case (node D' of Figure 6.4, where $g = 0$) the absence of the development of general resources makes these rights and safeguards more unstable. The workers do not have the same vested interest in their defense and the system is more likely to switch to a different set of rights and safeguards.

The entire argument can be reformulated by using the concepts of property rights and technological equilibria which we have developed in the preceding sections. An economic system may have multiple organizational equilibria in the sense that nodes A′, A, E, E′, C and C′ may all be institutionally stable equilibria even if some of them are inefficient. The organizational equilibrium which is, actually, achieved depends on the initial conditions of the system. These initial conditions can either be specified in terms of the initial technological conditions of the system or in terms of the initial system of rights (or safeguards). These two cases are described by Figures 6.5 and 6.6 which respectively describe technological equilibria and property right equilibria.

In the case of Figure 6.5 an initial technological specification of resources is such as to bring about an existence or an absence of safeguards and rights which reproduces the initial specification of resources. In the case of Figure 6.6, an initial set of rights and safeguards is such as to bring about a technological specification of resources which reproduces the initial set of rights and safeguards. Real-life systems could be in one of the equilibria considered in Figures 6.5 and 6.6 because of their different histories of technological and property rights' shocks. These shocks may determine new and different initial conditions which can reinforce and reproduce themselves creating different property rights and technological equilibria which may then show a remarkable institutional stability. This stability will imply that "history matters," in the sense that simple efficiency stories independent of initial conditions will be unable to take into account the full strength of this statement. Efficiency may also matter but it is always constrained by the past history of the system.

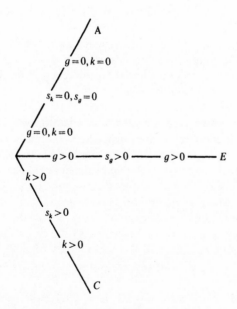

Figure 6.5   Technological equilibria

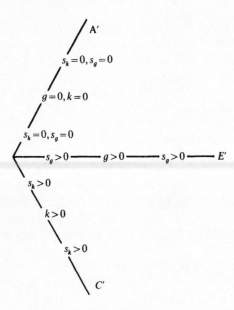

Figure 6.6   Property rights' equilibria

6   Conclusions

We may conclude and complete the argument by offering (very incomplete) suggestions about the implications of the analysis on two issues. The first is how the concepts developed in this chapter can be used to explain the diverging histories of the three major Western industrial economies. The second concerns the difficulty that more democratic organizations of production may find in establishing themselves, even if they are more efficient.

The concept of multiple technological and property rights' equilibria can help to explain the existence of alternative organizations of production which have characterized the histories of different Western industrialized economies. Some of them have shown greater efficiency at times but each one of them has shown a remarkable institutional stability in spite of its relative inefficiency. In particular, if we take the experience of the three major industrialized countries (the USA, (West) Germany, and Japan) there is no doubt that none of them can be characterized by the exclusive dominance of one type of organizational equilibrium. Each one of these countries is characterized by the co-existence in different sectors and for different resources of the three types of each of the equilibria which we have considered. Moreover, some arrangements are common to all of them.[25]

Still, on the basis of empirical work it is appropriate to say that Japan has been characterized by the existence of a relatively large sector of the economy where firms have developed safeguards and rights, such as job tenure and seniority rules, at firm level and by the fact that workers have invested quite a lot in firm-specific human skills.[26] At the same time, (West) Germany has been characterized by relatively well-developed occupational markets where job-specification rights in each firm belong to fairly centralized unions and employers' associations.[27] These institutions cooperate together with educational authorities for the development of their excellent system of vocational training. Here, workers seem to have invested more in general-purpose than in firm-specific skills and the existence of these skills makes it convenient to employ German workers in spite of their relatively high wages. By contrast, the USA seems to be the country where the dominance of Taylorism has been most pronounced and where a relatively large fraction of workers has been employed without safeguards and rights either at firm or at industrial level. These workers have often invested very little in either specific or general skills and have only the generic abilities which are required by the Tayloristic model of organization of production.

These different characteristics of three major industrialized countries have been remarkably stable in the post-war period. Simple efficiency explanations cannot elucidate this variety of experiences. By contrast, the dominance of one of these sectors in each one of these three countries seems to provide an example of one of the self-sustaining property rights – technological equilibria which we have considered in Figures 6.5 and 6.6. Moreover, this variety of experiences must mainly be due to the fact that these economies have gone through different property rights' shocks. For technological shocks, in the form of innovations changing the relative productivity of general, generic and firm-specific resources are more likely to have been shared by these economies.

Although an analysis of these property rights' shocks (as well as any proper analysis of real-life property rights' equilibria) is beyond the scope of this chapter, it is worthwhile to give an example of a "strong" property right shock which may have determined the different property rights and technological equilibria which have characterized the development of these economies after the war. Both Japan and (West) Germany, unlike the USA, lost the war and in both cases the local employers were punished for their war effort. Employers' rights were severely limited and the workers acquired some rights at the workplace. However, these rights were acquired at a more centralized level in Germany (where a strong party linked to relatively centralized unions was able to establish itself and defend the rights of these unions) and at firm level in Japan (where in 1950, after an initial honeymoon, centralized unions came under the attack of the occupying forces and were replaced by company unions[28]). As a consequence of this "strong" property rights' shock, the workers may have substantially invested in general resources (mainly in (West) Germany) and in firm-specific resources (mainly in Japan). These investments may have then reinforced and regenerated the initial sets of property rights creating two new different property rights – technological equilibria. Recent attempts by the USA to import the more efficient Japanese system are not endogenous to the USA (in the sense that they occur under the threat of Japanese competition) and are proving difficult and slow. This seems to imply that inertia and pre-existing property rights and technologies are important to explain the variety of organizations of economic systems – a variety that a simple efficiency story would fail to explain.

This brings us to the second point. Why is that democratic rights, such that workers have the necessary safeguards to invest in themselves and their working environment, come about only with great difficulty and resistance under capitalism? The answer suggested by this chapter should by now be obvious. Under capitalism there is a tendency to have "easy-to-monitor workers" and a tendency to under-invest in both firm-specific and general (not generic) human skills. This brings about an organizational equilibrium which may be remarkably stable in spite of its inefficiency. Democratic rights at the work-place and the technological specification of resources associated with them may be blocked by the ability of capitalist property rights to reproduce themselves.

Notes

I have received very useful comments from the discussant of my paper, Sam Bowles, and other participants in the workshop. In particular I wish to thank Gregory Dow, Herbert Gintis, Louis Putterman, Martin Weitzman, and Gilbert Skillman. I am also grateful, for useful comments and suggestions, to Marizio Franzini, Frank Hahn, Lionello Punzo, Michio Morishima, Robert Rowthorn, Hamid Sabourian, Alessandro Vercelli and Vinfried Vogt. After the SCASSS conference, I benefited from presenting this paper at the workshop on structural change held at the Certosa di Pontignano (Siena), at Queen's College (Cambridge) and at the Arbeitskreises Politische Ökonomie held at the Humboldt-Universität (Berlin). The paper draws extensively on Pagano (1991c) and I am grateful to *Economic Notes* for letting me use that material. The usual caveats apply.

1. The best general reader on the "New Institutional" and "Radical" views of the firm is Putterman (1986).
2. Although Radical Economists have drawn extensively from Marx and, in particular, from his analysis of the factory system, the Marxian analysis can also offer arguments in favor of the "efficiency view" entertained by New Institutional economics. Indeed, if we accept the Marxian view of the ultimate primacy of the development of productive forces over property rights, the Marxian approach becomes very close to that of New Institutional economics. By contrast, if we emphasize the Marxian analysis of the capitalist factory system, where capitalist property rights shape the quality and the direction of productive forces, then we can find many arguments which can be used to criticize the "effficiency view" of New Institutional economics. Cohen (1978) and Brenner (1986) are respectively the best examples of the first and the second Marxist philosophies of history. Roemer (1988) offers a very good survey of both. The Marxian analysis of the factory system was updated by Braverman (1974). Other radical economists, like Marglin (1974), Edwards (1979), Putterman (1982), Pagano (1985), Bowles and Gintis (1983) and (1986), Bowles (1985) and (1989b) have pointed out that the system of rights can shape and constrain the organization of production and technology.
3. A more formal approach stemming from asset-specificity can be found in Hart and Moore (1988) and (1990). In his textbook Kreps (1990b) considers the relation

between traditional microeconomic theory and transaction cost economics and observes how in transaction cost economics the firm, ceasing to be only an agent of the market economy, becomes also a "marketlike" agent alternative to the market itself.

4. The authority relation has been often seen as the only alternative to market relations. This limit to New Institutional economics and other analytical weakness of this approach are pointed out in Dow (1987). Another important limit to New Institutional economics is considered by Nutzinger (1982) where he argues that the transaction costs which characterize each institutional arrangement should not be considered to be independent of the coexisting institutions.

5. A limit to the New Institutional economics is that it has concentrated its attention on the market transaction costs which arise in an equilibrium situation. However, as Marx emphasized, the superiority of firm-type organization may be due to the disequilibrium costs which characterize market transactions (Pagano, 1992a). Another limit of this literature is that it considers only firms and not also standard markets as institutions, the existence of which has to be explained. On this point see Hodgson (1988).

6. The asset-specificity problem and the monitoring problems are strictly related. As Alchian (1984:39) observes,

Team production makes measurability of *marginal* products difficult, but not impossible. Even without team production, the contribution of one person in an exchange may not be economically measurable in all pertinent characteristics. If one party can gain by shirking in its performance, this *means* that the other party is made specific to the shirker by the circumstances. This mode of expression emphasizes the specificity of one resource to another, but it obscures the significance of measurement of performance. On the other hand, if measurement of performance is emphasized, then the significance of expropriability of coalition quasi-rents is obscured. Even if measurement were no problem at all, opportunistic behavior can occur blatantly because contracts are not costless to enforce, though I presume that without substantial expropriable quasi-rents of specific resources, blatant defiant cheating is not likely to be a serious problem.

Milgrom and Roberts (1990a) observe that the costs due to monitoring and asset-specificity are particular cases of bargaining costs.

7. "General" purpose resources may require a different type of safeguard and they should be distinguished from "generic" resources. In my opinion New Institutional economics is weak on both points. I will consider this problem in section 5. Until that point the New Institutional definition is accepted and used.

8. Of course, the specificity problem does not only arise between capitalist and workers but also among capitalists and workers. Leijönhufvud (1986) points out how the joint stock company arises as solution to the specificity problems among the owners of machines. Rowthorn (1988) and Pagano (1991a) suggest that "solidaristic corporatism" can be considered as a symmetrical solution for the workers. This solution is however much more difficult and unstable because, unlike capital, collective ownership of labor-power is in contrast with the condition of self-ownership which is at the foundation of individual liberties.

9. Capital is "difficult to monitor" when user-induced depreciation cannot be inferred by observing capital before and after it is used. Some information on the way capital has been used is therefore important in order to estimate its value after use. If the owners of the firm own the capital employed in the organization, then they have an incentive to

take care of their capital. When user-induced depreciation is difficult to monitor, the possibility of careless use makes the rental of "difficult-to-monitor capital" more expensive than its ownership (see Alchian and Demsetz, 1972a).

10. In other words different "technological trajectories" can be generated by alternative property rights structures. On the concept of "technological trajectories", see Nelson and Winter (1982) and Dosi (1988).

11. The use of specific inputs may not simply be technologically more efficient. It may also allow the production of commodities which other firms cannot easily imitate or reproduce. In other words, the specificity of the inputs may help the enforcement of "commodity rights." On this point see Bowles (1989b) who considers the interesting case of hybrid corn.

12. This argument will be completed in section 5, where it is shown that "classical capitalism" can inhibit the development of both "general" and "firm-specific" human skills and may be consistent only with the use of "generic" skills. I have considered the interpretations of Braverman's deskilling hypothesis in Pagano (1991b). Important developments as well as criticisms of Braverman include Edwards (1979), Littler (1982) and Bowles (1989b). A survey is offered by Thompson (1983).

13. An analysis of this point can be found in Pagano (1991a).

14. On the concept of workers' preferences and their unsatisfactory treatment in economic theory, see Pagano (1985).

15. A possible objection to this argument is that, instead of renting machines, the workers may borrow money, buy the machines and use them as collateral. Still, this objection can be answered by observing that firm-specific machines are less valuable as collateral than general-purpose machines because it is more difficult to liquidate them in case of bankruptcy. In both cases it will be more expensive to rent firm-specific capital than general-purpose capital.

16. On the advantages of horizontal monitoring see Aoki (1987, 1988) and Putterman (1982).

17. Again, difficult-to-monitor capital, like firm-specific capital, is less valuable as collateral than easy-to-monitor capital because it will be more expensive for the lender to monitor user-induced depreciation. Thus also in this case borrowing money and buying machines may not be a solution to the problem of difficult-to-monitor capital.

18. Ognedal (1990) considers one of these caveats: "unstable ownership" relations may characterize a system of joint ownership.

19. Some other reasons, which also imply that the existing property rights can have self-generating properties, are considered by Putterman (1982) and Levine (1992).

20. In order to simplify the analysis we assume that the production function is the same under capitalist and workers' ownership. Under these conditions the (only) way by which technology is "generated" by property rights is by fixing the K/L ratio.

21. I am implicitly assuming that prices reflect socially relevant costs, so that cost comparisons imply efficiency comparisons. While this assumption should not be taken for granted, it is justified by the fact that the purpose of the analysis is to show that, even in this case, we can get inefficient organizational equilibria.

22. The efficiency explanation of the industrial organization seems to be very weak on empirical grounds. Different countries (think of (West) Germany, the USA, Japan and Sweden) seem to have organized production in such different ways that a "pure" efficiency explanation of these differences seems difficult to accept. By contrast, property right–DS technological equilibria, which may be institutionally stable even when they are inefficient, are compatible with this variety of experiences. Although

any serious analysis of real-life economies is beyond the scope of this chapter, I will briefly consider this point in the concluding section 6.

23. On the potential instability of occupational markets see Ryan (1984) and Marsden (1986).

24. When the agents interact frequently, the enforcement of these rules and guarantees may be performed more easily and, sometimes, without the help of centralized institutions. In this case, we are more likely to be in the repeated game framework considered, for instance, by Axelrod (1984). This is likely to arise in the case of "local" markets whose actors are the members of an integrated community, or in the case of the "Marshallian" industrial districts. These circumstances may explain the vitality of small firms considered by Brusco (1982), Becattini (1987) and Piore and Sabel (1984) with particular reference to some Italian "local" experiences. Bowles (1990) argues that small communities having strong and continued interactions are more likely to develop moral rules than anonymous agents acting on "global markets." Since the extension of markets may destroy the institutional bases of "spontaneous" moral behavior, the "moral autonomy" of self-regulating markets must be reconsidered.

25. For instance, the organization of health care is typically such as to guarantee an occupational market for medical doctors which allows their mobility among different hospitals. The organization of the work of doctors and their common training and qualification is established by the union or the order of doctors together with employers. Dasgupta and David (1988) argue that, unlike technologists, scientists are organized on similar lines. A transition from what, in Pagano (1991a) I have called "unionized" capitalism and "company workers'" capitalism can be found in Elbaum and Wilkinson (1979).

26. See Aoki (1988) and Morishima (1982).

27. See Maurice *et al.* (1984) where they argue that, unlike France, (West) Germany has these characteristics.

28. See Ch. 5 of Morishima (1982), where he gives a detailed account of the rights acquired by the workers immediately after the war and of the consequences of the U-turn of the occupying forces in 1950.

7 Agency problems and the future of comparative systems' theory

MIEKE MEURS

1 Introduction

Recent events in the (former) Soviet Union and Eastern Europe have awoken the field of comparative economic systems from its quiet backwater. Spurred by the delegitimation of an undemocratic system which no longer delivered the goods, these changes challenged standard comparative systems' assumptions of placid, obedient workers, and unchanging economic and political systems.

The economic problems result from the inherent "shortage" character of centrally planned economies (CPEs) (Kornai, 1982), which causes input hoarding by managers, unfulfilled plans and a shortage of consumer goods, in turn weakening work incentives. The problems are also linked to the paternalistic, and often corrupt, nature of the state, which failed to represent citizens (Nove, 1983).

Underlying these failures are agency problems between owners and managers, between managers and workers, between producers and consumers, and between the state and citizens. These same four types of agency problems are common to all economies, although the specific forms they take in CPEs result from the particular institutional structures of these societies.

In spite of the importance of agency problems in CPEs, the agency-theoretic approach is conspicuously underdeveloped in the field of comparative economic systems. The dominant paradigms in the field have examined only one agency problem closely, the principal–agent problem between planners and managers. Other agency problems have rarely been addressed. Further, the planner–manager problem has been examined exclusively in the context of comparing problems arising under state ownership and central planning to that of an ideal market economy in which agency problems are assumed away.

It is argued, in Eastern Europe and much of the Western academic community, that the agency problems between owners and managers, and managers and workers result from the system of property rights – from the centralization of ownership in state hands and the exclusion of managers from decision-making and income streams. Property rights' reform is therefore seen as the key to overcoming these problems. A broader distribution of property rights, combined with the implementation of markets, is also expected to resolve agency problems between consumers and producers and is, occasionally, claimed to be sufficient to ensure a state responsive to citizens.

It is now well-known in the microeconomic literature, however, that agency problems are ubiquitous, avoided perhaps only in a system of petty commodity production. Thus, whereas the dominant comparative systems paradigms have provided important insights into the functioning of CPEs, they cannot provide a framework for evaluating and comparing the wide range of democratic and economic reforms now evolving.

A new framework should incorporate and extend agency-theoretic developments in other fields, to evaluate the impact of specific changes in property rights, and other institutions, on agency problems. Some recent comparative systems' work has begun to contribute to such a framework, addressing a wider range of agency problems and comparing the nature of problems and their resolution across institutional contexts. After reviewing the two dominant comparative systems' paradigms, three of the newer studies will be examined.

Even in the new work, however, a number of important issues remain unaddressed. Agency problems between the citizen and state, and between producer and consumer, have not yet been addressed. Further, little has been done to integrate relevant work from other, related fields, into a framework for evaluating the overall agency-related impact of a given reform. The challenge for future work in this area will be to generate such a paradigm.

2   Agency problems and comparative systems

2.1   Agency problems

Principal–agent problems may arise when: (1) a conflict of interest exists among parties to a contract, and (2) there are information asymmetries among the parties which render contract enforcement difficult. As a result of this situation, the principal, having the power to set the terms of the contract, searches for means to increase the likelihood of contract fulfillment. Means may include monitoring (which reduces information asymmetries), the implementation of shared rules (which reduces the conflict of interest) or, although this has not been widely recognized in the literature, through the modification of the preferences of either party (which can also serve to reduce conflicts of interest).

Where the conflicts of interest cannot be eliminated or a perfect monitoring scheme designed, a Pareto-optimal solution will not be achieved for agents pursuing dominant strategies (Hurwicz, 1972a). Agents with an incentive to "cheat" will misrepresent their utility functions, as well as their technical and other constraints, when defining the exchange.

Neither the conflict, nor the information asymmetry will be eliminated by movement from one form of property rights to another. Within capitalist firms, for example, the conflict of interest between owners and managers is widely recognized, although debate continues regarding the potential of stock markets and other institutional arrangements to attenuate this conflict (Fama, 1980; Stiglitz, 1985); problems of worker agency in capitalist firms have also been extensively examined (Bowles and Gintis, 1990; Akerlof, 1984). State-owned firms in market economies are known to face the same set of problems, often with fewer means available for attenuating the conflicts. Labor-managed firms face conflicts between the interests of individual workers and those of the collective as owner, replacing principal–agent problems with free-riding (Alchian and Demsetz, 1972b). Agency problems between consumers and producers, and between the state and citizens also persist, to different degrees, across the three contexts, although they are less frequently examined. The specific form of agency problems, as well as options for their resolution, will differ across economic systems, but the problems are ubiquitous.

Because agency problems occur in many economic and social relations, theory must permit comparisons between complete systems, taking into consideration the whole range of agency problems in each system. For example, in preparing for the change from central planning to private ownership in Eastern Europe it is important to predict the impact of this change on citizen–state relations and worker–management relations, as well as on management performance. It will also be important to analyze the impact of the form of resolution of one problem on others. For example, how might democratic control of the state affect the way in which worker agency problems are resolved? Finally, comparative evaluation will require a means of assigning values to the different constellations of agency problems and forms of resolution.

2.2   Agency problems in comparative systems

The field of comparative systems has developed two paradigms with which to analyze two of the problems described above. These will be referred to here as the *elicitation scheme* and *labor-managed firm* paradigms. While both paradigms offer important insights into particular problems, both fall short of permitting comprehensive analysis of the agency-related impact of property rights and institutional reforms.

The elicitation scheme paradigm was developed to analyze the principal–agent problem between planners and managers in a state-owned, centrally planned system. Whereas planners want managers to fulfill a plan maximizing total social output, managers are assumed to care only about maximizing their income. A coincidence of interests could apparently be generated by a sharing scheme linking managerial pay to output.

To maximize social production, however, planners must elicit information from managers about firm production potential and input requirements. If this information is then used to allocate inputs preferentially to the most productive firms, managers of less productive firms will have an incentive to lie about productive potential. Thus arises the intractable conflict of interest: planners want truthful information, but its provision may conflict with managers' goal of maximizing incomes.

Groves (1973) suggested a (now well-known) scheme which could overcome this problem by ensuring that managers could not manipulate their input allocations through false reporting. This incentive structure rewards agents according to the planners' expectation of the achievement of all other agents (based on their reports) and adds a lump-sum transfer not based on information given by that agent. With income decoupled from managers' individual performance, managers no longer have an incentive to lie about productive potential. Thus, for agents choosing a dominant strategy, this scheme could resolve the principal–agent problem.

The Groves scheme will not achieve Pareto-optimality, however, since it will not guarantee a balanced budget for the center (Hurwicz, 1975). The scheme is also vulnerable to manipulation by groups of managers, and to losing incentive compatibility if managers have preferences about firm output levels in addition to income (Conn, 1978).

In this basic model, it is the asymmetry of information about *production possibilities* which makes contract definition and enforcement difficult. The agency problem resulting from asymmetric information about *managerial effort* was introduced somewhat later, by Bonin and Marcus (1979), as an extension of the earlier model. In this model, effort has a disutility to managers but can serve to increase output and/or reliability of production, which planners desire. Using such a model, Miller and Murrell (1981) show that when managers can adjust their effort, there is no incentive scheme by which planners can simultaneously elicit accurate information about production possibilities and obtain output maximization, unless the planners have previous, extensive information about managers' utilities. In short, the work in the elicitation paradigm suggested that the marginal redistribution of property rights implied in sharing rules could not fully overcome principal–agent problems between planners and managers under reasonable assumptions. For the purpose of evaluating alternative institutional reforms in Eastern Europe, this paradigm has a number of shortcomings.

First, as previously noted, it does not address agency problems concerning workers or the state, two issues which have become central during the recent economic downturn and political upheaval. While a comparative examination of worker agency problems is important for its own sake, it would also clearly change at least some of the potential to overcome management problems. For example, much of the information which planners wish to elicit from managers must first be collected from workers, and elicitation schemes need to include incentives for this provision as well.

Secondly, the paradigm has not been oriented toward the necessary comparisons of owner–manager agency problems and associated inefficiencies, across forms of property rights and popular control. The paradigm has significantly increased our understanding of the impossibility of resolving management problems under central planning, but is only a small part of the necessary framework.

Thirdly, Pareto-optimality, used as a benchmark of efficiency in this work, is inadequate for the purposes of comparing different institutional arrangements. One reason for this is that the Pareto-principle is of little use in comparing some types of sub-optimal situations. Since principal–agent problems can be attenuated, but not eliminated, it is precisely the comparison of sub-optimal outcomes which is needed.

Another problem with the use of the Pareto-principle lies in its evaluation over a given set of preferences. Reforms of property rights and of democratic structures make changes in agents' preferences likely. For example, increased worker control of firms might reduce the disutility of work, allowing more effort to be provided at the same wage. This implies the possibility of a welfare-improving institutional change, even if Pareto-optimality could be shown for the previous arrangement.

Finally, the Pareto-criterion neglects the issue of feasibility. While institutional arrangements may be formally shown to offer only sub-optimal results, Williamson (1985) has argued that these must be compared to other real alternatives which, recognizing the ubiquitous nature of agency problems, as noted above, will also be sub-optimal.

Contributions within the elicitation scheme paradigm slowed after the early 1980s, when it was shown that no efficient solution to the incentive problem could be found under reasonable assumptions. Given the limited applicability of the paradigm to the evaluation of current reforms, it is likely to fade further from dominance in coming years. Many contributions of this paradigm are likely to be integrated into a new paradigm, however, since many of the problems of central planning exist also in large corporations in market economies.

A second paradigm has developed for use in analyzing Labor-Managed Firms (LMFs) (see, for example, Vanek, 1970; Ward, 1967). Although those working in this framework have focused on problems of *worker* behavior, they have generally not addressed the issue of agency *per se*. The free-rider problem is seen as characteristic of LMFs, and in the literature other potential sources of inefficiency have been emphasized, such as insufficient investment or employment, or slow adjustment to exogenous shocks. As was the case in the elicitation literature, perfectly competitive, agency-free market outcomes are used as the benchmark to evaluate the performance of LMFs, and the LMFs are found to be less efficient.

Recently, however, a few articles on LMFs have begun explicitly to examine worker agency problems across institutional contexts. Recognizing strategic behavior as a characteristic of all institutional contexts, the authors model the changing contexts as changing structures of strategic games. Only a handful of articles, and lacking a common set of questions or language, this work does not yet represent a fully developed paradigm. Still, by comparing agency problems and their resolution across institutional arrangements, the authors contribute to the formation of a paradigm with which to compare agency-related costs and benefits of different institutional structures.

The work of Ireland and Law (1988) is one example of the new approach. Rather than comparing outcomes in LMFs to a utopian vision of solved agency problems, their framework accepts agency problems as ubiquitous, and compares their form and degree of resolution across forms of property and control. Departing from the traditional comparative systems emphasis on the impact of property rights on material interests, Ireland and Law emphasize the impact of property rights on information asymmetries between principal and agent, and thus the range of strategies open to players.

Assuming that worker-owned firms and LMFs face the same worker preferences (including risk-aversion) and monitoring options as profit-maximizing, private firms (PMFs), Ireland and Law examine the efficiency with which the two firms will deal with worker agency problems (free-riding in the case of LMFs or shirking in PMFs) through monitoring. As has traditionally been the case, differing forms of ownership and control are represented by different maximands. But Ireland and Law also distinguish firms by differences in the set of feasible trades resulting from differences in information distribution.

Ireland and Law find that, if the LMF has homogeneous members and distributes the enterprise residual according to work, in accordance with the property rights of the worker-owners, the LMF will choose a more efficient level of monitoring than the PMF. The argument proceeds as follows. Since effort is immeasurable and creates disutility for (individual) workers, but always benefits the (individual or collective) owner, monitoring is desirable in both firms. In the LMF, workers collectively decide upon and hire a given level of monitoring, with the collective acting as a Stackleberg leader with respect to individual members. Under these conditions, the risk-averse workers are willing to trade reductions in risk of mispayment (due to inadequate monitoring or erroneous observation) for lower wages, choosing not to monitor all workers, but to monitor some of them carefully. Once this level of monitoring is established, workers respond to the combination of supervision and expected pay rates in a Cournot–Nash manner.

In the PMF, however, an information asymmetry arises which prevents this efficient solution. Since only the capitalist knows the actual level of monitoring, it is no longer possible for workers to exchange better monitoring (risk reduction) for lower wages. The trade is not credible since the capitalist will have an interest in minimizing monitoring costs. Instead, the owner will unilaterally set wages and monitoring so as to maximize profits subject to workers' reservation utility, and workers will respond to the combination of wages and monitoring, again in a Cournot–Nash manner.

A long-run solution to the level of monitoring for the PM firm, in the absence of market failures, would be to achieve the same supply of worker effort as in the LMF. However, since the set of feasible trades has been altered by the information asymmetries, capitalists will choose to casually monitor all workers. Under certain conditions, this will result in a reduced supply of effort in the PM firm, suggesting that the free-rider problem in a collectively-owned firm may be more easily solved than a principal–agent problem in a privately-owned firm. Although Ireland and Law avoid efficiency claims, due to the number of efficiency-related aspects of LMFs which are not addressed in their model, it can be argued that with respect to agency problems alone, the larger feasible set of trades open to LMFs provides potential efficiency increases.

Like Ireland and Law, MacLeod (1987) compares worker agency problems across capitalist firms and LMFs, modeling the differences as changes in the structure of a strategic game. Rather than grounding changes in information differences, MacLeod highlights the importance of workers' expectations of others' behavior, something which may be affected by the level of democracy in the firm or other ideological and cultural factors differing across firm types.

As in the previous model, the agency problem arises in the provision of work effort. In both capitalist firms and LMFs, workers are assumed to have utility for wages and disutility for effort. Since both firms have surplus-sharing incentive schemes, workers in both cases will do better if free-riding can be effectively overcome.

In evaluating the potential of a given sharing rule to attenuate agency problems, he suggests that capitalist firms and LMFs may differ in a fundamental way. The nature of the game varies, for MacLeod, because while he assumes that workers' behavior remains constant across firm types, he posits that their expectations of co-workers' behavior will vary. In an LMF, where production norms are collectively developed, workers expect their co-workers to adhere to the stated norms and goals. In a capitalist firm, they expect an "everyone for herself" strategy.

To capture these differences, MacLeod models effort provision as a cooperative game in the LMF, and as a non-cooperative game in the PMF. In the LMF, where workers respond to sharing schemes in a cooperative manner, he finds that an incentive-compatible sharing scheme can be defined. His scheme (one of many possible) would divide the work force into two teams and define a sharing rule in terms of (observable) output and prices. Effort is thus contracted implicitly. A team failing to meet its commitment would forfeit any surplus earned to the other team. This scheme will elicit effort levels that are a cooperative equilibrium, and thereby overcome the free-rider problem.

In the capitalist firm workers expect that their fellow workers, having developed no collective culture of work, will not behave cooperatively. Workers thus maximize utility by foregoing cooperative solutions and choosing the dominant, non-cooperative strategy. MacLeod argues that since, under surplus-sharing, if one worker is expected to shirk, it is rational for all workers to shirk, the dominant strategy response is for workers in this case to choose a low, rather than a high, level of effort. MacLeod shows that, under these conditions, there is no scheme with strictly positive effort levels under which individual utility maximization will maximize group utility. Incentive compatibility is therefore impossible to achieve, and free-riding cannot be overcome.

It is difficult to accept MacLeod's labeling of the non-cooperative firm as "capitalist," given the surplus-sharing pay scheme and emphasis on workers' utility in defining pay schemes. Still, the approach could be used to compare the resolution of agency problems in LMFs with differing levels of democratic control and worker cooperation. The salient point, regarding the impact of workers' expectations of each other's behavior on the resolution of the free-rider problem, should hold.

2.3   Labor, capital, and political power

While more suitable to the present task of comparing agency problems across forms of property and popular control of the firm, neither Ireland and Law nor MacLeod address the link between agency problems and popular control of the state. David Ellerman (1986a), in a work which does not deal specifically with agency problems, suggests a way in which the degree of resolution of citizen–state agency problems may affect other agency problems. Ellerman argues that the differences in survivability between LMFs and capitalist firms are not due to differential efficiency, but rather to the different contractual opportunities open to these two different firm types. His work suggests that democratic control of the state, which could be used to equalize the contractual opportunities open to the two types of firm, may be essential to the survival of LMFs. Such survival will, in turn, affect the kinds of agency problems faced within firms.

Ellerman begins by noting that although all producers are property owners, property rights are affected by a particular convention: that the hirer of inputs gets the residual – it is not divided among the owners of the many factors involved in production. The suppliers of the non-hiring factors, instead of being co-owners of the residual, are simply creditors. This is true no matter who hires whom. In capital-owned firms, capital has the right to appropriate the "whole products" produced, and to retain the residual after paying creditors.

But there is an important difference between the two firm types. Members of LMFs have the right to act as residual claimant only during their tenure in the firm (they will have no claim to residuals from contracts concluded after that), and they are forbidden to hire a specific class of input – other labor. Capitalist owners, on the other hand, may act as residual claimant over a tenure longer than that likely for any group of workers, should any future contracts be concluded, and capital is free to hire a full range of complementary resources.

Capital has no guarantee that it can capture these future residuals, however. People could, Ellerman suggests, resolve this power difference by legal fiat. By outlawing hired labor, expected contractual opportunities for capital will be limited to hiring itself out. Present value is then determined by the equivalent income-earning possibilities for the two firm types: selling out or taking the flow of sales of future services. Under these conditions, capital is on a par with labor.

Labor, faced with this possibility, might find it preferable. Or labor might prefer other forms of equalizing the competitiveness of different firm types. For our purposes, the important point raised by Ellerman is the potential relationship between agency problems between citizens and the state, and the predominant form of agency problem faced at the level of the firm.

3   Toward a new paradigm

To evaluate adequately the impact of property rights' reforms on the agency problems plaguing Eastern Europe economies, we require a framework broad enough to incorporate a range of agency problems and institutional contexts. The new work reviewed here makes important advances over earlier work, addressing agency problems in LMFs, and comparing these to problems of worker agency which would arise in a capitalist "twin." Perhaps, more importantly, these preliminary attempts appearing in the *Journal of Comparative Systems*, may represent the beginnings of a new comparative systems' paradigm, one particularly suited to current needs.

There remain, however, a number of issues as yet unaddressed within the field of comparative systems. Almost nothing has been done to examine agency problems between consumers and producers. Here, there is probably a relatively simple relation to market-oriented institutional changes. The heavy industrial concentration and shortage economy of Eastern Europe have left consumers with few means of enforcing the most minimal quality commitments on the part of producers. New firm entry and competition through market mechanisms may significantly disperse economic power, increasing the potential of consumers to elicit desired behavior from producers. But the impact of specific institutional arrangements on consumer power and firm agency have not been closely examined.

The impact of democratic institutions on state–citizen relations has not been adequately examined either. Formal examination of the relation between institutional arrangements and citizens' influence on state action will be an important complement to current work on the impact of different arrangements on public choice problems. Elections and recall, for example, may permit citizens to threaten state functionaries' jobs, and thereby elicit greater responsiveness to citizen interests. But which forms of democratic organization will best reduce the information asymmetries between citizens and the state, allowing citizens to exercise this threat? Roemer and Rosenthal (1979), and others, have modeled the impact of information asymmetries on citizen–state relations in a free market economy, but work of this type has not been extended to the field of comparative economic systems.

With respect to problems of worker agency, the work of MacLeod, and Ireland and Law on LMFs has illustrated important effects of this form of organization on agency problems. The impact of increasing workplace democracy on worker agency in capitalist or state-owned firms has been less extensively examined. In one attempt to model this (Meurs, 1989), I have examined the way in which a utility-increasing institutional change such as worker participation might affect the provision of effort by workers and the distribution of income within the firm.

Using a cooperative solution under the assumption that both workers and employer have good information about each other's behavior and stand to gain through cooperation, I show that participation may substitute for wages as a means of eliciting additional effort, but that this will not necessarily result in additional surplus for the employer, depending on the elasticities of response to increased participation of utility and effort, and on the marginal productivity of additional effort. This suggests that, while institutional change such as increasing workplace democracy may serve as one means of attenuating agency problems, such a change will not necessarily be welfare-improving. Other problems, such as the impact of worker participation on employment levels, and thus on the bargaining power of managers, remain to be examined.

In addition to the specific issues that remain to be addressed, a great deal of *comparative* work remains to be done. The excellent new work comparing problems of worker agency in PMFs and LMFs could be complemented by comparisons of other agency problems across systems of property rights, comparing, for example, the effect of specific sharing and monitoring schemes on managerial behavior across state, private, and worker ownership.

To evaluate the potential impact of property rights' reforms, however, comparisons must be extended to the whole set of agency problems involved in a system. For example, since the resolution of agency problems between owners and managers is likely to impact upon the resolution of problems between managers and workers, the two problems need to be analyzed simultaneously to capture effects on enterprise efficiency fully. Aoki (1984) has examined some of the relationships between agency problems between owners and managers, and managers and workers under a variety of institutional arrangements, but his work has not been integrated into comparative systems' analysis. Links to the state and to citizens remain to be examined.

To develop an integrated framework for analyzing agency problems across systems, a common language and set of research questions will need to be widely adopted. The existing comparative systems' paradigms offered the benefit a well-defined modeling framework within which researchers could debate results and build on existing work. A similar, well-defined framework will be important if work on distinct agency problems and systems is to be compared and aggregated. This will imply further research on, and eventual agreement about, the game-types and solution concepts which best represent different institutional structures (a problem noted by Conn in 1978). To date, the choice of methods appears quite arbitrary, and differing methods complicate comparisons of conclusions.

Finally, even if a common and integrated framework is developed, and solution concepts agreed upon, a framework will need to be developed for evaluating the costs and benefits of different forms of property and popular control. A framework suited to current tasks will focus on the comparison of feasible institutional states. But evaluation is likely to be problematic. Institutional changes may attenuate some agency or efficiency problems while exacerbating others. Institutional states can sometimes be compared using Samuelson or Scitovsky criteria (Feldman, 1980). In cases where these criteria do not offer a clear Pareto-ranking this, in itself, will be an important result – more significant than the conclusion that a certain state does not achieve the optimal results which could be achieved in an agency-free environment.

While providing no solutions to the many agency problems which have plagued Eastern Europe, the framework described here may permit a more detailed evaluation of the potential of different reforms to address them. At the same time, the integration of existing work on a range of agency problems will contribute to current debates on the potential of institutional reform to improve productivity in the capitalist economies of the USA and Western Europe.

Part III
Conditions for the success of the democratic firm

8 After the employment relation: problems on the road to enterprise democracy

LOUIS PUTTERMAN

1 Introduction

Suppose that there were a determined social consensus in favor of workplace democracy such that conventional employment relationships were ruled out by custom, by constitution, or by law. That is, assume that it has been decided that most enterprises will be so organized that the right to choose their boards of directors, managers, or other decision-making bodies and personnel, or directly to determine major enterprise policies, is assigned to their workers and only to their workers (including managerial personnel), on the basis of one worker, one vote. What problems should be anticipated, and how might these be dealt with by appropriate institutional design or policies? In this chapter, I attempt to apply the results of the theoretical and empirical literatures on worker-managed firms, along with some personal rumination, to the question of the costs and dangers of implementing enterprise democracy in a market economy.

The chapter is organized as follows. Section 2 briefly reconsiders the old question of why capital hires labor, in other words why worker-run firms are not the norm, in market economies. Section 3 is equally brief, giving a preliminary discussion of the question of society-wide institutional change viewed as a change in the regime of rights. The next three sections provide the core discussion of what past studies of self-management imply for the transition to an economy of worker-managed firms. Section 4 deals with issues of employment, membership rights, and product market behavior. Section 5 treats financing of worker-run firms and property rights in capital goods. Section 6 deals with some less standard topics, including decision-making mechanisms, work organization, and job satisfaction. Section 7 concludes the chapter by asking whether economic democracy ought in fact to be constitutionally mandated, and how costly the transition to such a system might be.

2 Why capital hires labor, revisited

An important question raised in this context is: "Can the fact that market economies disfavor internally democratic firms be explained on efficiency grounds?" A few years ago (1984), I attempted to argue that the efficiency explanations of the dominance of capitalist firms in the market economy offered by Williamson (1975, 1980), Alchian and Demsetz (1972a), and Jensen and Meckling (1979), fell short of their objectives. Alchian and Demsetz suggested that only a full claim on the enterprise's residual earnings could induce managers to undertake the monitoring of effort that is needed to give proper incentives to workers. I contended that that argument raised more questions than it answered, including why observed participatory firms often elicit high productivity and use fewer costly supervisors than do their conventional counterparts.[1] Williamson suggested that democratic firms would be inefficient in decision-making and would not assign workers to the jobs to which they were most suited. I contended that these arguments confused management structure with control rights,[2] that they assumed that democratic firms shunned specialization to a utopian degree while they overlooked the productivity advantages of selective "job enlargement," and that they neglected to consider the societal link between the available pool of skills and the dominant form of work organization (Bowles and Gintis, 1976; Putterman, 1982). Jensen and Meckling argued, among other things, that worker-run firms would squander whatever capital they might obtain from financiers. I suggested that that argument is directly undermined by their own assertion (Jensen and Meckling, 1976) that capital markets discipline managers by forcing firms to bear the costs of wealth-reducing discretionary behavior in the form of higher costs of capital.

Despite these criticisms, it was not my intention to suggest that labor hiring capital is dominated by capital hiring labor in the market economy due only to historical accident or because of a conspiracy by capitalists against workers. In my view, individual rationality and unequal distribution of skills and wealth combine to produce this result in several ways, the most salient of which have to do with risk-bearing and the financing of firms. On the one hand, suppliers of financial resources to business enterprises rationally seek safeguards on their investments; a share in control rights, such as that accorded to the stockholders of a corporation, is a relatively cheap way of meeting their requirements, from a pecuniary standpoint. On the other hand, an enterprise's workers have only limited resources to contribute to the financing of the production sector. In view of their typically low wealth and income positions, the foregoing of diversification with respect to their investments – a requirement of financing their own firms – would come at a high price. Unless workers highly value control rights, it is rational for them to diversify their financial portfolios and to let the enterprises in which they work be financed by various other individuals to whom control rights will be granted where expedient.[3]

Other factors seem likely to play a role as well. History matters in that today's skill distribution is shaped by the needs of yesterday's enterprise system and in turn influences the viability of tomorrow's competing organizational forms. Endogeneity of preferences is also related to the desire for control rights or participation on the part of workers: that desire may be non-existent or weak if workers are socialized into the expectation of subordination on the job, and are conditioned to viewing work as an acceptable sacrifice making possible increased consumption during leisure time. Raising the possibility that workers' valuations of autonomy are lowered by conditioning and socialization in a hierarchical industrial society is, however, problematic. To assert that workers would want what enlightened academics wish for them, if only they did not receive the wrong education, is both presumptuous and irresponsible. Although awareness of the endogeneity problem should sensitize us to the subtlety with which this issue must be approached, finding ways to identify just how much value workers themselves attach to participation in the workplace is an important problem facing sober designers of economic reforms.

I have argued that economic theory offers plausible explanations of why rational workers enter conventional employment contracts rather than forming capital-hiring firms in which they are their own bosses. But would individual rationality on the part of workers lead to institutional rationality for society as a whole? Here, problems may again arise if preferences have historical and systemic roots. There is also a distributional issue here: the "optimality" of any given competitive equilibrium is in a sense conditional upon the endowment distribution with which it is associated, and the same may be said for an institutional equilibrium that can in part be explained by workers' wealth positions and their resulting risk-bearing abilities. Another factor which I have alluded to in earlier papers is that the added cost of raising capital without according control rights to its suppliers is higher for a firm acting alone than it would be if the entire economy in which it participates had adopted this practice, so there is a collective action problem in the transition to workers' control (Putterman, 1982). Having said all of this, I would nonetheless conclude that there *is* indeed a *prima facia* case that control of industry by workers is inefficient in terms of workers' own value scales, in the sense that the most straightforward explanation of the observed job distribution would be to rely on such an inference. Those who are sympathetic to the idea of increased worker participation are obliged to contend with this problem in one manner or another, and ultimately that obligation entails going beyond the realm of theoretical exercise.[4]

3   Conceptualizing the transition to democratic enterprises

Although considerable numbers of worker-controlled enterprises have arisen in market economies, they have never accounted for more than a small share of employment and output. The popularity of participative approaches in the contemporary management literature (e.g., Lawler, 1986), the promotion of teamwork, gainsharing, and similar arrangements at numerous large firms such as the US company Proctor and Gamble, and the growing numbers of employee ownership and profit-sharing plans (Blasi, 1988; Blinder, 1990), could perhaps signal the dawning of an age of workplace democracy. Such a change, occurring without government intervention although with the partial stimulus of tax benefits (for ESOPs), might be largely attributable to the increased demand for less alienating work by more educated and higher-income workers (Rosner and Putterman, 1991), to the ascendance of human capital to the status of a pivotal productive factor (Schlicht, 1979), or simply to the quest for productivity enhancement in a world of heightened global competition.[5] However, the more widespread participative forms remain far removed from full democratization of the workplace. With the transition to a participatory economy by decentralized means still far from complete, proposals for promoting further movement towards such democratization through legislation and/or financial incentives are likely to remain on the political agendas of many nations.

One possible proposal is that there be a uniform transition from the conventional employment system to one of worker-controlled firms. Such a transition can be conceptualized as an augmentation of the bundle of "inalienable rights" granted to citizens by liberal societies. Here, the rights in question are that of autonomy as a producer, or of representation in any decisions regarding the management of production that must be taken collectively (due to its team character), and the related right to control the disposal of the products of one's labor. Ellerman (1986b) views these rights as "natural," arguing that an individual cannot escape responsibility for the consequences of his or her actions, and therefore cannot avoid responsibility for choosing those actions, cede entitlement to their fruits, or evade economic responsibility for any resources depleted in the process.[6] An alternative is to treat rights not as natural or pre-ordained but as reflections of values held by members of a society, capable of varying in time and place. A right of self-management may come to be viewed as worthy of social affirmation because it is believed to enhance the dignity of the individual, or to extend to the workplace the democratic principle of representation by the governed, or for some other reason.

It will doubtless be noticed that to extend to the worker the right to control the workplace and dispose of the net product of the production process is simultaneously to eliminate another right, the freedom to enter into a mutually desired agreement wherein the worker provides labor services to an employer and accepts that employer's authority in the workplace in exchange for monetary compensation. Exactly the same drawback accompanies all assertions of inalienable rights: the right of the people freely to elect their leaders prevents them from crowning a monarch; the right to be free from slavery prevents people from capitalizing their lifetime labor potential; an individual's right to vote cannot be sold, and so forth.[7] This hardly permits us to dismiss the problem, however. Presumably, people must weigh the costs of each inalienable right against its benefits, however intangible. Until there is broad social consensus that a right of self-management outweighs any losses of efficiency and/or of personal freedom which may be entailed, it seems unlikely that legal or constitutional provisions in favor of such a right, promoted by narrow interest groups, would produce desired and desirable results. Without such a social consensus, confirmed by an ongoing and open democratic political process, major changes in existing liberal property rights regimes would appear to be inherently unstable[8] or even dangerous.[9]

4   The labor-managed economy: labor and product markets

Let me return, now, to the assumption that there exists a determined social consensus in favor of workplace democracy, and that conventional employment relationships are ruled out either by custom, or by constitution or law, although perhaps with some exceptions. These exceptions might be (a) that there could be a period of candidacy before a worker is accorded membership status in his or her enterprise, (b) that an enterprise might contract with another enterprise for the delivery of temporary labor services, without according membership rights to the outside workers (who remain members of the sub-contracting firm), (c) that capitalist-style employment might be permitted in certain small-scale activities, and (d) that workers might share control rights with the state or other public bodies in certain very large enterprises. As indicated earlier, questions to be addressed are: what problems should be anticipated, and how might these be dealt with by appropriate institutional design or policies? In the present section, I take up questions relating to the employment of labor, membership rights, and the functioning of product markets, areas that have been the principal concerns of the theoretical literature since Ward (1958), Domar (1966), Vanek (1970), and Meade (1972a).

Probably the best-known finding of that literature is that a one-product firm seeking to maximize profit per worker, with the number of workers the sole variable input, will reduce membership and output in response to a price increase, and will have fewer (more) workers and produce less (more) output than a comparable capitalist firm when the latter is earning positive (negative) profits. Although any number of qualifications have been offered, the theoretical expectation of a less elastic product supply curve than the comparable capitalist firm survives most of these, even in long-run analysis.[10] However, while sharply backward-bending supply curves would certainly be worrisome, a little less elasticity of short-term supply hardly seems worthy of great concern.

I am afraid that it is not as easy to dismiss concerns about employment, labor allocation, and perhaps also supply by monopolies. As Labor-Managed Firms (LMFs) adjust their membership levels to maximize labor dividends in the face of shifting product prices, labor marginal products become more unequal: firms in profitable markets reduce membership and move to higher levels of labor marginal product, those in less profitable markets increase membership and move to lower levels of marginal product. Earnings for the same type of labor thus differ among industries, so workers in unprofitable industries will be seeking employment in profitable ones, but will find that firms are unwilling to accept them.

Such temporary misallocations of labor might still be a minor concern, and indeed a scarcely noteworthy price for self-management, if that innovation delivers as promised in the realms of worker satisfaction and technical efficiency, and if they are indeed temporary, and lead to appropriate adjustments. However, without free entry and exit into/from product markets, long-run adjustments by existing enterprises fail to address these inefficiencies. With labor's remuneration remaining endogenous to the firm and linked to the product price, profitable firms will choose more capital-intensive techniques, unprofitable ones more labor-intensive methods, and both labor and capital will be misallocated, since different firms will equate different factor- (shadow-)price ratios to different marginal rates of technical substitution. In fact, downward labor adjustments are likely to be more substantial in the long run, when they can be made through attrition. The industry's long-run product supply curve, assuming the number of producers remains constant, will continue to be inelastic. As new workers come into the labor force, they will have to join unprofitable firms which seek workers to share their debt burdens, and output of products the demand for which has declined may grow.

There are ways to address these difficulties by altering the institutional structure from that assumed in the models. One possibility is to require firms to accept all workers interested in joining them. This would redress the tendency for firms in high-demand industries to shrink or be stagnant while those in low-demand industries grow, although so long as net earnings were shared equally among workers in each firm, (i.e., earnings are profit shares rather than wages), the tendency to equalize earnings across firms would not imply equal marginal products of labor. In any case, the requirement that worker-run firms accept all applicants, or (less radically) all applicants meeting certain objective qualifications, would cause problems of its own, and might undermine strengths of the democratic enterprise form. For smaller firms especially, face-to-face relations and interpersonal compatibility might be a basis of both high productivity and work satisfaction, which could not be secure in the absence of the right to choose new members. It might be difficult, moreover, to include some qualities or abilities deemed important to specific jobs, in the set of "objective qualifications," so work force quality might be undermined by the free-entry rule. More importantly, workers' incentives to raise the profitability of their firms through hard work, technical improvements, careful marketing research, etc. could be severely weakened by the knowledge that such profits would have to be shared, *ex post*, with any rent-seeking newcomers who came knocking at the firm's doors. Finally, there is the social and philosophical point that without discretion over membership, firms would cease to be free associations of workers.

Another theoretical solution is to establish a market in "partnership deeds" or memberships in firms, with the price of membership to entrants being set by existing members and adjusting with supply and demand. While Sertel (1982b) and Dow (1986)[11] have proven that such a market would eliminate all perversities and inefficiencies of worker-run firms, assuming perfect information and competition, there are also reasons to question this approach. A membership fee can make it attractive for existing members of a profitable cooperative to accept new members when they would otherwise find it against their interests to do so. This result is achieved, however, precisely by means of financial discrimination between incumbent and joining members. Although the two solutions differ in terms of the resulting distribution of control and profit-sharing rights, the entrance-fee approach is in static financial terms distributively equivalent to hiring the new members at their opportunity wages rather than paying them an equal profit share, a practice which might be objectionable on normative grounds.[12] From a more practical standpoint, in a world of imperfect information, moral hazard, and imperfect capital markets, the membership market might end up discouraging the growth of successful firms because potential members could find it difficult to finance payment of the entrance fees. It is important to ask why the practice of bonding or up-front job purchase would be feasible in a labor-managed economy, whereas it does not appear to be so in a world of capitalist firms.

Temporary movement of workers among firms, for example in the form of agreements by one firm to supply labor to another while members in each firm continue to hold membership and to receive the average earnings of their original firm (not, for those temporarily transferred, the firm in which they are physically working), also solve the allocation problems in the short run (Sacks, 1977). However, they fail to suggest a mechanism for more long-run adjustments, and they might be thought unacceptable insofar as they create a kind of second-class worker, and a partial restoration of the conventional employment relationship.

In my view,[13] the most appropriate strategy for supporting the full and efficient employment of the labor force in an economy organized along the lines of workers' management is to facilitate free entry and exit of firms, in the sense both of *de novo* firm creations and full terminations, and in that of entry (exit) of existing firms into new (or out of old) product lines. This idea emerges quite directly from the theoretical literature, which shows that the inefficiencies of LMFs in short-run and long-run individual adjustment are sharply contrasted with their full efficiency in long-run market equilibrium, assuming free entry and exit. The challenge posed to policy-makers is to find adequate answers to the question of how entry and exit can be encouraged.

One of the traditional questions here is that of the incentives for entrepreneurship in a worker-run economy (Ben-Ner, 1987): if founders cannot capture a large part of the returns to entrepreneurship, who will bother identifying the profitable opportunities, and managing the start-up of firms where they exist? The problem here may be exaggerated, however, since special fees to entrepreneurs are not ruled out by worker control, which does not require equal pay for heterogeneous contributions of effort and know-how. Moreover, the relevant entrepreneurial attributes may be far less scarce than some would suppose, and an example of successful institutionalized entepreneurship with respect to the founding of new, viable cooperatives exists in the widely-known experience of the "empresarial division" of the *Caja Laboral Popular* of Mondragon (Wiener with Oakeshott, 1987). To be sure, the funding of start-ups is likely to raise problems unless appropriate financial institutions exist, but this can be addressed by institutions like the *Caja*, which will be discussed in the next section.

More critical to entry and exit are questions of monopoly, government intervention, and financial accountability, with respect to which nearly forty years of Yugoslav experience provide ample lessons on what *not* to do (Estrin, 1983; Prasnikar and Svejnar, 1991). Aside from diversification of existing firms, the basic entry mechanism in Yugoslavia has been local (including republican) government sponsorship. There has been limited exit, because such government sponsorship gives security even to unprofitable enterprises. Government objectives do little to assure that the enterprises created are the ones most needed from an economic standpoint. To increase the profitability of their investments, moreover, these governments have often afforded monopoly protection to their enterprises by closing borders to products imported from other parts of the country. The combination of monopoly and lack of financial accountability is believed to have taken a heavy toll on the efficiency of Yugoslav enterprises. Irrational allocation of capital stock, which is discussed further in the next section, has added to this inefficiency.

5   Finance and property rights in capital

There is undoubtedly still much room for controversy regarding the lessons of self-management literature, and of self-management experience, for the design of financial institutions and systems of ownership rights. Moreover, some disagreements over the philosophical acceptability of private ownership cannot be eliminated by appeal to either theory or practice. Nonetheless, both logic and experience seem to concur that a system of predominantly social or collective rights in capital is economically costly; and it is possible to argue that such a system is socially unnecessary if the goals of system design are focused on either workplace social relations and quality of working life, or on containing economic inequality.

Yugoslavia has been the main laboratory here, and its recent abandonment of the principle of social capital is telling. Furubotn and Pejovich showed early on (e.g., 1970) that if enterprise capital were owned by society or the collective, rather than by individual workers or financiers, there would be a disincentive to re-invest earnings in firms, except when the useful life of the capital goods to be acquired was shorter than the expected remaining job tenure of the average (more precisely, median) member of a firm's work force. They then connected this disincentive with the Yugoslav authorities' imposition of a requirement that firms replace all depreciating capital goods with others of equal value, with those authorities' political interventions to influence enterprise investment decisions, and with their tendency to pump cheap funds into the banking system to encourage otherwise unattractive enterprise investment. Social property rights in capital plus workers' management were thus asserted to have led both to inefficient capital allocation at sub-market-clearing interest rates, and to inflation. However, identification of these Yugoslav problems with workers' management as such, by those authors, has failed to convince most specialists.[14]

In (1970), Vanek argued for the separation of ownership and control rights in LMFs, suggesting that the failure of many producer's cooperatives historically could be attributed to collective capital (of which Yugoslavia's "social" capital represents one concrete example). Not only does collective capital ownership discourage retention of earnings for investment, according to Vanek, but an *ex post* view of the services of collective capital as "free" to the firm leads to inefficient long-run resource allocation, in his view. However, if investment funds are provided to firms out of individual savings, either directly in the form of bonds or other instruments (possibly owned by workers in the firm, among others) or indirectly in the form of bank loans, the loanable funds market should equilibrate with firms rationally borrowing to finance all projects but only those projects with expected rates of return higher than the rate to be paid to lenders. Private asset ownership and worker management of enterprises are fully compatible, according to Vanek, provided that there is a separation of ownership rights, which entitle the lender of funds to a financial return, and decision control rights, which are reserved to the worker members by virtue of their status as workers in the firm. The Mondragon cooperatives provide a partial example of such financing (see Wiener with Oakeshott, 1987, and my discussion in Putterman, 1990, Ch. 4) and suggest that excellent results might indeed be obtained from this kind of approach.

As I have mentioned above, one of the reasons why self-management rights might have to be mandated by law if they are to be widely realized, is that providers of finance will tend to give firms better terms if they are accorded powers to influence and/or monitor the firms' behavior. To obtain capital more cheaply and accordingly be able to earn higher incomes, many workers might therefore agree to share control rights with financiers.[15] Since in this chapter I assume that a regime of full workers' control is to be established and maintained, such outright codetermination is ruled out here. On the other hand, it is of interest to consider whether *de facto* influence by financiers would pose a threat to effective workers' control. For example, auditing of firms' books by bankers, and voluntary covenants that restrict a firm with respect to specific investment decisions, cannot be ruled out merely because workers retain control rights. More generally, large firms especially will find it critically important to maintain access to external sources of capital, so their decision-makers will have strong incentives to see to it that they have a reputation for assuring a good return on investment.

Earlier, I mentioned that workers in a worker-managed economy would have to bear more risk than those in a capitalist one. This is partly because one of the assurances that firms are more or less obliged to offer to external financiers is the commitment by internal decision-makers of some of their own wealth (Schlicht and von Weisäcker, 1977; Gui, 1985). Combined with the need to bear variations in enterprise earnings given the nature of labor remuneration in LMFs, this risk is one reason why many workers might opt for capitalist employment were it available. Assuming a social consensus ruling out that option, is there some way to reduce the risks involved? The theory of moral hazard provides a simple and familiar answer: that there exist unavoidable trade-offs between insurance and incentives. Thus, while governments might want to offer insurance schemes that help to smooth workers' income flows and/or put a floor beneath earnings in a given period, the more comprehensive the insurance, the more are workers' incentives to maximize current productivity attenuated. (Note that what permits capitalist firms to provide current income insurance to employed workers is that the corresponding moral hazard is reduced by taking decision-making out of workers' hands and imposing direct supervision.) However, this does not mean that the optimal amount of insurance is zero. For a risk-averse population, both insurance and high expected incomes are desirable, and trading some of the latter for some of the former is entirely rational.

My suggestions for efficient financing of a worker-managed economy assume that individuals can own financial assets and have a right to earn returns on those assets. Is this necessary, and is it socially acceptable? Perhaps we need not rule out the possibility of a solution that makes far less use of private ownership. For example, the government could tax a certain amount of people's incomes, and could funnel these savings into financial intermediaries that loan them on to firms according to assessments of expected returns.[16] Whether the system could be designed so as to give those intermediaries sufficient incentives to manage the funds well is problematic, but perhaps the efficiency losses could be kept at acceptable levels. Yet, further efforts in this direction are unnecessary unless we see something wrong with allowing private saving and private returns on assets. To be sure, some (e.g., Roemer, 1990) would argue that social control of capital is the essence of socialism and allows public direction of resources which is superior to a purely decentralized allocation. However, semantic problems aside, if some public mediation in the economy is desirable, it is not clear why this should take the form of direct control over savings, rather than use of indicative planning methods of the type practiced in many Western European economies today. Inequalities in the distribution of wealth which are deemed socially unacceptable can be addressed by means of redistributive taxation, including inheritance taxes. Private property in savings and, at least indirectly, in means of production, may be judged morally acceptable, partly as a reward to past labor, saving, and good investment decisions, but mostly as a vehicle for generating efficient utilization of the society's capital stock, with a clear understanding that ownership rights are not absolute, in that society retains the right to tax both income and wealth.

6   Participation, empowerment, and the workplace

Having discussed some of the standard economic issues of employment, product supply, and investment, I now want to turn to some of the more social aspects of enterprise democracy, and ask to what degree the human relations and developmental ideals that often lie behind advocacy of workplace democracy are likely to be achievable in a realistic worker-managed market economy, and what trade-offs might be involved in their achievement. The institutional rules of such an economy, as developed earlier, imply that firms are under the ultimate control of their workers, who have the right to decide collectively whom they will accept as colleagues; that there exist private property rights in productive assets, which entitle owners to negotiate for a financial return on funds or capital goods they supply to firms; that the basic coordinating mechanism of the economy is the competitive market, in which prices are freely determined; and that, in accordance with market principles (as applied in the workers' management context), labor incomes depend on the difference between enterprise gross revenues and enterprise non-labor input costs, with differentiation among workers according to skill, work hours, or other measures of labor contribution at least an open possibility.

The first topic to be addressed is that of worker participation in decision-making, beginning with a few remarks about its efficiency implications. One issue raised especially by critics of worker control rights (Jensen and Meckling, 1979) is the possibility that the problems of social choice mechanisms (Arrow, 1963) will vitiate any form of democratic management. However, worker control in the LMF and shareholder control in the capitalist corporation evince considerable parallels, e.g., in terms of (a) the relatively large number of persons holding control rights, and (b) the successful delegation of managerial and control functions to specialized personnel, and these parallels go a long way toward answering such concerns. Further encouragement that worker control rights need not imply managerial incompetence or anarchy may be drawn from some potential advantages of having workers rather than shareholders hold these rights: in particular, the greater direct involvement of workers than that of most shareholders in a company, and the jointness that may exist between their activities on the job and their abilities to vote knowledgeably. Parallelism breaks down in at least two respects that may be disadvantageous to workers' management, however. First, although similar types of scrutiny may come from potential lenders of funds, the relatively more closed nature of the group holding control rights may tend to reduce the amount and variety of outside surveillance of management, and its impact on the decision-makers (cf. Jensen and Meckling's, 1976, discussion of the role of financial analysts). Although incumbent workers themselves may oust their managers, no *outsider* has an incentive to search for mismanaged LMFs, due to the absence of the takeover possibility, and this eliminates another possible source of managerial discipline. Second, the one-man-one-vote restriction that applies to worker-members but not to corporate shareholders means that (in contrast to a controlling shareholder group, or to others who might consider a takeover bid) no one member has a greater incentive to scrutinize management than does any other, so all could conceivably be somewhat lax (i.e., there may be a free-rider problem with respect to the monitoring of managers).[17]

Independent of whether workers' control has a positive or negative impact on efficiency, on balance, is the question of whether the granting of formal control rights to workers will have much meaning to them in practice. It is widely agreed that direct democracy is too costly and unwieldy a method of making most decisions when the number of persons involved is large. Both to assure that decisions are made competently, and to reduce direct personal involvement in decision-making which is productive of neither immediate satisfaction nor income, virtually all worker-controlled firms can be expected to delegate some managerial responsibilities to specialist managers, and those with more than a few dozen workers are likely to adopt a formal structure that might include both representative councils or boards of directors, and top managers answerable to those bodies. Worker-members may well show somewhat greater interest in the way their firms are managed than do those in the analogous position, the shareholders, in a conventional corporation. But how effective will direct control rights be from the standpoint of raising workers' sense of involvement and control?

The two cases of worker control in relatively large firms of which I am aware both suggest that the effective *sense of control* is likely to be small when direct participation is limited. The Yugoslav case, as discussed by Wachtel (1973) and others, might be dismissed by some due to the undemocratic nature of the polity and the pervasiveness of political interventions; but Mondragon, which is an entirely independent set of cooperatives, seems to be a more difficult example to dismiss. Workers have gone on strike against "their" firms in both cases. Yugoslav leaders tried to encourage intra-firm democracy by minimizing the scale of the self-governing unit, creating Basic Organizations of Associated Labor within larger firms in the 1970s. In the larger enterprises of Mondragon, it was found necessary to borrow from participatory practices found in some otherwise conventional firms in order more effectively to involve workers in management.

Indirect evidence of the ineffectiveness of formal participation at the company level also comes from a large number of studies linking decision-participation with productivity in a wide range of firms, of which full LMFs represent an insignificant fraction. As summarized by Blinder (1990:13), these studies suggest that while "worker participation apparently helps make alternative compensa-tion plans ... work better ... and also has beneficial effects of its own ... giving labor a seat on the board of directors may be the least effective form of participation." If positive productivity effects are also indicators of efficacy from the standpoint of worker empowerment and involvement, then these studies suggest that participation at the shop floor level is more relevant to workers than is voting for company managers or board members.

On the whole, the evidence suggests that at a minimum formal control rights need to be accompanied by more direct forms of involvement at the shop floor level, and by some form of profit- or gain-sharing, if workers are to obtain psychic benefits from feeling themselves to be masters of their work, if participation is to lead to more consummate performance through identification with the goals of the enterprise, and if productivity is to benefit from an upward flow of information embodying workers' hands-on knowledge of the production pro-cess. The evidence that participation can have these effects is relatively strong, although it is possible to raise questions such as whether some of the observed effects result simply from the novelty of organizational change. The more troubling question for proponents of workers' control is whether one ought not to conclude from this evidence that *formal* control rights at the company level are simply irrelevant to workers. In my view, independent of whether fully-fledged workers' control is the best option in any global sense, drawing such a conclusion from the evidence just referred to seems unwarranted. The debate over the efficacy of shareholder control of management in corporations has raged unabated since the publication of Berle and Means (1932), but the consensus within the economics profession, which I view as sensible, is that managers are held meaningfully, if not perfectly, accountable to shareholders by a variety of mechanisms, of which voting and the takeover mechanism are an important last resort (Manne, 1965; Putterman, 1988a). By similar reasoning, I would expect that although managers in firms in which workers hold ultimate control rights would succeed in obtaining wide latitude to make business decisions on an ongoing basis, their ultimate recallability by workers would significantly affect the objectives that they pursue. Although having the right to recall management may not produce much immediate satisfaction or even a strong subjective sense of mastery over the firm on the part of rank and file workers, the reasons for workers to maintain the latter rights may be strengthened rather than weakened by the likelihood of managerial power. As I commented in response to Williamson a few years ago:

If workers are, to an important extent, tied to firms, and if managers, "having more complete information," have a "strategic advantage over everyone else," and "inordinate influence over both the value and factual premises of other members of the group," why should workers relinquish all controls over management? It would seem altogether irrational to [conclude] ... that since "hierarchy effectively obtains," there is no more reason for discussing workers' control over it. (Putterman, 1984:321; internal quotations from Williamson, 1975)

The second issue I wish to address here is whether worker-run firms are likely to deliver a distinctive bundle of workplace characteristics that would bring greater satisfaction and/or support enlarged personal development and more humane social relations. That work organization differs among firms, and that certain kinds of work organization have been associated with greater worker satisfaction and self-respect, seems to be supported by much research in industrial psychology, organizational behavior, and management (Lawler, 1986). The traditional, "Taylorist" style of work organization, as described by Lawler, Edwards (1979), and numerous other authors, entailed a highly refined division of labor within the enterprise and a minimal degree of discretion by the worker on the job, combined with substantial direct supervision. This type of job design seemed to be predicated on the assumption that the division of labor between owners, managers, and hired workers permitted no intrinsic motivation of labor, so that the worker could not be counted upon to use his or her judgment, and effort had to be obtained by supervision, by tying rewards and penalties (including possible dismissal) to observed performance, and by applicable technological measures such as machine-pacing and the assembly line. By (in effect) assuming that the worker is already alienated from the job, this type of work organization probably reinforces the sense of alienation. It makes the job as boring and repetitive as possible, giving the worker so little responsibility and so small a role in the production process as to make his or her identification with the result of production nearly impossible. And by robbing the worker of the chance to exercise discretion and consigning him (her) to strict subordination, it closes off avenues for the attainment of self-respect, dignity, and autonomy.

The logical opposite of such a job design is one in which the job is "enlarged" to include a fairly large number of tasks, in which the worker can develop a variety of skills on the job and not only can but must exercise judgment, and in which groups of workers cooperate in the production process as relative equals. Jobs having these characteristics are thought to reduce worker alienation by increasing the worker's sense of autonomy, by rendering the labor process less technologically self-estranging, and by reducing the sense of anomie that arises from social isolation (Rosner and Putterman, 1991). What is interesting is that, although the "Taylorist" approach seemed predicated upon the traditional capitalist employment relation, which eliminates worker concern with work's results by making the employer the sole residual claimant and possessor of control rights, non-employee-owned firms have been at least as innovative in the design of non-alienating jobs as have LMFs, many of which have been relatively conventional in these respects. The successes achieved in, for example, the innovative auto plants of the Swedish company Volvo, by plants of the US company Proctor and Gamble, and in some respects by many Japanese firms, suggest that worker control is neither necessary nor sufficient to guarantee the introduction and success of such changes. Instead, limited gain- or profit-sharing and shop floor level participation seem to provide adequate motivational bases, and do so without posing a real threat to control by non-worker owners. To be sure, it has often been remarked that middle managers and supervisors constitute a natural opposition to these programs, seeing their prerogatives and in some cases their jobs as threatened. However, the experience of Ulgor, the large Mondragon appliance manufacturer, and of other worker-run industrial firms, including most Israeli *kibbutz* industries in the 1960s and 1970s and Yugoslav state firms, shows that worker control is no guarantee of less alienating job designs.[18]

As with participation, then, the question of the attainability of less alienating, more (personal) growth-enhancing job designs under workers' self-management comes down, at least in part, to whether self-management provides any extra promise of movement in this direction, and whether it is at all necessary, or adds anything on the margin, insofar as better jobs are one's goal. To the extent that a degree of control over the workplace and a stake in the outcomes of work are needed in order to make enlarged jobs feasible, it can be seen that the shop floor participation and profit-sharing characterizing capitalist firms that have had some success in transforming work, is in a certain sense on a continuum with the complete worker control and residual claimancy characterizing LMFs, and the question, then, is whether the relationship of these features to job enlargement is monotonic in nature, or whether increasing worker control and residual claims might become harmful after some point. In my own view, it seems unlikely that worker control and residual sharing could become unconducive to job transformation in any direct sense. If worker-managed firms have not on the whole provided outstanding examples of humane work organization, this might be best explained by the fact that the emphasis in the founding of such firms has been upon making a novel organizational form viable in a rather alien environment. If organizational experiments are distributed randomly, one would expect to see few firms experimenting with *both* radical departures on the control and risk-bearing front, and radical departures in the sphere of job design. Given their relatively weak financial positions, which contrast sharply with the situations of corporations like Volvo and Proctor and Gamble, few worker-managed firms may have been willing to risk radical job innovation even if their members gave some thought to the issue.

One might argue that workers' self-management is unnecessary to job enlargement, and that since worker-managed firms are likely to exhibit various inefficiencies (as considered elsewhere in this chapter), promoting them is positively dangerous to the objective of job enlargement. A rather different point of view is possible, though. This would be to raise the possibility that worker autonomy is consistent with capitalist ownership and control only up to a certain point, and that corporations are likely to meet difficulties in sustaining more cooperative forms of organization at the shop floor level because of conflicts with the hierarchical nature of management.[19] From this standpoint, fully worker-run firms might turn out to have a deeper long-term compatibility with non-Taylorist work organization, and in an economy in which LMFs are sufficiently vigorous to undertake appropriate experiments, the design of non-alienating jobs would see its fullest flowering. It would not be inconsistent, however, to argue that an intermediate form, i.e., codetermination or partnership between labor and capital, would be at least as hospitable to job transformation; those who advocate such forms as globally more efficient will find nothing in my reasoning to rule out such claims.

I want to conclude this section by turning to a question that is in some respects considerably more abstract and philosophical than the others discussed here or elsewhere in the chapter. The question is whether any economic system in which markets are the primary vehicles of economic coordination can possibly reach a high level of achievement from the standpoint of human fulfillment and humane social relations.[20] Market competition, it has been argued, will drive worker-managed firms to behave like capitalist firms in all or most respects. For example, they will mimic a capitalist hierarchy to achieve efficiency in decision-making, and they will adopt inegalitarian pay structures as required to attract skilled workers and managers, to reward displays of effort and ability, etc. This being the case, how can workers' management improve the human condition?

The answer to this question partly hinges on how utopian we want to be in defining "a high level of achievement." No conceivable economic system will be capable of eliminating certain necessities associated with satisfying human material wants and needs, so a reasonable way of looking at the question is by thinking of "high levels" primarily in relation to the maximum that we think achievable under some feasible set of economic arrangements. Arguably there are undesirable features of contemporary civilization that can be attributed to the nature of a market system, such as tastes fostered by relatively unregulated advertising and the mass media supported by it. However, much that is unpleasant about economic life, like the need to undertake certain tasks and to schedule work at definite hours as opposed to when we happen to feel like it, reflects trade-offs that are probably unavoidable under any economic system. It would be possible for more people to perform only those tasks that they enjoy and to work only when they feel like it, but this would tend to entail sacrifices in material living standards that those people may or may not be prepared to make. I thus take the relevant question to be whether a market economy in which firms are under the ultimate control of those who work in them can negotiate the relevant trade-offs in the most efficient possible manner, from the standpoint of workers' welfare.

Much of the previous discussion in fact speaks to this issue. If worker control leads to inefficiency by means of inferior management, internal incentives, or allocation of investment funds, there is reason to be concerned about its ability to improve welfare in a global sense. On the other hand, if it is relatively efficient in the respects that concern most conventional economists, and in addition is capable of delivering increased protection of workers' interests and a higher quality of working life, then a favorable assessment would be appropriate. Insofar as the question is whether markets will drive worker-controlled firms to be exactly like conventional firms, I have already noted that even among capital-controlled firms, one observes enormous heterogeneity with respect to dimensions influencing workers' welfare, and the discussion of this section has suggested that worker-run firms may be capable of doing at least as well as the best conventional firms in these respects. Insofar as the question implies a belief in the potential superiority of a system in which the roles played by markets are fulfilled by some other set of mechanisms, the question is what these mechanisms are to be, and how they can be expected to perform. The present consensus about the relative virtues of market systems is so broad that it is probably unnecessary to present any additional defense here, in any case, space does not permit further discussion of this topic.

7   Conclusion

One can argue that worker-run firms might be just as efficient as conventional firms yet still be rare in market economies, among other reasons because there is a collective choice problem in the transition to a worker-managed economy. Perhaps the time has come, then, for proponents of workers' management to advocate the use of political means to mandate worker control in market economies. In my view, however, this would not be desirable. Any one country that followed this course today could be expected to meet with capital flight and the drying up of investment funds, would face difficulties in the fine-tuning of institutions for handling financial and property rights' questions, and would have to contend with open hostility from powerful economic agents and indifference from many others, including, perhaps, most workers. Use of legal or constitutional mechanisms to guarantee worker control rights may be a necessary condition for making workers' management the dominant institution in a market economy, yet such mechanisms seem to me to be by no means sufficient. Indeed, experiments with mandated self-management in industrial democracies are likely to be short-lived and to end up discouraging other such experiments by chalking up unhappy track records.

Since precipitous movements to mandate self-management are liable to produce negative results, the possibility of more evolutionary changes seems critical to the future of such a system. Groups of workers may be unlikely to seek control over their workplaces in view of the costs imposed by financiers (as well as various transitional problems relating to the existing backlog of skills and experience), and the desire to seek such control may be weak or lacking in the absence of contact with examples of successful workers' management. Yet evolutionary movement towards more practice of self-management and towards a consensus on its desirability may not be an impossibility. Factors pointing in this direction include the widespread interest in participation and team work at the shop floor level. As argued by Rosner and Putterman (1991), increasing levels of income and education, and more comprehensive social security nets which reduce the disciplinary impact of the threat of dismissal and thus induce firms to seek more intrinsic ways of motivating their workers, may be leading to the increasing incidence of less alienating work modes in many countries. Schlicht's (1979) argument about the increasingly pivotal nature of human capital as a factor of production is also relevant here.

If immediate mandating of self-management would be counter-productive, are there any positive steps that should be urged upon governments? One idea that might be advanced as not imprudent, in view of the lack of harm done in the (West) German case, is to promote formal codetermination in more countries, from the present standpoint as part of a transitional strategy (although it has been argued for elsewhere as an end in itself). Experience with worker participation in management may help to acclimatize people to the idea that workers can play such roles, making further movement towards worker control rights appear less radical and frightening. The assistance of governments or of private foundations in the formation of supportive financial institutions, partially modeled on the *Caja Laboral Popular*, might also play a role in the gradual growth of a cooperative sector, which could increase interest in, and improve attitudes towards, the prospect of an alternative economic order. When considering the provision of inducements to partially or wholly worker-controlled enterprises, however, two warnings strike me as being of particular importance. First, it seems to me to be critical to emphasize the conceptual separation between according control rights to workers by virtue of their role as producers, and the traditional tying of control rights to "ownership of the firm" (Putterman, 1988a). That is, it need not be assumed that workers must *buy* their firms in order to acquire control over them, since workers can in principle (albeit probably at some cost) hold control rights while contracting with non-controlling financiers for part of the required capital. Second, great caution needs to be exercised with regard to any proposal to use material inducements, such as taxes and subsidies, to encourage formation of more such firms. Among the gravest dangers for the formation of an efficient cooperative economy, in my view, is the development of financial dependency between enterprises and the state, since this is likely to undermine enterprises' financial accountability and generate the kind of "soft budget constraint" phenomenon so compellingly described by Kornai (1980).

Notes

1. Other questions are: what makes the monitor honest? (MacLeod, 1984); if monitoring is observable, why can't it be hired on a fee-for-service basis, and if it isn't, how does it induce effort? When is mutual monitoring, motivated by profit-sharing, superior to hierarchical monitoring with possible worker resistance?
2. Contrary to Williamson (1975, 1980), a worker-controlled firm can employ a decision-making hierarchy for operating purposes, even though it differs from a shareholder-controlled firm in that those holding ultimate control rights are labor rather than equity suppliers. More recently, Williamson (1988:22–23) appears to concede this point.
3. The finance argument might be developed in somewhat different ways while retaining the same overall implications. For example, Gintis (1989b) argues that differences in risk preferences between financiers and workers give rise to financier preference for firms run by managers accountable to them. In my view, Jensen and Meckling (1979) were correct in looking for major problems of labor-managed organizational forms in the sphere of finance, but they were not sufficiently explicit about the direct governance features of finance and ownership relations; see Putterman, 1988a.
4. This is not to deny the usefulness of models that provide theoretical arguments to the effect that worker-run firms could be rare despite manifesting superior efficiency. My point is that we all know that "[e]very model has a counter-model, and judgments about which models apply to which situations are ultimately empirical" (Weitzman and Kruse, 1990:96).
5. More participatory forms of organization may have had high efficiency potential but been rejected in a less competitive economic environment in which managers could protect their prerogatives even at some cost to company performance. An entertaining discussion along these lines is provided by Marglin (1979).
6. Ellerman makes the analogy with criminal law, arguing that just as a hired henchman cannot escape blame for a crime he helps commit, so it is impossible for a worker to escape responsibility for his labor and "its positive and negative fruits." He dubs these ideas "the labor theory of property," and emphasizes their distinctness from Marx's labor theory of value.
7. Such clashes of rights are discussed by Okun (1975) Ch. 1. A fascinating discussion of the implications of the inalienability of one's labor stock is presented by FitzRoy (1980:59–61).
8. Putterman (1988b).
9. Consider the results of efforts to trade such rights for other distributive and social objectives in the countries ruled by Marxist dictatorships. If the polity instituting workers' self-management can be assumed to remain democratic and to safeguard other conventional civil liberties, such extreme fears may be unwarranted. The safety of this conclusion would appear to depend in part, then, on the depth of economic democrats' commitments to a broader bundle of liberal values.
10. This is true, for example, for the cases of multiple products, multiple variable inputs,

and variable hours or effort per worker. As noted below, the objection that a real cooperative would not lay off members to achieve a small increase in earnings of those who remain (Vanek, 1970) loses some of its force when the longer-term question of replacing departing members is considered (Vanek, 1970:27–34; Estrin, 1983). For a general discussion, see Bonin and Putterman (1987:13–21).

11. See also Chapter 11 (by Dow) and 16 (by Fehr) in this volume.

12. To the extent that current worker-members' earnings are differentiated because of different degrees of participation in past entrepreneurial decisions, inequality of returns might be acceptable. The practical inseparability of "unearned" windfall profits from genuine entrepreneurial returns complicates matters, but is hardly unique to the LMF. It is important to point out that the idea of intra-firm egalitarianism that I am associating with labor-managed firms here is one of equal profit shares for workers providing qualitatively equal labor, *not* one of pay egalitarianism across skill grades or among workers judged to be unequally energetic or capable.

13. In which I follow Estrin (1983).

14. Relevant literature is discussed by Bonin and Putterman (1987:56–79 and 107–112).

15. See also the "dual control" approach to the Japanese firm proposed by Aoki (1990a) and that author's related discussion in Chapter 14 in this volume.

16. Note that the degree to which these savings should be viewed as "forced" could vary. Perhaps most individuals would willingly save, but need the government scheme to assure that others do their part, i.e., the situation is that of an "assurance game," as described by Sen (1967).

17. Hansmann (1990a, 1990b) hinges much of his explanation of the uncommonness of worker-run firms on a third difference: the fact that the number of concerns relevant to enterprise decision-making is larger for workers than for financiers, for whom the bottom line is financial return (possibly complicated by risk and a few other fine points). He argues that workers' preferences with respect to these concerns are likely to be heterogeneous, and that democratic decision-making is therefore costly.

18. Note, however, that relevant reforms are now actively on the agenda in at least the first two cases, see Whyte and Whyte (1988) and Rosner and Putterman (1991).

19. See again Marglin (1979). Similar themes emerge in *Business Week* (1989). Compare also Putterman (1982).

20. By asking this question, I address the concerns of doubters and opponents of market systems, who are unlikely to have read this far through a chapter of the present type; but let me imagine that there is enough of this doubter in other readers so that the discussion is not entirely beside the point.

9   Unions versus cooperatives

KARL OVE MOENE and MICHAEL WALLERSTEIN

1   Introduction

Why are labor unions in industrialized market economies more common than worker-owned firms? Throughout most of the nineteenth century, the primary goal of the labor movement was to build an alternative economy of cooperative associations that would eventually replace capitalist-owned enterprises. The dominant figure in the first wave of union growth in England in the 1830s was Robert Owen with his schemes of "villages of cooperation" and worker-managed factories. Among working class leaders in France in the 1860s, Pierre-Joseph Proudhon's anarchist vision of a society of decentralized producer cooperatives was far more influential than the socialism of Karl Marx. Even the German Social Democratic Party program called for government aid for the creation of workers' cooperatives until the adoption of the Erfurt Program in 1891 (Lindemann, 1983).

In the last decades of the nineteenth century, Marxists, who insisted that socialists must be dedicated to the attainment of political power, replaced the anarchists and communitarian socialists as leaders of the emerging working class movement (Przeworski and Sprague, 1986). However, it was not the socialist or social democratic party alone that triumphed as the expression of workers' hopes, but the combination of parties in the electoral arena and unions in the labor market. By 1980, union membership averaged 54 percent of the labor force in advanced industrial societies (Wallerstein, 1989). In contrast, membership in worker-owned firms in 1980 comprised only 2.5 percent of the non-agricultural labor force in Italy; even less in other European countries (Ben-Ner, 1988a, 1988b).

A plausible explanation of the success of union organizing relative to the formation of cooperatives is that organizing unions was easier. Establishing worker-owned firms requires capital to invest. Establishing unions requires militants. Given the scarcity of capital relative to activists within the early labor movement, the relative success of unions is easy to predict from economic principles. But the situation is different today. Unions now have substantial financial resources as well as access to capital markets. Indeed, in some countries the unions have their own bank. Over the course of an average worker's working life, the union dues paid by a firm's work force may well exceed the cost of buying a majority of the firm's stock.

Union leaders, however, have generally perceived workers' cooperatives as threats to union solidarity rather than as the fulfillment of their members' aspirations.[1] One explanation of union skepticism toward labor cooperatives points to the self-interest of union officials. It is certainly understandable, if not commendable, that union officials would show a certain reluctance "to embrace a system that would appear to deprive them of their *raison d'être*," (Elster and Moene, 1989:33). Yet one should not jump too quickly to the conclusion that union officials are acting contrary to the interests of their members in this regard. When union leaders decry cooperatives for undermining solidarity among wage-earners and driving down wages, their claims may have a solid economic foundation.

Many articles have been written comparing worker-owned firms with traditional capitalist firms. But worker-owned firms are rarely compared with firms whose wages must be negotiated with a union, the more relevant comparison for a (still) significant share of workers in advanced industrialized societies. In this chapter we compare, within the simplest possible model, the outcome of workers' ownership and wage bargaining at the industry level in terms of workers' income, the price and quantity of output, employment and the number of firms. To focus attention on the contrast between labor market power and ownership rights we assume that worker-owned firms and unions are identical in other respects. In particular, we assume that the worker-owned firm and the union have the same objective: to obtain the greatest possible income for their members. We assume, in addition, that both the union and worker-owned firms are internally egalitarian in the sense that all members are treated equally. Finally, we assume that neither direct ownership nor unionization has any impact on productivity other than the indirect impact that follows from induced changes in the capital-intensity of production.

The industry we study is characterized by a large number of possibly heterogeneous firms and free entry. Firms potentially differ in terms of their productivity. Differences in productivity could stem from some factor of production that cannot be duplicated without a reduction in quality. Such a factor of production could be superior raw materials, an advantageous location, skills acquired through "learning by doing," special engineering or scientific knowledge, or managerial expertise. In addition, we assume the industry is small relative to the aggregate economy such that the wage and employment in the industry affect neither the demand for the firms' output nor employment opportunities elsewhere.

2 Competitive capitalist equilibrium

The basic model consists of an industry in which two types of firms produce one homogeneous product. The firms differ according to their relative efficiency. Let the profits earned by each type of firm, π_i, be written in standard notation as:

$$\pi_1 = p\beta_1 F(L_1) - w_1 L_1 - C$$
$$\pi_2 = p\beta_2 F(L_2) - w_2 L_2 - C$$

(1)

with $\beta_1 > \beta_2$.

The two types of firms have identical fixed costs, C, and, except for the constant term β_i, identical production functions. The production function $F(\cdot)$ is assumed to have the usual properties with $F'(\cdot) > 0$ and $F''(\cdot) < 0$. There is a fixed number, n_1, of the more efficient firms, due to the fixed supply of whatever factor of production makes them more efficient. In contrast, there is free entry of firms with lower efficiency. Price is a function of total output:

$$p = p[n_1 \beta_1 F(L_1) + n_2 \beta_2 F(L_2)] \tag{2}$$

with $p'(\cdot) < 0$.

With a purely competitive labor market, the wage paid by either type of firm will be no higher than workers' reservation wage, r:

$$w_1 = w_2 = r. \tag{3}$$

As we are considering the consequences of the creation of workers' cooperatives or a union in one industry, holding prices and wages in other sectors constant, the reservation wage is assumed to be exogenous.

Profit maximization implies that employment in both types of firms is determined by the usual condition that the marginal revenue product equals the wage rate:

$$p\beta_1 F'(L_1) = r \tag{4}$$

and

$$p\beta_2 (F'(L_2) = r. \tag{5}$$

Finally, free entry of less efficient firms implies that profits of less efficient firms are driven to zero, or

$$p\beta_2 F(L_2) - rL_2 - C = 0. \tag{6}$$

We assume that demand is high enough for at least one of the less efficient firms to enter in the competitive capitalist equilibrium.

The competitive capitalist equilibrium is now fully described. We have four equations, (2), (4), (5) and (6), to determine our four endogenous variables, p, L_1, L_2 and n_2. Note that in the competitive capitalist equilibrium, more productive firms hire more labor and earn higher profits than less productive firms. Workers, however, are indifferent as to which type of firm they work for or, for that matter, whether they are employed in the industry at all.

3   Competitive equilibrium with workers' cooperatives

Now consider the same industry with workers' cooperatives instead of capitalist firms. Cooperatives are assumed to divide the net revenue of the enterprise equally among their members. Cooperatives are also assumed to be democratic and self-interested in the sense that the cooperatives seek to maximize their members' income.

In the long run, the income received by cooperative members in firm of type i, denoted y_i, is given by:

$$y_i = \max_{L_i} \left[\frac{p\beta_i F(L_i) - C}{L_i} \right]. \tag{7}$$

This is a long-run, rather than a short-run condition, since it is unlikely any cooperative would expel members in order to maximize the income of those who remain (Ireland and Law, 1982). Indeed, we have ruled out such expulsions with the assumption that the cooperative treats all members equally. In the long run, however, membership can be reduced by failing to replace members who retire or quit until the remaining members' income is as high as possible.

Employment in each cooperative in the long run is given by the standard condition for labor cooperatives that the marginal revenue product equals income per member:

$$p\beta_1 F'(L_1) = \frac{p\beta_1 F(L_1) - C}{L_1} \tag{8}$$

and

$$p\beta_2 F'(L_2) = \frac{p\beta_2 F(L_2) - C}{L_2}. \tag{9}$$

Free entry of firms with less efficient production now implies that new cooperatives will enter until the income of new cooperative members falls to the reservation wage, or

$$\frac{p\beta_2 F(L_2) - C}{L_2} = r. \tag{10}$$

The comparison of the equilibrium of cooperatives with capitalist firms is not independent of the path from one form of property to the other. In going from capitalist firms to workers' cooperatives, it matters whether the prior owners must be compensated by the new owners. Suppose, first, that no compensation is paid by the cooperative. Then the implications of workers' ownership can be derived by comparing equations (4)–(6) with equations (8)–(10). The results are summarized in Proposition 1.

Proposition 1
If cooperative members are not required to compensate the prior capitalist owners, the replacement of capitalist firms by labor cooperatives would have the following long-run effects: (a) Price and output in the industry would not change. (b) Employment in less efficient enterprises would not change. (c) Employment in more efficient enterprises would decline. (d) The number of less efficient enterprises would increase but total employment may be either higher or lower.

Parts (a) and (b) of Proposition 1 follow from the observation that the employment-setting condition and the zero-surplus condition for less efficient firms are equivalent in the cooperative and capitalist cases. Compare equations

(5) and (6) with equations (9) and (10). Regardless of ownership, new enterprises will enter the industry until the average product of labor is no greater than the reservation wage. Thus the price, aggregate output, and employment per enterprise among the less efficient firms are all uniquely determined by the assumptions of free entry and an exogenous reservation wage.

Parts (c) and (d) of Proposition 1 follow from a comparison of the employment-setting condition for the more efficient enterprises when organized as capitalist firms, equation (4), or cooperatives, equation (8). In the capitalist equilibrium, the more efficient firms employed more workers than the less efficient firms. The opposite is the case with workers' cooperatives. From equation (8) or (9) we have

$$\frac{dL}{d\beta} = \frac{F(L) - LF'(L)}{\beta LF''(L)} < 0.$$

The higher the productivity, the lower the long-run optimal employment for members of the cooperative. This is a variant of the well-known "perverse" response of cooperatives to a higher price (Ward, 1958). High productivity implies relatively lower fixed costs and lower fixed costs require fewer workers to share the burden. Since, with labor cooperatives, employment per more efficient firm is less while aggregate output and employment per less efficient firm is unchanged, the number of less efficient firms must be higher.

Thus, in the long-run equilibrium with labor cooperatives, the quantity produced is the same as in the competitive capitalist equilibrium, but at a higher aggregate opportunity cost. More workers are employed in the less productive enterprises and fewer workers are employed in the more productive enterprises. In addition, the industry is less concentrated with labor cooperatives. A larger number of enterprises implies higher aggregate fixed costs (or more capital invested).

Total employment may be either higher or lower than in the competitive capitalist equilibrium.[2] There is a loss of employment in each of the more efficient enterprises but a gain in the number of less efficient firms in the market. Thus workers' ownership with free entry may have opposite effects on employment at the firm and industry level. At the firm level employment is reduced. At the industry level employment might increase.

Workers in the more productive firms clearly receive a higher income when the firms are organized as cooperatives. The workers now capture the rents that previously went entirely to the shareholders. Workers in the less productive firms, however, receive the same income in the long run no matter who owns the enterprise.

In the absence of a break with legality, however, capitalist owners who lose their firms must be compensated. Of course, the capitalist owners could be compensated by the government using general tax revenues, in which case the assumptions of Proposition 1 are appropriate. But it is reasonable to require that the compensation of the old owners be paid by those who receive the benefits of ownership: the members of the cooperative. This implies that the fixed costs for the cooperative must include payments to service the debt incurred in buying the firm. If capital markets are perfect, a cooperative that borrowed sufficient funds to pay the market price for a firm would have new fixed costs of

$$C_i^w = \pi_i + C$$

per period. In this case, we have Proposition 2.

Proposition 2
If labor cooperatives are required to fully compensate the prior owners, then the formation of cooperatives would have no effect on price, employment or income.

The fixed costs increase only for the more efficient enterprises, since the less efficient firms earn zero profits. The income of workers in the more efficient cooperatives can be written as

$$y_1 = \max_{L_1} \left[\frac{p\beta_1 F(L_1) - [p\beta_1 F(L_1^c) - rL_1^c]}{L_1} \right]$$

where L_1^c denotes the employment level under capitalist ownership. Cooperative members must earn at least as much as the reservation wage, or

$$y_1 \geqslant r.$$

Combining these last two equations and writing the cooperative's optimal employment level as L_1^w, we have:

$$p\beta_1 F(L_1^w) - rL_1^w \geqslant p\beta_1 F(L_1^c) - rL_1^c.$$

But under capitalist ownership, employment is chosen to maximize the RHS of the last equation. The best workers can do is to choose the same level of employment as the capitalist owners. Therefore,

$$L_1^w = L_1^c \quad \text{and} \quad y_1 = r.$$

With perfect capital markets, the market price of the more efficient firms contains the present discounted value of future rents. If members of the cooperative must pay the full market price, they have to pay the capitalized value of the future stream of rents in order to obtain the rents. In this transaction, workers (and employers) neither gain nor lose.

4   Capitalist equilibrium with collective bargaining

The alternative to competitive labor markets that a significant proportion of workers have chosen, where workers are free to choose, is not producers' cooperatives but unions. The promise of trade unionism is that workers can obtain a share of the rents through collective bargaining without paying the economic or political costs of obtaining a share of ownership. In addition, trade unions that can set wage levels throughout an industry can generate additional rents as the industry is pushed up its demand curve.

The unions' bargaining goal is assumed to be the highest possible wage for its members. This implies that an efficient contract would allow employment to be chosen unilaterally by employers. We also assume, at first, that the union is strong enough to unionize new entrants. Later we discuss the typical case in the USA where new entrants successfully resist unionization.

Without presenting one of the standard models of collective bargaining, it suffices for our purposes to assume that the outcome of collective bargaining is a uniform wage that is higher than workers' reservation wage:

$$w_1 = w_2 = w \quad \text{with} \quad w > r. \tag{11}$$

If no single firm can influence the wage bargain by its choice of employment, a reasonable assumption in industry-level bargaining, each firm will set employment to maximize profits taking the union wage as given. This yields the usual conditions:

$$p\beta_1 F'(L_1) = w \tag{12}$$

and

$$p\beta_2 F'(L_2) = w. \tag{13}$$

The zero profit condition for the less efficient firms, provided the wage is low enough for some less efficient firms to enter the market, is

$$p\beta_2 F(L_2) - wL_2 - C = 0. \tag{14}$$

The comparison of the collective bargaining equilibrium with the competitive capitalist equilibrium is summarized in Proposition 3.

Proposition 3
In comparison with the competitive capitalist equilibrium, collective bargaining at the industry level has the following effects: (a) The price of output is increased and the quantity produced is reduced. (b) Employment in each type of firm is reduced. (c) The number of less efficient firms that enter the market may be either higher or lower but total employment in the industry is less.

From the zero-profit condition (14) we have:

$$\frac{dp}{dw} = \frac{L_2}{\beta_2 F(L_2)} > 0 \quad \text{and} \quad \frac{dp}{dw}\frac{w}{p} = \frac{wL_2}{p\beta_2 F(L_2)} < 1. \tag{15}$$

Since the wage is higher with a union, the price must also be higher if any of the less efficient firms are able to enter the market. Since the elasticity of the price with respect to the wage is less than one, the real product wage, w/p, also rises. A higher real product wage implies, from equations (12) and (13), lower employment in both types of firms.

The impact of a higher wage on the number of less efficient firms that enter the market, however, depends on the elasticity of price with respect to output, the elasticity of the demand for labor with respect to the real product wage and the wage share. It is possible that the number of firms that enter the market is higher with the union. One way to understand this result is to note that the union lowers relative fixed costs, C/p, as it raises relative variable costs. Another way to understand this possibility is that the union, by inducing a reduction of employment and output, creates monopoly rents. It is possible that employers receive a sufficient share of the rents created such that profits go up when wages increase up to some limit. Higher profits attract new entrants until the newcomers' profits are driven to zero. Aggregate employment, however, always declines.[3]

With industry-wide bargaining, the intra-industry allocation of labor is efficient. However, the interindustry allocation of labor is not. By raising wages, the union forces the industry to raise prices and curtail production. It is obvious that workers in less efficient firms are better off with the union than in workers' cooperatives since $w > r$. Such workers can obtain higher incomes only by reducing aggregate production and creating monopoly rents. The income comparison of workers in the more efficient firms is less obvious, as Proposition 4 makes clear.

Proposition 4

If the union is weak in the sense that $w \to r$, workers in the more efficient firms would have higher incomes in cooperatives provided they did not have to pay the market price for the firm. If, however, the union is strong in the sense that $w \to \bar{w}$ where $\bar{w}$ is the wage level at which the more efficient firms earn zero profits (and the less efficient firms do not enter the market), workers earn higher incomes in collective bargaining than they could in workers' cooperatives.

The first part of the Proposition is obvious since $y_1 > y_2 = r$ (see equations (7) and (10)). To demonstrate the second part of the Proposition, it is sufficient to write the definition of $\bar{w}$:

$$p\beta_1 F(L_1) - \bar{w}L_1 - C = 0 \quad \text{or} \quad \bar{w} = \frac{p\beta_1 F(L_1) - C}{L_1}$$

and the first order condition for employment

$$p\beta_1 F'(L_1) = \bar{w}.$$

Note that these last two equations are identical to equations (7) and (8) describing workers' cooperatives. Since workers' income in the cooperative is an increasing function of price, and since the price with collective bargaining exceeds the competitive price of the equilibrium with workers' cooperatives, workers are better off in the union.

5   Bargaining rights versus property rights

If unionized firms are mentioned at all in the literature on cooperatives, they are typically subsumed as a species of worker-owned firms. For example, Drèze's book on the theory of labor-managed firms contains the assertion that unions can be understood "as enforcing [upon the capitalist firms] the very decisions that workers themselves would reach under labour management" (1989:3). Worker-owned firms may be equivalent to unionized firms with exceptionally strong unions in special cases. As a general statement, however, this view overlooks fundamental differences between the impact of collective bargaining and workers' ownership on both workers' income and industry structure.

The essential trade-off for workers in comparing membership in a cooperative and membership in a union is that the union provides a smaller share of a larger pie. In a cooperative, workers obtain all of the rents. But, without barriers to entry, the rents are limited to the intrinsic advantages some firms have in production. With unionization, total rents in the industry are increased as monopoly rents are created. Moreover, the pie grows as the union's share grows, since the higher the union wage, the greater the curtailment of production. If the union is sufficiently strong to capture all of the rents, that is to drive the profits of the efficient firms in the industry to zero, the union has captured all of a bigger pie and its members are clearly better off than they would be in a competitive market regardless of ownership. The stronger the union, the less likely are union members to favor workers' cooperatives.

The entire discussion of the impact of collective bargaining so far has been premised on the assumption that the union is able to organize the work force of new entrants in the industry. This premise is clearly inappropriate for the USA where new entrants fight unionization with increasing success. If new entrants are not unionized, competition would eliminate the union from the less competitive firms. In this case, where the union contract covers only workers in the more efficient firms, the impact of the union is much reduced. Price and quantity produced would be the same as in the competitive equilibrium, as would employment in each less efficient firm. Employment would still be less in each more efficient firm, which implies that more firms would enter the market. The industry would become less concentrated, as in the case with workers' cooperatives.

Now if we imagine the union wage rising as high as possible without forcing any of the more efficient firms out of business, the income of union members will approach the income of cooperative members (provided, as always, that the cooperative members did not have to purchase their firm at its market price). In this case, and only in this case, does the equilibrium with industry-wide bargaining converge to the equilibrium with workers' cooperatives as the unions' influence on wages increases.

The mixed case with both unionized capitalist firms and labor cooperatives is also possible. The entry of labor cooperatives in a unionized industry would reduce the price and lower wages of union members in the same manner as the entry of non-union firms. Thus unions have good reason to oppose the formation of new cooperatives and to insist, if possible, that any cooperatives that do enter pay union wages. In contrast, the unionization of capitalist firms or an increase in union strength benefits existing cooperatives by reducing production and raising price. Therefore, cooperatives have reasons to support unions, even while unions oppose cooperatives. In fact, members of cooperatives in Norway generally join the union, i.e. pay union dues, even though they do not use union services (Lindkvist and Westenholz, 1987).

Our conclusions should not be taken to be more general than they are. We have assumed that cooperative ownership does not affect productivity except insofar as cooperatives choose a different mix of factor inputs. Many advocates of cooperatives base their case precisely on the contrary claim that cooperative ownership enhances productivity, either because worker-owners have better incentives to work hard or because of the absence of intrinsic conflicts of interest between workers and owners. In addition, there are reasons why workers might prefer cooperatives even if their expected income was higher in a strong union. To the extent that cooperatives are more likely to rely on attrition rather than layoffs when cut-backs are desirable, cooperatives provide greater security of employment (Moene, 1989). Cooperatives also provide security of a different kind when workers are able to replace managers who have lost their confidence.

Moreover, we have compared labor and cooperatives only within a particular industry structure where potential entrants are less efficient than the industry average. The assumption of only two categories of firms is harmless. The same results could be obtained in a model with k categories, as long as all potential entrants are in the kth category. The assumption that all potential entrants have the same productivity, however, is restrictive. Indeed, the possible variations of industry structure are almost endless. Firms might differ in their fixed costs instead of, or in addition to, their variable costs. The number of firms might be small enough that oligopolistic price-setting is a more reasonable assumption than simple price-taking behavior. Recognizing the interaction of the way workers are organized and the industry structure limits the applicability of any single model but increases the richness of the conclusions that can be derived. It is unlikely that the economic and distributional effects of either unions or labor cooperatives would be the same in all industries.

Finally, comparing cooperatives and unions within one industry is different from comparing the two forms of organization at the level of the aggregate economy. Monopoly gains of unions at the industry level entail costs that are paid, in part, by workers in other industries. Moreover, in aggregate the costs exceed the benefits. Thus union members would be more likely to benefit from the simultaneous introduction of workers' cooperatives in all industries than in their industry alone. However, workers in industries with a low elasticity of demand, for example, might still prefer the general equilibrium with unions to the general equilibrium with labor cooperatives. Moreover, the benefits from increased competition are not restricted to union members. The benefits will be shared with unorganized workers, the self-employed and all who do not participate in the labor force. Even at the national level, unions' opposition to cooperatives may be consistent with the rational self-interest of union members, as well as the rational self-interest of union leaders.

158   *Karl Ove Moene and Michael Wallerstein*

Notes

We thank Steinar Holden, Bertil Holmlund and the participants in the conference for helpful comments. This chapter presents a special case of the model developed in our paper in the *Journal of Comparative Economics* (Moene and Wallerstein, forthcoming).

1. One exception to this generalization can be found in the early views of Solidarity in Poland. Solidarity's 1981 program declared that "the socialized enterprise should be the basic organizational unit of the economy. It should be controlled by the workers' council representing the collective and should be operatively run by the director appointed through competitions and recalled by the council ... [T]he prices of most goods and services should be fixed by supply and demand" (Solidarity, 1981). However, by the time that Solidarity formed the government in 1990, its earlier preference for workers' cooperatives over capitalist ownership had been reversed.

2. Let $L = n_1 L_1 + n_2 L_2$ and hold total output, $n_1 \beta_1 F(L_1) + n_2 \beta_2 F(L_2)$, and L_2 constant. Then $dL/dL_1 > (<)0$ if $\beta_1 F'(L_1) < (>) \beta_2 F(L_2)/L_2$. At the competitive capitalist equilibrium, $\beta_1 F'(L_1) = \beta_2 F'(L_2) < \beta_2 F(L_2)/L_2$. At the equilibrium with labor cooperatives, however, $\beta_2 F(L_2)/L_2 \to \beta_2 F'(L_2) < \beta_1 F'(L_1)$ as $C \to 0$.

3. From equation (2) we have

$$\frac{dp}{dw} = p'(\cdot)\left[n_1 \beta_1 F'(L_1)\frac{dL_1}{dw} + n_2 \beta_2 F'(L_2)\frac{dL_2}{dw} + \beta_2 F(L_2)\frac{dn_2}{dw} \right].$$

Using equations (12), (13) and (15), this last equation can be rearranged to yield:

$$\frac{dn_2}{dw} = \left(\frac{dp}{dw}\right)\frac{1}{L_2}\left[\left(\frac{dp}{dw}\right)\frac{1}{p'(\cdot)} - \left(\frac{w}{p}\right)\left(n_1 \frac{dL_1}{dw} + n_2 \frac{dL_2}{dw} \right) \right]$$

which can be either positive or negative. Let L represent total employment in the industry, or $L = n_1 L_1 + n_2 L_2$. Using the last equation and recalling that n_1 is a constant, we obtain

$$\frac{dL}{dw} = \left[1 - \left(\frac{dp}{dw}\right)\left(\frac{w}{p}\right) \right]\left(n_1 \frac{dL_1}{dw} + n_2 \frac{dL_2}{dw} \right) + \left(\frac{dp}{dw}\right)^2 \frac{1}{p'(\cdot)} < 0$$

since $(dp/dw)(w/p) < 1$ by equation (15) and (dL_1/dw), (dL_2/dw) and $p'(\cdot)$ are all negative.

10 Demand variability and work organization

DAVID I. LEVINE

1 Introduction

While worker participation in decision-making has been a popular topic in the business press for much of the last decade, substantive participation by workers remains relatively rare in the USA (Levine and Strauss, 1989). Many economists have concluded that the low incidence of participatory arrangements in the USA implies that such arrangements are inefficient – for if participation were a good idea, then the market would favor companies with participation (Alchian and Demsetz, 1972a; Jensen and Meckling, 1979; Williamson, 1980).

The argument that "survival of the fittest" implies efficiency is not correct if there are externalities from work organization – that is, if one company's choice of work organization affects the costs of other firms. Several examples of such externalities are presented in Chapters 1, 11, and 6 in this volume (by Bowles and Gintis, Dow, and Pagano, respectively; see also my survey article with Tyson, 1990).

The current chapter focuses on a single externality of participatory work organizations, a macroeconomic externality that stems from the tendency of participatory workplaces to avoid layoffs when product demand declines. To see the basic argument, consider two fictitious auto plants X and Y. Plant Y has a highly trained work force and a participatory work organization with a no-layoff pledge. Its competitor in the auto industry is plant X, which utilizes a traditional US labor relations system. At both X and Y nominal wages are set once a year. Plant X lays off workers whenever there is a downturn in demand. Plant Y, on the other hand, avoids layoffs during downturns by retraining workers, freezing hire, transferring workers within the firm, and ultimately hoarding excess labor.[1]

Plant Y's no-layoff pledge is relatively expensive when recessions are frequent and deep. In these cases, plant X's use of layoffs gives it a cost advantage over the long run.

There is also feedback from the firm's employment system to the macro-economy. Recessions are deeper when many companies have layoffs (X-style). Layoffs lead to lower spending on consumer goods by X workers, resulting in further layoffs at stores in its area, and eventually affecting producers around the world. On the other hand, recessions are shallower when many firms avoid layoffs (Y-style). Since the costs of running participatory systems increase as the variability of product demand increases, policies that reduce this variability will tend to encourage such systems. Because Y firms are not rewarded by the market for their function as an automatic stabilizer, the economy underprovides firms which avoid layoffs.

This chapter explains why participatory firms avoid layoffs and presents a model of externalities of workplace organization. The empirical section employs three data sets to show that companies high in participation and training also tend to have long-term employment relations.

2   Literature review

The argument made in the current chapter has two parts, each of which has been made separately in the literature: first, long-term employment relations will lower the multiplier; second, long-term employment relations (and other investments that increase fixed costs) may raise productivity at high output levels, but raise costs in a slump.

The first part of the argument was made by Vanek, who assumed that labor-managed firms tended to avoid laying off workers. Thus, an economy populated entirely by such firms will have a very small multiplier in the face of negative demand shocks ([1972] 1977).

The second part of the argument was presented by Rebitzer and Taylor, who argue that when product demand is uncertain, firms will choose to guarantee employment to a sub-set of workers, and hire contingent workers at the margin (1988). The contingent workers, because of their shorter time horizons, work with lower effort. As in the current chapter, workers with employment security are more productive when working, but are costly when demand is low.

The current chapter combines these two parts by showing how reducing demand variability reduces the costs of providing employment security, and how employment security can reduce demand variability. There is a growing literature on macroeconomic spillovers from the *level* of activity of a firm (Cooper and John, 1988); this chapter focuses on macroeconomic spillovers from the *variability* of activity of a firm.

To the extent that workers with employment security become a fixed cost, this argument is related to recent work on irreversible capital investment. Ramey and Ramey (1990), for example, argue that economic fluctuations reduce average productivity because they reduce companies' incentives to invest. They provide evidence that in more periods when output has been more variable, its growth rate has been lower. Their empirical evidence is consistent with the model in this chapter.

2.1   *Justifying the assumption that participatory firms avoid layoffs*

After fifty years of research, it is clear that participation *sometimes* has a potentially beneficial effect on productivity; nevertheless, most US participatory plans do not lead to sustained increases in corporate performance (Levine and Tyson, 1990). One reason for the failure of many US plans is the lack of job security and of long-term employment relations.[2]

There are several distinct reasons that successful participatory systems usually avoid laying off workers. Most directly, workers are unlikely to cooperate in increasing efficiency if they fear that higher productivity will jeopardize their jobs. Guarantees of job security reduce fears that higher productivity will lead to layoffs. On the other hand, there have been several cases when the fear of layoffs has inhibited the success of participation (Kochan, Katz and Mower, 1985:290); there is also a long tradition of industrial relations research where workers have resisted productivity improvements that might reduce labor demand (e.g., Mathewson, 1931; Roethlisberger and Dickson, 1939).

Workers with job security have a longer time horizon and are more likely to forego short-term gains to build a more effective organization. Participation will work only if employees choose to share their good ideas, and if managers reward workers for increased productivity. In the short run, the dominant strategy is for workers to disguise the fact that they have found a productivity-improving technique, and to enjoy more on-the-job leisure. Similarly, the company's short-run dominant strategy is to deny that productivity has increased, and to avoid increasing pay. As the literature on repeated games suggests, only long horizons can convince both players to cooperate, and to forego short-run gains for long-term success.

To the extent that participation relies upon work group cooperation and employees monitoring one another, long-term employment relations are essential. The longer an employee expects to be in a work group, the more effective are group-based rewards and sanctions as motivators. Furthermore, employees with long time horizons will be less likely to try to pump up current accounting profits at the expense of long-run profits.

The case study literature on labor-managed firms shows that these participatory workplaces rarely lay off worker-members (although temporary workers are laid off). It appears that fairness considerations constrain these enterprises from reducing the workforce via layoffs. More generally, participatory firms try to instill a sense of membership and community in all employees, and layoffs are inimical to such an environment.

Finally, participatory firms often make large investments in the selection, socialization, and training of workers. If workers are to contribute to more decisions, they will need more skills and more information. From the firm's point of view, long-term employment relations are necessary to recover the higher investment in human resources that accompanies participation.

2.2   Examples

There are numerous examples of firms that provide high levels of employment security as part of a package of policies to ensure the success of participation. In the USA, IBM, Hewlett-Packard, and the NUMMI Toyota–GM joint venture automobile plant are important cases.

Each of these companies has gone to extensive efforts to avoid layoffs. During the 1972–1975 slowdown, IBM transferred 17,000 workers, completely retraining 7000 of them (Bolt, 1983:120). During the early 1980s, Hewlett-Packard adopted hiring freezes, shortened work weeks, the elimination of perquisites, and so forth, while other firms were engaging in mass layoffs (Ouchi, 1981:118). Later in the decade, NUMMI sent its entire workforce into retraining during a time when one union official declared that General Motors (the previous owners of the plant) "would have closed the second shift" (Nano, 1988).

The relationship between participation and long-term employment relations appears to be causal, not merely correlational. A typical comment is by an IBM executive:

Our people, by using their minds as well as their hands, have cut two thirds of the hours that go into manufacturing our product ... That achievement would have been impossible without productive and committed employees. And much of their commitment stems from the security they know is theirs through our practice of full employment. (Bolt, 1983:116)

At Hewlett-Packard, the long-term employment relations have been integral parts of the personnel policies that have led to "the lowest voluntary turnover rate, the most experienced workforce in the industry, and one of the highest rates of growth and profitability" (Ouchi, 1981:118).

As will be discussed below, full-employment policies are also common in other successful examples of worker participation such as large firms in Japan, and the Mondragon worker cooperative network in Spain.

3   The model

The basic story can be illustrated with a macroeconomic model that permits work organization to affect both productivity and the cost of adjusting labor demand. Firms come in two types, X and Y. X firms lay off workers when demand declines. Y firms have high levels of training and participation and enjoy high productivity, but also maintain full employment regardless of the state of demand.

The model makes traditional Keynesian fix-price assumptions, with prices normalized to unity. Companies are symmetrically rationed in the output market. When demand is low, companies can either hoard labor, or lay off excess workers.

Product market
Aggregate demand (AD) is the sum of consumption (C) and autonomous spending (A):

$$AD = C + A. \tag{1}$$

A crucial assumption of the model is that the propensity to spend out of wages is greater than the propensity to consume out of profits. Let W equal the wage, and L employment. Consumption is assumed to increase with wage income, with a marginal propensity to consume c out of wage income:

$$C = cWL. \tag{2}$$

Results are unchanged if either unemployed people have non-zero consumption from savings or unemployment insurance, or if the marginal propensity to spend out of profits is non-zero, as long as the marginal propensity to spend out of wages is greater than the propensity to consume out of profits.

This assumption about the relative propensities to consume out of wages and profits is supported by substantial recent research on consumer behavior standards; this research finds that a high proportion of consumers either are liquidity-constrained or follow rules of thumb that lead to high marginal propensities to consume (Thaler, 1990). Profit recipients are unlikely to be liquidity-constrained, while companies typically require lead time to change their investment plans, leading to a modest short-run propensity to spend out of profits, controlling for sales (Keynes, 1930; Marglin, 1984).

Autonomous spending (A) is assumed to equal A_1 in good states, and $A_1 - \delta$ in bad states. Each state occurs with probability equal to one half.

Production
Production occurs in factories, each of which has a capacity of $\hat{L}$ workers, where $\hat{L}$ is assumed to be small with respect to the total labor force. (The size of a single firm is assumed to be sufficiently small that integer problems are neglected in the analysis below.) Productivity (Γ) varies according to the work organization of the firm. X firms, which engage in layoffs when demand is low, have productivity Γ_x. Y firms guarantee full employment and have productivity Γ_y, where $\Gamma_y > \Gamma_x$. Up to the capacity limit, production exhibits constant returns to scale, with labor as the only variable input, implying a production function

$$Q = \Gamma L. \tag{3}$$

3.1   Equilibrium with only X firms

Labor market
Wages are set exogenously equal to W_x. Assume that A_1^x is such that there is full employment in good states.

The use of an exogenous wage avoids two complications of a competitive labor market. First, in the model that follows, some firms that do not rely on long-term employment relations would be able to pay a very low wage; they would be able to hire workers only in bad states, since all of their workers would move to higher-paying firms in times of full employment. If the fixed costs of operating a firm (i.e., the costs that must be paid in both good and bad states) are high, low-wage firms that operate only in bad times would be unprofitable. Adding such fixed costs and permitting the low-wage strategy complicates the model without modifying the basic point. (Weitzman, 1989, works through a model with low-wage firms that hire only in bad times.)

A related complication with endogenous wages is that Y firms that offer employment security would like to pay lower wages, with the wage difference acting as a payment for the insurance against layoff. This insurance contract is not feasible.

When workers are mobile after the level of autonomous spending (A_1 or $A_1 - \delta$) is observed then, although Y firms guarantee employment in bad times, they are unable to extract a compensating differential from their workers. If Y firms paid a wage lower than the market wage, they would lose all of their workers during good times, and become like the low-wage firms described in the preceding paragraph. Furthermore, as noted above, Y firms typically have large investments in their workers, and cannot afford the high turnover rates that accompany a low-wage strategy.

Equilibrium

In equilibrium, aggregate demand equals output:

$$AD = Q. \tag{4}$$

Solving equations (1) through (4) yields

$$Q = \mu A, \tag{5}$$

where μ is the multiplier:

$$\mu = 1/(1 - cW_x/\Gamma_x). \tag{6}$$

Let Q_1^x ($= \mu A_1$) equal output in good states, while output in bad states equals $Q_1^x - \mu\delta$.

Expected profits for an X firm in an environment where all other firms are also X firms equals

$$E(\pi_x^x) = (1 - W_x/\Gamma_y)(Q_1^x - \tfrac{1}{2}\mu\delta). \tag{7}$$

In the expression π_x^x, the subscript "x" refers to this firm's choice to use the X strategy; the superscript "x" refers to the environment being populated by other X firms.

3.2   One Y firm in an X world

Consider the introduction of a single Y firm into an economy populated solely by X firms. The expected profit of a Y firm in an X economy equals

$$E(\pi_y^x) = (1 - W_x/\Gamma_y)(Q_1^x) - \tfrac{1}{2}\mu\delta.^3 \tag{8}$$

The single Y firm will go out of business if its profits are below those of its competitors. Equations (7) and (8) imply that Y firms will have lower profits than X firms in an X environment (i.e., $E(\pi_y^x) < E(\pi_x^x)$) whenever

$$(2Q_1^x - \delta)(1 - \Gamma_x/\Gamma_y)/\delta < \mu. \tag{9}$$

This inequality represents two counteracting effects: Y firms do better as their productivity advantage increases (Γ_x/Γ_y falls), but they do worse as the number of workers they must hoard increases (i.e., when δ or μ increase).

3.3   Equilibrium with only Y firms

Assume that the wage in the equilibrium with only Y firms equals W_y, and that A_1^y is such that there is full employment in good states.

As before, aggregate demand equals the total of consumption plus autonomous spending, but now consumption is invariant to the realization of the shock to autonomous spending:

$$AD = cW_y(Q_1^y/\Gamma_y) + A. \tag{10}$$

Because Y firms do not lay off workers, the Y environment has a multiplier equal to unity, smaller than in the case with X firms. Expected profits for a Y firm in this economy equals

$$E(\pi_y^y) = Q_1^y(1 - W_y/\Gamma_y) - \tfrac{1}{2}\delta. \tag{11}$$

3.4   Introduction of an X firm

The expected profits of a single X firm in an environment populated by Y firms is

$$E(\pi_x^y) = (Q_1^y - \tfrac{1}{2}\delta)(1 - W_y/\Gamma_x). \tag{12}$$

If the expected profits of an X firm in a Y world are lower than that of a Y firm, then the Y equilibrium is stable. The specific condition is:

$$1 < (2Q_1^y - \delta)(1 - \Gamma_x/\Gamma_y)/\delta. \tag{13}$$

Examination of the two inequalities (9) and (13) shows that it is possible for two equilibria to exist. If both inequalities are satisfied, then in an environment populated by X firms aggregate demand is too variable for a Y firm to survive. At the same time, in an environment populated by Y firms demand is more stable; with more stability, the productivity advantage of Y firms outweighs the cost of hoarding labor. In a Y environment, it is X firms that are unable to survive.[4]

An approximate example gives the sense of the model. If the multiplier is 2 and the range of the shock is zero to 10 percent of full employment GNP, Y firms are less profitable in an X world unless they are at least 10 percent more productive (to make up for the 20 percent of workers that Y firms hoard in bad times). On the other hand, in a Y world when the multiplier drops to one, Y firms are more profitable than are X firms whenever their productivity advantage is at least 5 percent. For the ranges of $(\Gamma_y - \Gamma_x)$ between 5 and 10 percent, both equilibria are possible.

3.5   Continuous distribution of Γ_y

The results are somewhat modified if there is a distribution of Γ_ys. In this case, some companies with very high productivity when adopting participation will find it profitable to switch to Y work organization even if all other firms choose X (Levine and Parkin, 1993).

The results with a distribution of Γ_ys imply that the Nash-equilibrium proportion of firms choosing the Y technology will be inefficiently low. (If certain stability assumptions are not met then there are two equilibria, and the results are similar to those discussed above with discrete Γ_y.) The marginal firm trades off the productivity advantage of Y workers with the costs of hoarding labor during downturns, and ignores the positive macroeconomic externalities that hoarding labor provide.

The welfare results are identical to those of other models with macroeconomic spillovers.

Agents, in choosing their strategy, do not take account of their influence on the payoffs of others; hence symmetric Nash equilibria are inefficient relative to the set of feasible allocations ... A coordinated increase in the strategies of all players would be welfare improving. (Cooper and Jon, 1989:448)

In the language of this chapter, the market underprovides Y workplaces.

In the model with continuous distribution of Γ_ys, in most cases stabilizing aggregate demand will not cause a discrete shift in regime (as occurred with a single value for Γ_y). Instead, each reduction in the exogenous variability of demand will increase the proportion of Y firms that survive. As with standard Keynesian models, stabilizing aggregate demand reduces recessions; here, there is a further effect where stabilizing demand permits more firms to introduce participation and to increase their levels of training. Thus, stabilizing demand raises average productivity, and (because the Y firms hoard labor) leads to further stabilization of demand.

3.6   Discussion

Limitations of the model
The model specified above has made numerous strong assumptions. As noted above, the cost disadvantage of Y firms will be smaller to the extent that X firms must pay higher unemployment insurance premia after layoffs and must pay higher wages to compensate for the risk of layoff, and to the extent that hoarded labor at Y companies are at least somewhat productive when they perform maintenance tasks or undergo training.

The stabilizing effects of Y firms are reduced to the extent that Y firms reduce the employment of contract and part-time employees and at sub-contractors, and to the extent that many companies have high propensities to invest out of cash-flow, controlling for sales and capacity utilization.

The stabilizing effects of Y firms are also reduced to the extent that Y firms reduce hours, while maintaining employment. Because liquidity constraints on workers are less severe in the face of job sharing than in the face of layoffs, Y firms that use partial playoffs will still stabilize aggregate demand compared to firms that engage in traditional layoffs.

The model discussed above ignores persistent industry- or company-specific shocks, when layoffs are the efficient response. Incorporating such shocks moderates the conclusion that full employment security is optimal. The basic result remains that the free market will have too many layoffs and inefficiently few *Y* firms, since firms ignore the macroeconomic externality that their layoffs create.

A novel economy of scope
This analysis points out a novel economy of scope for labor-hoarding firms. Specifically, *Y* firms will be more successful if they are members of a network that permits workers to shift from one group to another within the network. Such transfers lower the cost of maintaining full employment policies.

Both large US companies with employment security and the large corporate groups (*keiretsu*) in Japan follow this practice extensively (Gerlach, 1987; Abegglen and Stalk, 1985, Ch. 8; Koike, 1988; Foulkes, 1980). For example, IBM is diverse enough that slowdowns in one segment of the firm are often offset by growth in others, so transfers can alleviate the need for layoffs. (Frequent transfers have led some employees to remark that IBM stands for "I've Been Moved.")

The participatory firms do not need to be integrated large firms, but can be networks of firms that attempt to hire each other's surplus labor. The Mondragon network of worker-owned enterprises in the Basque region of Spain produces a diverse set of products, and has been highly successful.

An emphasis on job security raises potential difficulties for the long-run coexistence of cooperatives with conventional capitalist enterprises. To cope with possible shifts in demand, the diverse product mix of Mondragon is essential to facilitate the transfer of labor between enterprises experiencing different fortunes. (Bradley and Gelb, 1983:71)

4   Statistical evidence

Empirical evidence that participation is most common in the presence of long-term employment relations is found using three data sets: a 1982–1983 survey of manufacturing plants and workers in Indiana; a 1988 General Accounting Office survey of Fortune 1000 employee involvement efforts; and a 1989 survey of US automobile suppliers.[5] These regressions do not reflect causal relations; they merely measure whether participation and training occur in conditions characterized by stable employment and product demand.

4.1   Data

Indiana survey
The data are from 1982–1983 surveys of manufacturing establishments in the Indianapolis area in the USA. 140 US establishments were contacted, and 52 (37 percent) provided usable data. Within each establishment, a structured interview was conducted with top management personnel, and arrangements were made to administer a questionnaire to a sample of full-time, non-temporary employees.

In the Indiana survey participation was measured by membership in quality circles and by the number of group meetings a month a worker attends on company time to talk about work problems. A possible interaction of these two measures was also included, in case quality circles were effective only if they met frequently.

The data set contains four measures of training: the time required to train someone for the job (0 = "A few hours," 6 = "Five years or more"); separate questions concerning the importance of formal and informal learning and firm on-the-job (OJT) training as sources of skills (0 = "Never had," 4 = "Very important"); and the level of agreement that "My job makes me keep learning new things," (1 = "Strongly disagree," 5 = "Strongly agree"). The first three measure whether a job requires high OJT, while the third measure focuses on whether the job is currently providing OJT.

The regressions also include three measures of autonomy: "My job lets me decide the speed that I work" (same codes); "My job gives me freedom in how to do my work" (same codes); and "My job does not let me participate in decisions that affect me" (reverse coded so 1 = "Strongly agree," 5 = "Strongly disagree").

Long-term employment relations were measured by the workers' responses to: "The security [on my job] is good" (1 = strongly disagree, 5 = strongly agree). Additional controls include age, age^2, education, tenure, tenure^2, gender by marital status interaction, and six occupational controls.

The means and standard deviations of the main variables are presented in Table 10.1.

GAO Survey

In the summer of 1987 the GAO surveyed 934 companies – the Fortune 500 industrial and the Fortune 500 service companies – concerning their employee involvement efforts. (The actual number of companies surveyed was less than 1000 because of acquisitions, mergers, etc.) Responses were received from 476 private firms (51 percent) covering about 9 million full-time employees. Approximately one-third of the firms did not want their data analyzed by non-GAO investigators, leaving a sample of 326 corporations.

The surveys were filled out primarily by the Vice President of Human Resources (or equivalent title), or by the Director of Employee Involvement (or equivalent title).

The participation measures in the survey include: the proportion of workers who are currently involved in self-managing work teams, job enrichment, quality circles, other employee participation groups, mini-enterprise units, and union–management quality of worklife committees. An index of participation is the sum of the seven participation measures.

There are two types of training measures: first, the sum of the proportion of workers who in the last five years have received formal training on each of the following: group decision-making, leadership, understanding business (e.g., accounting), statistical analysis, and team building; and second, the proportion of workers who have received cross-training.

Table 10.1. *Descriptive statistics*

	Mean	Std Dev.
Indiana survey (Individual level variables):		
The security [on my job] is good (1 = strongly disagree; 2 = disagree; 3 = undecided; 4 = agree; 5 = strongly agree).	3.35	0.49
I take part in a quality circle (1 = yes).	0.23	0.11
Number of group meetings a month attended on company time to talk about work problems.	2.01	4.31
Interaction (product) of previous two measures.	0.96	3.15
Time to train someone to do your job (0 = few hours; 1 = few days–week; 2 = several weeks; 3 = 2–5 months; 4 = 6 months–1 year; 5 = a few years; 6 = more than 5 years).	2.42	1.71
Importance of formal on the job training (0 = never had; 1 = not at all important; 2 = a little; 3 = somewhat; 4 = very).	3.35	0.91
Importance of informal on the job training (same codes).	3.51	0.85
My job makes me keep learning new things (1 = strongly disagree; 5 = strongly agree).	3.53	1.21
My job gives me freedom in how to do my work (same codes).	3.55	1.02
My job lets me decide the speed that I work (same codes).	3.27	1.14
My job does not let me participate in decisions that affect me (reverse coded: 1 = strongly agree; 5 = strongly disagree).	2.80	0.23
GAO survey		
The proportion of workers who have employment security, where employment security, is defined as a company policy designed to prevent layoffs (1 = none; 2 = 1–20 percent; 3 = 21–40 percent; 7 = all).	2.99	2.40
Index formed by summing the proportions of workers who participate in the following employee involvements programs: survey feedback job enrichment/redesign quality circles, other employee participation groups, union–management quality of work life councils, mini-enterprise units, and self-managing work teams (for each measure, same codes).	13.43	4.78
The proportion of workers with cross-training (same codes).	3.08	1.22
Sum of proportion of employees receiving formal training in group decision-making, leadership skills, business skills, quality/statistical analysis, team-building skills (for each measure, 1 = 0–20 percent, 5 = 81–100 percent).	8.72	3.11
Supplier survey		
The length of contract with the customer of this product (0 = No contract; 5 = Greater than 5 years).	2.95	1.58
The degree of availability the customer would have in switching to another supplier (1 = Easy; 5 = Hard).	3.28	1.25
Percent of production workers that actively participate in some form of employee involvement program (1 = 0 percent; 4 = 67–100 percent).	3.04	0.87

The measure of long-term employment relations in the survey is a seven-point scale of the proportion of workers who have employment security, defined as "a company policy designed to prevent layoffs." Additional controls include proportion union, a dummy variable for zero unionization, and a constant.

Supplier relations survey

In the Spring of 1989 a survey was mailed to virtually every domestically-owned first-tier supplier to manufacturers of cars and light trucks in the USA. There were 453 responses (47 percent response rate) with no obvious response biases. The target respondent was the Divisional Director of Marketing or Director of Strategic Planning. Because many companies supply their customers with several different types of products, respondents were asked to answer the survey for *one* customer using *one* product that was typical of their company's output.

The participation measure in this study is the percent of production workers who actively participate in some form of employee involvement program (1 = 0 percent; 4 = 67–100 percent).

The measurement of long-term employee relations in this data set is indirect, and relies upon measures of long-term *customer* relations. The hypothesis tested is that suppliers with long-term contracts are better able to offer long-term employment relations. If this is so, then employee involvement should be more prevalent in companies with long-term customer relations.

There are two measures of customer relations: the response to "What is the length of your contract with the customer of this product?" (0 = No contract, 5 = Greater than five years), and the response to "Please estimate the degree of availability your customer would have in switching to another supplier" (1 = Easy, 5 = Hard). The latter specifically excludes legal considerations such as the existence of long-term contracts.

Additional controls include the log of employment, a measure of the technological complexity of the product, and the union status of production workers.

4.2   Participation, training, and employment security

This section uses the three data sets to measure the extent to which training and participation is more common in companies with increased job security. Unfortunately, the measures of participation in some of these regressions (e.g., quality circle membership) do not measure the theoretical construct of *substantive* participation, since most quality circles in the US lead to little control by workers (Levine and Strauss, 1989).

Indiana survey

Every measure of participation and of training was positively related to perceived job security in a regression (Table 10.2). Furthermore, most of the regressors are statistically significant at the 5 percent level (all except the importance of formal and informal OJT, the number of meetings per month, and the interaction of the meetings variable with QC membership).

Table 10.2. *Indiana survey*

Dependent variable = Agreement with "The Security [on my job] is good."

	Coefficient	Standard error
I take part in a quality circle (1 = yes).	1.75**	0.056
Number of group meetings a month attended on company time to talk about work problems.	0.007	0.007
Interaction (product) of previous two measures.	0.009	0.010
Time to train someone to do your job.	0.017**	0.014
Importance of formal on the job training.	0.070	0.031
Importance of informal on the job training.	0.045	0.032
My job makes me keep learning new things.	0.100**	0.020
My job gives me freedom in how I do my work (same codes).	0.165**	0.024
My job lets me decide the speed that I work (same codes).	0.121**	0.021
My job does not let me participate in decisions that affect me (reverse coded: 1 = strongly agree; 5 = strongly disagree).	0.117**	0.021
R^2	0.170	
N	2592	

Notes: * = Statistically significantly different from 0 at the 5 percent level.
        ** = Statistically significantly different from 0 at the 1 percent level.
Standard errors are in parentheses.
Additional controls include age, age^2, education, tenure, tenure^2, gender by marital status interaction, and six occupational controls.

The estimated effects are fairly sizable. Increasing each of the three autonomy measures by 1 standard deviation corresponds to a 0.40 point (about a third of a standard deviation) increase in perceived job security. Increasing each of the four training measures by 1 standard deviation corresponds to a 0.25 point (about a quarter of a standard deviation) increase in perceived job security.

The results are robust to changes in specification. Neither adding controls for firm characteristics such as industry and union status nor restricting the sample to workers (i.e., dropping supervisors and managers) changes the results.

GAO survey
The most direct evidence that downturns in demand hurt participatory efforts comes from the questions concerning barriers to employee involvement efforts. "Worsened business conditions" is cited as a barrier to employee involvement efforts by 45 percent of the respondents, with 14 percent claiming that it is a barrier to a "great" or a "very great" extent. Furthermore, short-term

Table 10.3. *GAO survey*

Dependent variable = The proportion of workers who have employment security

	1	2	3
Index formed by summing the proportions of workers who participate in the following employee involvement programs	0.0824** (0.0291)		0.0614† (0.0530)
Sum of proportion of employees receiving formal training in group decision-making, leadership skills, business skills, quality/statistical analysis, team-building skills (for each measure, 1 = 0–20 percent; 5 = 81–100 percent).		0.0295 (0.0454)	−0.0136 (0.0530)
The proportion of workers with cross-training		0.4814** (0.1236)	0.4530** (0.1335)
R^2	0.052	0.095	0.099
N	263	290	263

Notes: Additional controls include proportion union, a dummy variable for union = 0, and a constant.
† = Statistically significantly different from 0 at the 10 percent level.

performance pressures (which worsen during downturns when performance measures are declining) are cited as a barrier by 87 percent of the respondents, and as a "great" or a "very great" barrier by 45 percent.

There is additional evidence in this data set that firms with employment security are more likely to introduce employee involvement experiments. The first column of Table 10.3 regresses the proportion of employees enjoying employment security against several controls and an index measuring the total amount of participation in the company (i.e., the sum of the seven participation measures). The coefficient on the participation index is positive and significant at the 0.01 level. The coefficient is modest: a 2 standard deviation increase in the participation index (about 9.6 points, or an increase in participation of about 25 percent of the workforce on each of the seven policies) corresponds to a 0.8 increase in the measure of job security (about 16 percent of the workforce).

The second column in Table 10.3 replaces the participation index with a training index and a measure of cross-training. The former's coefficient is small and not significant, while the measure of cross-training is both large and highly significantly related to employment security (0.48 (0.12), $P < 0.01$). The final column includes both participation and the two training measures. None of the coefficients move very much, but the significance level of the participation index drops to the 5.1 percent level.

Similarly, in results not shown, including measures of company employment

Table 10.4. *Supplier survey*

Dependent variable = Employee involvement (percent of workers in some form of employee involvement program)

	1	2
The length of your contract with the customer of this product (0 = No contract; 5 = Greater than 5 years).	0.0948** (0.0396)	
The degree of availability your customer would have in switching to another supplier (1 = Easy; 5 = Hard).		0.0043 (0.0379)
R^2	0.0456	0.0337
N	337	337

Notes: The independent variables measure long-term customer relations and are related to long-term employment relations. Additional controls include a constant, the proportion of the work force in a union, a measure of the complexity of the product, and log(employment).

can reduce the statistical significance of the coefficient on the participation index, although its size is not changed. Furthermore, if each measure of the participation index enters individually, an F-test cannot reject the hypothesis that the coefficients on the participation measures are all zero.

Supplier relations survey
Employee involvement efforts are substantially more common in firms with long-term customer contracts (Table 10.4). Moving from no contract to a contract over five years in length corresponds to a roughly 15 percent higher (2 standard deviations) increase in the proportion of workers who actively participate in some form of employee involvement.

These results were similar when the controls for size, technology, or union were deleted, when the contract length variable was unravelled and entered as a set of dummy variables, and when the regressions were re-run using multinomial logit regressions that relax the assumption that a move from no workers in a quality circle to 1–33 percent involved is the same as a move from 1–33 percent to 34–66 percent. On the other hand, the presence of non-contract barriers to switching supplies were not useful in predicting employee involvement efforts. Again, these results were robust to a variety of changes in specification.

Summary
It is encouraging to be able to replicate findings with several data sets. In all three data sets, the presence of employment security is correlated with employee participation and training.

Each data set has severe problems with measurement, and while most of the coefficients are of the predicted sign, many are small or not statistically significant. Nevertheless, these results in total present a suggestive case that firms with high levels of participation and of OJT also have employment security. Correspondingly, the theoretical point that demand fluctuations are particularly costly for participatory firms is supported by these data.

5   Conclusions

The theory and evidence presented above is consistent with past research that "strongly suggests employment security policies have desirable macroeconomic consequences and therefore warrant support of national policy makers" (Kochan, MacDuffie and Osterman, 1988:141). Economists' typical policy advice is to subsidize goods with positive externalities. Unfortunately, any simple subsidy on "participation" would encourage firms merely to go through the motions of participation, and therefore have little impact. In spite of this problem, a *contingent* tax subsidy on training in labor--management cooperation and in dispute resolution could be effective. The key is to make the subsidy contingent upon implementing a variety of additional policies that are only valuable to a firm that is serious about participation. Such a policy is discussed in Levine (1992b).

Firms with employment security are particularly successful if there are few and shallow declines in demand for output: that is, if industry demand is less variable, if aggregate demand is less variable, and if there is high average growth in the industry and economy. While these are helpful conditions for all firms, these conditions are particularly favorable to firms that use participation and that engage in high levels of training.

Granting partial unemployment insurance for partial layoffs (i.e., job sharing) and releasing Jobs Training Partnership Act funds for workers who have not yet been laid off would reduce the current subsidy that labor-hoarding firms pay to firms that lay off workers. Such policies stabilize aggregate demand, encourage companies with long-term employment relations, and (in this model) increase average output. Both Motorola and Hewlett-Packard, for example, have made extensive use of short-time compensation for job sharing in the states where it is available. (Policies that encourage work sharing also stabilize the macro-economy by spreading slowdowns across more workers and, therefore, reducing liquidity constraints.)

The model in this chapter is one of many examples of why the free market may not lead to an efficient organization of work (Levine, 1991a, 1991b; Bowles and Gintis, 1990). If the market imperfections discussed in this literature are found to be important, then government policies that improve the training of the workforce, promote worker participation in decision-making, and encourage employment stability can help stabilize the macroeconomy, increase productivity, and increase equity.

Notes

Sam Bowles, Bill Dickens, Jonathan Leonard, Gil Skillman, Larry Summers, Marty Weitzman, and Janet Yellen made helpful comments, as did participants at seminars at the UC Berkeley Macro-Labor Seminar, Industriens Utredningsinstitut (IUI), and the SCASSS Conference on Democracy and Participation. I have also benefited from reading the related research by Richard Parkin.

1. Y plants do not completely stabilize employment to the extent that they lay off part-time and contract employees, reduce the amount of work that they contract outside the firm, and reduce work hours.

2. While economic crises can prod management, workers, and unions to initiate participatory experiments, demand stability reduces the costs of maintaining participation. Levine and Strauss (1989) survey the numerous other reasons why participatory plans often fail.

3. The model makes the extreme assumptions that layoffs are costless to X firms, while hoarded labor are valueless to Y firms. Actually, the costs of layoffs include severance pay, increases in unemployment insurance taxes, hiring costs when employment increases, and so forth. Less tangibly, firms with layoffs increase worker discount rates and lose their reputation for caring for workers (Bolt, 1983). On the other hand, Y firms use slack time to retrain workers, perform maintenance tasks, and utilize workers at low-value tasks. In a classic case of the latter, Mazda sent its line workers door-to-door to sell Mazda automobiles during slack times – a strategy that met with surprisingly high success.

   The calculations above assume that the markup is greater than one over the probability of low demand. Otherwise Y firms hire only the number of workers needed to produce in times with low demand, and receive lower profits because of the missed sales in good times. The welfare results remain substantially unchanged.

4. There is also an unstable mixed equilibrium, which is not discussed further.

5. The Indiana, GAO, and Supplier data sets were kindly made available to me by Jim Lincoln of UC Berkeley, the General Accounting Office, and Sue Helper of Case Western Reserve. Lincoln and Kalleberg (1990), Levine and Kruse (1991), and Helper (1990) discuss the data sets in more detail.

11 Democracy versus appropriability: can labor-managed firms flourish in a capitalist world?

GREGORY K. DOW

1 Introduction

A growing body of econometric evidence suggests that worker participation in firm decision-making increases productivity (Defourney, Estrin and Jones, 1985a, 1985b; Jones and Svejnar, 1985; Estrin, Jones and Svejnar, 1987). Labor-managed firms (LMFs), however, have only a marginal place in Western market economies. LMFs most commonly engage in professional, craft manufacturing, or service activities where capital requirements are modest. The principal exceptions involve worker takeovers of capitalist firms (KMFs) in financial distress (Ben-Ner, 1988a, 1988b).

At first glance, this situation seems paradoxical: why should the bulk of production activity in market economies be organized in hierarchical capitalist firms, when worker control appears to have a significant positive impact on productivity? Writers who have addressed this question can (at some risk of caricature) be classified as *skeptics* and *proponents*. Skeptics draw normative conclusions from evolutionary outcomes: if contemporary economies are dominated by capitalist firms, then such firms must have some efficiency advantage relative to more democratic rivals. Authors who have expressed this view include Nozick (1974, Ch. 8), Jensen and Meckling (1979), and Williamson (1985). Skeptics often grant that the LMF might have merit in the specialized niches where it has already proven viable (Hansmann, 1988, 1990a, 1990b), but doubt that widespread adoption of this organizational form would provide net social benefits.

Proponents of the LMF place less weight on the verdict of the market, although they are encouraged by the recent upsurge in the LMF population relative to capitalist firms (Ben-Ner, 1988a). They also take heart from favorable empirical findings about LMF productivity performance. Proponents, however, face a serious analytic dilemma: why would a socially attractive organizational form persistently fail to thrive in a laissez-faire environment? For both practical and intellectual reasons, those who advocate public intervention on behalf of the LMF must supply convincing answers to this question.

In this chapter I show that defective investment incentives can place the LMF at an evolutionary disadvantage relative to the KMF.[1] The proposition that LMFs may underinvest is not new: this point has been made by Jensen and Meckling (1979), for example. A more interesting result (reported in section 4 below) is that the LMF can outperform the capitalist firm on static and dynamic welfare measures, while nevertheless losing the evolutionary race in the long run. I also show that the private value of the KMF to its owners can exceed the corresponding value of its LMF twin, so that even if the LMF is socially preferred, workers may not buy out capitalist firms. Rather, the members of existing LMFs may gain by selling out to capitalist investors.

The model developed here builds upon an existing literature concerned with market failures that may impede LMF formation or growth (Ben-Ner, 1988b). Two hypotheses are prominent in this literature: first, that the LMF is disadvantaged in the credit market relative to KMFs (Gintis, 1989a, 1989b); and, second, that workers are deterred from joining LMFs by the income risks connected with residual claimant status (Drèze, 1989). A closely related thesis is that capitalist firms represent a response to moral hazard in the borrower/lender relationship (Eswaran and Kotwal, 1989).

However, even if all biases in access to credit or insurance were somehow removed, LMF investment behavior would still require more attention than it has thus far received from proponents. In an earlier paper (Dow, 1986) I showed that LMFs will mimic the investment decisions of conventional neoclassical firms if there is a competitive market for LMF membership rights. At least in principle, this institutional arrangement rescues the LMF from the horizon and common property problems emphasized by Jensen and Meckling. But this earlier paper failed to address two other key issues: why the LMF might have an efficiency advantage over the KMF, and why KMFs could nonetheless dominate in a market economy. The present analysis suggests answers to these latter questions.

Section 2 outlines the necessary background assumptions and explains how the LMF could acquire a static efficiency advantage relative to its KMF twin. Section 3 characterizes the investment behavior of each organizational form. These preliminary results are used in section 4 to compare KMFs and LMFs on three distinct dimensions: social value, private value, and growth rate. The main formal conclusion is the LMF Dominance Theorem in section 4.2. This theorem shows that the LMF can be socially preferred even when the private value of capital is larger in the KMF and the KMF grows more rapidly. Section 5 identifies some possible reasons for LMF underinvestment, and discusses policy remedies.

2 Output choice, expected dividends, and organizational form

In sections 3 and 4, I will develop a simple growth model to compare the investment behavior of KMFs and LMFs. Here I take up the preliminary task of determining the static return per unit of capital in each organizational form. Background assumptions are presented in section 2.1. Analyses of the KMF and LMF follow in sections 2.2 and 2.3 respectively.

2.1 The static choice environment

Consider a firm with a given capital stock K. Capital and labor are combined in fixed proportions so that $L = K$ is also the number of workers employed by the firm. The firm chooses output $q \geqslant 0$ per unit of capital after a technological shock $x \in X$ has been revealed. All agents are risk-neutral. Each worker bears an effort disutility $c_L(q, x)$ which cannot be shifted to any other agent by means of contracts. A depreciation cost of $c_K(q, x)$ per unit of capital is borne by the owner(s) of the firm's capital stock. The reservation payoff of each agent (worker or owner) is normalized at zero. The supply of labor to firms is infinitely elastic at this utility level. The price of output is unity.

Assumption A1

For each state $x \in X$, the functions $c_K(q, x)$ and $c_L(q, x)$ are defined for all $q \geqslant 0$, twice continuously differentiable, strictly increasing, and strictly convex in q, with $c_K(0, x) = c_L(0, x) = 0$.

Assumption A2

Define the *surplus function* by

$$s(q, x) \equiv q - c_K(q, x) - c_L(q, x).$$

We assume that for every state, there is an output interval $0 < q < q_0(x)$ on which total surplus is positive.

Figure 11.1 shows the shape of the surplus function for an arbitrary state x, as well as the output $q^*(x)$ maximizing total surplus per unit of capital. This output level provides a useful benchmark for subsequent efficiency comparisons between the KMF and LMF.

2.2   Expected dividends in the KMF

The owner of the KMF's capital stock is a residual claimant who supplies no labor. Within a given period, the sequence of events in the KMF is as follows:

(a) A per-worker wage $w \geqslant 0$ is announced by the owner.
(b) A work force of size $L = K$ is hired by the owner.
(c) The random shock $x \in X$ is revealed to all agents.
(d) A per-worker output $q \geqslant 0$ is chosen by the owner.

The wage is not contingent upon output or the state of the world. Piece rates are excluded on the assumption that outside enforcers cannot verify output quality. Wages are invariant across states of the world because it is too costly to revise the wage whenever a new state is revealed. The employment contract thus involves an authority relationship where employees accept the directions of the firm's owner in exchange for a fixed wage payment (Simon, 1951; Masten, 1988).

For any given wage/state pair (w, x), the owner selects the output $q(w, x)$ at the production stage which solves

$$\max_{q \geqslant 0} q - c_K(q, x) - w \tag{A}$$

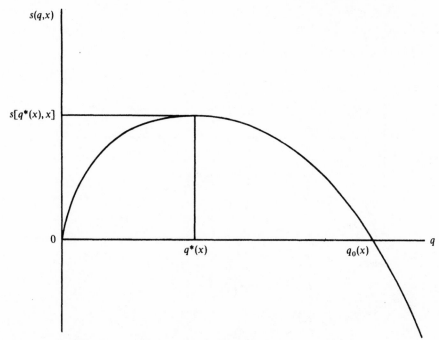

Figure 11.1   Surplus per unit of capital in state x

subject to:

$$w - c_L(q, x) \geqslant 0.$$

The objective function in (A) is the owner's payoff per unit of capital. Because the input ratio is fixed at unity, this is also the owner's payoff per employed worker. The constraint in (A) requires that workers receive at least their reservation utility *ex post* in every state; otherwise, workers will leave the firm at the production stage. The existence and uniqueness of the output $q(w, x)$ are guaranteed by Assumption A1.

Figures 11.2(a) and 11.2(b) illustrate the solution of problem (A) when the labor participation constraint is non-binding or binding respectively. In Figure 11.2(a), the owner adopts the unconstrained optimum $\hat{q}(x)$ corresponding to state x, and each worker receives a rent $w - c_L[\hat{q}(x), x] > 0$. In Figure 11.2(b), the owner chooses the highest output level allowed by the constraint, and each worker's payoff is driven down to the reservation level of zero.

Upon substituting the output $q(w, x)$ back into the objective function, the owner chooses a wage level *ex ante* to achieve

$$\pi_K \equiv \max_{w \geqslant 0} E_x \{q(w, x) - c_K[q(w, x), x] - w\}. \tag{B}$$

The wage plays two distinct roles in problem (B): it determines the level of output in those states where the labor participation constraint binds, and it transfers

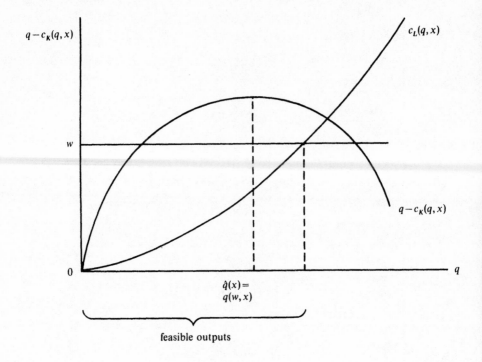

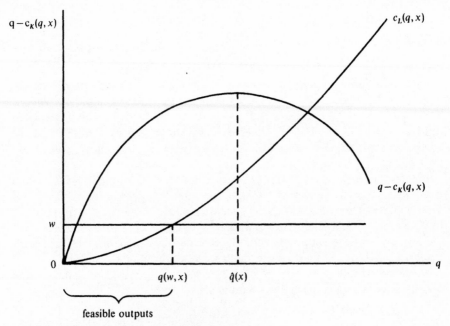

Figure 11.2   The labor participation constraint
(a) Non-binding labor participation constraint
(b) Binding labor participation constraint

surplus from the employer to workers in states where the constraint does not bind. Since the capital stock and the capital/labor ratio are exogenously given, the wage which maximizes the owner's expected payoff per unit of capital in (B) also maximizes total expected profit. The *ex ante* payoff π_K is the *expected dividend* for the KMF. The dividend is nonnegative because $w = 0$ is always feasible. A zero wage gives zero output in every state due to the constraint in problem (A).

It is useful to contrast the KMF dividend π_K with the payoff π^* obtained by maximizing total surplus *ex post* in every state:

$$\pi^* \equiv E_x \{q^*(x) - c_K[q^*(x), x] - c_L[q^*(x), x]\}. \tag{C}$$

We recall from Assumption 2 and Figure 11.1 that $q^*(x)$ uniquely maximizes the surplus expression $s(q,x)$. The following theorem summarizes the relationship between π_K and π^*.

KMF dividend theorem

(a) Suppose the surplus-maximizing output $q^*(x)$ is adopted in every state $x \in X$. If the resulting effort disutility level $c_L[q^*(x), x]$ is invariant across states, then $\pi_K = \pi^*$.
(b) If the disutility $c_L[q^*(x), x]$ varies across states of the world, then $\pi_K < \pi^*$.

Proof
Available from the author upon request.

In general, the capitalist firm departs from the output rule $q^*(x)$ which maximizes expected social surplus. Because the wage is independent of output, the KMF owner fails to internalize the effort disutility $c_L(q, x)$ when choosing an output in problem (A). It is true that the owner is obliged to consider effort costs if the constraint in (A) is binding. But even so, the wage is rigid across states of the world, and in general there is no wage which simultaneously induces surplus maximization in all states. The KMF thus deviates from the first-best output level $q^*(x)$ in some states. Since the situation described in part (a) of the theorem is exceptional, I assume $\pi_K < \pi^*$ hereafter.

The expected dividend π_K represents the entire social return from the KMF if the labor participation constraint $w \geqslant c_L(q, x)$ in problem (A) is binding in every state. In this case, all surplus goes to the owner of the firm because the payoffs of workers are identically zero. But if the strict inequality $w > c_L[q(w, x), x]$ holds for some x, where w is the optimal wage in problem (B), the workforce captures a rent in state x. The dividend π_K is then less than the full surplus generated by the KMF, since π_K reflects only returns which are appropriated by the owner of the firm. This point is addressed in greater detail in section 4.

2.3   Expected dividends in the LMF

The LMF differs from the KMF in that the firm's capital stock is owned collectively by the work force, who take over the residual claims previously held by external capital suppliers. Workers also determine output collectively using some democratic choice procedure. The total revenue of a LMF having the capital stock K, net of depreciation costs, is

$$[q - c_K(q, x)] \cdot K.$$

This net revenue is shared equally among the work-members of the LMF. Because $K = L$ due to the assumption of fixed production coefficients, each worker's payoff net of effort disutility is

$$s(q, x) \equiv q - c_K(q, x) - c_L(q, x).$$

This is the firm's total surplus per unit of capital as defined in Assumption A2. Since capital stock and membership size are fixed in the short run, in any given state x the current members unanimously favor the output level which solves

$$\max_{q \geqslant 0} q - c_K(q, x) - c_L(q, x).$$

The LMF output policy is therefore given by $q^*(x)$. This policy yields the positive surplus $s[q^*(x), x]$ shown in Figure 11.1.

Because each LMF member is a residual claimant, there is no counterpart to the KMF's *ex ante* wage choice in problem (B). The LMF dividend π_L per unit of capital is simply the expected payoff per worker when total surplus is maximized *ex post* in each state:

$$\pi_L = \pi^* \equiv E_x \{q^*(x) - c_K[q^*(x), x] - c_L[q^*(x), x]\}.$$

Comparing this with the analysis in section 2.2, we find that the LMF has a static efficiency advantage over the KMF since $\pi_K < \pi^*$.

Unlike its KMF twin, the LMF selects a first-best production level in every state of the world because each member correctly internalizes the effort cost c_L.[2] The key difference between the two modes of organization is that capitalists do not work in the firms they own, and therefore ignore effort disutilities at the production stage (unless the labor participation constraint is binding in a particular state). Since the wage in the capitalist firm is independent of output and inflexible across states of the world, the roles of capital and labor supplier must be integrated to obtain a first-best static result. The creation of a LMF with collective capital ownership accomplishes this.[3]

3   Investment incentives and organizational form

3.1   The dynamic choice environment

Time is discrete. All agents maximize the expected present value of their consumption streams using the common subjective discount factor

$$\rho^* \equiv \frac{1}{1 + r^*} \in (0, 1)$$

where $r^* > 0$ is the market interest rate. A typical firm (KMF or LMF) obtains a stochastic dividend π_t per unit of capital in each period t, and incurs costs of adjusting its capital stock. Firms solve dynamic optimization problems having the general form

$$\max_{\{g_0, g_1, \ldots\}} E \sum_{t=0}^{\infty} \rho^t [\pi_t - I(g_t)] K_t \tag{E}$$

subject to $K_{t+1} = g_t K_t$ for all t with K_0 given.

The technological shocks $x_t \in X$ discussed in section 2 are taken to be independent and identically distributed across periods so that the π_t are also i.i.d. $I(g_t)$ is investment expenditure per unit of capital. The choice variable $g_t \geqslant 0$ is called the *growth policy* of the firm in period t. The firm adopts the same growth policy in every period due to the stationarity of problem (E).

Investment expenditures per unit of capital are assumed to be a quadratic function of the firm's growth policy:

$$I(g) \equiv \theta(g - \tau)^2$$

where $\theta > 0$ and $0 < \tau < 1$. The assumption $\tau < 1$ implies that over time the firm's capital stock will decay toward zero in the absence of investment expenditures.

3.2 Investment incentives in the KMF

If KMF ownership shares are traded on a competitive stock market, the firm's owners in each period will unanimously support present value maximization. We set $\rho = \rho^*$ in problem (E) because the KMF owners discount future dividends at the market interest rate r^*. The expected dividend in each period $E(\pi_t) \equiv \pi_K$ is derived using the analysis of section 2.2.

Let A_K be the maximized present value of a unit of capital in the KMF. This present value satisfies the recursive equation

$$A_K = \max_g \{\pi_K - I(g) + \rho^* g A_K\}. \tag{1}$$

For an arbitrary growth factor g, the present value of one unit of capital A_K equals this period's expected cash flow $\pi_K - I(g)$ plus the discounted value of g units of capital next period, each having the value A_K by stationarity.[4] Upon choosing g optimally in equation (1), we obtain the *KMF growth policy*[5]

$$g_K = 1/\rho^* - [(1/\rho^* - \tau)^2 - \pi_K/\theta]^{1/2}. \tag{2}$$

Solving for the present value of a unit of KMF capital gives

$$A_K = \frac{2\theta}{\rho^*} (g_K - \tau). \tag{3}$$

Whenever the dividend π_K is positive, we have $g_K > \tau > 0$. Net expansion of the firm requires $g_K > 1$. Net expansion and the requirement that g_K be a real number together imply

$$(1/\rho^* - \tau)^2 \geq \pi_K/\theta > (1/\rho^* - \tau)^2 - (1/\rho^* - 1)^2. \tag{4}$$

There always exist positive values of the ratio π_K/θ such that these two inequalities are satisfied.

A social planner interested in maximizing the present value of total surplus would choose the output $q^*(x)$ in each period to obtain the expected payoff π^* per unit of capital, as in section 2. The planner would then solve problem (E) using the discount factor ρ^* and $E(\pi_t) = \pi^*$. The resulting first-best policy g^* is

$$g^* = 1/\rho^* - [(1/\rho^* - \tau)^2 - \pi^*/\theta]^{1/2}. \tag{5}$$

Comparing this with g_K in (2) we find that $g_K < g^*$ whenever $\pi_K < \pi^*$. The KMF uses the correct discount factor ρ^*, but since its average dividend π_K falls short of the theoretical maximum π^*, its growth rate is below the first-best growth rate g^*.

3.3   Investment incentives in the LMF

Although its owners discount future returns correctly, the KMF's growth is hampered by a low static dividend. LMFs suffer from the converse ailment: while their static output choices are first best, they often discount the income of future members too heavily. The resulting tendency toward underinvestment offsets the static efficiency advantage of the LMF, and may depress its growth rate below that of capitalist rivals.

I assume that an exogenous fraction $\beta \in [0, 1]$ of the LMF work force stays with the firm in each period, while the remaining workers quit or retire.[6] Let P be the price paid by each new LMF member upon joining the firm.[7] The expected present value A_L of a typical LMF member can be written as

$$A_L = \max_{g} \{\pi^* - I(g) + \rho^*[(g - 1)P + (1 - \beta)P + \beta A_L]\}. \tag{6}$$

Equation (6) has the following rationale. The LMF dividend per worker is π^* from section 2.3. Each existing member expects to receive this payoff in the current period t, net of *per capita* investment expenditure $I(g)$. An investment $I(g)$ in period t creates $g - 1$ new jobs in period $t + 1$ (per period-t member). The revenue from entrance fees paid by new recruits is shared equally among the members from period t, each of whom therefore receives $(g - 1)P$ at the start of period $t + 1$. These payments go to period-t members regardless of whether such individuals stay or leave in period $t + 1$. Apart from these new positions, it is necessary at the start of period $t + 1$ for the firm to fill $(1 - \beta)$ vacancies per period-t member, due to the attrition of existing members. This process yields additional revenue of $(1 - \beta)P$ per period-t worker. A typical period-t worker remains a member with probability β, and receives the present value A_L in period $t + 1$ by stationarity. Each worker leaves the firm with probability $1 - \beta$, and workers who exit obtain zero utility in subsequent periods. All workers use the subjective discount factor ρ^* to evaluate any payment or present value to be received in period $t + 1$.[8]

Since the firm cannot charge potential members more than the expected value of participation, we must have $0 \leqslant P \leqslant A_L$. If $P < A_L$, memberships are sold at a discount and incoming workers enjoy a rent. This positive payoff attracts an applicant queue to the LMF, much as workers will queue up when labor receives a rent in the KMF. Writing $P \equiv \mu A_L$ and collecting terms in (6) gives

$$A_L = \max_g \{\pi^* - I(g) + \rho^*[g\mu + \beta(1 - \mu)]A_L\}. \tag{6'}$$

This can be recognized as a variation on the KMF equation in (1), where the KMF dividend π_K has been replaced by the LMF dividend π^*. Future returns are now discounted in a more complex fashion which reflects potential membership discounts ($\mu < 1$) as well as the possibility that current members may leave the firm ($\beta < 1$). Note that the fraction μ of the present value A_L which must be paid by new members is treated as an exogenous parameter in (6').

Current LMF members will favor investment policies which maximize the expected present value of their membership rights.[9] For this reason, the membership will unanimously support the *LMF growth policy*[10] associated with equation (6'):

$$g_L = 1/\rho_L - [(1/\rho_L - \tau)^2 - \pi^*/\theta]^{1/2} \tag{7}$$

where

$$\rho_L \equiv \mu\rho^*/[1 - \rho^*\beta(1 - \mu)]. \tag{8}$$

The maximized present value of membership in the LMF is

$$A_L = \frac{2\theta}{\mu\rho^*}(g_L - \tau). \tag{9}$$

An LMF which sells memberships at their full value (setting $P = A_L$ or equivalently $\mu = 1$) adopts the first-best growth policy g^* described by equation (5). This follows because $\mu = 1$ implies $\rho_L = \rho^*$ in (8), so that the LMF uses the correct social discount factor to compute its growth policy g_L in (7). The retention rate β has no effect on investment behavior in this case. Since the LMF dividend is π^*, we obtain the first-best result $g_L = g^*$. This confirms that competitive membership markets induce the LMF to adopt value-maximizing investment policies (Dow, 1986).[11]

Now suppose instead that new workers pay less than the full value of their membership rights (that is, $\mu < 1$). It follows from equation (8) that the effective discount factor ρ_L used to compute the LMF growth policy in (7) is less than ρ^*, so that the LMF places insufficient weight on future dividends. Since ρ_L is increasing in β when $\mu < 1$, we also find that a LMF with greater membership stability invests more rapidly, all else being equal. But regardless of the retention rate, the LMF growth factor g_L is always lower than the first-best level g^* when $\mu < 1$.

Section 4 shows that if LMFs do not price membership rights at their full market value, LMFs may be socially superior to KMFs while simultaneously growing more slowly than their capitalist rivals. In section 5, I discuss some factors which may keep the price of membership from being bid up to a market-clearing level.

4   Evolutionary outcomes and welfare comparisons

4.1   Private and social values

The private values of the KMF and LMF per unit of capital are respectively A_K and A_L from equations (3) and (9) in section 3. These values need not coincide with social values for two reasons. In the KMF, the private value A_K does not incorporate rents captured by workers (if any), since these do not appear in the private dividend π_K (see the remarks at the close of section 2.2). In the LMF, on the other hand, the private value A_L may not fully reflect rents to be appropriated by future members.

To correct for these omissions we define the *social values* of the KMF and LMF (per unit of capital) as follows:

$$B_K \equiv \sum_{t=0}^{\infty} (\rho^*)^t (g_K)^t [\bar{\pi}_K - I(g_K)] = \frac{\bar{\pi}_K - I(g_K)}{1 - \rho^* g_K} \qquad (10a)$$

$$B_L \equiv \sum_{t=0}^{\infty} (\rho^*)^t (g_L)^t [\pi^* - I(g_L)] = \frac{\pi^* - I(g_L)}{1 - \rho^* g_L}. \qquad (10b)$$

The modified dividend $\bar{\pi}_K$ in (10a) is the total surplus generated per unit of capital in a KMF, regardless of whether this surplus flows to workers or to owners.[12] It is easy to see that $\pi_K \leqslant \bar{\pi}_K \leqslant \pi^*$. No such modification is needed for the LMF since π^* is already the full surplus generated by the firm. Payoffs in both (10a) and (10b) are discounted using ρ^*. Since one unit of capital expands in each period by the factor g_K (g_L) in the KMF (LMF), it is also necessary to apply an appropriate growth factor to the surpluses generated by each organizational form.

Clearly $A_K \leqslant B_K$ (the private value of the KMF cannot exceed its social value) because $\pi_K \leqslant \bar{\pi}_K$. Equality holds if and only if workers capture no rents in the capitalist firm. A less obvious result is that $A_L < B_L$ when $\mu < 1$. The private and social values of the LMF diverge when membership rights are sold at a discount, because incoming workers appropriate rents upon joining the firm. The current members thus fail to capture the full value of the returns generated by their investment expenditures. When $\mu = 1$, future surpluses are fully capitalized into the entry fees paid by new members, and hence $A_L = B_L$ (the private and social values of the LMF coincide).

4.2   The LMF dominance theorem

We are now ready to address three fundamental questions in the theory of the labor-managed firm:

(a) Under what conditions will evolutionary forces bring about an economy dominated by LMFs in the long run?
(b) When will a unit of capital have greater *private* value in the LMF sector than in the KMF sector?
(c) When will a unit of capital have greater *social* value in the LMF sector than in the KMF sector?

First consider question (a). If $g_L > g_K$, then individual LMFs will grow more rapidly than their KMF counterparts. In the long run the LMF sector will dominate, unless new KMFs form more rapidly than new LMFs. On the other hand, $g_K > g_L$ implies that the LMF sector will account for a vanishingly small fraction of the economy-wide capital stock in the long run, in the absence of persistently high rates of entry by new LMFs.

The evolutionary question can alternatively be viewed as an issue of institutional stability. If $g_K > g_L$ then a capitalist economy would be secure against invasion by LMFs. Any LMFs which did form would be condemned by their slow growth to remain at the fringes of the capitalist world. On the other hand, if $g_L > g_K$ then an already existing LMF economy would have no reason to ban "capitalist acts between consenting adults" (Nozick, 1974), since rapid LMF expansion would quickly overwhelm isolated instances of deviant capitalist behavior.

Question (b) bears on the private incentives of workers and owners to convert firms from one mode of organization to another. If $A_L > A_K$ then the owners of a capitalist firm will be inclined to sell out to their work forces. By reorganizing the firm as a LMF, workers will generate a private value A_L per member, which is larger than the firm's value as a capitalist enterprise. The reverse inequality means that the members of an existing LMF can gain by selling out to capitalist investors.

Finally, question (c) deals with the net social benefits of the two organizational forms. If $B_L > B_K$ then society as a whole can be made better off (in a Kaldor–Hicks sense) by transforming KMFs into LMFs. The converse inequality implies that capitalist firms are socially preferred. Needless to say, distributional judgments are also highly relevant in making welfare comparisons of this sort, but here I am concerned with the aggregate surplus generated by each organizational form.[13]

LMF advocates have long claimed that democratic management by workers is socially preferable to capitalist enterprise, in spite of evidence that LMFs fail to thrive in competition with capitalist rivals. LMF critics, on the other hand, have often argued that the evolutionary dominance of KMFs is evidence for their social superiority over LMFs. The following theorem adds weight to the argument of LMF advocates by establishing that LMFs can be socially preferred even when they grow less rapidly than KMFs, and have a lower private value per unit of capital.

LMF dominance theorem

Fix π_K and π^* and assume $0 < \pi_K = \bar{\pi}_K < \pi^*$ (that is, workers in capitalist firms obtain no rent, and the KMF dividend π_K falls short of the LMF dividend π^*). Fix the social discount factor ρ^*, and assume $\beta = 0$ (there is complete turnover in LMF membership from one period to the next). We derive the following results by varying μ, the share of the LMF membership value A_L which must be paid as an entry fee by incoming members:

(a) There is a unique value of μ (denoted by μ^e) for which the growth rates of the KMF and LMF are equal ($g_K = g_L$).
(b) There is a unique value of μ (denoted by μ^p) for which the private values of the KMF and LMF are equal ($A_K = A_L$).
(c) Either
   (i) There is a unique $\mu^s \geqslant 0$ for which the social values of the KMF and LMF are equal ($B_K = B_L$), or
   (ii) $B_K < B_L$ holds for all $\mu \geqslant 0$; in this case, we write $\mu^s = 0$.
(d) It can be shown that $0 \leqslant \mu^s < \mu^p < \mu^e < 1$.
(e) It can also be shown that

$$g_L \gtreqless g_K \quad \text{when} \quad \mu \gtreqless \mu^e$$
$$A_L \gtreqless A_K \quad \text{when} \quad \mu \gtreqless \mu^p$$
$$B_L \gtreqless B_K \quad \text{when} \quad \mu \gtreqless \mu^s.$$

We call $E \equiv [\mu^e, 1]$ the region of *evolutionary dominance* for the LMF. $P \equiv [\mu^p, 1]$ is the region of *private LMF dominance* and $S \equiv [\mu^s, 1]$ is the region of *social LMF dominance*.

These three regions are illustrated in Figure 11.3. The region where the LMF is evolutionarily dominant is smallest, and is contained within the set where the LMF dominates in private value. The largest set is that of LMF social dominance.

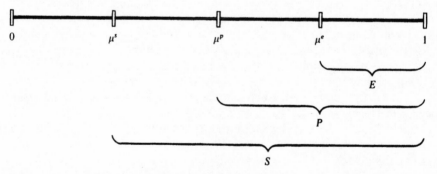

Figure 11.3 Dominance relations and the price of LMF membership
E = evolutionary dominance of LMF, P = private dominance of LMF, S = social dominance of LMF

Proof
Available from the author upon request.

4.3   Implications of the LMF dominance theorem

Ignoring boundary cases, Figure 11.3 indicates that one of the following four situations must arise:

(a) $\mu \in E$. In this situation the LMF is socially preferred, and wins the evolutionary race. Since the LMF is also privately preferred, workers have an incentive to buy out the assets of capitalist firms where they are employed.

(b) $\mu \in P$ but $\mu \notin E$. For somewhat greater membership discounts the LMF remains socially desirable and privately beneficial but it no longer wins the evolutionary contest with the KMF. Socially preferred results are achieved in the long run only if individual agents can counteract the evolutionary process by converting KMFs directly into LMFs. If not, evolutionary forces will drive the economy in the wrong direction.

(c) $\mu \in S$ but $\mu \notin P$. When LMF membership rights are priced at a still lower level, the LMF remains socially desirable but it is no longer possible to rely on private incentives to undo evolutionary outcomes. The worker-members of existing LMFs will perversely attempt to sell their firms to capitalist investors, despite the inferior social performance of the KMF. Such private transactions serve only to reinforce the prevailing evolutionary bias toward capitalist firms.

(d) $\mu \notin S$. When $\mu^s > 0$, LMFs can discount membership rights so heavily that LMFs lose their efficiency advantage over KMFs. However, if $\mu^s = 0$ then even LMFs with an open admission policy are socially preferred to KMFs.[14]

Before concluding, we briefly sketch two extensions: to the case where workers obtain rents in the KMF, and to the case where the expected tenure of LMF members exceeds one period.

Labor rents in the capitalist firm
When labor rents are absent, as assumed in the LMF dominance theorem, we have $\pi_K = \bar{\pi}_K$ and $A_K = B_K$ (the private and social values of the KMF are identical). If we keep the "social dividend" $\bar{\pi}_K$ constant while transferring some surplus to the work force, we have $\pi_K < \bar{\pi}_K$. Since all investment expenditures are borne by capitalists but the returns must now be shared with workers, the firm grows less rapidly. This reduction in the KMF growth rate g_K diminishes both the private and social value of the KMF.

A second effect arises because rents appropriated by workers are counted in the social value of the KMF (B_K) but not in the owner's private value (A_K). This opens up a previously excluded possibility, namely $A_K < A_L < B_L < B_K$. Private incentives then encourage worker takeovers of capitalist firms $(A_K < A_L)$ despite the social superiority of the KMF $(B_L < B_K)$. This suggests that caution is needed in evaluating worker buy-outs when the firm's work force already extracts significant rents due to unionization or firm-specific human capital. This is especially true in cases where private and social values do not diverge much for the LMF.

Extended LMF membership ($\beta > 0$)
The expected tenure of LMF members is positively related to investment incentives through (7) and (8), and to the private value of membership through (9). Other things being equal, LMFs which cannot price memberships at their full market value ($\mu < 1$) gain by taking steps to retain existing workers. This stimulates growth, raises the firm's private value to its own membership, and increases its social value. A higher private value has the beneficial side effect that LMF workers are less tempted to sell out to capitalist investors in cases where this is socially undesirable. Positive β values do not, however, alter the qualitative results stated in the dominance theorem.

4.4   Evolution and efficiency

Two conclusions stand out. First, evolutionary forces do not inevitably favor socially desirable modes of organization. This point is fundamentally important, because skeptics who infer the inefficiency of the LMF from its current marginal position almost always rely on evolutionary arguments (Dow, 1987, 1988b, 1993b; Williamson, 1987). Such arguments neglect the possibility that LMFs may not internalize some of the social benefits they provide. In particular, outside workers who are lucky enough to be chosen for membership usually obtain a rent. For this reason, it is entirely possible for LMFs to outperform KMFs on standard welfare criteria while simultaneously growing more slowly.

Any comparison between capitalist and labor-managed firms is a comparison between second-best alternatives. The dilemma for the LMF arises not from its inefficiency *per se*, but rather from the precise nature of its departure from first-best performance. Because its liabilities involve problems of underinvestment, the LMF is poised to lose an evolutionary contest before it starts. To phrase the matter another way: the easiest hurdle for the LMF to surmount is that of social superiority. It is more difficult for the LMF to generate the same private value of capital as a KMF, and hardest of all for the LMF to thrive in an evolutionary competition against capitalist rivals.

It is important to recognize that these results do not hinge in any essential way on the assumptions about wage rigidity used in section 2.2. This is only one way in which LMFs could acquire a static productivity advantage over KMFs. Even if this specific hypothesis were to fail, the LMF could still help strengthen work incentives, lower supervisory costs, or make better use of worker information about the production process. So long as the KMF's disadvantage is static while the LMF's disadvantage is dynamic, the general argument of this section will remain intact.

The second conclusion worth highlighting is that even when it is socially desirable to transform KMFs into LMFs, there may be no private incentive to do so. Indeed, if LMF members do not capture all of the surplus enjoyed by future worker cohorts, it may be privately beneficial to reorganize as a capitalist firm, so that current members can appropriate expected future returns as capital gains. Such organizational transformations sacrifice the interests of future LMF members, and can prove perverse when the static efficiency of the KMF is inferior to that of the LMF.

In a number of recent cases, KMFs have been sold to their work forces (Ben-Ner, 1988a). In light of the dominance theorem, there is a presumption that worker buy-outs which are privately profitable ($A_L > A_K$) will also prove socially beneficial ($B_L > B_K$), except perhaps where workers already enjoy substantial rents under capitalist management. Conversely, there are cases where LMFs have sold out to capitalist firms: the plywood cooperatives of the US Pacific Northwest furnish examples (Bellas, 1972). Here the dominance theorem provides a more ambiguous verdict: a privately profitable LMF sell-out ($A_L < A_K$) could result in net social losses ($B_L > B_K$). Some skepticism about the efficiency of private organizational arrangements is warranted in such cases.

5 Failures in the market for LMF membership

LMFs generally operate in capital-intensive industries only under special conditions (such as a worker takeover of a failing capitalist firm). Even when KMFs and LMFs compete directly, LMFs seem averse to the use of capital inputs. In a study of the US plywood cooperatives, for example, Berman and Berman (1989) found that LMFs have lower capital–labor ratios than capitalist firms operating in parallel input and product markets.

It is usually suggested that this phenomenon reflects some LMF disadvantage in the credit market. The analysis here points toward an alternative hypothesis: LMF underinvestment may derive not so much from an *inability* to finance the membership's desired growth policy as from a bias toward *undervaluation* of investment returns. Such biases will arise whenever incoming members pay an entry fee less than the full private value of membership. We are therefore led to investigate forces which might prevent potential members from bidding entrance fees up to a market-clearing level (see Ben-Ner, 1988b: 301–304 for a closely related discussion).

5.1 Credit market imperfections

The most obvious suspect is credit rationing. Constraints of this sort can operate at the level of the individuals who seek to become members of a LMF, rather than as direct restrictions on LMF investment expenditures. Low personal wealth and restricted borrowing could keep many workers out of the membership market. This is especially true for LMFs in capital-intensive industries, where the implicit present value of collectively-owned physical assets will bulk large in the price paid for LMF membership.

Membership markets have a further peculiarity: workers are placed in the position of borrowing against future labor income. Due to prohibitions on indentured servitude and the illiquidity of individual claims on the LMF capital stock, it will generally be difficult to secure a loan using the membership right itself as collateral. Analogous problems arise for educational loans, whose collateral is the present value of increased labor income in the future. Since there is no way of ensuring that students will work at lucrative jobs after graduation, banks are reluctant to finance a university education. This problem is handled in practice by having government agencies bear default risks either directly (through government loans), or in less direct ways (such as guaranteeing the loans extended by private banks).

To the extent that credit rationing operates at the level of the firm as a whole, rather than for individual workers, it may help to clarify the ways in which bankruptcy rules apply to LMFs. If individual workers can shed all responsibility for the collective debts of the LMF simply by leaving the firm, private lenders will understandably hesitate to finance LMF investment. A membership market must therefore be accompanied by clear rules governing the liabilities of individual members for collective debts.

5.2   Insurance market imperfections

Another common hypothesis about underinvestment by the LMF is that it stems from worker risk-aversion, in conjunction with failures in the insurance market. Since the model used in this chapter assumes risk-neutral preferences it is not possible to give a formal argument here, but a few remarks can be made.

A LMF membership right is similar to an ownership share in a capitalist corporation, except that workers cannot diversify risk by holding membership rights in many firms simultaneously. The members of a LMF can therefore be expected to seek out other ways of insuring themselves against the income risks associated with residual claimancy. One way of doing this is to sell the firm's assets to a group of risk-neutral capitalists in exchange for the expected present value of the firm reorganized as a KMF.

Section 4, however, described situations where the expected value of a LMF exceeds its expected value when reorganized as a KMF, even in purely private terms. In such cases, converting the LMF into a capitalist firm could be a peculiarly inefficient way of insuring workers. A better solution might be to leave the firm in the hands of its work force, while rectifying the problem of missing insurance markets in a more direct manner (perhaps through government income supports for workers adversely affected by industry-wide shocks).

5.3   Informational asymmetries and indivisibilities

Workers who seek employment in a capitalist firm do not need to estimate the expected present value of the firm. It is enough for workers to know that their reservation utilities can always be secured through exit if need be. A worker who wants to buy a LMF membership right, however, must form some opinion about the prospects of the firm. It is quite likely that incumbent workers will have better information about such matters than an outsider. Because of the resulting adverse selection problem, firms which do have favorable prospects may be unable to capture their full private value through transactions on the membership market.

Of course, traders in a capitalist stock market routinely cope with similar problems of inside information. But unlike a stock market, where claims on the firm are highly divisible and can be traded instantaneously, the LMF membership market involves lumpy assets that are traded rather infrequently. Apart from the problem of high search costs, this aggravates adverse selection problems by reducing the informational content of market prices.

5.4   Egalitarianism

The proposal that LMFs should treat membership as a saleable commodity raises deep philosophical issues about the objectives of workplace democracy. Marketable membership rights may imply a degree of individual property ownership that is inconsistent with some rationales for the LMF (Putterman, 1988a). Two points need to be kept in mind in this connection. First, the key feature of the LMF is democratic worker control over the production process. Marketability of memberships does not compromise this objective. Second, private ownership of membership deeds does not mean that individual workers can walk away with "their" share of the firm's assets whenever they please. The use of collective assets is a matter to be settled through democratic governance procedures.

There remains an issue of income distribution. Some LMF advocates who do not oppose private share ownership *per se* are nevertheless troubled by the implication that new members will not reap any net benefit from their association with the firm. The LMF with competitive membership markets is an "inegalitarian" cooperative in the terminology of Meade (1972b), because usually only founding members can capture economic rents (Dow, 1986).

There is clearly a trade-off between investment incentives and the goal of sharing rents with future workers. The greater the surplus reserved for future members, the smaller will be the number of jobs created through the growth of existing LMFs. When pressed too far, efforts to equalize the incomes of insiders and outsiders (e.g., through open membership policies) can doom the entire LMF sector to perpetual marginality.

There are other ways to promote egalitarian objectives which do less damage to the prospects of the LMF sector. Taxes and transfers remain available as devices for the redistribution of income. Beyond this, one could facilitate formation of new LMFs through the provision of credit, insurance, and technical support services, with the goal of making LMF membership widely available throughout the economy. There is no conflict between charging a competitive price for membership rights in ongoing LMFs, on the one hand, and maximizing the opportunities for workers to join or organize new LMFs on the other.

The main recommendation which arises from this discussion is simply that new LMF members should pay competitive entry fees in order to stimulate adequate investment by incumbent workers. But it is equally important to address the market imperfections that are likely to limit the size of such entrance fees. Appropriate measures could include the direct extension of government credit to workers, or guarantees to private lenders who finance worker membership fees; paycheck deduction schemes to help new workers stretch out the payment of their admission fees over prolonged periods of time; systems to monitor the membership market for possible fraud and ensure full disclosure of relevant financial risks borne by LMF members, with procedures to minimize adverse selection and moral hazard problems; and technical or managerial support for the formation of new LMFs in promising market niches.

At the present stage of our understanding, there is no way to know which of these measures will yield the largest payoff. Indeed, some of these suggestions may ultimately prove misguided or unworkable. What is clear, however, is that no invisible hand guarantees the efficiency of current organizational arrangements. By modeling, and hopefully quantifying, the trade-offs involved, the economics profession may provide some sorely-needed policy insights. In the end, we may find that democracy and efficiency are not incompatible aspirations, but rather mutually reinforcing aspects of a humane and productive economy.

Notes

Sam Bowles and Herb Gintis provided valuable editorial advice. I am indebted to Avner Ben-Ner, Ernst Fehr, Stephen Jones, Louis Putterman, and Gil Skillman for comments on earlier drafts. This work was supported by the Social Science and Humanities Research Council of Canada. All opinions are those of the author.

1. Two types of LMF should be distinguished: those which lease physical assets from outside capitalists (the pure-rental case), and those where assets are owned collectively. Here I limit attention to LMFs with collective capital ownership. Elsewhere I show (Dow, 1993a) that the pure-rental LMF is unlikely to emerge in capital-intensive industries, because investors will find it difficult to recoup sunk set-up costs when this organizational form is adopted.

2. The LMF may also have other efficiency advantages, including enhanced work incentives, reduced labor supervision costs, greater willingness to share information with management, and less resistance to workplace innovation. Private worker information about the production process is examined by Dow (1988a, 1989). Work incentives and supervision in the LMF are modeled by Dong and Dow (1991, 1993) and Dow (1991). Related discussions appear in FitzRoy and Mueller (1984), Ben-Ner (1988b), and Hansmann (1990a, 1990b).

3. This logic is familiar from transaction cost theories of vertical integration (Klein, Crawford and Alchian, 1978; Williamson, 1985, Chs. 4–5; Grossman and Hart, 1986).

4. Investment expenditures are borne by the owners of the KMF, who ignore labor rents (if any) in choosing a growth policy.

5. The negative root is used in (2) since otherwise we obtain $\rho^* g_K > 1$. The resulting

present value is unbounded. It can be shown that whenever a real solution for g_K exists, growth policies with unbounded present value must have non-positive cash flows $\pi_K - I(g)$. Such policies can be ignored.

6. Labor turnover has no effect on KMF behavior because workers can be replaced whenever necessary at zero cost.

7. Skeptics sometimes argue against the notion of markets for LMF membership by observing that capitalist firms seldom require employees to pay entrance fees (even where workers appear to capture *ex post* rents). Dow (1991) shows that firm-side moral hazard may prevent the KMF from charging an entry fee, without imposing similar disabilities on the LMF.

8. Notice that in equation (6) the only way incumbent members can benefit from investment expenditures is by charging an admission fee to new workers as the capital stock expands. This is an artifact of the fixed coefficients assumption, which implies that extra units of capital are useless to the current work force. A model with variable input ratios would be more complex, but would give similar qualitative results.

9. LMF members unanimously support the output rule in section 2.3 and the investment policy in section 3.3 because worker heterogeneity has been suppressed. When workers in a LMF have conflicting interests, issues of democratic procedure become more significant. Hansmann (1990a, 1990b) argues that the diversity of worker interests is the main impediment to more widespread adoption of the LMF organizational form.

10. Condition (4) is easily modified to show that for suitable positive values of the ratio π_L/θ there is a real solution $g_L > 1$. As in the KMF case, existence of a real solution for g_L implies that any growth policy having an unbounded present value must have a non-positive cash flow.

11. The LMF membership market is isomorphic to capitalist stock markets. In each case, future returns are capitalized into the market price of ownership shares, so that current owners support present value maximization regardless of their own expected tenure with the firm. A competitive LMF membership market also cures the perverse comparative static behavior which would otherwise result from maximization of income per worker (Sertel, 1982b; Dow, 1986; Fehr, 1992). Related ideas appear in Meade (1972b) and Barzelay and Thomas (1986).

12. Formally, $\bar{\pi}_K \equiv E\{q(w,x) - c_K[q(w,x),x] - c_L[q(w,x),x]\}$ where $q(w,x)$ solves problem (A) and w solves problem (B) in section 2.2. The inequality $\pi_K \leqslant \bar{\pi}_K$ follows from the labor constraint in problem (A), which implies $c_L[q(w,x),x] \leqslant w$. The inequality $\bar{\pi}_K \leqslant \pi^*$ follows from the fact that the output rule $q^*(x)$ maximizes *ex post* surplus in every state.

13. This focus on total surplus is motivated by the emphasis in transaction cost economics on aggregate efficiency measures (Dow, 1987, 1993b).

14. When $\mu = 0$ the LMF allows its capital stock to decay toward zero. However the LMF can still dominate socially if its dividend π^* is large enough relative to the KMF surplus $\bar{\pi}_K$.

Part IV
Productivity, distribution, and power

12 Cooperation, conflict, and control in organizations

AVNER BEN-NER

1 Introduction

A multitude of individuals and entities ("participants") have a stake in any organization. Resource suppliers, for example, have an interest in how an organization functions because their own well-being is affected via their remuneration. Likewise, the welfare of the users of an organization's output is affected by price, quality and other decisions made in the organization. The interests of various participants with a stake in the same organization are both intertwined and divergent. Participants seek both to maximize the total return from their common transactions (i.e., the size of the surplus that can be distributed among them) and to maximize their respective shares in the surplus. The desire to maximize total surplus amounts to maximizing productivity and technical efficiency and minimizing production and transactions costs; this draws participants together and drives them to cooperate. The goal of maximizing individual shares propels participants to conflict with each other (either individually or in groups), possibly to the detriment of the size of the total surplus.

Incentives for both cooperation and conflict exist because participants must often bear some costs in moving from one organization to another and because participants who have already collaborated together, having developed relationship-specific human and physical capital, are capable of generating more value than other combinations of participants (Aoki, 1984; FitzRoy and Mueller, 1984).

Cooperation and conflict characterize all organizations. Likewise, control is employed universally. Different organizational structures, production technologies and environments are associated with different degrees of cooperation and conflict and with different methods of control. The importance of cooperation, conflict and control has been long recognized in the literature on organizations. In economics, the neoclassical paradigm regards the organization as the place where different inputs cooperate to maximize the size of that surplus, while the Marxian paradigm considers the conflict between owners of capital and workers over the distribution of the organizational surplus as the core of the organizational problem.[1] A growing literature, anchored in agency and game theories and transaction cost economics, emphasizes conflict among various participants in organizations and views control as the response to it (see Williamson, 1985; Hart and Moore, 1990; Dow, 1989). However, this strand of the literature understates both the genuine incentives for cooperation in organizations as well as the power of the strategic tools available to controllers to structure organizations so as to foster cooperation and reduce conflict. These elements have been emphasized by sociologists and industrial relations specialists who focused on the makeup of positions in organizations and the specific tools available to those who occupy them (see Hill, 1981; Pfeffer, 1981; Dickson, McLachlan, Prior and Swales, 1988; DiMaggio, 1988; Edwards, 1990).[2]

This chapter builds on these and other contributions to develop an embryonic theory of the structure of organizations, focusing on the interplay between cooperation, conflict and control.[3] The theory provides a framework for the analysis of entire organizations as well as diverse specific practices in them. In order to preserve space and to hint to its generality, the theory is presented in abstract terms. To inject a measure of concreteness, the undertone of the discussion focuses on relations between labor and management.

Some of the main points of the theory are summarized in the following three propositions: (1) control arises in response to both cooperation and conflict; (2) control is exercised through organizational design; (3) control is held by participants who derive the greatest net value from its exercise.

The flow of the chapter's argument is as follows. First, key concepts are defined and discussed in section 2: organizational structure is defined in terms of positions which determine the actions in which their occupants can engage as well as their interests, whereas cooperation, conflict and control are defined in terms of the consequences of participants' actions. In section 3 familiar incentives for cooperation and conflict are stated and the proposition that both cooperation and conflict lead to the exercise of control is demonstrated. Section 4 examines the choice of organizational structure, its constituent positions and their attendant tools of actions and interests; this constitutes the design of organizations. The design depends on the identity of those who control them, because the position of controllers affects the extent of cooperation and conflict and the specific ways in which control is exercised. Section 5 explores the value and costs of exercise of control to different participants and establishes the organizational and external factors that affect the allocation of control, such as the power of incumbents, the skills of different participants, and the nature of technology available to the organization. Concluding remarks are made in section 6.

2   Definitions

2.1   *Organizational structure, positions, and interests*

Organizational structure consists of the rules and regulations that determine which positions exist in an organization, what is their formal function, who will carry them out, and when. A *position* is defined by the actions that can be undertaken by its occupants.[4] A position has three important dimensions: role in supply of inputs or demand for output, location in the structure of units, and place in the division of labor.

Supply-side participants supply resources; they may be workers, managers, providers of equity or debt, banks, parent organizations, the state or suppliers. Demand-side participants use the output; they may be clients, customers, donors, the state, or sponsors. There may also be hybrid participants that provide more than one type of input (e.g., worker-owners) or that are on both the demand and supply sides (e.g., commune members). The second dimension of a position regards the location of participants in the organizational structure of units, such as work groups, teams, departments, divisions, unions, and committees. The place of participants in the division of labor is the third dimension, represented by the specific tasks which participants perform, such as different aspects of planning, production, administration, monitoring, risk-taking, information processing and marketing.

All participants have an interest in the organization's well-being since their utility depends on it. However, the level of utility is also tied to a participant's organizational position. Participants therefore have an *interest* in the organizational structure because it affects the utility they can obtain. Because of the multiplicity of organizational positions, and because organizational positions have many facets, divergence as well as unity of interests is simultaneously created. The interests of participants thus criss-cross the organization in a lattice fashion.[5]

2.2　　Cooperation, conflict, control, and organizational tools

Definitions of cooperation, conflict and control are often derived from the goals, intentions or actions of participants, or from the rules that govern their interactions. The following working definitions are based on the actions of participants; motives for engaging in certain actions are discussed later.

Cooperation and *conflict* entail actions that foster and harm, respectively, the interests of some participants other than their initiators. *Control* entails actions that affect the choice of actions by participants in the organization. Control by A over B means that A engages in actions which induce B to choose actions he or she would otherwise not choose;[6] analogously, A has control over his or her own actions if B does not control A's actions. The ability to exercise control depends primarily on a participant's position in the organization. The three dimensions of a position determine what actions are available to its occupants and incorporate such determinants of control as ownership of the organization, possession of crucial inputs (e.g., skills and information) and the ability to deploy them, force, assignment of decision-making power, access to organizational tools that help wrest control away from others, and the ability to bargain for some control.

Participants typically exercise only incomplete control because they have access to only a limited set of actions, and have only partial effect on the actions of other participants. Joint control by participants A and B over C can therefore be interpreted as follows: A and B engage in actions that together affect the choice of actions by C. Thus control can vary in degree and it will be useful to distinguish between *ultimate control* and *attenuated control*. The wielders of ultimate control, the principals (controllers), determine the main actions of other participants, whereas participants with attenuated control, agents, have only limited influence over the actions carried out in an organization.[7]

An organizational position consists of a list of *tools* (*actions*) its occupants have at their disposal.[8] These tools are drawn from broad classes, which include, for example (a) work (including buying or selling), (b) planning, coordination and administration of activities, (c) assignment of tasks and determination of promotion ladders, (d) monitoring of actions, (e) determination of prices (external or transfer prices and compensation schemes), (f) collusion and the formation of coalitions, (g) communication and negotiation, (h) unilateral action, (i) sharing, hiding and manipulation of information, (j) manipulation of participants' objectives, (k) fulfillment of agreements, (l) making of investments (including training), (m) shirking of responsibilities, (n) consent, and (o) technology.

Although classes (a), (b), (g) and (n) contain tools that can be employed mainly for cooperation, and tools in (h) and (m) can be used mainly for conflict, most tools can be used for both cooperation and conflict. These tools are termed *mixed*, in contrast with *pure* cooperative or conflictual tools.[9] Pure cooperative tools always increase the size of the organizational surplus, whereas pure conflictual tools at best have no effect on the surplus. As for tools of control, subsequent discussion will indicate that they exist in almost every class.

Some actions cannot be costlessly observed except by those who engage in them. Such actions are termed *unobservable* tools. Observability is not immutable but often depends on technology and the willingness of interested participants to bear costs to observe or hide actions.

Control tools that are deployed in similar ways or in combination with each other may be termed collectively a *control mechanism*. Three main control mechanisms employed are commonly identified: the market, trust, and authority (Bradach and Eccles, 1989).[10] These mechanisms share some tools and are interdependent. The *market* control mechanism entails the use of various prices to provide incentives for participants to act in certain ways. Prices within an organization (e.g., wage and salary scales, piece rates, transfer prices) are typically set by participants via the control mechanism of authority, though these prices function to control the actions of participants through market-type incentives. The *trust* control mechanism entails actions that induce participants to act in ways that are inconsistent with their short- or long-run self-interest (not necessarily both) but which accord with controllers' (stated or inferred) wishes. In the game-theoretic sense trust may reflect "enlightened self-interest;" in the social psychological sense trust is the diffuse loyalty participants have to other participants, entailing a moral rather than a calculative commitment to the interests of these participants (Fox, 1974; Gambetta, 1988). Trust may be unilateral or mutual. The *authority* control mechanism entails the direct selection of actions to be carried out by participants (Simon, 1951).[11]

2.3   Organizational design

The choice of organizational structure and of the combination of the three mechanisms of control constitutes *organizational design*. Organizational design is therefore the grand architectural act committed by controllers, who define the positions that exist in an organization, and the mechanisms through which participants in an organization will be induced to carry out their designated functions. As the analysis in the remainder of the chapter suggests, organizational design is not unilateral, but is the result of the actions of organizational participants, among which controllers are the most powerful.[12]

3   Control as a consequence of incentives for cooperation and conflict

This section examines a two-person prisoner's dilemma game to provide some basic insights into incentives for cooperation and conflict.[13] The example is used to illustrate how various tools and mechanisms of control are deployed in support of cooperation, control, or both. Broader considerations are introduced in the next section, where organizational design is analyzed.

Consider the two-participant organization represented in the numerical example in Figure 12.1 as a game in strategic form. Each participant may engage in one of three actions; a pair of actions is denoted by σ^i, where i is the cell number, counting from left to right by rows. Participants' payoffs are marked in the conventional way, with their sum representing the surplus of the organization.

Participants' incentives in this organization are clearly mixed. On the one hand, the participants have an incentive to cooperate by choosing the actions that lead to the greatest organizational surplus attainable from their collaboration. This consideration induces both participants to prefer actions associated with σ^5. On the other hand, they have an incentive to conflict over the distribution of the surplus by selecting actions that maximize their individual payoffs. This consideration induces A to favor σ^2 and B to prefer σ^4. The actual outcome depends on whether the participants are engaged in a cooperative or non-cooperative relationship, in the game-theoretic sense.

A non-cooperative relationship arises if participants do not communicate with each other, or do not coordinate their actions. In this event, participants will

		Participant B		
		b_1	b_2	b_3
	a_1	2,2	6,1	1,0
Participant A	a_2	1,6	5,5	2,1
	a_3	0,1	1,2	4,4

Figure 12.1   The two-participant organization as a prisoner's dilemma

undertake actions that result in lower payoffs than those feasible with agreements based on communication.[14] But even if participants do communicate and coordinate their actions, they will still conclude only *self*-enforcing agreements. Such agreements have the feature that after actions are chosen and agreed upon, participants maximize their respective payoffs by honoring the agreement. If either participant has an incentive to deviate from the promised action, the agreement is not self-enforcing and will not be made in the first place. While agreements on σ^1 or σ^9 are self-enforcing, the superior outcome (σ^5) cannot be reached via self-enforcing agreement.[15]

In a cooperative relationship participants communicate and make binding and enforceable commitments, hence any σ^i is feasible, including σ^5, which maximizes the surplus. The question of the surplus distribution is not settled, however, and incentives for conflict remain.

3.1   *Cooperation and conflict-induced control: the production of trust*

Non-cooperative behavior emerges more easily than cooperative behavior because the latter requires special organizational arrangements to support the credibility of commitments, facilitate communication among participants, and help reach and enforce agreements. Nevertheless, participants have incentives to control non-cooperative behavior despite their incentives to conflict. Trust is one important control mechanism used to steer participants towards cooperation.

Trust may be a product of participants' long-lasting relationship. Repeated interaction among participants allows for retaliation against those who deviate from agreements and for the evolution of reputations, as well as for the development of common language and symbols, leading to the development of trust which induces participants to engage in actions a_2 and b_2, respectively (as the "folk theorem" in game theory suggests). Long-lasting relationships may be encouraged, for example, by tenure systems and internal labor markets within organizations, or by stable and continuous associations within the ethnic, cultural, ideological or similar community from which organizational participants are drawn. Trust can also be generated through training, indoctrination, social assimilation and similar tools affecting participants' psychological predisposition. Participants who trust each other's promises for action may engage in actions associated with σ_5.[16]

Trust, in both the psychological and game-theoretic senses, can be employed in response to incentives for cooperation, as illustrated above. Trust may be used also for conflictual purposes, with controllers seeking to alter agents' preferences (psychological predisposition) in order to align their interests with those of principals. The tools of trust employed in an organization thus depend on the identity of controllers. If A and B control the organization jointly, they will aim to produce trust in the most economical way to achieve σ^5. If, however, A is the principal, he or she will seek to employ trust to induce B to engage in b_2 (and A will adopt a_1).[17] This requires B's partial abdication of personal judgment and placing of trust in A's hands. Suspension of personal judgment may be facilitated and encouraged by specialization of knowledge and information among the participants (not strictly part of the numerical example), which reduces the basis for rational decisions by agents.[18]

3.2 Cooperation and conflict-induced control: authority

Consider now the authority mechanism of control. Suppose A is the principal and has authority in the organization. If authority entails only the power to select the actions that participants must perform, then A will aim at combination σ^2 by performing a_1 and order B to do b_2. A more expansive exercise of authority comprises also the ability to appropriate the surplus. Such control is the surest way to attain the highest payoff. If B must simply comply, then A would choose σ^5, with the maximum surplus of 10, paying B the minimum compensation necessary to keep him or her in the organization. It is therefore evident that every participant desires to gain control over actions in the organization.

However, if participants are assured that authority will not be used to serve conflictual goals (to tilt the distribution of the surplus against them), they will seek to assign control *qua* authority to some participants. The following sub-sections illustrate this point in the context of specific control tools associated with authority; it is also shown there how authority is used for conflictual purposes.

3.3 Cooperation-induced control: authority exercised via administration

Participants have a unity of interests with respect to the size of the surplus produced in the organization. In order to promote this goal, participants' work must be specialized and coordinated, tasks and information have to be allocated, transfer prices and wages that elicit desirable actions (i.e., market control) must be determined, and other functions must be fulfilled. This range of activities is often collectively termed "administration."[19] Administration is an important form of exercise of authority.

The task of administration cannot, in most cases, be carried out alone by a single individual for reasons of bounded rationality. Consequently, some delegation of responsibilities is necessary, often resulting in a hierarchy with several tiers. The organizational structure of the hierarchy will be designed to maximize the total surplus.

3.4 Cooperation and conflict-induced control: authority exercised via monitoring

Individual input or output is monitored in all organizations. Such monitoring is undertaken in conjunction with output- or input-dependent remuneration (market control) and disciplinary schemes such as dismissal, suspension and promotion (authority control). The function of monitoring is performed by some participants in the organization, is relegated to specialized technology (e.g., time clocks), or is embedded in technology that has additional functions (e.g., computers).

The common explanation for the near ubiquity of monitoring is that agents will shirk their responsibilities under the veil of asymmetric information; that is, conflict induces control via monitoring. However, such monitoring is not welcomed by the monitored. The cooperative motive to maximize the size of the surplus also contributes a reason for participants to want monitoring, in order to prevent shirking and promote an optimal internal allocation of resources (though each participant will still want to be personally exempt from being the subject of monitoring). However, since monitoring is applied to all occupants of certain positions, the support for monitoring by agents is not assured because the weight of the conflict motive may dominate the cooperation motive. Hence principals will seek to use monitoring to support market and authority-based control, whereas agents may resist it.[20]

3.5   Cooperation and conflict-induced control: authority exercised via the design of positions

All participants have an interest in a design of positions that maximizes the total surplus. For purposes of cooperation, the structuring of positions and the allocation of participants to them is based on strictly cooperative considerations of the kind discussed in the theory of teams (Marschak and Radner, 1972). However, generalized cooperation whereby each participant seeks cooperation with respect to all participants cannot emerge (see section 4 below). Therefore, *some* conflict exists in all organizations. Principals will structure organizational positions so as to align agents' interests with their own, to give themselves access to tools that favor their interests, and to provide agents with a minimum of conflict tools.

Agents contest the control of principals and will seek to wrest away some of it, by employing the tools that are available to them by virtue of their positions. The fight over control focuses on the details of positions and the tools that can be employed by their holders. Consequently, attenuated control may be successfully appropriated by agents. This may even become a formal part of the organizational structure, as is the case when employee representatives are brought onto the board of directors.

4   The exercise of ultimate control: organizational design

The previous section has established the existence of motives for both cooperation and conflict, and has demonstrated that goals related to both are pursued through control. In view of the common origins of cooperation, conflict and control, the design of organizational structure by controllers is guided by complex considerations. In this section it is argued that organizational design balances considerations connected with the desire to promote cooperation, the cost of gaining cooperation, the mixed nature and uncontrollability of some organizational tools, the costs and benefits of using different tools, the lattice of interests created by organizational positions, and the relative effectiveness and cost of employing different control mechanisms. The discussion assumes the existence of controllers, whose identity is examined in the next section.

4.1 Promotion of cooperation

Controllers obviously seek to engage agents' cooperation in order to enhance their own objectives. However, since the objective of controllers is neither promotion of cooperation nor elimination of conflict but maximization of their utility, they will generally not seek to obtain agents' full cooperation. Instead, they will balance the gains from cooperation with the costs of attaining it and will choose control tools with this calculus in mind. This simple principle is illustrated by the familiar result from agency theory that the profit-maximizing incentive scheme offered by the principal typically does not eliminate all shirking by the agent. In other words, it might be too expensive (and thus undesirable) to engage agents' full cooperation. (Additional considerations are discussed below.)

4.2 Mixed and unobservable tools

While the motives for the use of control are decomposable into cooperation and conflict, many tools are mixed, and some mixed and pure tools are unobservable by principals. The unobservability of mixed and conflict tools poses problems for both agents and principals. Agents must decide how to employ unobservable tools in view of the double effect of mixed tools on the organizational surplus, whereas principals must design positions in view of what agents may do with the tools attached to the positions they occupy.

Agents will always use cooperation tools (pure cooperative and the cooperative aspects of mixed tools); these, it will be remembered, increase the total size of the pie and do not diminish their payoffs. They will use conflict tools only as long as the net change in their payoff due to their employment is positive. The discriminate use of strikes by employees provides a familiar example.

Principals will always try to assign cooperative tools to all positions, and will never design positions that give agents access to pure conflict tools. However, they will assign mixed tools to positions if the cooperative aspects are expected to produce results which outweigh the negative consequences of the possible use of the conflictual aspects. Unobservable mixed tools will be the target of attempts to make them observable; when observability is impossible or very costly, trust control may be attempted.[21]

In response to changes in technology and in relative prices of various control tools, principals may have incentives to invest in transforming mixed tools into pure cooperative ones, and to observe previously unobservable tools. Parallel comments apply to agents' considerations. Hence positions will be redesigned in response to various changes within and without the organization.

4.3   The lattice of organizational interests

Participants act on their interests which, for given preferences, are determined by the positions they occupy in the organization. In designing an organization, principals consider the effects each position will have on its occupiers' motives for cooperation and conflict, both with principals *and* with other participants.

Principals seek but cannot design positions that generate *only* cooperation with them, for the following related reasons. First, the separation between principals and agents precludes the complete eradication of motives for conflict. Second, the cost of eliciting complete cooperation through position design may be prohibitive. Third, the three dimensions of positions generate a lattice of interests that creates some divergence of interests between principals and agents; the total elimination of conflict motives may preclude the use of valuable division of labor, structuring of units, or allocation of risk, work and other supply-side functions. Fourth, despite the fact that mixed unobservable tools provide their occupiers with some conflictual actions in addition to the cooperative ones, the existence of motives for cooperation may nonetheless make the value of these tools positive for controllers (despite the expectation that the conflictual actions will also be used).

Principals seek to design positions that induce agents to cooperate *with each other*, since this would maximize the organizational surplus. However, this is not fully feasible for the reasons enumerated above. Cooperation among agents will sometimes be intentionally thwarted by principals who structure positions so as to inhibit the formation of coalitions of agents that may pursue their own group interests. One important way of achieving this objective is through the creation of agent positions that, in addition to interests in cooperation with each other and the principals, also (a) have mutually conflicting interests, and (b) have tools at their disposal to pursue these interests. The lattice of interests thus crafted in an organization is intended to balance the consequences of the persistence of conflict of interest between agents and principals, which calls for the prevention of the formation of adverse agent coalitions through the fostering of conflict among agents, with the need to secure cooperation among agents and with principals. Many of these issues are presented, albeit in an attenuated form, also in organizations composed only of principals.[22]

4.4   Trade-offs between different control mechanisms

The market, authority and trust mechanisms of control may complement and substitute for each other. For example, participants may be induced to carry out certain actions because they are rewarded for their performance, their employment is contingent on fulfilling orders, they believe that a request initiated by principals should be honored, or some combination of the above.

The marginal cost of deploying each mechanism is generally increasing; that is, the marginal product of a mechanism in terms of eliciting compliance with the goals of principals is declining. For example, in order to eliminate more of the consequences (in type or degree) of an agency relationship it is necessary for the principal to provide a rapidly increasing share of the surplus (indeed, as remarked earlier, it is rare that incentive schemes are designed so that they result in either theoretical models or in practice in the elimination of all negative consequences of agency problems). Similarly, reliance on authority alone to induce agents to accomplish certain tasks may require increasingly elaborate monitoring schemes as well as detailed determination of what agents need to do. Likewise, the use of only trust to get agents to act in certain ways may require very large and expensive investments in trust building. Consequently, controllers will combine control mechanisms in a similar way to the combination of different inputs in production geared to maximization of profits.[23]

Differences in positions suggest that they will be controlled via different mixes of control tools. For example, Armstrong (1989) argues that the establishment of trust is expensive and time-consuming. Investment in trust relations is therefore directed more heavily toward senior management, who have access to many mixed unobservable tools which are very expensive to control through other mechanisms, rather than toward other employees, whose actions can be controlled more cheaply through market and authority control tools.

4.5   Some examples

Consider the treatment of information in organizations. Principals will seek to structure positions so as to allocate information to those who will use it most effectively to increase the size of the organizational surplus. However, this cooperative motive is entangled with conflict incentives since agents with access to certain information may use it to enhance their claim on the surplus at the expense of the principals. Principals, therefore, will structure positions so as to balance these two considerations, and consequently the stronger the conflict motive, the less useful information will be allocated to agents. It is for this reason that an increase in access to information by workers has been found to occur in firms that are transformed from conventional to worker-owned firms. In conventional firms the conflict of interest between workers and owners induces owners to limit the amount of financial, technical and product information that workers possess to the detriment of the total surplus.[24] In worker-owned firms, this conflict is reduced (but not eliminated) as all participants are principals; consequently, information flows more freely to enhance the organizational surplus (Manning, 1989).

Agreements that may be desirable to all participants may not be concluded because of asymmetric information. Because the refusal to engage in certain agreements often harms the interests of all participants, an incentive exists to share information. Participants may therefore forego some conflict tools in favor of cooperation. One means of sharing information is effected when agents willingly submit themselves to monitoring. Symmetrically, principals may relinquish some of their controlling rights in order to provide agents with directly verifiable information that can serve as basis for superior agreements and

understandings. This can be achieved, for example, through employee representation on the board of directors of conventional firms. Agents and principals may
therefore share some information while at the same time guarding and
manipulating other information.

Another illustration is provided by the issue of investment in physical and
human capital. Participants' decisions on investments balance their beneficial
impact on the size of the organizational surplus (the cooperation motive) and
their detrimental impact on investors' share in it due to loss of bargaining power
induced by the sunk cost (the conflict motive). The conflict motive reduces the
level of investments; for instance, investments that may enlarge the organizational surplus are partly foregone in conventional firms because they enhance the
bargaining power of workers and therefore reduce owners' profits (Grout, 1984;
Moene, 1988). In worker-owned firms, this particular consideration is absent,
enabling more favorable investments.

The design of positions provides an illustration of the lattice of interests
attending the organizational structure. In many conventional firms the division
of labor is very fine and is accompanied by detailed job classifications. This
generates a "dense" lattice of interests and makes it harder to create broad and
powerful coalitions of agents against principals.[25] In worker-owned firms there is
a coarser division of labor and job classifications are less detailed.[26] Another
crucial difference is exhibited by the dual organizational structure employed in
worker-owned firms: on the one hand, workers participate in strategic decision-
making (of the kind reserved to the board of directors in conventional firms), but
on the other the authority mechanism is used to implement the goals set by
workers. While dual structures are used also in some conventional firms, the
definition of workers' positions as agents is not fundamentally altered (Kanter,
1983).

It is a commonplace that the three control mechanisms discussed earlier are
simultaneously employed in organizations. The trade-off among the mechanisms
is discussed by Armstrong (1989) and Bradach and Eccles (1989) in studies of
contemporary organizations. North (1990b) observes a trade-off that varies
across societies and changes over time based on a historical analysis; Ben-Porat
(1980) compares the heavier reliance on trust within families with the more
prominent role of market and authority control in business firms. Finally, the
degree of reliance on control mechanisms depends on the degree of conflict and
cooperation in organizations, which is affected by the extent of separation
between principals and agents. As remarked already, in worker-owned firms
employees are the principals, which induces an internalization of conflict that is
not attainable in conventional firms. As a result, in worker-owned firms control is
motivated more by cooperation than in conventional firms, with attendant
differences in organizational structure (Ben-Ner, 1988a).

5   The allocation of ultimate control in organizations

This section presents a preliminary investigation of the considerations underlying the allocation of ultimate control. Controllers may occupy any organiza-

tional position. In fact, although many organizations in market economies are controlled by a sub-set of participants on the supply side – owners of capital who do not work in their own firms – ultimate control is often wielded by participants in other positions as well. For instance, the roles of labor and capital suppliers are combined in worker-owned firms, partnerships, and sole proprietorships. Demand-side participants hold control rights in consumer cooperatives and non-profit organizations, and also in conventional firms which were formed through forward vertical integration by customers. Thus contemporary experience suggests that control rights do not necessarily or "naturally" reside with a single type of participant.

Control has value for those who wield it because it enhances their interests – hence control is desirable. However, both the acquisition of control and its exercise entail costs. Control will therefore be appropriated by those for whom it yields the greatest *net* value. Both the value and costs of control vary across participants with different positions and depend on a number of organizational and external variables.[27]

The *value of control* is greater the better the controllers' ability to promote cooperation rather than conflict. Such ability is affected by organizational skills and experience (or the capability to engage the services of others with such attributes), and by the organizational position of participants. The position of controlling participants is important because it determines the extent of the lattice of interests (including the overlap of interests between them and other participants). The value of control over specific areas of an organization also varies with participants' position; for example, control over working conditions may be more valuable to a worker than to others. In addition, participants may not be indifferent to the mere exercise of control: as in the political arena, there are those who may prefer not to be controlled by others, not even by benevolent rulers (even when they believe that they are motivated by the desire for cooperation).

The *costs of control* are related to participants' ability to exercise various tools of control, which in turn depends on their skills and experience as well as on their organizational position. Workers, for example, are more apt to observe each other than other participants, but less able to exercise financial control directly. The most important cost of control is probably incurred during the attempt to gain access to it. Given a *status quo* with some incumbent controllers, control may be transferred in one of two ways. In a cooperative environment it can be transferred, for example, to the highest bidder. Importantly, this is predicated on the effective functioning of institutions outside the organization itself, such as financial markets on which contestants may borrow funds for the purchase of control. In an organization where cooperation is mixed with conflict, such a transfer mechanism may not be feasible and attempts will be made to gain and retain control by also using conflict tools. Since incumbent controllers determine the organizational structure, they may arrange it so as to impose large costs on wresting away control. This is the celebrated "power of incumbency."[28]

The *net value of control* thus depends on its costs relative to the gains from its exercise. The net value differs for holders of different positions, and may even be negative. For example, suppliers of a minor input to an organization may not gain enough from being involved in organizational control to merit the costs, whereas it may pay to banks with major debt holding to share ultimate control with other participants. Although the value of control net of the costs of exercising it may be larger for contesters of control than for incumbents, the cost of acquisition of control may tip the balance of the net value in favor of incumbents. Workers, for example, may face large acquisition costs due to the strategies employed by owners already in control, although once in control, their net gains may be greater than those of owners of capital.

Finally, the identities of ultimate controllers are not fully interchangeable. Occupiers of some positions may assume roles that other participants cannot: for example, workers can supply capital in lieu of capital suppliers, whereas the latter are less likely to be able to provide their labor actually to displace workers. Similarly, consumers may be able to make production decisions, but owners cannot make consumption decisions for their firms' customers.

The variables which are external to individual organizations but which influence the allocation of ultimate control in them can now be summarized. These variables include: (1) the economic and legal systems which affect who may engage in organizational control, what are its bases, and what are the rights associated with it; (2) the history of participants in terms of occupation, wealth, values, and the like; (3) the identity of incumbent controllers; and (4) the available technology of production, which affects the positions needed in the organization and their content, the extent of opportunities for cooperation and conflict as well as the tools to act on them, the control possibilities embedded in the technology, and therefore the net value of control to different participants.

In sum, control rights are not necessarily vested in participants who could exercise it most effectively. "Natural" as well as strategically erected barriers to entry, the power of incumbency, historical legacies, and the advantage of first-movers are some of the main reasons control may be vested in the "wrong" hands. It is the conflict among principals and agents that may prevent the achievement of Pareto-optimal solutions that entail the assignment of control to those who can use it to generate the largest organizational surplus. When these and other factors are fully accounted for, the assignment of control to participants is likely to follow the calculus outlined above.[29]

6   Conclusions

The objective of this chapter has been to examine the criteria behind the design of organizations, focusing on the relationship between cooperation, conflict. and control. The theory developed suggests that each organizational position consists of a set of "tools" which define what its occupiers should and should not do, and also determine the "interests" of its occupiers. The structure of positions in an organization generates a lattice of interests, which in turn engenders both cooperation and conflict among participants in the organization. *Both* cooperation and conflict create incentives for control; some tools of cooperation-induced control differ from those of conflict-induced control. Those who control organizations therefore structure positions in view of the importance of tools and interests associated with them, and choose a set of control mechanisms that promotes their own interests.

Consequently, the identity of those who hold ultimate control – essentially, the controllers' organizational position – determines the organizational design, that is, the structure of positions and the combination of control tools and mechanisms. Organizational design will thus be different, for example, in bank-controlled versus shareholder-controlled firms, capital-owned versus worker-owned firms, seller-controlled versus consumer-controlled firms, and so forth. Variations are also introduced by the nature of available technologies and other factors that affect the tools that can be employed in different positions and the comparative costs of different control mechanisms. Thus, for instance, in more closely-knit groups trust control can partly substitute for market and authority control, whereas in highly "transparent" economic activities market control may make investments in trust redundant.

Finally, the assignment of control to different organizational participants follows the principle of allocation to the highest-net-value user. This calculus must, however, incorporate the costs of transfer of control imposed by the power of incumbency and by other barriers in situations characterized by conflict, as is the case in most organizations where principals and agents are separate entities. In such situations control is not necessarily held by those who maximize the organizational surplus.

This chapter's theory of cooperation, conflict and control, presented in general and fairly abstract terms, has implications for empirical research on organizations. In particular, the theory calls for (1) a careful documentation of various tools associated with different positions (including both "shoulds" and "should nots") and an analysis of the interests they generate, (2) an examination of different mechanisms of control and the tools employed in their support, and (3) a comparison of positions and of control mechanisms in different types of organization (e.g., conventional versus worker-owned firms). The first point holds the key to structural sources of cooperation and conflict, whereas the second indicates how an organization responds to both. The third point is indispensable since little can be learned from *actual* practices (which do not reveal what *could have been* done); comparison across types of organization is an alternative to counterfactual theorizing. Since cooperation enhances the organizational surplus and conflict frequently reduces it, an empirical study of organizational design in different typs of organizations will also highlight their comparative-productivity attributes.

Notes

Valuable comments were made by Victor Devinatz, Herbert Gintis, Egon Neuberger, Tone Ognedal, Woody Powell, Ekkehart Schlicht, Jan Svejnar, Theresa Van Hoomissen and participants at the "Conference on Corporate Governance" at the University of Minnesota (1990). A seed grant from the Conflict and Change Center at the University of Minnesota is gratefully acknowledged, as is use of research facilities at the Center for Urban Affairs and Policy Research at Northwestern University.

1. Putterman (1988a) quotes Robertson's characterization of firms as "islands of cooperation like lumps of butter coagulating in a pail of buttermilk" (1930:85). For an elaborate characterization of different approaches to conflict and cooperation, see Bowles (1985).

2. Williamson (1985) is a rare exception among economists in dealing with the function of some positions and the tools that can be employed by their occupants.

3. In linking contributions from economics with those from sociology and social psychology, this chapter answers (to a limited degree) Baron's (1988) call for informing economic analysis of the employment relationship with insights from other social sciences disciplines. The influence of Baron (1988) on this chapter will be obvious to the reader.

4. A position thus includes both formal and informal actions that can be undertaken by its holders. This combines what Mackenzie (1986) calls "regular" and "virtual" positions.

5. For example, among supply-side participants, a worker's utility depends on his or her productive activities via the wage, working conditions, and effort exertion, a manager's utility depends on his or her supervisory and administrative activities via salary, working conditions and effort, whereas a provider of capital is concerned with monetary returns to investment. A supplier's utility depends on the price and quantity combination it secures from customers. The structure of units affects the attitude of a division's management about the various elements of the division's performance. A participant's place in the system of jobs affects his or her interest in more profitable versus more skill-enhancing technologies.

6. This is the common social sciences definition of control and power (see, e.g., Dahl, 1957; Bowles and Gintis, 1990). Control has often been used synonymously with power, authority, influence and other related concepts. As will be argued shortly, authority is just one, albeit important, mechanism of control in organizations. Most distinctions between control and power made in the literature serve little analytic purpose (e.g., Manz and Gioia, 1983). Power in the game-theoretic usage may be regarded as a global measure for the consequences of the deployment of control actions; see Binmore, Rubinstein, and Wolinsky (1985) and Harsanyi (1977) on bargaining power, Shapley (1953) on power indices, Moulin and Peleg (1982) on the effectivity function approach, and Barry (1989) for a review of different solution concepts. For a discussion of the bases of power from a different perspective (though leading to similar conclusions), see Pfeffer (1981). For a detailed discussion of control from a social–psychological perspective, see Tannenbaum (1976).

7. By this definition, delegated and discretionary control constitute examples of attenuated control, as does the right of unions, wrested away from management, to control certain aspects of the workplace. Bowles and Gintis (1990) relate ultimate control ("short-side power") to excess supply of workers. Principals and agents may sometimes be the same participants in an organization. For example, in worker-owned firms this distinction is eliminated. However, for the purpose of generality of the analysis, the distinction between the two types of participants will be retained with the understanding that it may accommodate the possibility mentioned here.

8. The two terms will be used interchangeably, according to contextual and grammatical convenience.

9. Mixed tools are "undecomposable" in the sense used by Hurwicz (1960). Most organizational tools seem to be mixed. For example, information can be transmitted accurately to help its receiver, or be manipulated to cause harm. Similarly, a hammer may be used to perform a productive task, or to sabotage another tool.

10. Related terminology (in the sociological tradition) includes remunerative, normative and coercive power; see, for example, Etzioni (1975).

11. Authority is often defined as legitimate decision-making power. However, within the theoretical framework of this chapter authority need not be legitimate; in fact, it may be continuously contested.

12. This definition of organizational design is closely related to those offered in the literature. In particular, Tirole (1988) views organizational design as the game played between the organization's members. Mintzberg (1979) focuses on both coordination mechanisms and the division of labor as major components of organizational design. A somewhat narrower definition, focusing mainly on positions, is suggested by Huber and McDaniel (1986) and Malone (1987).

13. There are obvious pitfalls in motivating general propositions with simple examples. For instance, with more than two participants there cannot be completely opposed interests, an important point in understanding behavior in organizations. Nevertheless, the example in Figure 12.1 helps identify important issues in an easy way.

14. Agent A will probably mix a_1 and a_2 with equal probability, and B will mix b_1 and b_2, also with equal probability. The expected payoffs can be calculated on this basis.

15. For example, once the superior outcome has been agreed upon, participant A has an incentive to carry out action a_1 for a payoff of 6 instead of 5 which would result from a_2 under the assumption that B carries out b_2. Anticipating that, participant B will not go along with the agreement that yields the best joint outcome. This is a classic prisoner's dilemma situation.

16. For diverse discussions of the production of trust in organizations, see Fox (1974), Sen (1977), Axelrod (1984), Shapiro (1987), Kreps (1990a), Gambetta (1988), Armstrong (1989), Bradach and Eccles (1989) and Williamson (1990). Trust can be also generated through the legal enforcement of agreements by a third party. This requirement is predicated on a third party's ability to verify participants' actions (or their direct consequences) and to impose penalties in the event of reneging on agreements.

17. For related discussion and examples, see Fox (1974); on joint control, see Purcell (1979).

18. Thus "the boss knows better" may be true not only because the boss needs to know better in response to surplus-enhancing specialization, but also because greater knowledge may be interpreted (at least by uninformed subordinates) at the source of broad decision-making ability that should be respected and trusted.

19. Administration was appositely compared by Marx to the conducting of an orchestra: "All combined labor on a large scale requires, more or less, a directing authority, in order to secure the harmonious working of the individual activities, and to perform the general functions that have their origin in the action of the combined organism, as distinguished from the actions of its separate organs. A single violin player is his own conductor, an orchestra requires a separate one. The work of directing, superintending, and adjusting, becomes one of the functions of capital, from the moment that the labor under the control of capital, becomes co-operative" (Marx, 1967:50).

20. Alchian and Demsetz (1972a) fail to distinguish between cooperation and conflict, and erroneously conclude that all participants desire monitoring. They also state that members of worker-owned firms will *also* be interested in monitoring, whereas the argument in the text suggests that in fact they are *more* likely to do so than participants

in conventional firms. However, the form of monitoring will differ considerably; for example, worker-owned firms are likely to employ mainly mutual monitoring whereas conventional firms will rely on monitoring by specialized agents.

21. See Fox's (1974) parallel discussion of trust employed to control high-discretion tasks. "Professional ethics" are often invoked as a trust control tool for many unobservable activities, including mental ones.

22. The implications of complicated lattices of interests may be gleaned from the Yugoslav case at the national level (Ben-Ner and Neuberger, 1990). Changes in the definition of the positions of Yugoslav republics and of individual enterprises, entailing the addition of some mixed tools (such as compulsory participation in negotiations on the determination of various economic variables) have also profoundly altered their interests. This has probably exacerbated the conflict among various participants (regional political units and enterprises) during the 1970s and 1980s, and increased their ability to act in their own interests, creating havoc in the economy. The Yugoslav reality approximates an organization composed only of principals.

23. Various control-related phenomena can be examined by using standard analysis from the theory of the firm. For example, the existence of a stock of trust due, for example, to family relations among participants, can be analyzed as a situation in which the firm is endowed with a given quantity of a certain input, which will influence in obvious ways the use of other inputs – control tools.

24. Surplus is lost for two principal reasons. The division of labor will be excessive relative to cooperation because principals seek to reduce the amount of information held by any individual agent. In addition, in their search to improve their information basis, workers may strike and engage in other surplus-damaging activities. See Ben-Ner and Jun (1991a) for a detailed discussion of information-sharing in conventional firms.

25. For related analyses, see Gintis (1976), Roemer (1979), and Bowles (1985).

26. See Davy's (1983) discussion of the change in the structure of positions in a firm after it has been transferred to the control of its workers.

27. Only a sketch of the calculus of assignment of control will be presented here. For more detailed analysis, see Ben-Ner (1986, 1988), Hansmann (1988), Ben-Ner and Van Hoomissen (1991) and Ben-Ner and Jun (1991b) on the assignment of control to labor versus capital on the supply side, and to supply-side participants versus demand-side participants.

28. One example is provided by the practice of "poison pills" in takeover "battles." Another example (the empirical validity of which is debated) is the deskilling of workers to prevent them from being able to acquire effective control in firms (Braverman, 1974). The concept, critical to the understanding of the identity of controllers, has been largely ignored so far in the social sciences (Williamson, 1990).

29. The reader will note the difference between this statement and the "Coase theorem" (Coase, 1960).

13 Wage bargaining and the choice of production technique in capitalist firms

GILBERT L. SKILLMAN and HARL E. RYDER

1 Introduction

Does it matter who owns and directs the means of production? In particular, does the structure of ownership and command influence the choice of production technique in any important way? Given complete and competitive markets, the answer to the latter question is "no," as illustrated by the first welfare theorem for production economies: existence of Walrasian equilibrium implies that only efficient techniques are adopted, no matter how ownership is divided or who directs production. This is an example of what Bowles and Gintis (1988) have termed the principles of "neutrality of property assignment" and "irrelevance of command."

These principles may not be supported in the absence of complete and competitive markets. In this chapter, we explore the implications of distributional conflict in labor markets for the choice of production techniques in capitalist firms. Such conflicts stem from possible bilateral monopoly conditions arising from the presence of significant mutual costs of exit from given employment relationships. Potential sources of exit cost in labor markets derive from such problems as search, factor-specificity, asymmetric information, and task idiosyncrasy, which are frequently encountered in such markets.

We study the distribution of production rents in capitalist firms as a bargaining relationship between owners of firms and the labor teams they employ. Following the seminal work of Rubinstein (1982), we model the relationship as a game in extensive form in which bargaining proceeds over real time and is costly to the participants. We relate equilibrium outcomes to the structure of ownership, and suggest that the choice of production technique in capitalist firms may be driven by considerations of bargaining power as well as of efficiency.

Finally, we discuss the implications of our analysis for the choice of production technique under alternative social arrangements including worker ownership of firms. We close by considering directions for future research.

2 The bargaining game

We represent distributional conflict in a capitalist firm as a bilateral bargaining relationship between the owner of the firm and the labor team it employs in which each worker bargains with the owner over his or her individual wage. This construction reflects the assumption that owners of capital inputs (or their proxies) hire labor inputs, and not vice-versa,[1] and the assumption that workers do not collude in bargaining with the firm. We consider the strategic implications of collective bargaining below. All parties can exit the relationship, but the firm owner enjoys the strategic option of replacing any sub-set of the labor team subsequent to disagreement in bargaining. In contrast, each worker can choose only to bargain or exit the relationship entirely.

The cost of exit to the firm is captured by the idea that its incumbent workers have accumulated firm-specific human capital which is diminished when any incumbent worker is replaced.

Thus, we imagine a bargaining process between firm K and its incumbent labor team L, consisting of workers $i = 1, 2$. Let bargaining periods be denoted $t = 0, 1, 2, \ldots$, and let x_i represent the wage suggested for worker i in a given period, no matter who makes the offer. Correspondingly, we can write $x = (x_1, x_2)$, the vector of wage offers in a given period, and $x_L = \Sigma_i x_i$, the total wage offer in a given period.

Let z_{jm} represent j's response to m's offer, where either j or $m = K$ (but not both), and $z_{jm} \in \{Y, N, E\}$ for all j, m; the elements of the set denote, respectively, acceptance, rejection, and exit. Further, let $z_K = (z_{K1}, z_{K2})$ and $z_L = (z_{1K}, z_{2K})$.

If the firm exits bargaining with an incumbent worker, it replaces that worker in production with an outsider who is paid the reservation utility $a_L \geqslant 0$, assumed to be the same for all workers, incumbent or otherwise. Thus, we assume a strategic disparity between incumbent and potential workers, in that the latter's pay is determined by a Walrasian market process.

The surplus to be bargained over is denoted $V_n, n = 0, 1, 2$, understood as the gross rent generated when there are n incumbents in the labor team undertaking production; it is assumed that production commences only after all bargaining has concluded. To capture the notion that exit is costly to the firm owner, we assume $V_2 > V_1 > V_0$. In addition, we assume that the firm owner prefers producing with no incumbents to not producing at all, other things being equal.

Bargaining is assumed to proceed as follows. Bargaining commences in period $t = 0$ with incumbent workers 1 and 2 making simultaneous offers to K, who responds to both offers simultaneously.

If worker i's offer is accepted, i.e., $z_{Ki} = Y$, bargaining concludes between that worker and the firm owner, and the worker receives the agreed-upon x_i after production takes place. If the firm owner chooses $z_{Ki} = E$, the worker is replaced and receives a payoff of a_L (not paid out of the firm's surplus).

If one and only one worker's offer is rejected, i.e., $z_{Ki} = N$, $z_{Kj} \neq N$, $i \neq j$, bargaining continues between the worker whose offer is rejected and the firm owner, beginning with the latter's counter-offer in period $t = 1$. This bargaining sub-game is structurally equivalent to the Rubinstein two-person bargaining game with exit. The surplus to be divided in this case depends on the disposition of bargaining with worker $j \neq i$: if $z_{Kj} = Y$, $V_2 - x_j$ is to be divided, and if $z_{Kj} = E$, the surplus V_1 is contested.

Finally, if both offers are rejected, i.e., $z_K = (N, N)$, the firm in period $t = 1$

makes simultaneous counter-offers to the members of L, who respond simultaneously. The consequences of the nine possible values of z_L are as in the initial bargaining round, except that a worker who uniquely rejects the firm's offer commences subsequent bilateral bargaining with the firm owner in period $t = 2$, and subsequent to $z_L = (N, N)$ the workers make simultaneous offers to K, as in period $t = 0$. This process continues until all bargaining is concluded or both incumbents are replaced.

Bargaining is assumed to be a costly activity. We employ the "fixed bargaining cost" version of Rubinstein's bilateral model: each rejection of an offer imposes a cost of $c_i > 0$ on the players who continue bargaining[2] (a worker whose offer has been accepted incurs no additional bargaining costs). Assume $c_1 = c_2 = c_L$.

It will be useful for the subsequent argument to differentiate bargaining sub-games. Precise identification would require a specification of the history of play leading up to each sub-game; however, for our purposes it will be sufficient to indicate the player(s) making offer(s) at a given decision node, and the response $z_j, j = L, K$, which immediately precedes that node.

Accordingly, let Γ denote any sub-game which commences with members of the labor team making simultaneous offers to K, noting that this also refers to the game itself and that for $t = 2\tau, \tau = 1, 2, 3, \ldots, \Gamma$ can be reached only by successive plays of (N, N).

Let Γ^K denote the sub-game which commences with K making simultaneous offers to both workers. This is first reached in period $t = 1$ subsequent to a play of $z_K = (N, N)$ at $t = 0$. The sub-game is subsequently encountered at periods $t = 2\tau + 1, \tau = 1, 2, 3, \ldots$, via an uninterrupted series of (N, N) responses.

Let $\Gamma^K(z_K)$ be a bilateral bargaining sub-game immediately preceded by response z_K, noting that K makes the first offer in any such sub-game. The value of the surplus to be bargained over and the identity of K's bargaining opponent will be indicated by the specification of z_K; for example, in the first round of $\Gamma^K(E, N)$, K initiates bargaining with worker 2 over the distribution of V_1.

Similarly, let $\Gamma(z_L)$ denote a bilateral sub-game immediately preceded by response vector z_L in which a worker first makes an offer to K. Once again, the identity of the worker and the size of the surplus to be divided will be indicated by specifying z_L; for example, in the first period of $\Gamma(N, Y)$, worker 1 initiates bargaining with K over the surplus $V_2 - x_2$, where x_2 is the offer previously accepted by worker 2.

A detail of the extensive form described above is presented in Figure 13.1.

The solution concept we adopt in analyzing this game is that of sub-game perfect equilibrium, which requires that candidate strategies satisfy Nash-equilibrium on all proper sub-games. The intuitive force of this condition is to permit as equilibrium strategies only those to which players can credibly commit. It is this restriction to credible strategies which drives the strong results of the Rubinstein approach; a continuum of equilibrium points can be found for bargaining games such as the one constructed above if players can be presumed to commit to strategies which are not subsequently rational to carry out (an

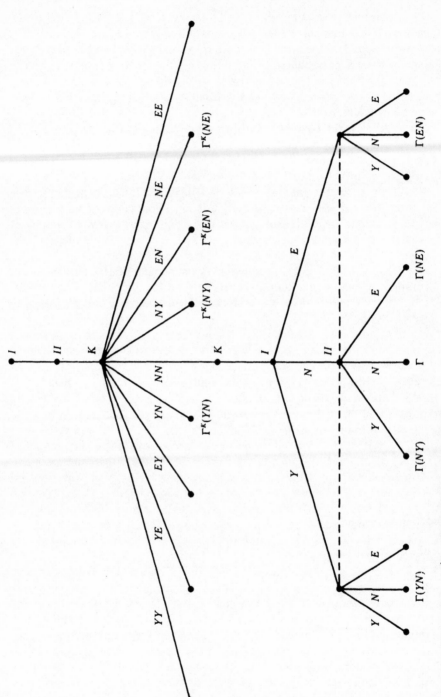

Figure 13.1 A detail of the multilateral bargaining game

example of this is a "bad-faith bargaining" strategy in which a player insists on receiving (virtually) the entire surplus, without regard to the strategies of the other player).

Denote the set of equilibrium payoffs to player j (net of previously incurred bargaining costs) on sub-games Γ, Γ^K, $\Gamma(z_L)$, and $\Gamma^K(z_K)$ respectively by Π_j, Π_j^K, $\Pi_j(z_L)$, and $\Pi_j^K(z_K)$, with respective elements π_j, π_j^K, $\pi_j(z_L)$, and $\pi_j^K(z_K)$.

Attention is now turned to the solution of this bargaining game.

3   Bargaining outcomes and the firm's choice of technique

In this section, we first indicate the logical structure of the solution, and then discuss implications of the equilibrium outcomes for the choice of production technique in capitalist firms. For expositional focus we subsequently narrow attention to a particular case of the three-person game. The general solution and its proof are available from the authors.

3.1   Equilibrium in the two-person sub-games

The solution technique for sub-game perfection involves establishing equilibria wherever possible on the proper sub-games of Γ, and then using backward induction to derive optimal strategies in the first round of play, based on expectations of subsequent equilibrium play and making use of the recursive structure of the game.

The sub-games $\Gamma^K(z_K)$, $\Gamma(z_L)$, reached by asymmetric responses to joint offers such that one offer is rejected, are structurally equivalent to the two-person bargaining games first studied by Rubinstein, augmented by the exit options discussed above. Solutions to these games are already known.

Stated generically, the solution to the sequential bargaining game with players α and β (with α making the first offer), bargaining costs (c_α, c_β), and gross surplus V is such that

$$\Pi_\alpha = \begin{cases} \{V - a_\beta\} & \text{if } c_\beta > c_\alpha \\ \{\min(a_\alpha + c_\beta, V - a_\beta)\} & \text{if } c_\alpha > c_\beta \\ [\min\{(a_\alpha + c_\beta, V - a_\beta)\}, V - a_\beta] & \text{if } c_\alpha = c_\beta. \end{cases} \tag{1}$$

Note that the player with lower fixed bargaining cost essentially receives the entire surplus (exactly so in the limit as $\max_i c_i \to 0$). This strong result rather offends intuition and is perhaps the chief weakness of the fixed bargaining cost model.[3]

Applying the generic results reported in (1) to the two-person sub-games defined in the present game (and letting $a_L = 0$), we find

$$\Pi_K^K(E, N) = \Pi_K^K(N, E) = \begin{cases} \{V_1\} & \text{if } c_L > c_K \\ \{\min(V_0 + c_L, V_1)\} & \text{if } c_K > c_L \\ [\min(V_0 + c_L, V_1), V_1] & \text{if } c_L = c_K; \end{cases} \tag{2a}$$

222   *Gilbert L. Skillman and Harl E. Ryder*

$$\Pi_K^k(Y,N) = \Pi_K^k(N,Y) = \begin{cases} \{V_2 - x_j\} & \text{if } c_L > c_K \\ \{\min(V_1 - x_j + c_L, V_2 - x_j)\} & \text{if } c_K > c_L \\ [\min(V_1 - x_j + c_L, V_2 - x_j), V_2 - x_j] & \text{if } c_K = c_L, \end{cases}$$
(2b)

where x_j is the wage to be paid to the worker whose offer was previously accepted;

$$\Pi_i(z_{iK} = N, z_{jK} = Y) = \begin{cases} \{\min(c_K, V_2 - V_1)\} & \text{if } c_L > c_K \\ \{V_2 - V_1\} & \text{if } c_K > c_L \\ [\min(c_K, V_2 - V_1), V_2 - V_1] & \text{if } c_L = c_K; \end{cases}$$
(2c)

and

$$\Pi_i(z_{iK} = N, z_{jK} = E) = \begin{cases} \{\min(c_K, V_1 - V_0)\} & \text{if } c_L > c_K \\ \{V_1 - V_0\} & \text{if } c_K > c_L \\ [\min(c_K, V_1 - V_0), V_1 - V_0] & \text{if } c_L = c_K. \end{cases}$$
(2d)

(If $a_L > 0$, then the indicated payoff ranges to i are increased by a_L, and those for K decreased by a_L.)

In each case, the payoff to the opponent of the indicated player j is simply the surplus to be shared *less* π_j, since bargaining concludes immediately (the sole exception is when $c_L = c_K$, in which case equilibria exist which do not involve immediate acceptance; in that case, the supremum of the opponent's equilibrium payoff set is the relevant surplus minus π_j, see Rubinstein, 1982). For example, the unique payoff to K on $\Gamma(Y,N)$ for $c_K > c_L$ and $a_L = 0$ is $V_2 - (V_2 - V_1) = V_1$.

With these results, we can specify the consequences of all values of z_K and z_L except (N,N). Solution of the entire game will require an analysis of the latter option; this problem is addressed in the next sub-section.

3.2   Solution to the three-person game

The solution to the complete game depends on the relative values of c_L, c_K, $(V_1 - V_0)$, and $(V_2 - V_1)$. We focus on the case which yields results of interest to the present discussion; the general solution to the game is available from the authors.

Thus, in what follows we assume

$$c_L < c_K < (V_2 - V_1) < (V_1 - V_0).$$
(3)

The first inequality guarantees that workers enjoy bargaining power; as suggested by the results for the two-person sub-games, the firm reaps essentially the entire rent if $c_K > c_L$, and may do so if $c_K = c_L$.

The second inequality is merely for convenience. It will emerge in any case when we evaluate the solution in the limit as $c_K \to 0$.

The strategic significance of the third inequality will be made apparent in the following discussion. It implies that the firm's cost of exit in terms of foregone gross rent is increasing in the number of incumbents replaced.

Given (3), equilibrium exists and is such that bargaining concludes immediately with the firm accepting both workers' offers. Evaluated in the limit as $c_K \to 0$, the unique payoffs to K and L are simply

$$x_L^* = 2a_L + 2(V_2 - V_1)$$
$$\pi_K^* = V_2 - x_L^* = 2V_1 - V_2 - 2a_L. \tag{4}$$

To get a sense of why this result obtains, consider the strategic options faced by L and K at $t = 0$. For any offer x, K can choose from among nine responses, as illustrated in Figure 13.1. The payoffs to each response are fully determined by (2) and (3) and by making use of the recursive structure of the game. Thus, given x at $t = 0$, we can unambiguously determine K's optimal response. It is straightforward to show that, given (2) and (3), responses EN, NE, YN, and NY are strictly dominated, and thus will not be chosen by K in any case.

Now consider the options faced by a worker, say worker 1, in selecting an opening round offer, given K's expected response. Ignoring the possibility that K chooses NN for a moment, the worker avoids being replaced and receiving payoff a_L only if K finds it optimal to select YY or YE. It is straightforward to show that this implies that the worker can demand *at most* $x_1 = a_L + (V_2 - V_1)$. Explicit consideration of the NN option does not significantly change this conclusion (and the difference disappears in the limit as $c_K \to 0$).

Similar reasoning shows that the workers together can expect to receive *at least* $2a_L + 2(V_2 - V_1)$ (how this total is to be divided is not uniquely determined). Thus, given that equilibrium exists (which is easy to demonstrate), the solution is as given in (4).

The significance of the third inequality of (3) in the above is that for any x the firm strictly prefers replacing just one incumbent worker to replacing both. Thus, the effect of the assumption is to render the firm's "divide and conquer" threat credible.

Therefore, the sense of the solution given in (4) can be stated as follows: given that workers have bargaining power and the firm's "divide and conquer" threat is credible, the firm's equilibrium payoff is strictly decreasing in V_2, the maximum attainable gross rent.

Alternatively, if the structure of V_n is interpreted as due to firm-specific skills, the result indicates that the firm's equilibrium payoff is strictly declining in the marginal product of embodied firm-specific skill, for given V_2.

3.3   Implications for the firm's choice of production technique

Imagine now that a potential firm owner is considering the choice of production technique prior to entering a given line of business, and suppose that alternative techniques are represented by the pair (V_1^k, V_2^k), $k = 1, 2, 3, \ldots, M$. If fully aware of the subsequent strategic consequences of this choice, will the prospective owner necessarily choose the most productive technique, i.e., that which yields the maximal value of V_2?

As indicated by (4), the answer is "no": depending on the set of available techniques, the owner may rationally choose to sacrifice V_2 if the value $(V_2 - V_1)$, the cost of replacing one incumbent, is thereby reduced by at least half as much, other things being equal. For example, the profit-maximizing firm would choose $(6, 8)$ over $(5, 9)$.

The result can be generalized so as to provide a theory of labor demand in bargaining environments. It is straightforward to show that for labor teams of size $n \geqslant 2$, equilibrium exists such that the firm's payoff for given n is

$$\pi_K^* = V_n - n((V_n - V_{n-1}) + a_L)).$$

(This is a generalization of (4). However, we do not know if this equilibrium payoff is unique for all n; we assume in what follows that it is.)

To see the implications of this outcome for the choice of labor team size, let us proceed as if n were continuously-valued and $V_n = V(n)$, a twice continuously differentiable function such that $V' > 0$ for all n.

The social payoff to n is given by

$$V(n) + (m - n)a_L, \tag{5}$$

where $m \geqslant n$ is the size of the labor pool from which the firm hires. In contrast, if the firm chooses n in light of consequent bargaining outcomes, it solves

$$\max_n V(n) - n(V'(n) + a_L). \tag{6}$$

The social optimal choice of n solves $V'(n) = a_L$; however, given an interior solution to (6), the firm chooses n to solve $-nV''(n) = a_L$. The firm's choice is thus efficient for all values of a_L only in a special case that $V(n)$ is an affine transformation of $\log n$.

4   Discussion

We have shown that, under plausible conditions, rent-seeking motives may distort a capitalist owner's choice of production technique. In this section we consider whether this perversity can be alleviated under feasible complementary or alternative social arrangements. We consider three such arrangements: contracting, collective bargaining, and worker ownership of firms.

4.1   Contracting

To focus the discussion, we assume that workers acquire a bargaining wedge only after entering employment relationships, as in the attainment of firm-specific human capital. Thus initial hires might occur under competitive conditions. Clearly, the argument we have advanced suggests that there is scope for Pareto-improving agreements which could, in principle at least, be reached at the point of initial hire. The inefficiencies considered above could be avoided with the use of sufficiently complete contracts.

However, short of involuntary servitude, the contractual arrangements necessary to preclude "opportunistic" behavior of the kind we have described may be seriously hampered by problems of verifiability and enforcement. For example, workers could conceivably stipulate that an efficient technique be used in exchange for a promise to accept a lower wage than that made possible by bargaining in its presence. However, effective enforcement of this arrangement presumes that courts can distinguish among alternative techniques which may differ, say, only in the degree of task idiosyncrasy.

Furthermore, it is difficult to imagine enforceable contractual language which could prevent workers from re-opening negotiations so as to take advantage of the bargaining power ensured by the efficient technique.

Alternatively, the firm might "sell" jobs with bargaining advantages, setting the price so that workers just achieve their reservation wage in present value. However, this does not eliminate the firm's perverse incentives in the choice of technique, and is hampered by possible liquidity constraints faced by workers.[4]

The argument may be illustrated by a comparison to "transaction costs" analysis as exemplified by the work of Williamson (1975, 1985). The presumption in that literature is that organizational innovations are adopted to minimize or avoid transactional dysfunctions similar to the type we analyze here, and are thus Pareto-improving. If, however, rent-seeking motives also inform the choice of organizational form, and complete contracting is difficult or infeasible (a central premise of the transaction cost approach), then it is less clear that adopted organizational forms yield Pareto-improvements.

4.2   Collective bargaining

Our theoretical results are based on the assumption that workers do not collude in bargaining, so that the firm can feasibly threaten "divide and conquer" bargaining strategies. True collective bargaining, i.e., collusion in making and responding to offers, deprives the firm of this option and thus eliminates the perverse motives in choice of production technique (if asymmetric responses to wage offers are excluded, the equilibrium payoff to the firm under the conditions stated in section 3.2 is always $V_0 - 2a_L$).

However, explicit consideration of worker collusion does not fundamentally alter the strategic relationship between firm and workers; the firm would still gain were it able credibly to pursue the "divide and conquer" strategy. The firm thus has the incentive to invest in obstructing worker collusion. Whether or not it pays the firm to act upon this incentive depends on such factors as the legal status of collective bargaining and the resources workers invest in maintaining collusion.

Our analysis yields the striking implication that unionization may actually improve productive efficiency in the "long run" by offsetting the perverse incentives which stem from the firm's "divide and conquer" option. However, the strength of this conclusion depends on the extent to which rent-seeking behavior is deterred, and not simply redirected.

4.3   Worker ownership

Would perverse incentives in the choice of production technique similar to those discussed in section 3.3 necessarily arise if, contrary to our initial assumption, workers owned the firms and hired capital inputs? Or might worker-owned firms be superior on these grounds?

A complete answer to these questions would require analyses of two qualitatively distinct bargaining problems. On the other hand, there is the essentially bilateral relationship between firm owners and input suppliers who do not share in ownership, an example of which is analyzed in the present chapter. There is an essential asymmetry in this relationship in that it represents bargaining between suppliers of different inputs. On the other hand, there is the potentially multilateral bargaining relationship among input suppliers of a certain type (here, physical or human capital) who are also co-owners of the firm and must collectively determine the production technique to be employed.

Under some conditions, worker-owned firms may avoid the perverse incentives generated when capitalist owners bargain with workers. This is due to a basic asymmetry in the characteristic of the two inputs, physical capital and human capital ("labor power"). Human capital is necessarily embodied in its supplier; therefore workers always enjoy the *potential* to exploit bargaining power which emerges from the imperfect fungibility of their asset (due to firm-specificity, search costs, etc.).

This is not necessarily the case for suppliers of physical capital, which is clearly not embodied in the supplier. Furthermore, capital in its liquid form cannot be firm-specific. Thus, the strategic nexus between *ex ante* competitive supplier and *ex post* bargainer can for the most part be broken by "hiring" capital in the form of credit, rather than, say, renting physical capital or issuing equity claims. In that case worker-owned firms may indeed be able to avoid the perverse incentives identified in our analysis.

There remains the question of the multilateral bargaining relationship among firm owners, and the implications of its solution for the choice of production technique. Earlier work on the multilateral bargaining problem suggests that its solution is qualitatively quite distinct from that of the bilateral problem, including the presence of multiple equilibria in general (see Binmore, 1986; Sutton, 1986).

It is therefore difficult to predict the implications of multilateral bargaining among supplier-owners for the problem we identify without further analysis. Note, however, that to the extent that labor inputs are homogeneous, worker-owners each receive the same bargaining advantages yielded by the production technique, so that there is correspondingly less immediate incentive to manipulate the choice of technique on strategic grounds.

Clearly further research is needed on this issue and the larger question of why, if labor-owned firms are indeed more efficient, they do not triumph as the dominant ownership form in market economies. For explorations of the latter issue, see Chapters 11 and 1 in this volume, by Dow and by Bowles and Gintis, respectively.

5   Conclusions

We advance strategic bargaining analysis as a powerful framework for exploring the consequences of property rights and organizational structure in non-classical economic environments. It is not meant, however, as a substitute for other approaches to this issue. Such concerns as the provision of efficient effort incentives are to some extent necessarily foreign to the strategic bargaining approach, and are more appropriately addressed in the context of transaction costs or asymmetric information models.

Thus, a central part of the research agenda is to work towards a comprehensive framework for the study of organizational structure which is sufficiently flexible to address a range of strategic and normative concerns. Some intriguing suggestions as to how to proceed with this agenda are found in Chapters 4 and 6 in this volume, by Hurwicz and Pagano, respectively.

Notes

Gilbert Skillman acknowledges helpful comments by Karl Moene, Herbert Gintis, and Stephen Jones.

1. Why this might be so is an important problem which has not been satisfactorily resolved. Putterman (1984) provides a survey of the issue. Dow (1993a) offers a bargaining-theoretic account, while Eswaran and Kotwal (1989) develop an explanation on the basis of moral hazard in credit markets. See also Chapter 6 by Pagano in this volume for a re-examination of the issue in a novel light.

2. This assumption is unappealing in some respects, as discussed in section 3.1 below. We choose this representation of bargaining costs because it allows us to sidestep issues concerning the temporal coordination of production and distribution which arise when only one worker's offer is accepted. To see that similar results arise in "time-discount" settings, see Jun (1989), who solves the problem alluded to above by making strong assumptions about the timing and disposition of production when total agreement is delayed by asymmetric bargaining responses.

3. However, our central result, that firms have rent-seeking incentives in the choice of production technique, does not depend on the fixed-cost specification; see Jun (1989), the results of which imply similar conclusions in the "time-discount" setting.

4. A detailed discussion of a related issue, employee bonding, is found in Dickens *et al.* (1989). Several arguments given there against the feasibility of bonding apply in the present context as well.

Part V
Ownership, participation and capital markets

14 The motivational role of an external agent in the informationally-participatory firm

MASAHIKO AOKI

We need decentralization because only thus can we ensure that the knowledge of particular circumstances of time and place will be promptly used. But the man on the spot cannot decide solely on the basis of his limited but intimate knowledge of the facts of his immediate surroundings. There still remains the problem of communicating to him such further information as he needs to fit decisions into the whole pattern of changes of the larger economic system. (F. Hayek, 1945)

1 Introduction

This chapter deals with incentive issues involved in workers' collective participation in information-processing (e.g., problem-solving on manufacturing site, horizontal coordination, on-the-job learning, R&D) in the context of large firms. In exploring this theme, it specifically tries to make the following two points: first, the critical basis of "workers' power" in the firm in accord with internal and allocative efficiency lies not so much in the "democratic rule" *per se* that workers' majority voting (or unanimous will) is explicitly applied to management decisions (or selection of management) of the firm. Nor does it lie in the workers' exclusive property rights which allow them to appropriate all gains arising in the associated firm. Rather, workers' power is derived more fundamentally from their ability to generate information value through active, collective participation in information-processing within the firm. By "workers' power," I mean their capacity to have due influence over management decisions relevant to their own economic welfare, learning opportunities, membership status in the firm, etc.

The second point to make is that, in spite of the desirability of enhanced workers' role in internal information-processing, there are a few incentive reasons for pure workers' self-management of the large, informationally-participatory firm to be practically difficult and even undesirable. These incentive difficulties exist independently of possible needs for external financing of large-scale investment and for insuring risk-averse workers. More positively, the chapter suggests that the existence of an external agent sharing in the value generated by the informationally-participatory firm in a particular contractual form may provide a positive incentive effect on workers without the complete destruction of their participatory and property rights.

The organization of the chapter is as follows. Section 2 summarizes reasons why the emergent market and technological conditions in the global market have

made active participation of workers in internal information-processing impera-
tive for the competitiveness of firms, which leads to the conceptualization of the
P-network (the large, participatory information network internalized within
firms) and that of the P-value (participatory information network-specific rent)
in section 3. Although the essential point of this section has already been made in
my previous works (Aoki, 1986, 1988, 1990a, 1990b; also see Itoh, 1987; Milgrom
and Roberts, 1990b), it is nonetheless indispensable for the development of the
theme of the present essay.

Section 3 addresses three incentive and monitoring issues specifically relevant
to the participatory firm: the possibility of undersupply of effort in teams, the
difficulty of designing a consensus-based personnel scheme, and the possible
tendency toward underinvestment. It discusses some measures proposed by
theorists of worker-controlled firms, such as cooperative reciprocity, equity
contracts, and membership markets, to cope with these problems under
worker-controlled management and points out reasons why these solutions may
not be workable for the firm internalizing P-network, even if they may in theory
be so for the small technological black box of the neoclassical type.

Section 4 designs a scheme of the distribution of the P-value between the
members of the P-network and an external agent which combines features of
sharing contract and fixed wage contracts, and examines conditions under which
this device may have a positive motivational impact on the members of the
P-network.

Section 5 provides a couple of institutional interpretations for the proposed
scheme. It derives some analogy from German–Japanese-type bank–firm
relationships as well as alluding to the importance of designing appropriate
financial institutions in the process of transforming ex-socialist economies into
participatory market economies.

2   The value of participatory information-processing

As is well known, in a seminal paper on information economics, Hayek (1945)
argued that the price system can respond to the apparently opposing requisites
for the best use of knowledge in an economic system: the desirability of the rapid
utilization of "local" knowledge, on the one hand, and the systematic need of
"global" communications of relevant information among individual decision-
makers (planners), on the other. Prices are "sufficient statistics" of the whole
pattern of changes for the purpose of efficiently coordinating decentralized
planning by many individual agents. The price mechanism may thus be regarded
as a much more "informationally efficient" planning system, to use a phrase of
Hurwicz's (1960), than central planning. A series of recent world events seems
unequivocally to endorse this contention.

But considerable time has passed without the recognition of the importance of
a cursory reference by Hayek to the "half-way house" between decentralized
market planning and central planning. By this he meant "the delegation of
planning to organized industries, or, in other words, monopoly" (Hayek,

1945:521). It is curious, however, that he identified the "delegation of planning to organized industries" only with monopoly, and did not elaborate on it. In practice, however, a large proportion of planning in the price system is delegated to large firms, whether they are monopolies or not. Some of those large firms constitute even more complicated planning systems than a small planned economy producing a relatively small number of simple products.

Although Hayek was himself not explicit, most economists seem ready to identify the information-processing structure of the firm as a variant of "central" planning system, i.e., hierarchy (possibly modified by some kind of decentralized measures such as internal transfer pricing, the so-called "M-form" divisionalization). That is, strategic management decisions such as on investment, diversification, the scale of output, etc. are decided upon centrally by top management, and an implementation plan is successively decomposed through layers of management hierarchy until it is finally given as a command to the operational level.

Central planning within a particular firm may not be efficient in practice, due to the limit of managers' information-processing capacities at various levels (Geanakoplos and Milgrom, 1991), the lack of "high-powered incentives" (Williamson, 1985) provided to them, inappropriate hierarchical decomposition in the organizational design, etc. But this possibility would not bother the Austrian, neoclassical, or transaction cost economists much, because inefficient enterprise planning systems would be weeded out through the competitive selection by markets. The state monopoly of the central planning system is bad, but multiple central planning by competing firms is efficiency-compatible. The political implications of the command–obedience relationship associated with central planning within the firm are not troublesome either for those economists, because anybody who does not like a particular boss has the freedom of terminating the relationship at will without prejudice and penalty under the conditions of perfect competition in the labor market.

The traditional structuring (or at least economists' perception of it) of the firm as a central planning system (hierarchy) may have been connected with the relatively smaller importance attached to unplanned "change" in the heyday of mass production of standardized products. When a small number of large producers controlled stable segments of markets for standardized products, demand projection could be fairly accurate. In such situations, the task of drawing up a comprehensive plan governing all activities within the firm could be manageable. Detailed production plans could then be laid down for fairly long periods in advance and closely adhered to. Also the factory for mass production could be designed in such a way as to utilize the maximum economies from single-purpose machines and the minute division of work for specialized skills. Under such schemes, small "changes" in market demands or emergent irregularities on the factory site could be dealt with by adjustments in buffer inventories, without modifying the basic plan. Although Hayek contested the then "fashionable" belief that "changes, or at least day-to-day adjustments, have become less important in modern times" (Hayek, 1945:523), what he seemed to be primarily concerned with was the importance of constant struggle by the manager to keep costs down. No particular mention was made about the use of "the knowledge of particular circumstances of time and place" by "the man on the spot" within the context of large firm organizations, such as workers on the shop floor, service and sales personnel in the marketing division.

There have emerged economic conditions in the global market, however, under which the informational efficiency of central planning within the large firm has become problematical without some fundamental modifications, so that the knowledge of "the man on the spot" may be more efficiently utilized. The increasing integration of relatively segregated national markets into global markets has been making producers' competition more fierce, on the one hand, and consumers' demand patterns as well as their choice opportunities more diverse, on the other. Oligopolistic market power within a national boundary is increasingly contested by foreign base competitors and producers must compete on a global scale for diverse consumers' demands embedded in different cultural heritages, but also proliferated by increasing international communications and consumers' aspirations.

In such a situation, important variables determining firms' competitive strength are certainly not limited to the capacity to reduce costs by the exploitation of economies of specialization, scale, and scope. The capacity to respond to continually changing demands quickly and without costly inventories are becoming crucial factors for firms desiring to compete in those markets. The capacity to create "changes" in production processes to make the production facility more flexible, as well as in products to capture consumers' interests in quality improvement and product innovation, is another such factor. Some authors, such as Piore and Sabel (1984), seem to suggest that these capacities are more closely connected with firms of relatively smaller size than were typical in the heyday of mass production (e.g., mini-mills in the American steel industry, the horizontal alliance of small firms in the garment industry in Plato, entrepreneurial venture firms in Silicon Valley and along Route 128). But I am interested in whether those capacities to respond to exogenous changes, and to create changes endogenously, can be nurtured in the industry where the efficient large-scale coordination of activities needs to be achieved in the intra-organizational context.

Flexible and speedy productive response to continually changing market conditions requires:

(1) the collection of precise information regarding the pattern of demands (variety, quantity, time) at the site where demands are generated;
(2) the quick transformation of this information to production scheduling at the relevant production site;
(3) the quick discovery and solution of emergent problems which may disrupt continual production processes at the site where they occur; and
(4) continual fine-tuning in the coordination of production and supply scheduling among inter-related shops as well as with suppliers.[1]

It is not difficult to see that these requirements necessitate the best use of knowledge of particular circumstances of time and place held by "the man on the spot" as well as the quick communication of information regarding the whole pattern of changes among relevant people. My presumption is that neither the decentralized price system nor centralized coordination through the hierarchy can fully meet these tasks satisfactorily, and that some kind of system of participatory information-processing within the firm, that is, decentralized knowledge utilization on site combined with non-hierarchical communications for mutual coordination, is necessary.

In previous works (Aoki, 1988, 1990a), I have presented some institutional examples of horizontal coordination within firms among people on the spot within the framework of "indicative" central planning of management. I have also constructed an analytical model capturing the essential characteristics of such institutional practices and investigated conditions under which it may be informationally more efficient than central planning based only on prior knowledge of management (Aoki, 1986, 1990b). Learning by people on the spot about their "particular circumstances" and making that information available to a larger system in an organizationally useful way is, of course, not costless. People's time, effort, and attention may be diverted to activities that are not operationally productive, and economies of specialization available in central planning may be sacrificed. Political, sociological, or ethical reasons aside, the replacement of central planning by a system of participatory information-processing may not be worthwhile, therefore, in markets that are fairly stable or subject to frequent drastic changes. In these cases, the value added by the best use of local posterior knowledge may not match the cost of doing so. But, in between, where market conditions are continually changing, but not drastically, the value of information net of costs of local learning and horizontal communications may become worthwhile to pursue.

Since the value of information is created not by management alone, but also by the participation of people on the spot, i.e., workers, they may acquire power to influence management decisions by the threat of non-cooperation. This situation has, however, a very different efficiency implication from the case in which the union exercises bargaining power over a share in oligopolistic rents of the firm through the monopsonic control of labor supply (Aoki, 1990b). The information value created by the system of participatory information-processing represents genuine economic value (producers' and consumers' surplus), unavailable through either the price system or delegated central planning. I also contend that a solid foundation of participatory power of workers may be sought in their positive role in such an economically productive undertaking. But why, then, do workers not seem to appropriate the whole value of the system of participatory information-processing? In other words, why do worker-controlled firms not flourish more? In the next section, we address these questions from the incentive point of view.

3   The incentive difficulties of pure workers' control

In order to discuss the issues proposed at the end of the previous section, it is helpful to conceive the *firm* as a coherent complex of a system of information-processing, a system of incentives or a personnel administration scheme (sub-divided into a reward scheme and a task assignment scheme), and a mode of control over management. As systems of information-processing, we can conceive of two prototypes: traditional central planning and the system of participatory information-processing (i.e., the system of on-the-spot information processing and horizontal coordination complementing central planning based on prior knowledge of management). We refer to the large-scale system of participatory information processing as the *P-network* for short. Also, the net information value generated by the P-network is referred to as the *P-value*. It does not include either the normal rate of return to physical assets utilized therein nor workers' outside opportunity wages. It is that part of the firm's value added which is available only in the context of the P-network, and may assume negative values when a traditional hierarchy integrating marketable resources performs relatively better.

We define *pure workers' control* of the firm by the following two requisites: (1) the total P-value (net of a fixed obligation arising out of debt contracts for financing investments) is shared entirely among workers; and (2) a personnel administration scheme and crucial management decisions, such as on employment and investment, are decided in the sole interest of incumbent workers (e.g., through their majority voting or by the manager elected by them). The questions we face in this section can then be formulated in the following way: can the P-network be placed under workers' control without spoiling its informational efficiency and disturbing economy-wide allocative efficiency? If so, what kind of personnel administration scheme among participants of the P-network is agreeable to workers? We are going to discuss three incentive reasons why an answer to the first question is likely to be negative.

3.1   Does the sharing of P-value provide sufficient incentives?

The operation of a P-network requires teamwork, cooperative communications, and horizontal coordination on the part of workers. It may be difficult to meter precisely individual contributions to the generation of P-value in such a system, and there may arise the familiar problem of moral hazard (or what Arrow calls "hidden action"). The provision of the entire P-value to workers (i.e., the sharing of P-value among workers) does not necessarily provide effective incentives for teamwork in the P-network. Efficiency requires that each individual supplies effort at such a level that the marginal disutility cost of effort is equated with the marginal P-value product. However, if workers behave selfishly under the sharing scheme (where individual share parameters are differentiable with respect to the P-value), each individual may stop the amount of effort supply at that level at which the marginal disutility cost of own effort is equated with the marginal

P-value product of own effort times his/her share parameter (which is less than one). An undersupply of effort may thus result. If a change in the effort supply of each individual is reciprocated by all other individuals participating in team-work, either through mutual monitoring and/or collective mores, this problem can be mitigated. But, if the reciprocity is not perfect, the problem still remains.

Holmstrom (1982) proposed an ingenious device that may resolve this moral hazard problem in teams. He argued that a first-best effort expenditure in teamwork under uncertainty can be approximated by the introduction of the following group penalties. If the team output exceeds a certain critical value of team production, workers may exhaust the total value (*less* a fixed obligation) among themselves. If the total value falls short of the critical level, however, positive penalities, specified *ex ante*, are imposed on all workers in the team so that the total payment becomes less than the full value (net of fixed obligation). In other words, if and only if underperformance results, an outside agent administering this scheme expropriates a substantial portion of the output. By an appropriate choice of a critical value, the first-best solution can be approximated arbitrarily closely and, in effect, the chance that the full output (net of fixed obligation) is exhausted among workers in team becomes very high. In the next section, we adapt Holmstrom's essential idea to the design of a realistic incentive contract for the P-network members.

3.2   Why is workers' control over a personnel scheme difficult?

In the P-network where information-processing (including decision-making and problem-solving) is delegated to lower levels of functional hierarchy and direct coordination among people on the spot is sanctioned, room for local collusion within a sub-set of the P-network may become greater, and there is no guarantee that such local collusion is consistent with the pursuit of the goal of a larger system. One measure to cope with this problem would be to rotate workers (managers) across various work units periodically and prevent them from associating with particular local interests detrimental to the pursuit of the global goal of the maximization of P-value (Tirole, 1986:202; Aoki, 1988, Ch. 3). Such a practice, however, necessitates a more centralized personnel administration system than the one under which personnel decisions concerning hiring, discharge, and job assignment of workers are delegated to the immediate supervisor of the posts concerned.

There is another, more positive, reason why an organizational approach to personnel administration (human resource development program) is more desirable for the firm internalizing the P-network. Workers' capacity for on-site information-processing and communication consistent with the organizational goal may be acquired only over time in the context of a specific network. Incentives for long-term learning may be provided by ranking workers and paying differential shares in the P-value according to the degree of advancement in learning over time (Aoki, 1988, Ch. 3). Also, although individual potential and motivation for continual learning may not be known to the firm at the outset of employment (adverse selection or what Arrow calls "hidden information"), screening workers by observed performance on a step-by-step basis through a promotional scheme is known to be effective to cope with this problem (MacLeod and Malcomson, 1988).

The efficient operation of the P-network thus seems to require a systematic personnel administration characterized by organizational job allocation and rank hierarchy of pay – which we refer to as the *H-personnel scheme* for short. As Knight (1921) said, the essence of controlling a decision is to control the selection of people who make the decision. In this vein, it may be said that, in spite of decentralization in information-processing, a firm is able to preserve its organizational effectiveness and integrity through the organizational, rank-hierarchical approach to personnel administration. This is one instance of the manifestation of what I called the *Duality Principle*.[2]

But the H-personnel scheme may not be completely agreeable from the viewpoint of egalitarian values. As the size of the P-network gets larger, more refined, and intricate, it is inevitable that the network will come to include a variety of workers within it whose aspirations, whose potential capacities to contribute to the generation of P-value, and whose tangible as well as intangible benefits derived from the associated H-personnel scheme may become quite diverse. Also, the administration of the promotion scheme as a screening device may be improved by biasing the promotion criterion in favor of the workers with better prior credentials and past performance, rather than placing everybody on an equal footing in promotional competition (Meyer, 1991). Further, there arises a possibility that a participant of the "firm" other than internal members of the P-network will expropriate a proportion of the P-value through the creation and administration of the H-personnel scheme. Is it possible for the workers of the P-network to remedy these situations? That is, is it possible for them to purchase the P-network, run a more egalitarian personnel administration scheme agreeable to everybody, and distribute the entire P-value (net of fix debt obligations) among themselves on consensus basis?

The reservation wage of each individual at which he or she agrees to form the new pure worker-controlled firm and to make at least an equal effort therein as in the current firm may be private information, because individuals derive unverifiable benefits under the current H-personnel scheme in the form of different promotion perspectives, non-pecuniary benefits associated with rank differentiation as such (e.g., prestige), etc. Suppose that the decision as to whether or not to create a new worker-controlled firm and, if so, what type of reward scheme is to be created, can be made on the basis of everybody's true reservation wage. In order for the truthful revelation of the private information to be compatible with everybody's incentives, however, information premia need to be paid (the Revelation Principle). As the number of workers in the original firm gets large and they become heterogeneous in their reservation wages, the aggregate amount of such premia may become very large (Mailath and Postelwaithe, 1990). In addition, if workers of a lower-paid type demand more egalitarian wages in alignment with the reservation wages of workers of a higher-paid type, total aggregate wages to be paid at the worker-controlled firm may well exceed the limit of residual P-value available for redistribution by its formation. More fundamentally, the egalitarian treatment of workers may even reduce the total amount of P-value, because such a scheme may reduce the learning incentives of high-capacity workers.

It may be concluded, then, that, in spite of the increasing potential power of workers and the good intentions of worker-control advocates, it may be difficult in practice for the firm-internalizing P-network and H-personnel scheme to be transformed into pure workers'-controlled management. As the size and heterogeneity of workers in the firm increases, it may become possible for an agent external to the P-network to appropriate some portion of P-value without risking the possibility of a workers' takeover of the firm (Mailath and Postelwaithe, 1990). However, I do not necessarily interpret this expropriation as simple exploitation. The administration of an H-personnel scheme does not itself produce P-value but, as the Duality Principle indicates, it is indispensable for the operation of the P-network to be effective in motivating members' efforts, reciprocal behavior, and learning within it. Also, individual workers come and go, but in spite of individual turnover, knowledge generated within the P-network may be stored in corporate memory (e.g., as work customs and rules at the shop, files in the office) and the collective use of such common knowledge may often be more efficient than the decentralized use of more refined individual knowledge (Cremer, 1990). It is suggested then that the well-run, incentive-compatible H-personnel scheme and the corporate memory constitute important economic assets specific to the firm which exist independently of incumbent workers and that the referred external agent may be interpreted as the personification of such assets.

In the next section, I construct a simple model in which the partial expropriation of P-value by an agent external to the P-network contributes to the restraint of free-riding by the members of the P-network and, accordingly, to their increased material welfare. The model assumes the homogeneity of the members, but I hope that it may help us to understand why under certain conditions the abandonment of the first requisite of pure workers' control will actually enhance workers' material welfare through incentive effect.

3.3   Can the workers' myopia be cured by a market device?

Even if payments to individual workers according to their performance and attributes do not (cannot) exhaust the total P-value, there remains the possibility of distributing the residual among incumbent workers on a simple *per capita* basis or according to a sharing rule unrelated to individual performance. Let us discuss an incentive difficulty unique to such schemes.

First, consider the case of *per capita* distribution of the residual and suppose that the firm tries to maximize (the present value sum of) *per capita* income. A well-known problem associated with such a scheme is the possibility of underinvestment. In order to see this point in the simplest form, suppose first that the technology of the firm and the efficiency of the P-network is such that P-value can grow at the same rate as a fixed combination of work force and physical assets. Suppose also that growth costs, including investment in equipment, training, advertisement, etc. are to be internally financed. Then the gross P-value per workers would remain constant even if the firm invests in growth, but current capital expenditure for growth needs to be entirely borne by incumbent workers and will thus depress their incomes after growth-cost expenditures. Workers may therefore become growth-averse. Potential benefits of growth of the firm, such as new employment opportunities (the admission of new members to an expanding P-network), increasing returns to firm-specific assets, and the generation of new consumer surplus, may thus remain unexploited.

There may be a few factors that mitigate this problem. Incumbent workers may benefit from growth by adopting capital-biased technology and/or by realizing labor-saving technological progress. The firm may also differentiate the distribution of residual P-value among workers according to pure seniority, so that senior workers get larger shares of growth dividends while making newcomers bear growth costs. Incumbent workers may also reduce their own burden of growth costs by relying upon debt financing and having the future cohorts of workers share the repayment of debts. But these factors may not entirely resolve the problem of underinvestment by the worker-controlled firm.

Economists such as Drèze argue, however, that there is no intrinsic problem with workers-controlled management: "under a minimal assumption, the sets of allocation that can be sustained as [Walrasian] competitive equilibria and as labour-management equilibria are identical" (Drèze, 1989:24). But the dynamic version of this neoclassical equivalence proposition must presuppose that the firm maximizes the weighted average of wealth of all types of workers, that is, including the future cohorts of workers. But how can the future cohorts of workers be represented in the process of management decision today?

Further, the neoclassical equivalence theorem is derived from the assumption that the workers are perfectly mobile among workers-controlled firms, while rents imputed to existing facilities can be adjusted externally so as to equalize value added per worker across firms. These two mechanisms supposedly entail the same income for workers equivalent to market-clearing wages. The perfect mobility of workers between firms in the present context is questionable, however. Because they become assets specific to a particular P-network internalized therein (i.e., they are "network-specific" assets), their value may be lost if they move individually and not collectively. Also, as Drèze himself recognizes, even if workers are perfectly mobile without losing their value, there will be no incentive for workers to raise productivity, if rents are automatically raised when value added per worker rises above its level elsewhere (Drèze, 1989:28).

Other economists, such as Sertel (1982b) and Dow (1986), propose that the creation of new markets for membership in the firm may resolve the problem of the absence of voice of future cohorts of workers in a way analogous to equity markets. Membership involves perpetual rights to a certain share in residual

P-value so that its value reflects the present value sum of the share in the entire future stream of residual P-value. Workers can realize its value by sales upon retirement from the firm. Under certain conditions, then, workers unanimously support the rate of investment which maximizes total membership value and, it is claimed, that rate becomes equal to the Walrasian equilibrium rate realized through stock-price maximization.

There is no guarantee, however, that a person who is willing to invest in membership is the one who is most qualified as a member of the P-network and the problem of adverse selection (hidden information) may become acute under such a scheme: less capable and less motivated workers may bid up the price of membership and, after entry to the firm, they may shirk, yet be able to reap a share in residual P-value, while more qualified workers may be denied membership because of the lack of initial wealth. As mentioned already, in order to cope with this adverse selection problem, it is a good strategy for the administrator of an H-personnel scheme to select workers on the basis of prior knowledge (Meyer, 1991). But such a strategy is clearly not compatible with the free-market competition of potential workers for membership.

4 The P-value-enhancing role of an external agent

In previous sections, I have emphasized that the incentive scheme based on status differentiation among workers – the H-personnel administration – may be essential for the development of human assets conducive to the efficient working of the P-network. It is probable that this administration is reciprocally monitored by workers (e.g., through the union, the work council, the grievance committee, the informal reputation mechanism) for the sake of fairness, industrial democracy, the prevention of management abuse, etc. but complete internal control by workers is unlikely because of the difficulty of consensus-making among heterogeneous workers, as well as not being desirable from the dynamic allocative efficiency point of view. As a consequence, the requisites of worker-controlled management may remain unsatisfied. Specifically, an external agent who extracts a portion of P-value without directly participating in the P-network may become viable. However, can such an external agent play any positive role, for example, in motivating the internal members of the P-network?

This section explicitly introduces interactions between the internal P-network members and an agent external to the P-network in the motivational dimension. For simplicity's sake the model makes an important compromise with the point emphasized so far by assuming the homogeneity of workers participating in the P-network. Albeit simple, the model clarifies an incentive effect of the sharing of P-value between the P-network members and the external agent, that is, the provision of external incentives for the internal members of the P-network who may otherwise tend mutually to free-ride on team production.[3]

Let us suppose that there are n identical numbers of the P-network and let $f(P, \mathbf{a})$ be the probability density function of output P of P-value, conditional on a vector of action $\mathbf{a} = (a_1, \ldots, a_n)$ taken by P-network members $i = 1, \ldots, n$, where f is symmetric and continuously differentiable in $\mathbf{a}$, with $f_i(P, \mathbf{a}) = \partial f / \partial a_i$. For any $\mathbf{a}$ with $a_i = a_j$ for all i and j, we assume that there exists $\hat{P}(\mathbf{a})$ such that $f_i < 0$ for $P < \hat{P}(\mathbf{a})$ and $f_i > 0$ for $P > \hat{P}(\mathbf{a})$, which implies that an increase in individual effort always decreases the probability of P-values in the lower tail (see Figure 14.1). It is to be remembered that by definition, P-value does not contain either the normal rate of returns to physical assets used by the network or the normal wage available outside, and therefore can become negative.

Suppose that each member of the P-network has the identical quasi-linear utility function:

$$U(w_i, a_i) = w_i - v(a_i)$$

where w_i is the share of the ith member in P-value ($i = 1, \ldots, n$). Let us denote the expected value of the external agent's share in P-value by R:

$$R = P - \Sigma_i w_i.$$

The Pareto-efficient network effort $\mathbf{a}^*$ requires that

$$\max_a E[P - \Sigma_i v(a_i)] \Rightarrow E_i P(\mathbf{a}^*) \equiv \delta E P(\mathbf{a}^*)/\delta a_i = v'(a_i^*)$$

for all i.

First consider that the external agent receives a fix income $\bar{R}$ regardless of the actual realization of P-value and the n-identical members become residual claimants with equal shares. Suppose that there is incomplete reciprocity of efforts among team members either through reciprocal monitoring and/or the mores of cooperation so that we have

$$da_i/da_j = k \quad \text{(for all } j = i)$$

where $0 < k < 1$.

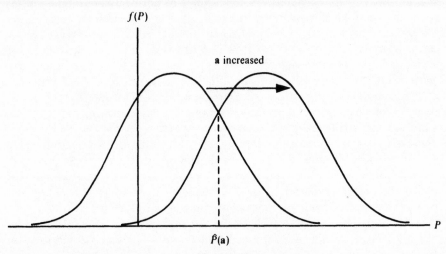

Figure 14.1   Net information value and individual effort

Then the incentive-compatibility, or Nash-equilibrium, requires that

$$\max_a E[(P - R)/n - v(a_i)] \Rightarrow H(k)[E_i P(\mathbf{a}^N)] = v'(a_i^N)$$

for all i, where $H(k) = [1 + k(n - 1)]/n \approx k$ for large n. Evidently $a_i^N < a^*$. The question we now raise is: does there exist any alternative sharing scheme to fill the gap, i.e., to approximate the Pareto-efficient production a^* more closely than a^N?

Assume that $\hat{P}(\mathbf{a}^N) > 0$ and let us consider the following simple contract in the neighborhood of $\mathbf{a}^N$ (see Figure 14.2):

For $P < 0$ and $P > \hat{P}(\mathbf{a}^N)$, $\quad w_i = (s/n)P$

For $0 \leqslant P \leqslant \hat{P}(\mathbf{a}^N)$, $\qquad w_i = 0$

where $0 < s < 1$. If the P-value is negative or greater than $\mathbf{a}^N$, then each P-network member participates in the sharing of loss or gains, with share parameter s/n. In the intermediate range, each member gets zero P-value (i.e., receives only the income equivalent to what is available in the external market). This contractual form may be considered as a mixture of a fixed-income contract for the intermediate range of P-value and sharing contracts for the upper and lower ends of P-value. We refer to this contractual form below as the *hybrid contract*.

The residual goes to the external agent and its expected value will equal:

$$R(\mathbf{a}) = (1 - s)E(P(\mathbf{a})) + sT(\mathbf{a})$$

where

$$E(P(\mathbf{a})) = \int Pf(P, \mathbf{a})dP \quad \text{and} \quad T(\mathbf{a}) = \int_{[0, \hat{P}(a^x)]} Pf(P, \mathbf{a})dP.$$

In this scheme, the Nash-equilibrium condition of a member's effort choice will become:

$$sH(k)\{E_i(P(\mathbf{a})) - T_i(\mathbf{a})\} = v'(a_i)$$

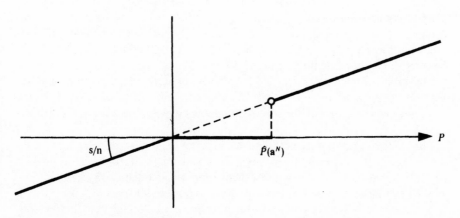

Figure 14.2   A hybrid contract

where $T_i(\mathbf{a}) = \partial T_i(\mathbf{a})/\partial a_i$. Note that in the neighborhood of $\mathbf{a} = \mathbf{a}^N$, $T_i(\mathbf{a}) < 0$ by construction. Choose s so that $R(\mathbf{a}^N) = \bar{R}$ for a given claim $\bar{R}$ by the external agent. It is clear that if $s\{E_i(P(\mathbf{a}^N)) - T_i(\mathbf{a}^N)\} > E_i(P(\mathbf{a}^N))$, the hybrid contract can improve upon the effort expenditures by P-network members. This condition is satisfied if

$$\frac{E(P(\mathbf{a})) - R}{E(P(\mathbf{a})) - T(\mathbf{a})} > \frac{E_i(P(\mathbf{a}))}{E_i(P(\mathbf{a})) - T_i(\mathbf{a})}$$

at $\mathbf{a} = \mathbf{a}^N$, which is always possible if the amount of $\bar{R}$ is not excessively high. The hybrid contract will thus make the members of the P-network better off by eliciting efforts approximating the optimal level more closely in comparison to the case of their being residual claimants.

5   Institutional remarks

Section 4 showed that the existence of an agent external to the P-network who shares the P-value (positive or negative) with the internal members may have positive incentive impacts on the latter in curbing their free-riding. The external agent in the model is reminiscent of that in Holmstrom's model which imposes penalties on team members when the outcome of the team (P-network in our terms) is in the worst state either because of their shirking or through simple bad luck. Our model may be interpreted in such a way that the external agent imposes penalties when the production of P-value is not sufficiently high, i.e., when the realized value of P falls on the region $[0, \hat{P}(\mathbf{a}^N)]$, although it mitigates the burden of the internal members when the realized P-value is too small (i.e., when negative), which has some negative incentive effect but a positive insurance effect.

One important criticism raised against the Holmstrom model is as follows: the external agent has a better chance to get group penalties when members of the team shirk. If the external agent itself is a selfish income-seeker, therefore, there may be incentives for it to collude with some members of the team secretly, and to induce them to shirk in exchange for the promise of sharing the expropriable penalties with them (Estrin and Kotwal, 1984). Our model has a similar problem. The external agent is better off when the realized P-value is a little bit less than $\hat{P}(\mathbf{a}^N)$ in comparison to the case when it is a little bit greater than $\hat{P}(\mathbf{a}^N)$, because the R-schedule under the hybrid contract exhibits a discontinuous drop at that point. If the level of realized P-value is not verifiable, a dispute may arise between the internal members and the external agent regarding what is the real state, and whether or not the internal members are qualified for the sharing of P-value.

But the above point may not be such a big problem. If the arrangement itself is secret and non-observable/verifiable, how can the external agent credibly commit to make such side payment? In my opinion, an intrinsically more difficult problem with the Holmstrom model is that it is hard to find, in the context of firm organization, a reasonable institutional interpretation for the assumed external agent which imposes penalties on team members and enjoys higher income, when the team has actually performed badly. In contrast, our external agent may be given a reasonable institutional interpretation. It may be the management who administers the incentive scheme in the trust of internal members of the P-network. Management assures a fixed-income equivalent to the opportunity wage to the members as far as the P-value is non-negative. In addition, it promises them a bonus payment equivalent to sP/n, if P-value exceeds the critical value $\hat{P}(\mathbf{a}^N)$. If realized P-value becomes negative, it asks the internal members partially to bear the brunt of the depressed state, while absorbing the remaining loss out of reserves. If production is repeated over time and stochastic elements affecting the output of P-value are independently, identically distributed over time, adequate reserves should be accumulated over time as far as the hybrid contract is designed in such a way that $\hat{P}(\mathbf{a}^N) > 0$. If management defaults on the payment of bonus in spite of the realized P-value exceeding the critical value $\mathbf{a}^N$, the reputation of management may be damaged. In any case, if management's income level is related to that of internal members, then it ought to be in the long-term interest of management to adhere to the formula specified by the hybrid contract.

Another possible interpretation of the model is that the external agent is a bank-like financial institution – let us call it the *B-agent* – which provides various services, including monitoring, in exchange for the expected return R (in addition to the normal rate of return to the supply of financial resources, if any). Suppose that the B-agent is assured of the fixed payment of $(1 - s)\hat{P}(\mathbf{a}_N)$ from the P-network (the firm) and, on top of it, participate in share $(1 - s)$ of incremental value $P(\mathbf{a}) - \hat{P}(\mathbf{a}^N)$, as far as the realized P-value exceeds $\hat{P}(\mathbf{a}_N)$. Suppose that if the realized P-value falls short of the critical value $\hat{P}(\mathbf{a}^N)$ and the P-network (the firm) cannot meet the fixed obligation without sacrificing its share, a mechanism is triggered to transfer control rights from the internal management (a member of the P-network in this case) to the B-agent. After the transfer the B-agent reduces the payment to the internal members to zero or even negative in the case of negative realized P-value.

A difficulty arising in this institutional set-up roughly corresponding to the Estrin–Kotwal point is this: if the realized P-value is not verifiable, then the internal members of the P-network (the internal management of the firm) may resist the transfer of control rights by paying the fixed obligation even when the realized P-value is smaller than, but in the close neighborhood of, $\hat{P}(\mathbf{a}_N)$. In this interpretation, the schedule of payments to the B-agent, defined as the residual P-value after the total payments to the internal members according to the hybrid contract, may be regarded as a financial contract mixing debt contracts (the fixed obligation) and equity contracts, with the threshold of bankruptcy (in the sense of control right shifts) at $\hat{P}(\mathbf{a}_N)$.

We may draw a certain analogy between the above institutional interpretation and bank–firm relations in Japanese–German practice. In Japan and Germany, the main bank or the Hausbank usually maintains more comprehensive relations with the customer firm than described in the economists' model of arm's-length debt contracts. The bank normally combines stockholding with creditholding, which enables the bank to take over management of a failing firm at relatively cheap cost, while enabling it to reap a higher income from a well-run firm in the form of dividends and capital gains not possible under a fixed-claim contract.

Another interesting aspect of the Japanese–German bank–firm relationship is that it cannot be characterized as a unilateral control relationship, but rather is a kind of partnership in the normal state of affairs. Namely, as far as the firm is run well, the bank normally does not interfere with management decisions explicitly, although it is ready to exercise control rights over management of a badly-run firm and inflict penalties on the insiders (managers and employees) in the form of wage/bonus cuts, layoffs, discharges, social humiliation, etc. It is the potential threat of such penalty imposed on managers, as well as on workers associated with the firm on a long-term basis, that stimulates internal efficiency. And this effective silent partnership also prevents management from engaging in complete collusion with incumbent employees in management decisions and compels it to pay heed to the long-run viability of the firm by investing for the future.

Management may thus be interpreted as engaged in effect in the pursuit of dual goals when the firm is run well, striking a balance between the investor's interests as represented by the bank and employee's interests as represented by the union or other type of work organizations.[4] Such dual control over management more clearly manifests itself in the codetermination at the German firm in which representatives from the bank and the union share seats on the supervisory board with the authority of appointing top management, but may be considered as implicit in the so-called Japanese management style as well (Aoki, 1984, Part III; 1988, Ch. 5).

The essence of these common features of Japanese–German bank–firm relationships (i.e., shared control over internal management in good states and the transfer of control to the bank and loss-bearing by the insiders in bad states) is captured by the above interpretation of hybrid contracts. The interpretation suggests that desirable external incentives for the firm-internalizing P-network may be provided by its relation with the responsible financial institution which makes credible threats of takeover in the event of bad states, but behaves circumspectly otherwise. Exclusive reliance on equity contracts or debt contracts would not provide good incentives for the firm where workers play active participatory roles in information processing.[5]

The argument of this chapter may also shed light on the issue of the transition of a socialist economy to a market economy. Our model suggests that, if the mores of collective efforts and reciprocity in the socialist firm is real and is to be inherited in its gradual transformation to a P-network-type organization, a proper external disciplinary mechanism has to be provided, possibly by a responsible banking institution. As Kornai has argued forcibly for some time, one crucial problem of the socialist economy was that the threat of disciplinary action by the state bank on badly-managed state firms was never carried out in earnest. The state bank tended to respond to *ex post* needs of badly-run firms out of political expediency, creating the so-called "soft-budget" problem (Kornai,

1980, 1986), which is precisely the opposite to what our model suggests the external monitor should do.

Notes

1. The capacity to create changes, i.e., to develop process or product innovation may require, besides scientific and/or engineering competence, the following:

   (1) entrepreneurial capability to perceive new market potential from the observation of existing markets and to translate it to a new product concept;
   (2) the effective feedback of information regarding consumers' reactions, opinions, etc. available at the site where products are marketed and serviced to the manufacturing site for engineering changes or to the development laboratory for new product design; and
   (3) the effective feedback of engineering knowledge available at the manufacturing site to the development laboratory for process redesign.

2. The Duality Principle states: in order for the firm to be internally integrative and organizationally effective it is necessary that centralization and decentralization be dually combined in its information-processing aspect and its personnel administration aspect. That is, either its information-processing aspect or its personnel administration aspect needs to be centralized (hierarchical), but not both. If both aspects are centralized, the firm organization becomes too authoritarian. If both aspects are decentralized, the firm becomes disintegrative. According to this Principle, firms which rely upon a market-oriented, decentralized personnel scheme require a centralized, hierarchical information structure; see Aoki (1990a).

3. The model does not explicitly deal with the distribution of controlling rights over management (the selection of management). But, I have shown elsewhere (Aoki, 1984) that, when the sharing of firm-specific gains are involved between the insiders (employees) and the outsiders (investors), it is efficient and power-equilibrating for management to make decisions according to the weighting rule: maximize the weighted average of the collective objectives of the insiders and the outsiders, with weights given by their respective *distributive* shares. Therefore, one may say that the sharing model introduced below implicitly implies the sharing of control over management between the P-network members and the external claimant to a share in the P-value. If so, the proposed model may also suggest a way to address the third incentive problem discussed above, i.e., the myopia of incumbent workers in investment decisions.

4. See n. 3 above.

5. The bank–firm relation of the Japanese–German type is not without problems, however. The fear of a bank's takeover or the strong preference for independence from the bank by management may lead inside management to pursue the excessive promotion of reciprocated work efforts among workers as well as the accumulation of "free cash flow" (Jensen, 1986) in excess of that required for the efficient growth of the firm organization. There is ample casual empirical evidence attesting to such a tendency in the Japanese economy.

15   Unstable ownership

TONE OGNEDAL

1   Introduction

Many countries seem to favor mixed ownership as a way to make firms democratic. Employees are therefore induced to buy shares in the firm where they work. Among other things, this may reduce the conflict between labor and capital as both groups get interests as shareholders in the firm.

A crucial point for the proposers is often that the shares should be purchased and held by the individual worker, not by an organized group of workers. There should, for example, be no restrictions on each employee's trade of shares. A free individual purchase and sale of shares, however, may be inconsistent with a stable mixed ownership structure. Employee-owners may have the opportunity to avoid equal profit-sharing with the other owners. They can, for example, allocate the income of the firm to higher wages and fringe benefits for themselves, instead of paying out profit to all the shareholders. To pursue their own interests in the firm, the employees need the majority of shares. As a consequence, the external owners also want the majority of shares to prevent a non-value-maximizing policy. Hence, there may be a struggle for control over the firm between the two groups.

The conflict may not be solved through a free market for shares and a market for corporate control. On the contrary, restrictions on the trading of shares may be necessary to obtain a stable ownership structure. The initial majority owners as a group have no interest in selling their control over the firm for less than a full compensation for their loss from the takeover. However, there is a conflict between collective and individual rationality. When each shareholder is assumed to be free to sell and purchase shares, he can be "bribed" to sell shares even if this is against the collective interests of his group. The result may be an inefficient ownership structure, where the profit of the firm is not maximized.

Restrictions on the purchase and sale of shares may prevent takeovers that favor one group at the expense of other owners. In most countries, the legislation requires equal treatment of all shareholders in a takeover. In addition, countries like the UK and Norway do not allow restricted offers. Legal restrictions, however, may be difficult to enforce. Shareholders sometimes have self-imposed restrictions on the individual purchase and sale of shares. The shares may, for example, be collectively owned, as is often the case with employee-owned firms.

A distribution of the firm's surplus that favors one group of owners is against the firm legislation in most countries if the policy is not announced before the shares are sold. It may, however, be extremely difficult to prove to a court that the majority has exploited the minority by illegal means.

In the present chapter, I consider only the conflict between external and employee-owners. However, the problem applies to all firms where some stockholders can avoid equal profit-sharing with the other stockholders if they control the firm. One example may be a situation where a peer group of shareholders owns all the shares in firm A, and a majority of the shares in B. As majority owners in B, the peer group can decide that firm B should buy firm A. If firm B pays a price above the market price for these shares, some of B's profit is transferred to the peer group instead of being shared among all the stockholders.

The model is outlined in section 2. The approach taken in the present chapter is based upon cooperative game theory, where a stable ownership structure is one which cannot be blocked by any coalition. The problem is analyzed as a one-shot game. In section 3 the results for the general case are given. The consequences of restrictions on the sale and purchase of shares are investigated in section 4. Some concluding remarks are given in section 5.

2   The model

I consider a firm that is jointly owned by its workers and external stockholders. The number in each group is N and E respectively. The workers initially have a fraction α of the shares. It is assumed that the shares are equally distributed among the workers, such that each of them owns α/N of the total stock. Similarly, each of the external owners has $(1 - \alpha)/E$ of the stock. One share gives one vote. It is assumed that 50 percent of the shares is necessary and sufficient to control the firm. The surplus can either be distributed as dividends or as wages and fringe benefits. Dividends must be distributed to all the stockholders according to their share of the total stock. Moreover, I assume that wages, fringe benefits, etc. have to be shared equally among all the workers.

The value added (after tax) in the firm may depend on its governance structure. When the firm is run as an ordinary capitalist enterprise the value of the surplus after deduction of normal wages is set equal to 1. When the workers control the firm, however, the value of the surplus above normal wages is $1 + \beta$. Hence, in the case where β is positive there exists a labor-management gain that can be distributed among the workers, while there is a labor-management loss in the case where β is negative.

There are several reasons why the value of β may actually differ from zero. A positive value of β captures, for example, the case where worker ownership increases productivity, as argued by Vanek (1970) and others. Several empirical studies support this hypothesis, as for example Estrin and Jones (1988). A negative value of β indicates that worker ownership reduces productivity, as argued by Alchian and Demsets (1972a). When the workers control the firm they may run the firm as a capitalist firm, implying that $\beta = 0$. The surplus must then be distributed as in a capitalist firm. Hence, if β is negative the workers have the choice between 100 percent of a low surplus and a lower share of a higher surplus.[1]

β may also be influenced by tax rules. If, for example, the tax rate on wage incomes is higher than on capital income, β may be negative. If the opposite is true, β may be positive.

Finally, a negative β may be due to the fact that a given sum paid out as fringe benefits may have a lower value than the same amount paid in cash.

Both types of shareholders are free to form any coalitions. A shareholder can also break out of a coalition and form a new one if he can profit by this. I define $V(n,e)$ as the income a coalition of n employees and e external owners can guarantee itself, irrespective of what the owners outside the coalition do.

The income of a coalition is the dividends or wage increases that are received from the firm. If the coalition has the majority of the shares, it can choose to pay out the surplus in the way that is most profitable for the coalition. The income for the rest of the shareholders is the residual.

The external owners obviously prefer to distribute the surplus as dividends, since they do not benefit from high wages and fringes. The workers, however, have two alternatives: in a labor-managed firm the workers share the total surplus $1 + \beta$. This surplus is allocated to the workers as wages and fringe benefits. If, on the other hand, the workers choose to run the firm as a capitalist firm the surplus is equal to 1. This surplus must then be shared between all the owners as in a traditional capitalist firm, such that the workers get α. The workers therefore choose labor-management as long as $1 + \beta \geqslant \alpha$. If $1 + \beta < \alpha$, all shareholders agree to run the firm as a capitalist firm and distribute the surplus as dividends.[2]

For individual owners we define:

x_i = the payoff for an employee owner

= dividends or wages and fringes

+ net income from the sale of shares.

y_j = the payoff for an external owner

= dividends

+ net income from the sale of shares.

Side payments between members of a coalition are transferred by the sale of shares. Suppose that a majority coalition (n, e), i.e., a coalition of n workers and e external owners, pay out the whole surplus as wages. The payoff to the external owners in this coalition is the income they obtain from the sale of shares to the employee-owners.

There is a stable ownership structure if and only if there exists an outcome such that no stockholders can profit by forming new coalitions, i.e., that no group try to buy shares to obtain control over the firm. In technical terms a stable solution is an outcome $x_1, \ldots x_N, y_1, \ldots y_E$ such that:

$$V(n,e) \leqslant \sum_n x_i + \sum_e y_i \quad \text{for all possible } n, e. \tag{2.1}$$

The set of outcomes satisfying (2.1) is the core of the game. The condition says that no group of stockholders can accept a lower total income than what they can obtain if they form a coalition together. From this it follows that no individual stockholder can accept a lower income than he could obtain by staying alone. Further, a coalition of all the stockholders obtains the maximum profit, $V(N, E)$. More formally, it follows from (2.1) that

$$v(n_i) \leqslant x_i \quad \text{for all } i$$
$$v(e_j) \leqslant y_j \quad \text{for all } j. \tag{2.2}$$

$$V(N, E) = \sum_N x_i + \sum_E y_j. \tag{2.3}$$

Since it is impossible to obtain more than $V(N, E)$, (2.3) must be an equality.

In the following I show that an outcome satisfying (2.1) exists only if the workers control the firm initially, and only for some particular values of α and β. In all other cases, the core is empty and the ownership structure is unstable.

3   Instability

To check whether or not a mixed ownership structure is stable, one has to investigate each of the following four cases:

(I) $\alpha \geqslant 0.5, \quad \beta \geqslant 0$

(II) $\alpha < 0.5, \quad \beta \geqslant 0$

(III) $\alpha \geqslant 0.5, \quad \beta < 0$

(IV) $\alpha < 0.5, \quad \beta < 0$

(I) is the case where the firm is initially controlled by the workers, and there are gains from labor-management. In case (II) there would be gains from labor-management, but the firm is initially controlled by the external owners. In (III) there is a loss from labor-management and the workers have the majority of shares. Finally, in (IV) external owners control the firm and labor-management gives rise to a loss.

The conditions for stability given by (2.1) should be applied to each of the cases (I)–(IV). Since I want to demonstrate under what conditions the core is empty, it is sufficient to find *one* violation of (2.1). It is assumed that any coalition with majority can decide to pay out the profit in the way that is most profitable for the coalition. That means, for any of the cases (I)–(IV):

$$v(n, e) = \max \left\{ \frac{n}{N}\alpha + \frac{e}{E}(1 - \alpha), \frac{n}{N}(1 + \beta) \right\}$$

$$\text{for all } n, e \text{ s.t. } \frac{n}{N}\alpha + \frac{e}{E}(1 - \alpha) \geqslant 0.5. \tag{3.1}$$

If $\dfrac{n}{N}\alpha + \dfrac{e}{E}(1 - \alpha) < \dfrac{n}{N}(1 + \beta)$, the most profitable for a majority coalition (n, e) is to pay out the profit as wages. Hence, external owners' income from their shares comes only as side payments. The interpretation of this case when $\alpha < 0.5$

initially, can be as follows: The e external owners sell their shares to the n employee-owners. This gives the workers the majority. The firm's surplus $1 + \beta$ is paid out as wages. Side payments to the external owners are the income from their sale of shares.

Similarly, if $\frac{n}{N}\alpha + \frac{e}{E}(1 - \alpha) > \frac{n}{N}(1 + \beta)$, it will be most profitable for the majority coalition (n, e) to pay out the surplus as dividends.

In this section I consider only the cases with many small shareholders, such that both N and E at least exceed 2. The results for collective employee ownership ($N = 1$) or one external owner ($E = 1$) are given in section 4.

I now consider each of the cases (I)–(IV) separately. Since the proofs are similar in all four cases, only the proof of case (I) is elaborated.

(I)   Worker-controlled firm with labor-management gains

Proposition 1

For $\beta \geqslant 0$ and $\alpha \geqslant 0.5$ the core is empty for all α and β such that $\alpha < (1 + \beta)/(1 + 2\beta)$. Worker control in a firm with labor-management gains is a stable ownership structure if and only if $\alpha \geqslant (1 + \beta)/(1 + 2\beta)$.

Proof

If there is an outcome in the core, this must be one which gives nothing to the external owners. To see this, we use (3.1) and (2.1). From (3.1) we get:

$$v(N, 0) = v(N, e) = 1 + \beta \tag{3.2}$$

since $1 + \beta$ is the highest possible income. Inserting (3.2) in (2.1) gives one of the conditions for a stable solution:

$$\sum_N x_i = \sum_N x_i + y_j = 1 + \beta \quad \text{for all } j. \tag{3.3}$$

(3.3) implies that

$$y_j = 0 \quad \text{for all } j. \tag{3.4}$$

Let n^* be defined by

$$\frac{n^*}{N}\alpha + (1 - \alpha) = 0.5,^3 \tag{3.5}$$

i.e., to obtain majority, the E external owners must buy the shares from at least n^* employee owners. Hence, from (2.1), (3.1) and (3.4) we obtain:

$$\sum_n x_i \geqslant \frac{n}{N}\alpha + (1 - \alpha) \quad \text{for } n \geqslant n^*. \tag{3.6}$$

If the core is not empty, it can be shown that at least one outcome must give the same income to all the workers.[4] That means there is an equilibrium outcome iff:

$$nx \geqslant \frac{n}{N}\alpha + (1 - \alpha) \quad \text{for all } n \geqslant n^* \tag{3.7}$$

which implies

$$Nx = \sum_N x_i \geqslant \alpha + \frac{N}{n}(1 - \alpha) \quad \text{for all } n \geqslant n^*. \tag{3.7'}$$

(3.3) and (3.7') imply that a solution exists if and only if

$$1 + \beta \geqslant \alpha + \frac{N}{n^*}(1 - \alpha) \tag{3.8}$$

where n^* is given by (3.5). If (3.8) holds for n^*, it will certainly hold for all $n > n^*$.

Substituting n^* from (3.5) into (3.8) gives the condition from Proposition 1:

$$\alpha \geqslant \frac{1 + \beta}{1 + 2\beta} \tag{3.9}$$

which is the combinations of α and β that are consistent with a solution. If α and β are high enough to satisfy (3.9), the firm will remain worker-controlled. The higher the values of α and β, the more expensive is a takeover for the external owners. When the labor-management gain β is large, the workers get a high income from running the firm themselves. Consequently, it is expensive for the external owners to bribe the n^* workers that are necessary to get external control over the firm. Similarly, if the workers' fraction α of the shares is large, the number of shares the external owners must buy to get control is also large. To buy the majority of shares is therefore expensive for them.

The combinations of α and β that ensure permanent worker control are given in Figure 15.1. For reasonable values of β, the workers need a large fraction of the shares to keep control. If for example the labor-management gain is 30 percent ($\beta = 0.3$), a stable solution requires that the workers have at least 81 percent of the shares. A more equal distribution of the shares requires improbably high gains from labor-management. To obtain a stable ownership with $\alpha \geqslant 0.6$, for example, the labor-management surplus needs to be three times the capitalist surplus.

As long as (3.9) is not satisfied, any outcome can be blocked by a coalition. Since $\beta > 0$, it is impossible that all the workers can benefit by selling their shares to the external owners. However, when α and β are not too high (cf. (3.9)) the external owners are willing to pay n of the workers more than $(1 + \beta)/N$ each, such that they benefit by selling. By the same argument, it is impossible to give compensation such that no-one prefers to sell, since it is impossible to give each worker more than $(1 + \beta)/N$. Hence, when (3.9) is not satisfied the initial ownership structure cannot constitute an equilibrium. However, an external takeover cannot lead to a solution either. Any distribution of the profit that follows from a takeover by the external owners can be blocked by a coalition of all the workers. With external control of the firm, the workers can at most obtain the capitalist surplus equal to 1. This outcome can be blocked by a coalition of all the workers since they obtain $1 + \beta$ under a labor-management regime. Since each of the employees wants to sell, the competition between them may drive the price

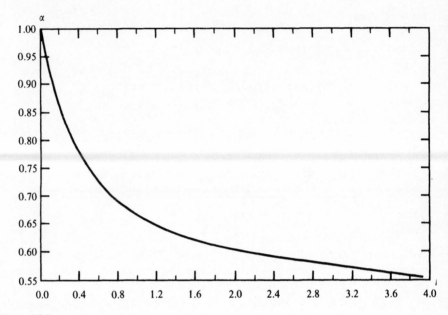

Figure 15.1

down to the reservation value α/N. This is less than what each of them can obtain in the coalition $(N, 0)$. Hence, the coalition $(N, 0)$ can block any distribution following from a takeover by the external owners.

(II)   Capitalist firm with labor-management gains

Proposition 2
For $\beta \geqslant 0$ and $\alpha < 0.5$ the core is empty.
There is no stable ownership structure in a firm with labor-management gains, initially controlled by external owners. To obtain the majority of shares, the employees must buy the shares from at least e^* of the external owners, i.e.,

$$\alpha + e^*(1 - \alpha)/E = 0.5,$$

Since $\beta \geqslant 0$, the coalition of all the workers and e external owners can obtain more than under external ownership. Hence, the coalition (N, e^*) can block the coalition of all the external owners. Further, if the workers obtain control the value of the external shares becomes zero. Any coalition (N, e^*) where the external owners get more than zero can therefore be blocked by a coalition of e^* other external owners and all the workers. Intuitively, the external owners underbid each other in order to obtain at least something for their shares.

However, any outcome where the external owners together obtain less than

$1 - \alpha$ can be blocked by the coalition of all the external owners, which obtains $1 - \alpha$.

(III)   Worker-controlled firm with loss from labor-management

Proposition 3
For $1 > 1 + \beta > \alpha$ and $\alpha \geqslant 0.5$ the core is empty and there is no stable ownership structure. For $1 + \beta < \alpha$, any ownership structure is stable.

If $1 + \beta < \alpha$, the workers run the firm as an ordinary capitalistic firm and pay out the profit as dividends. There is therefore no reason for the external owners to achieve control over the firm. Hence, if $1 + \beta < \alpha$ the ownership structure is stable.

For $1 + \beta > \alpha$, however, any ownership structure is unstable. This result may seem contra-intuitive at first glance, since the external owners are willing to pay a price such that all the workers can benefit by selling. However, the problem is that each worker will try to benefit by selling individually. The external owners are willing to pay more per share if they buy only the majority shares than if they buy more. Hence, there is a potential gain for those n^* workers who break out of the $(N, 0)$ coalition, and sell individually. Any outcome where the workers distribute the profit between them in one way or another can be blocked by a coalition (n^*, E). However, all outcomes following from a takeover by the external owners can also be blocked. Intuitively, as each worker tries to sell individually, the competition between them drives the price down to their reservation level α/N. This is less than what each of them can obtain if they form a coalition and sell as a group, which will give them at least $(1 + \beta)/N$. The theory does not predict which group will get the majority.

(IV)   Capitalist firm: Loss from labor-management

Proposition 4
For $0.5 < 1 + \beta < 1$ and $\alpha < 0.5$ the core is empty and there is no stable ownership structure. For $1 + \beta < 0.5$, any ownership structure is stable.

When $1 + \beta < 0.5$ the workers do not benefit by allocating the profit to higher wages if they obtain the majority. Hence, the ownership structure is stable in this case. If for some reason the workers buy the majority of the shares, they pay out the profit as dividends. There is therefore no reason for resistance against worker control over the firm.

If $1 + \beta > 0.5$, however, any ownership structure is unstable. As long as $\beta < 0$, the external owners as a group cannot benefit by selling the majority to the workers. However, the employees are willing to pay a high price to e^* shareholders to obtain a majority, such that any external owner wants to sell. Hence, any outcome under external majority can be blocked by the coalition (N, e^*). By the same arguments as in sections (I)–(III), however, any outcome where e^* external owners get more than zero and the remaining $E - e^*$ get zero can be blocked. Intuitively, external owners underbid each other to sell shares that give zero return under worker control. However, coalition $(0, E)$ can obtain $1 - \alpha$. All outcomes that give the group of external owners less than $1 - \alpha$ can therefore be blocked by this coalition. Since any outcome can be blocked, the core is empty in this case.

An efficient takeover market does not solve the problem with unstable ownership if it is not combined with restrictions on the sale and purchase of shares. The effects of a takeover market can be studied within the model by assuming that one or more of the external owners is able to purchase control over the firm. Since such an assumption is just an interpretation of the model, it does not alter any of the conclusions. It follows that a takeover market is not sufficient to obtain a stable and efficient ownership structure.

4   Restrictions on the trade with shares

The assumption that shareholders are free to form all possible coalitions means that there are no restrictions on individual purchases and sales of shares. Restrictions on purchase or sale of shares imposed by governmental legislation or by binding agreements among groups of shareholders can, however, make mixed ownership stable.

4.1   Restrictions on the individual sale of shares

Labor-managed firms often have restrictions on their members' sale of shares. Workers may not be allowed to sell their shares individually, at least not to external owners. Sometimes the shares are collectively owned by the workers. With such self-imposed restrictions on the individual sale of shares, employee-ownership will be a stable outcome if $\beta > 0$ and the workers control the firm initially ($\alpha \geqslant 0.5$). If $\beta < 0$ or external owners control the firm, however, there is no stable outcome even when the workers trade their shares collectively.

Similarly, a group of external owners can form a group that trades their shares only collectively. With only one external owner $\beta < 0$ and $\alpha < 0.5$, the ownership structure is stable. If $\beta > 0$ or the firm is controlled by the workers initially, however, there is no stable ownership structure even when there is only one external owner.

4.2   Restricted offers not allowed

If restricted offers are allowed, an investor can limit his offer to a certain fraction of the shares. This makes it easier to obtain control since the acquirer can offer a higher price when the offer can be restricted to the number of shares necessary to obtain a majority. In many countries, however, restricted offers are not allowed for shareholders who obtain more than a certain fraction of shares after the purchase. All shareholders must be given the same offer. Analytically, this rules out the coalition between the acquiring group and only a fraction of the incumbent majority owners, if such a coalition will get more than a certain percentage of the shares.

If external owners want to take over a worker-controlled firm they must offer to buy all the shares. External owners are willing to pay 1 for 100 percent of the shares, while the workers' valuation of the firm is $1 + \beta$. Hence, a takeover will take place if and only if $\beta < 0$. Similarly, the workers will take over a firm controlled by external owners if and only if $\beta > 0$. Hence, when restricted offers are not allowed, takeovers take place as long as they increase the value of the firm. Moreover, the resulting ownership structure is stable.

There are, however, several reasons why laws against restricted offers may not be effective. An acquirer may hide his takeover by purchasing some of the shares through other shareholders. If, for example, he is not allowed to purchase more than 30 percent by restricted offers, he can buy 30 percent himself and the rest be formally held by his family and friends.

Second, a group of owners may cooperate about a takeover. It is, however, difficult to prove that a takeover is coordinated as long as the shares are bought individually.

Third, an acquirer may announce an unrestricted offer with a low price such that incumbent owners do not want to sell. A group of incumbent owners, however, are tacitly offered additional payments for selling their shares. The offer can then in effect be a restricted offer.

4.3   Equal treatment of all shareholders

In countries like the USA the buyer is allowed to restrict his purchase to a certain fraction of shares, but not to a limited group of shareholders. All shareholders must be treated equally. As a consequence, the buyer must purchase *pro rata* from all shareholders if he does not want to buy all the shares that are tendered, i.e., he must buy the same fraction of the shares from each shareholder. Equal treatment rules out all coalition except for the one containing all shareholders, (N, E). It then follows from (2.3) and (3.1) that $V(N, E) = \max(1, 1 + \beta)$.

Hence, there is a stable ownership structure where the owners with the highest valuation of the firm have the majority of shares. The intuitive explanation is that all shareholders get the same proportion of the takeover price and the after-takeover value when the shares are purchased *pro rata*. Hence, the incumbent owners will not sell unless the takeover price exceeds the current value of the firm.

The buyer may avoid equal-treatment restrictions by tacit agreements with a group of shareholders. The public offered share price is chosen so low that no shares will be tendered. A group of shareholders, however, are "bribed" to sell by additional benefits.

5   Conclusions

Worker participation through purchase of shares can lead to unstable ownership when the trade with shares is unrestricted. With restrictions on the purchase of shares, however, mixed ownership can be stable. Furthermore, even without restrictions there are some factors that may lead to stable mixed ownership.

First, if the number of shareholders is large, coalition formation may be difficult, at least among external owners. Even if, for example, external owners are exploited in a worker-controlled firm, they may be unable to cooperate to take control over the firm. Further, each owner is so small that she has no incentives to buy worker shares individually. This situation is similar to the free-rider problem in value-increasing takeovers, analyzed by Grossman and Hart (1980).

Second, mixed ownership may be viable if the shareholders take their long-run interests into account. To finance new investments it may, for example, be necessary to issue shares. If external owners expect to be exploited as co-owners in a worker-controlled firm, however, they may not be willing to invest in such firms. Hence, it may be optimal for the workers not to exploit those external owners who have already bought shares in the firm, in order to get external investors in the future.

The problem of unstable ownership applies to all firms where a group of owners can obtain a share of profits higher than their share of votes. The problem also arises when a majority group have other goals for the firm than maximum net present value. Such goals seem to become more frequent as cross-ownership between firms increases.

Even when all the owners are workers in the firm, the problem may arise. Heterogeneous labor can lead to conflicts about distribution. With different types of labor, the remuneration of different jobs is likely to be a conflict issue. Workers of each type may want to distribute more of the firm's surplus as payment to their type. Each group may therefore try to obtain control over the firm. Job rotation may, however, solve the problem, since then each worker's total pay will be an average of the pay for each job.[5]

Notes

I am grateful to Michael Hoel, Aanund Hylland, Karl Ove Moene and Michael Wallerstein for valuable discussions and advice in the preparation of this chapter.
1. It makes little difference if we assume that the workers do not have the opportunity to run the firm as a capitalist firm and get a surplus equal to 1. The workers then sell the firm to the external owners if $1 + \beta < \alpha$, due to low productivity under worker control.
2. In the case investigated the workers can obtain more than half of the profit only when they control half of the shares. However, the analysis can easily be generalized to the case where both groups have this possibility. Further, there may be more than two competing groups. In the extreme case, any coalition of owners can use a majority position to obtain private benefits.

3. n^* is just an approximation for the lowest *whole* number n^{**} defined by $\alpha n^{**}/N + (1 - \alpha) \geqslant 0.5$. This approximation does not affect the conclusions if N is sufficiently large (i.e., $N > 5$), which is assumed. When N is interpreted as the number of workers, the cases with very few workers ($N < 5$) are not interesting. However, at the end of this section we analyze the case where $N = 1$ is interpreted as a worker-union. It is obvious that when $N = 1$ the approximation in (3.5) cannot be used.

4. The proof is available from the author for the interested reader.

5. This point was suggested by Ugo Pagano.

16 The simple analytics of a membership market in a labor-managed economy

ERNST FEHR

1 Introduction

The defining feature of a Labor-Managed Firm (LMF) is that the ultimate decision-making rights are assigned to the workers. From this we can expect that the decisions of the LMF conform to the interests of the (majority of) worker-members.[1] But which worker-members do we mean? In an intertemporal context we must distinguish between the *ex ante* members of period t and the *ex post* members of period t. The *ex post* membership consists of the *ex ante* members who remain with the LMF and those additional workers who join the LMF during the period. They will be the *ex ante* members of period $t + 1$. It seems obvious that the *ex ante* members make the decisions in any given period because those who are not yet members of the LMF can hardly be given a direct say in firm decisions. To be more precise: assume that decisions are made at the beginning of the period. Only those who are a member of the LMF at that time, i.e., the *ex ante* members, can participate in these decisions while those who join the LMF later are excluded.

Beginning with Ward (1958), Domar (1966) and Vanek (1965) the larger part of the economic theory of the LMF *assumes* that LMFs maximize the (present value of) *per capita* income of *ex post* members. A recent example is Drèze (1989).[2] The LMF is thus assumed to act in the interests of its *ex post* members in any given period. But why should *ex ante* members take into account the interests of *ex post* members? What is the institutional mechanism that leads to the maximization of *per capita* income of *ex post* members? These questions become even more important when we consider the well-known implications of this assumption for efficiency (see, e.g., Bonin and Putterman, 1987:13–18): first, the marginal value product of labor will in general exceed the reservation wage. As a result the LMF produces less output with less workers than its profit-maximizing capitalist twin. Moreover, involuntary unemployment and unexploited gains from trade prevail. Second, in the one input–one output case the Illyrian LMF decreases output and employment if the output price rises. As a consequence the output market equilibrium in Illyrian labor-managed economies (LMEs) may be unstable. Third, marginal value products of labor are not equalized across firms and industries, which gives rise to an inefficient allocation of labor.

Most papers which assume the maximization of income per *ex post* member are silent on the above questions. To the best of our knowledge we do not know of any microfoundation of this assumption, that is, of an analysis that *derives* it from the interests of utility-maximizing *ex ante* members. And we doubt that such a foundation is, under competitive conditions, possible. The reason for our scepticism is that as long as the choices of Illyrian LMFs are different from those of the competitive profit-maximizing twins, *ex ante* members can increase their welfare by imitating the choices of the latter. This follows simply from the fact that the profit-maximizing twin exploits all gains from trade while the Illyrian LMF does not, which gives *ex ante* members an incentive to reap these gains.

In this chapter we *derive* the behavior of the LMF from the interests of *ex ante* members. We draw on the work of Sertel (1982a, 1982b, 1987) and Dow (1986) and discuss several extensions. The essential idea of Sertel and Dow is the "introduction" of tradable membership rights. With tradable rights the *ex ante* members can reap all gains from trade. We show that the maximization of the income of *ex ante* members generates the same firm behavior as the maximization of profits. It follows that the above-mentioned inefficiencies of the Illyrian LMF vanish. Moreover, given our institutional framework, the employment choice of *ex ante* members is shown to be *unanimously* supported by *ex post* members. Our analysis deals in detail with the entry and exit payments which are associated with membership adjustments and examines the behavioral implications of our legal structure in the case of a loss-making LMF. We show that "our" LMFs apply the same short-run shut-down condition as Walrasian firms. The equilibrium of a labor market consisting only of LMFs is determined. It is argued that the LME absorbs aggregate shocks automatically and exhibits permanent full employment. Even if we introduce rigidities in the membership deed price-nominal (real) shocks do not cause unemployment and output losses. Membership markets for differently qualified workers and some implications of the introduction of unequal *income* shares are studied. In the final section we summarize our arguments and mention some possible solutions to the problem of how to share and/or insure firm-specific risks.

2   A legal structure for labor-managed firms

Being a partner in a capitalist firm is usually associated with the following rights and duties:

(i)   The right and the duty to supply capital

(ii)   The right to a profit share and the duty to share in losses; very often these shares are proportional or identical to the share of the capital supplied

(iii) The right to participate in the determination of the company's decisions either indirectly and/or directly via active and/or passive voting rights

(iv)   The right to transfer the partnership rights to other (possibly new) partners and protection from dismissal by other partners.

In this chapter I consider the following legal structure of LMFs:

(i′)   Each member of the LMF has the right and the duty to supply labor of a pre-specified quality.

(ii′)   Each member has the right to a share of the residual income and the duty to assume a share of the liabilities of the firm. The exact share may but need not be proportional to the quantity and quality of labor supplied.

(iii′)   Each member has the same active and passive (voting) rights regarding the determination of the firm's policy; in particular, the "one-person-one-vote" rule prevails.

(iv′)   No member can be dismissed against his or her will if the membership duties (e.g., to supply labor or refrain from stealing LMF property) have not been violated. The membership of the LMF is acquired through the purchase of a membership deed and expires when the deed is sold to the firm (i.e., the collectivity of the remaining members) or to a new member. The membership deed specifies the rights and duties listed in (i′)–(iii′).

(v′)   The set of workers and the set of members of the LMF coincides.

It is assumed that the economy is populated by F LMFs and by N^0 homogeneous labor suppliers who, if employed, provide one unit of labor.[3] The fth firm's production possibilities are determined by the strictly concave production function

$$g^f = g^f(n^f, K^f)\quad g_n^f > 0, g_{nn}^f < 0. \tag{1}$$

Output g^f is sold at a competitive price p. Each firm employs K^f units of capital which costs r per unit of K^f. We do not consider the adjustment of the capital stock, i.e., it is assumed to be given at K^f. Since each member of the LMF supplies the same quantity and quality of labor the residual

$$R^f = pg^f - rK^f \tag{2}$$

is shared equally by all n^f members. The income of each member is, therefore, given by

$$y^f = R^f/n^f. \tag{3}$$

The alternative income of each worker is given by w, that is, each labor supplier can earn a return of w for one unit of labor supplied elsewhere. Those who know the Illyrian theory of the LMF may wonder whether such alternative income possibilities will generally exist in an economy which consists only of LMFs. But as will be shown below "our" LME is a full-employment economy which gives every worker the possibility to get a job as an LMF member at the competitive return w.

As it is well known the Illyrian firm maximizes y^f by the choice of n^f. y^f is maximized if it equals pg_n^f (see Figure 16.1). It is obvious that if there is some excess supply of labor and in case of $y^f > w$ the members of the Illyrian firm do not exhaust all possibilities of increasing their income. They could employ additional workers at the competitive return w and share the marginal gains of $(pg_n^f - w)$. If, initially, there are m^f members each of them would gain $(pg_n^f - w)/m^f$ for each worker employed in addition.

It may be argued that such an income discrimination violates the principle of equal membership rights. This argument is, however, wrong, or at least

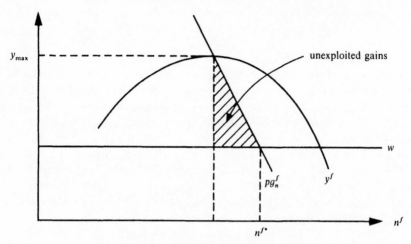

Figure 16.1   *Per capita* income maximization in the Illyrian firm

one-sided, because equal membership rights should also take account of the fact that "old" members have presumably contributed to the existing stock of physical and human capital by past entrepreneurial decisions. Viewed from this perspective the principle of equal membership rights is more likely to be met if those who are responsible for the present income-generating capacities of the LMF have the right to appropriate the gains of their past decisions but must also bear the losses when they occur. The legal structure of the LMF laid down at the beginning of this section meets this criterion: once a worker has acquired membership status she has the same rights and duties as the other members. But if the LMF is profitable[4] a price must be paid by newly hired members in exchange for the right to a profit share. On the other hand if the LMF makes losses it must compensate those who become members because they cannot be made responsible for the losses (and are of course not willing to bear them).

3   Demand and supply for membership rights

Following Sertel (1982a, 1982b, 1987) the demand price for membership deeds of the fth LMF is given by

$$d^f = y^f - w. \tag{4}$$

d^f is the maximum willingness to pay for a membership deed; if somebody pays d^f s/he is indifferent between accepting or rejecting the offer to become a member of the fth firm because his/her net income will be $y^f - d^f = w$. The supply price of a membership deed is given by the minimum payment to the firm that is required to induce the current members to accept a new member. Since the new member gets paid y^f and increases the revenue by pg_n^f the loss to the incumbents of admitting one more member is given by

$$s^f = y^f - pg_n^f. \tag{5}$$

In Figure 16.2(a) d^f and s^f are illustrated for a profitable LMF while Figure 16.2(b) shows an unprofitable LMF. Consider first the case of a profitable LMF. If the number of initial members is given by m_o^f the LMF would be willing to employ new members even if they pay nothing because m_o^f is below the Illyrian size of the LMF. Beyond the Illyrian size, however, new members are costly for the LMF[5] and s^f becomes positive. As long as $d^f > s^f$ workers are willing to join the firm and the LMF is willing to increase membership. At equilibrium $d^f = s^f$ which means that $pg_n^f = w$. The marginal condition for employment is thus the same as in a Walrasian firm and the common assertion that profitable LMFs employ less labor than the profit-maximizing twin is true only in the absence of a market for membership deeds.[6]

4   Membership adjustment and the shut-down condition

It is interesting to ask whether the LMF can engage in price discrimination. If new workers of a profitable LMF know that the optimal employment level is at n^{f*} (see Figure 16.2(a)) they can derive the average income $y(n^{f*})$. They are, therefore, not willing to pay $d^f > d^f(n^{f*})$ for the membership because net income would then fall below w:

$$y^f(n^{f*}) - d^f < y^f(n^{f*}) - d^f(n^{f*}) = w.$$

The LMF is of course not ready to sell membership deeds for less than $s^f(n^{f*}) = d^f(n^{f*})$. Thus, if the agents in the membership market are perfectly informed and are price-takers with respect to w self-interested behavior on both sides of the market forces them to accept an agreement at $d^f(n^{f*})$.

New members of a profitable LMF have to pay $d^f(n^{f*}) > 0$ for their membership. But what happens if the current membership, say m_1^f, exceeds n^{f*}? In this case, it is useful to reinterpret the s^f- and d^f-schedules. Each member is now willing to pay s^f to those who leave the firm because s^f is the marginal gain of a membership reduction whereas the minimum payment required to persuade a member to leave is given by d^f (because leaving causes a loss of $y^f - w$). Since $s^f > d^f$ at m_1^f those who leave can be compensated.

No member is willing to leave for less than $d^f(n^{f*}) = y^f(n^{f*}) - w$ because if s/he is paid less, i.e., $d^f < d^f(n^{f*})$, s/he is worse off than those who stay with the firm. If each leaving worker gets paid $d^f(n^{f*})$ his/her income is

$$w + d^f(n^{f*}) + [d^f(n^{f*})(n^{f*} - m_1^f)/m_1^f] = y(n^{f*}) + [d^f(n^{f*})(n^{f*} - m_1^f)/m_1^f],$$

which is exactly equal to the amount received by those who remain. Notice that all current members, that is also those who leave, share the costs of compensating the leavers. These costs are captured by the term in the brackets above. The consideration above makes it clear that a member who leaves for less than $d^f(n^{f*})$ loses relative to the remaining members. The latter, however, would lose

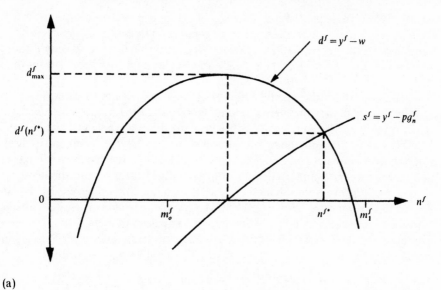

(a)

(b)

Figure 16.2   The value of membership in a profitable firm

(relatively) if they paid more than $d^f(n^{f*})$. Hence, in order to achieve a membership reduction on the basis of a voluntary agreement all agents must be made indifferent between staying and leaving, and this is possible only if those who leave receive $d^f(n^{f*})$ for their willingness to give up their share of the residual R^f.

Next we consider the membership adjustment for an unprofitable LMF. If $d^f = y^f - w < 0$, each member would prefer to leave the LMF. Within our legal structure this is, however, not possible because in order to leave the LMF the member has to find somebody who is willing to buy his/her membership deed. But nobody is willing to pay a positive price for the deed. Instead the LMF has to pay new members compensation in order to induce them to join the firm.

Assume, for example, that the current membership is given by m_o^f in Figure 16.2(b) which is below n^{f*}. The LMF cannot persuade $(n^{f*} - m_o^f)$ outside workers to join the firm unless it is willing to pay each of them $-d^f(n^{f*})$. New members are then indifferent between joining and not joining because their income is given by $y^f(n^{f*}) - d^f(n^{f*}) = w$. The "old" members will earn

$$z^f(n^{f*}) = y^f(n^{f*}) + [d^f(n^{f*})(n^{f*} - m_o^f)/m_o^f]. \tag{6}$$

The term in the brackets is negative because $d^f(n^{f*}) < 0$. Since fixed costs rK^f which have to be paid by the members irrespective of whether g^f is positive or zero the m_o^f members of the LMF agree to shut down the firm (temporarily) if

$$z^f(n^{f*}) < w - (rK^f/m_o^f) \tag{7}$$

holds. The RHS of (7) represents the income of the current LMF members if they work elsewhere. Notice that the m^f members still own their membership deeds, which forces them to pay the fixed costs rK^f even if they work elsewhere. This is implied by property (ii >) of "our" legal structure. Inserting (2), (3) and (4) into (7) and rearranging terms yields

$$\frac{pg^f(n^{f*}) - rK^f}{n^{f*}} \cdot \frac{n^{f*}}{m_o^f} + w(1 - (n^{f*}/m_o^f)) < w - (rK^f/m_o^f)$$

which simplifies further to

$$pg^f(n^{f*}) - wn^{f*} < 0. \tag{8}$$

Hence, we arrive at the conclusion that all m_o^f members agree to shut down the LMF if the revenue does not cover the competitive job return for n^{f*} workers. Since n^{f*} is determined by the marginal productivity condition $pg_n^f(n^{f*}) = w$ this is, of course, exactly the shut-down condition for a profit-maximizing twin acting in a competitive environment.[7]

It remains to discuss the case of a membership reduction for an unprofitable LMF. Suppose that current membership is at m_1^f in Figure 16.2(b). Since $d^f(m_1^f) < 0$, members were happy if they could work elsewhere; they are even willing to pay in order to leave the LMF. A reduction by one member saves the LMF $s^f(m_1^f) > 0 > d^f(m_1^f)$. As long as s^f is positive the LMF gains from a reduction even if those who leave pay nothing. If each leaving member pays

$-d^f(n^{f*})$ to the LMF leavers and stayers are again equally well off, that is, they share the costs of adverse business conditions equally. Those who remain earn

$$z^f(n^{f*}) = y(n^{f*}) + [d^f(n^{f*})(n^{f*} - m_1^f)/m_1^f]$$

and those who leave get

$$w + d^f(n^{f*}) + [d^f(n^{f*})(n^{f*} - m_1^f)/m_1^f] = z^f(n^{f*}).$$

Thus $-d^f(n^{f*}) > 0$ is the only price at which the membership reduction can be achieved wholly on a voluntary basis. For if leavers pay less, that is, if $-d^f < -d^f(n^{f*})$, those who stay, i.e., the constituency of the LMF, are worse off and are, therefore, not willing to take back the membership deeds of the leavers, whereas if the inequality is reversed nobody is willing to leave.

5   LMF-maximand, comparative statics, and turnover

The analysis in the preceding section shows that *ex ante* members receive always an income of

$$z^f(n^f) = y^f(n^f) + [d^f(n^f)(n^f - m^f)/m^f] = y^f(n^f) + v^f(n^f). \tag{9}$$

We can distinguish four cases:

(1) Expansion of a profitable LMF: new members pay $d^f > 0$, i.e., $v^f > 0$.
(2) Contraction of a profitable LMF: leaving members get paid $d^f > 0$, i.e., $v^f < 0$.
(3) Expansion of an unprofitable LMF: new members get paid $-d^f > 0$, i.e., $v^f < 0$.
(4) Contraction of an unprofitable LMF: leaving members pay $-d^f > 0$ to the firm, i.e., $v^f > 0$.

In all four cases the entry and exit payments are determined by the equilibrium price of the membership deed. All *ex ante* members are treated equally and receive z^f while new members always get the competitive return w. Inserting (2), (3) and (4) into (9) and rearranging terms leads to

$$\begin{aligned} z^f &= (1/m^f)[pg^f(n^f) - wn^f - rK] + w \\ &= (1/m^f)\Pi + w. \end{aligned} \tag{10}$$

We know already that "our" LMF chooses the profit-maximizing employment level. The behavior of the LMF can, therefore, be derived from the assumption of profit-maximization. This is confirmed by expression (9) and (10), which indicate that profit-maximization can itself be derived from the maximization of income of *ex ante* members under conditions of a competitive membership market. Or put differently: the LMF maximizes the income of its current members by acting like a Stackelberg leader *vis-à-vis* new (or leaving) members, that is, it maximizes z^f as given in (9) subject to $d^f = y^f - w$. This is tantamount to profit-maximization since m^f and w have to be taken as given. This implies, of course, that the LMF inherits the comparative static properties of Walrasian firms. In particular, a rise in fixed costs rK^f leaves employment unaffected. It reduces "only" the income of the current members. A rise in p induces an increase in n^f while a higher w leads to a reduction of n^f.

From expression (10) we can also derive that the employment choice is independent of the initial membership level. Thus, if we asked the *ex post* members about their preferred level of n they would *unanimously* support n^{f*}. This sounds surprising because – as Figure 16.1 illustrates – n^{f*} deviates from the level of n^f that maximizes the income of *ex post* members y^f. In the presence of our LMF constitution *ex post* members (of a profitable LMF, say) must, however, take into account the payments that have to be made to leaving members. In equilibrium $\delta y^f/\delta n^f = -\delta v^f/\delta n^f < 0$ holds: a reduction of n^f increases y^f but since d has to be paid to "dismissed" members it reduces v^f by the same amount. n^f-reductions are, therefore, not in the interest of *ex post* members.

So far, we have discussed adjustments of the membership size but not the problem of entry and exit of members at a given size of the firm. It is clear from the legal rules of section 1 that a member can leave only if s/he is able to sell the membership deed (possibly at a negative price). The deed may be sold to the LMF or to a new member directly. As in capitalist partnerships, admitting a new member may or may not be subject to the agreement of the old members. It seems useful that old members have at least the right to reject a new one if the new one is not as skilled as the leaving member. It is, however, clear that (in a world of imperfect information) this right might render the position of the LMF *vis à vis* a leaving member too powerful. Alternatively, one can imagine a right to sell the membership to the LMF at the competitive (possibly negative) membership price. Or, what is just the other side of the coin, the duty of the LMF to buy membership deeds from leaving members at the competitive price. The LMF is then free to sell the deeds to a new member of its choice. In our perfect information model the assignment of such rights does not matter because one can always determine the equilibrium membership price unambiguously. Under conditions of imperfect and asymmetric information, however, this may be difficult and different turnover-related membership rights may give rise to very different outcomes. To derive the distributional and the efficiency implications of different rights assignments is an important task of future research.

6   Labor-market equilibrium and shock absorption properties

The preceding sections showed that each LMF adjusts employment according to the marginal productivity condition $pg_n^f(n^f) = w$. Denoting $(g_n^f)^{-1}$ by h^f and remembering that each LMF takes w and p as given allows us to derive aggregate labor demand N^d as

$$N^d = \sum_{f=1}^{F} h^f(w/p). \tag{11}$$

Assuming that a sum of $\tilde{w}$ is required to compensate a worker for the disutility of one unit of labor, aggregate labor supply can be written as

$$N^s = \begin{cases} 0 & \text{if } \tilde{w} > w. \\ N^o & \text{if } \tilde{w} \leqslant w. \end{cases} \tag{12}$$

(12) deserves some further explanation because as we have seen z^f may fall below w and there is no barrier that it might not fall even below $\tilde{w}$. If all firms provide their current members with an income above $\tilde{w}$, each member prefers to remain in the labor market. If, however, $z^f < \tilde{w}$, members prefer to leave the labor market. But according to our legal system they cannot escape from the burden of the loss. This implies that $[w - (rK^f/m^f)] \geqslant [\tilde{w} - (rK^f/m^f)]$ is the appropriate labor-market participation condition for a member of an LMF. Even if z^f is below the RHS of the above inequality members of LMFs will stay in the market; they will then of course shut down their firm (temporarily) but leaving the market would render them (weakly) worse off. In Figure 16.3 we depict a short-run labor-market equilibrium of the LME. Since LMFs behave like Walrasian profit-maximizing firms it is not surprising that it is a full-employment equilibrium which is of course also Pareto-efficient.

It seems worthwhile to point out that adverse shocks to aggregate labor demand or aggregate labor supply lead to an *automatic* adjustment of workers' incomes, deed prices and, thus, of the competitive return to a job. Whereas in capitalist economies it is easy to imagine contractual rigidities that lead to a violation of Walrasian assumptions, in a LME, with a membership market

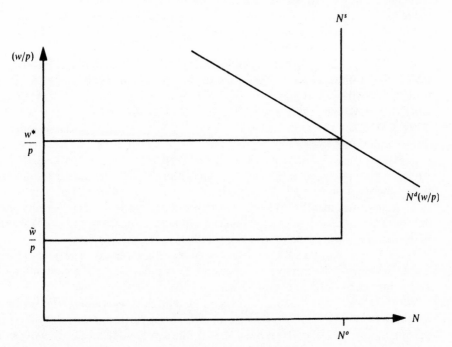

Figure 16.3 The value of membership in an unprofitable firm

rigidities are much harder to think of because workers are not hired for a contractual wage but become members of the LMFs and receive a contractual *share* of the residual. Their incomes adjust automatically if shocks occur.

The only source of price rigidity in the labor market we can plausibly think of is the deed price d. Imagine, for example, that there is a small volume of trades in membership deeds and that all transactions in the membership market for a particular LMF involve this LMF. Since there are virtually no transactions between insiders and potential new members which do not involve the LMF there is no market price for a deed which is established independently of the LMF. In such a situation there is only the "official" deed price which is set by the LMF, and which may not change continuously with economic conditions.

So let us assume that d is fixed (in nominal terms) at d_0 in the short run. What happens under this assumption if the LME is hit (in a state of full employment) by a *negative* nominal demand shock which reduces p (and r) from p_0 (r_0) to $\lambda p_0 \equiv p_1$ ($\lambda r_0 \equiv r_1$), $\lambda < 1$. In each firm y decreases from y_0 to $\lambda y_0 \equiv y_1$ and the marginal value product falls to $\lambda p_0 g_n$.[8] Before the shock the net income of a new worker is given by $w_0 = y_0 - d_0$. Since d is kept fixed and y decreases by $(1 - \lambda)$ percent the return from a job, $y - d$, decreases by more than $(1 - \lambda)$ percent, that is, $p_1 g_n \equiv \lambda p_0 g_n > \lambda y_0 - d_0$. But the RHS of this inequality represents the cost of a new worker to the LMF which has, therefore, an incentive to *increase* n. We assumed that the shock occurred at full employment and, hence, no LMF can satisfy its membership demand unless it poaches members from other firms by reducing d below d_0. In the long run LMFs will bid up the costs of a worker by reducing d to $\lambda d_0 \equiv d_1$ which gives $w_1 = y_1 - d_1 = \lambda w_0 = \lambda y_0 - \lambda d_0$.

Next let us examine the consequences of a *positive* nominal demand shock ($\lambda > 1$):y and pg_n increase by $(\lambda - 1)$ percent whereas d is fixed at d_0. This leads to $p_1 g_n \equiv \lambda p_0 g_n < \lambda y_0 - d_0$, that is, all LMFs prefer to lay off members. Given our LMF constitution this is not possible unless individual members agree upon being laid off. They will, however, sell their membership deed only if leaving the LMF does not render them worse off relative to those who remain. But since in all other LMFs the marginal value product is given by $p_1 g_n < \lambda y_0 - d_0$ this is impossible. Other LMFs pay a maximum of $p_1 g_n$ which gives a leaving member who gets a deed price of d_0 a net income of $[p_1 g_n + d_0 + d_0(n - m)/m]$. Those who stay receive $[\lambda y_0 + d_0(n - m)/m]$ which is larger. Thus no member is willing to sell the deed and no LMF succeeds in reducing its membership.

The above arguments lead to the surprising conclusion that *even if the nominal deed price is rigid nominal demand shocks will not cause unemployment*. A LME with membership markets exhibits, therefore, appealing shock-absorbing features. It behaves like a Weizmanian profit-sharing economy. The government is able to control inflation by restrictive monetary policy without creating output and employment losses.

What about real shocks? Suppose the LME is hit by a *negative real shock* which reduces g_n by $(1 - \lambda)$ percent at any level of n. This in turn reduces $g(n)$ by $(1 - \lambda)$ percent at any level of n. If d is fixed at d_0 in the short run the cost of a worker is reduced from $y_0 - d_0 = [(pg - rK)/n] - d_0$ to $y_1 - d_0 = [p\lambda g - rK)/n] - d_0$. As in the case of a negative nominal demand shock the cost of a worker decreases by more than $(1 - \lambda)$ percent and each LMF has an incentive to expand membership because $p\lambda g_n > y_1 - d_0$ prevails. If we assume a positive (g- and g_n-increasing) supply shock (i.e., $\lambda > 1$) LMFs would like to reduce membership at the deed price d_0. But as in the case of a positive nominal demand shock no current LMF member is willing to sell his/her deed at a price of d_0. So again we arrive at the important conclusion that productivity shocks do not cause unemployment even if the deed price is kept rigid at d_0.

7 Membership markets for different types of labor

Suppose the LMF needs different qualifications. The number of members with labor of type 1 (2) is denoted by n_1 (n_2). The production function is given by

$$g = g(n_1, n_2).\tag{1'}$$

Both types of labor exhibit positive and decreasing marginal products. The competitive return for a job of type 1 (2) is labeled w_1 (w_2). At first sight it seems obvious that if the productiveness of n_1- and n_2-workers differ, assigning the same rights to the residual to them might generate allocative inefficiencies. In the presence of a membership market this presumption is, however, wrong. One can give differently qualified workers identical residual rights without any distorting effect. Moreover, as we will see below, one can assign *any* distributional weight to a particular membership deed without causing an inefficiency. The reason for this is very simple. Membership prices reflect different distributional shares in such a way that new members will always receive their competitive return, w_1 or w_2. Therefore, it is in the interest of the current members, whatever their composition, to employ labor of type 1 (type 2) until the marginal productivity condition $pg_1(n_1, n_2) = w_1 [pg_2(n_1, n_2) = w_2]$ holds.

To show this in more detail let a_1 (a_2) be the distributional share of type 1 (type 2) members. Then $(a_1 n_1 + a_2 n_2)$ reflects the weighted labor input and the residual income per weighted labor input is given by

$$x \equiv [pg(n_1, n_2) - rK]/(a_1 n_1 + a_2 n_2).\tag{13}$$

The residual income of each member is given by $y_1 \equiv a_1 x$ or $y_2 \equiv a_2 x$, respectively. It follows that the demand prices for labor are defined by

$$d_1(n_1, n_2) = a_1 x(n_1, n_2) - w_1.\tag{14a}$$

$$d_2(n_1, n_2) = a_2 x(n_1, n_2) - w_2.\tag{14b}$$

The supply price of a type 1 job (type 2 job) is given by the income loss of the LMF if it creates one more type 1 job (type 2 job):

$$s_1 \equiv -n_1(\partial y_1/\partial n_1) - n_2(\partial y_2/\partial n_1).$$

$$s_2 \equiv -n_1(\partial y_1/\partial n_2) - n_2(\partial y_2/\partial n_2).$$

Using the definitions of x, y_1 and y_2 we get

$$(\partial y_1/\partial n_1) = \dot{a}_1(pg_1 - y_1)/(a_1 n_1 + a_2 n_2).$$

$$(\partial y_2/\partial n_1) = a_2(pg_1 - y_1)/(a_1 n_1 + a_2 n_2).$$

$$(\partial y_1/\partial n_2) = a_1(pg_2 - y_2)/(a_1 n_1 + a_2 n_2).$$

$$(\partial y_2/\partial n_2) = a_2(pg_2 - y_2)/(a_1 n_1 + a_2 n_2).$$

Inserting these derivatives into the definitions of s_1 and s_2 yields

$$s_1 = y_1 - pg_1 = a_1 x - pg_1. \tag{15a}$$

$$s_2 = y_2 - pg_2 = a_2 x - pg_2. \tag{15b}$$

Equating supply and demand prices leads to the marginal productivity conditions

$$pg_1(n_1, n_2) = w_1. \tag{16a}$$

$$pg_2(n_1, n_2) = w_2. \tag{16b}$$

It is important to stress that the derivation of the marginal productivity conditions as the relevant conditions for the employment choice is completely independent of the size of a_1 or a_2. Thus, in the presence of a membership market any distribution of residual income is compatible with efficiency. This result holds because any change of a_1 or a_2 is accompanied by a change of equilibrium membership prices in such a way that the cost of a new member is equal to the competitive return w_1 or w_2, respectively.

8   Differential income shares for identical workers

The analysis in the preceding section is easily applicable to the case of differential shares of identically qualified workers. All that has to be done is to reformulate the production function as $g = g(n) = g(n_1 + n_2)$; n_1-workers get a share of a_1 while n_2-workers are paid $a_2 x$. Of course, x now contains the above production function. The supply price of a job for a worker with share a_i is defined as $s_i = a_i x - pg_n$, his/her demand price by $d_i = \bar{a}_i x - w$. At equilibrium $pg_n(n) = w$ holds.

For the current members it is irrelevant whether new members receive a large or small share because the membership price adjusts accordingly. The same holds true for new members. They always have to pay a price (or receive a compensation if losses prevail) which reduces their net income from the job to the competitive return.

Notice that the assignment of different income shares does not imply that the one-person-one-vote rule is violated, or that members are treated differentially with respect to other rights. By the introduction of differential income shares it is possible to reduce the membership price for particular workers to zero. The existence of liquidity constraints and imperfect capital markets is, therefore, no argument against a membership market. If some workers cannot afford to pay a high membership price they are assigned a share a_1 such that $d_1 \equiv a_1 x - w$ $= a_1 x - p g_n \equiv s_i = 0$ holds at equilibrium.

9   Summary and conclusions

The Illyrian theory *assumes* that LMFs maximize income per *ex post* member. We have argued that this assumption is not rooted in the interests of *ex ante* worker-members who have the decision-making power. Under the LMF constitution of section 2 all *ex ante* worker-members unanimously agree upon the choice of the efficient employment level because this choice maximizes *their* income. Moreover, all *ex post* worker-members unanimously support (*ex post*) this decision of *ex ante* members. There can, therefore, be no doubt that the legal rules laid down in section 2 constitute a firm structure which deserves the term "labor-managed." Under conditions of perfect competition the existence of a membership market does away with all inefficiencies of the Illyrian LMF. Not only will the allocation of labor be efficient but underinvestment effects (see Dow, 1986; Fehr, 1991) and the so-called "horizon problem" which has been emphasized by Furubotn (1979, 1980) will vanish as well.

With tradable membership rights the *ex ante* members share the successes and the failures of the enterprise while the newcomers will not have to bear the burden of present losses but will also be excluded from a share of present profits. In our view, this mechanism is also morally appealing because on average it assigns losses and profits to those who have been responsible for them.[9] In the short run a loss-making LMF will shut down if and only if the profit-maximizing twin shuts down.

We have assumed throughout the existence of a complete market system with perfectly competitive markets. Although we do not believe this assumption to be realistic, we can give two justifications: first, the great majority of contributions in the field of LMF theory rest on the (often implicit) assumption that labor management is a deviation from perfect competition in a complete market system. The best example is again the Illyrian theory which implicitly assumes the absence of membership markets – to say the least. But there is also a large number of papers on investment and financing in LMFs which do the same (see, e.g., the papers quoted in section I.2. in Bonin and Putterman, 1987). It is trivially true that if we compare such an imperfect LME with a perfect Walrasian economy (which is very often identified with a capitalist economy (CE)) the former will exhibit deviations from a first-best allocation. One implication of the work of Sertel, Dow and of this chapter is, however, that such a comparison is biased in favor of CEs and that the efficiency advantage of Walrasian economies is due not to the principle of labor management but to the arbitrary neglect of a membership market.

Second, in our view, it is wrong to think that so-called equivalence theorems[10] do not allow us to make an affirmative case in favor of LMEs. Although both perfectly competitive LMEs and CEs will implement an efficient allocation, they will in general not implement the same allocation because in LMEs the right to a share of pure profits is restricted to worker-members. Moreover, even if the two systems arrive at the same allocation one may prefer the "LME" allocation because in a LME decisions are made by those who are directly involved in the production process and are thus for a large part of their lifetime directly affected by the choice of working conditions and production plans. Since "most human beings prefer to have a say in decisions regarding the activities in which they are personally involved" and since "the quest for self-determination is deep rooted in human psychology" (Drèze, 1989:8), giving those who are most directly affected by decisions the right to decide may be regarded as a good in itself.[11]

Having said all this I hasten to concede that future research should concentrate on the examination of LMEs and CEs in imperfect market environments (see Chapters 11 and 1 in this volume by Dow and Bowles and Gintis, respectively). Our comparison of capitalist and labor-managed monopsonies in Fehr and Sertel (1991) and the introduction of efficiency wage effects in Fehr (1990) can be regarded as another step in this direction. We show that a labor-managed monopsony employs more workers than a capitalist monopsony and that even the efficient employment level may be an equilibrium of the former. Moreover, in the case of a sequentially discriminating LMF monopsony the employment choice is always efficient. If one allows for efficiency wage effects, the rate of equilibrium unemployment may (but need not) be lower in a LME than in a capitalist economy.

In the presence of a membership market it is also possible to solve distributional problems without distorting the allocation. In the preceding section we have shown that the membership price is positively related to the worker's share of the residual income. This means that liquidity and credit constraints are no argument against the implementation of a membership market. If capital markets are imperfect and credit rationing does not allow workers to pay a positive price for their membership one can always adjust their share a_i such that the equilibrium membership price is zero.

Although we have not dealt with the problems of uncertainty and risk-bearing in this chapter, we want to make a few remarks on this issue. It is generally acknowledged that the *allocation* of risk is one of the most important problems in a LME (see, e.g., Drèze, 1976, 1989). With regard to the aggregate risks "our" LME economy, however, does well. Since a LME with a functioning membership market is a full employment economy there is essentially no unemployment risk. This economy has similar properties as Weitzman's share economy: it is permanently in a state of full employment because adverse shocks to aggregate demand or aggregate supply lead automatically to an adjustment of nominal incomes y and this in turn automatically changes the nominal price of membership deeds. But notice that even if the deed prices are fixed, shocks are not capable of causing unemployment under the constitutional rules laid down in section 2. This is the Weizmanian feature of "our" LME.

Aggregate risks are properly socialized in "our" LME while firm- or industry-specific risks may pose considerable problems. To some extent the membership market may prove to be beneficial in this respect, too. For if a worker is more risk-averse than his/her fellow members s/he may opt for a low share a_i. A low share of the residual is not only associated with a lower membership price but also with a lower income risk. Thus, by the choice of a_i one can partially insure members against the risk of income fluctuations. One can imagine that risk-neutral or less risk-adverse members of a LMF insure their more risk-averse members. The latter pay their insurance premium by accepting a residual share/membership price combination that drives their income below the competitive spot return w while the former receive the premium in the form of an extra share.

Since we did not analyze the problems of risk allocation formally we can say nothing definite about the efficiency properties of a membership market in this respect. If it solves this allocation problem inefficiently, non-voting equity shares might be introduced or the government could implement a membership insurance. Since unemployment does not seem to be a big problem this insurance could replace (or complement) the unemployment insurance. A membership insurance might, for example, guarantee a member of an LMF λ percent of the competitive return w, i.e., if his/her firm makes losses which cause income z to fall below λ percent of w, the insurance pays the difference between z and λw. This suggestion, of course, needs further investigation; problems of moral hazard and adverse selection wait in the background. The latter could be dealt with by the legal requirement that each LMF or each LMF member has to be insured. The former problem will, however, remain. But is it not inevitably connected with almost any insurance?

Notes

1. Throughout this chapter we exclude agency problems by assumption. The management of the LMF will, therefore, act in the interests of the majority of workers.
2. For the rest of the chapter we call LMFs which maximize income per *ex post* member Illyrian LMFs. In addition, we assume decreasing returns to scale and that the state does not tax away the pure profits accruing to LMF members.
3. Throughout we neglect the integer problem associated with this assumption and use partial derivatives w.r.t. employment as approximations of the change in the value of a function if employment changes by one unit.
4. A LMF is called profitable if $y_{max} - w > 0$; it is unprofitable if this inequality is reversed.
5. The LMF is defined by its current membership which is in this case m_o^f. The Illyrian size is given by the level of n^f which maximizes y^f or d^f.
6. In Fehr (1990) I show that in the absence of a membership market egalitarian LMFs may employ *more* labor than the capitalist twin with positive profits if efficiency wage effects prevail.
7. Of course the long-run shut-down condition is given by $z^f(n^{f*}) < w$.
8. For notational convenience we assume for the rest of the chapter identical firms. The argument below does not hinge on this assumption since in a full-employment equilibrium the marginal product is the same in all LMFs and a change in p therefore causes the same change in the marginal value product in each LMF.

9. Stochastic elements are of course also responsible for what a member earns in a LME. But this is true for any type of economic system. In our view the tax/transfer system should compensate people for their good luck or their bad luck.

10. By an "equivalence theorem" we mean the following: "The set of allocations that can be implemented as an equilibrium of a perfectly competitive capitalist (Walrasian) economy can also be implemented as an equilibrium of a perfectly competitive LME."

11. Imagine that a central planner implements the same allocation as a Walrasian economy. I suspect that people prefer the "Walrasian" allocation because it is sustained by their own choices. Kornai (1988) argues forcefully that freedom has not only instrumental but also intrinsic value. Given that in modern economies the vast majority of people work in enterprises it makes a difference whether firm decisions are taken *by* themselves or whether they are taken by capital-owners if freedom of choice does have an intrinsic value.

Part VI
Political democracy and economic democracy

17 Investment planning in market socialism

IGNACIO ORTUÑO-ORTIN, JOHN E. ROEMER and
JOAQUIM SILVESTRE

1 Introduction

Despite the fact that the phrase "market socialism" has a respectable history, dating back to Lange's (1938) famous contribution in the Austrian debate, there has been little formal economic theorizing on the nature of market socialism.[1] We take market socialism to be a system of economic organization in which (1) the state has the authority to influence the pattern and levels of investment across sectors; (2a) most, if not all, resources are distributed via markets; (2b) citizens, in particular, earn income from labor that is traded on markets; (3a) firms are publicly owned, which means that profits are distributed to members of the population in proportions that are politically determined; and (3b) firms maximize profits. In this chapter, we depart from much contemporary literature (e.g., Miller, 1990 and Estrin and LeGrand, 1989, but not Brus and Laski, 1990), and do not consider the presence of worker-managed firms to be a necessary condition of market socialism.

Given the above characterization of market socialism, two kinds of question naturally arise. The first concerns the *consistency* of the five characteristics listed above. For example, can one design institutions which will assure that firms maximize profits while at the same time distributing profits diffusely among the population rather than concentrating firm ownership in the hands of stockholders who can trade stock? Is it possible for the government to control the distribution of corporate profits, without interfering with profit-maximization? It is largely these questions that have animated the debate on market socialism in recent years. The second kind of question concerns the *flexibility* of market socialism. Assuming that the incentive problems raised by the first kind of question can be solved, to what extent can a market socialist economy differ from a capitalist economy? In particular, what scope is there for planning in an economy where most private goods are allocated through markets? If the answer to the second question were "very little," then there would be little reason to advocate a market socialist economy. Social democracy, a system with significant redistribution of income but in which investment decisions are still made by capitalists, would be no different from market socialism, and probably easier to implement.

Our focus in this chapter is on the second kind of question. Our modeling choice has been to treat the structure of investment as the planning objective, although we could have chosen other objectives instead, such as the level of employment or the structure of employment across industries. Our treatment of the problem is classical: we attempt to characterize the class of investment vectors that can be implemented in a market economy if the government has available various types of price and quantity instruments. We have chosen investment as the focus, for we believe it is arguably the aspect of capitalist economies that most justifies intervention. In large economies, at least, investment leads the business cycle. Furthermore, there are significant externalities, both positive and negative, associated with investment that may justify government intervention.[2] We do not debate here with those who argue that government intervention in the investment process can only lower social welfare from what it would be without intervention.

Let there be an investment-good industry, sector 0, and N sectors which use the investment good as an input and produce consumer goods. The economy exists for two periods; in the first period, firms place orders for the investment good which will increase their productivity in the second period. In a private-ownership model of the economy, there will be a Walrasian equilibrium in which a certain vector of investments $\bar{I}^W = (\bar{I}_1^W, \ldots, \bar{I}_N^W)$ is attained in the consumer-good industries. The socialist state, however, wishes to implement a different vector of investments, say $\bar{I}$.

How can the center implement the sectoral investment $\bar{I}$? We assume that it has available various price or quantity *instruments* and various options for *taxation*; as summarized in Figure 17.1, we characterize the class of implementable investment vectors for three combinations of these instruments, indicated by the filled-in cells of Figure 17.1.

We view Lange's (1938) *On the Economic Theory of Socialism* as the direct ancestor of our own study. Despite the claimed parentage, Lange's concerns were quite different from ours. He facilely remarked that the center could set the interest rate to implement the level of total investment that it wants to attain in the economy – that was the extent of his concern with the implementation problem, as we have defined it. In section 4 we present a model which generalizes Lange's suggestion. The set of instruments consists of N discounts on the market interest rate – one for the firm in each consumer-good sector. Taxes are levied on firm profits to balance the deficit of the central bank. Firms borrow to finance investment; they maximize profits in the presence of markets for all commodities. Each citizen receives, as well as wage income, a fraction of total after-tax profits, what Lange called the social dividend, which is determined by some political process.

Lange did not study the set of implementable investment vectors, but was concerned with the calculation of prices. He remarked that the prices of consumer goods could well be set by markets, but the prices of investment goods were too important to be left to the market, and should be set by the center *equal to their values at market equilibrium*. Evidently, he believed that disequilibrium in the investment-goods' sectors was too destabilizing for the economy, and that a considerable advantage of socialism over capitalism would be the setting of these prices by the center instead of the market. Thus, he proposed a tâtonnement mechanism by which the state could calculate prices that would converge, he

instruments		
prices		quantities
consumption goods	investment goods	
	Lange model (i)	direct investment model (i)
sales-tax model		

(row labels: **corporation tax**, **sales tax**)

Figure 17.1   The class of implementable investment vectors

assumed, to equilibrium.[3] In the literature that followed Lange (notably, Arrow and Hurwicz, 1958, and Arrow, Block and Hurwicz, 1959), the question of the convergence of tâtonnement was studied rigorously. But the basic issue of implementation has never been raised in the literature on market socialism.

Economists have since become less interested in tâtonnement, because of the results of Debreu (1974) and Sonnenschein (1973a, 1973b) demonstrating that on the space of economic environments, the convergence of the tâtonnement process to Walrasian equilibrium is the exception rather than the rule. In our chapter, we study only the existence of equilibrium. We think of the center as setting the values of its instruments, and then view the existence of an equilibrium at those parameter values as a stylization of the conventional wisdom that "the market finds equilibrium."[4]

There is an important inconsistency between the motivation of our study and the models exhibited below. In the models, there is no uncertainty, there is a complete set of futures markets, and there are no externalities. But it is precisely uncertainty, the lack of futures markets and insurance markets, and externalities, which motivate influencing the investment vector of an economy away from its laissez-faire value. Our apology consists in conjecturing that the conclusions about planning that we arrive at here will be preserved in more realistic and complex models.

Incentive issues related to asymmetric information and the politics of a market socialist society are beyond the scope of the present chapter; for discussion of these issues and their relation to the models of this chapter, see Bardhan and Roemer (1992).

In organizing the chapter, we have followed the practice of Sen (1971). Sections 2 through 6 present the analysis informally and verbally; the asterisked sections with the same numbers which follow present the formal definitions and theorems. Proofs are available separately (Ortuño-Ortin, Roemer and Silvestre, 1991).

2   The economic environment

There are $N + 1$ sectors in the economy and two time periods. There is one firm in each sector. Firm 0 produces the only investment good in the economy, and operates only in the first period. Firm j $(j = 1, \ldots, N)$ produces a consumption good in each period. In the first period, each of the $N + 1$ firms has a production function with only labor as an input. We view the capital stock as already fixed, and unchangeable in the first period. During the second period, the production for each consumer-good firm is a function of investment and labor. These firms place orders for the investment good in period one, and make their investments in period two.

There are M citizens, each with a utility function defined over the N consumption goods in each period: there are $2N$ arguments in each utility function. In particular, we assume for simplicity that labor (or leisure) is not an argument in the utility function: each citizen offers the entire endowment of his labor in each period, so long as the wage is positive. There is only one kind of labor in the model; thus, differential skill is only imperfectly modeled as differential labor endowment. Each citizen has an entitlement to a share of profits of each firm, his "social dividend." In principle, there can be $M(N + 1)$ such shares. In a socialist economy, the government may opt to set simply a share of *total* profits going to each citizen, and so there would be only M such shares delineated: we call this the *simple socialist case*. The setting of shares, in any case, is the outcome of a political process. (Lange suggested that a household's social dividend be proportional to its size. We shall comment on this below.) In the *general case*, which includes that of a capitalist economy with government intervention (a social democracy), the shares of profits going to citizens vary across firms as well.

The timing of economic activity is as follows. Wages are paid at the end of each production period, and commodities are sold at the end of the period in which they are produced. Profits are paid to citizens at the end of the period in which they arise. Consumer-good firms order the investment good during the first period, but investment is not accounted as a cost of production until the second period, for it enters into production only then. Since firms must distribute (or turn over to the state) profits at the end of the first period, they must borrow to finance investment, because the investment good must be purchased at the end of the first period. Citizens, on the other hand, consume in each period, and also save in the first period; an equilibrium condition in the economy will be that total savings of citizens equals total investment of firms. At the end of the second period, firms pay back principal and interest, and citizens count the matured loans with interest as income in the second period.

Total labor in the first period must be allocated between the production of the investment good and consumer goods. The larger the fraction of its labor an economy allocates to investment, the smaller its consumption will be in the first period, and the larger it will be in the second period, since investment augments the production of output in the second period. A government which seeks to raise levels of investment, in this model, is thus concerned to replace first-period consumption with second-period consumption.

3   Constrained Walrasian equilibrium: a command-market-thought experiment

Suppose the government, which wishes to implement a given vector of investments across sectors, were able costlessly to monitor firms. A natural way of accomplishing its goal would be as follows: to command each consumer-good firm to invest exactly the desired amount, and to allow markets to do the rest. We call the market equilibrium associated with this procedure an *exactly-constrained Walrasian (ECW) equilibrium*. It is, formally speaking, a set of prices and an allocation which constitute a Walrasian equilibrium, with one restriction: that each consumer-good firm has no choice but to invest in the way commanded. In particular, it might well be at such an equilibrium that some firms register negative profits, for they are being commanded to invest more than they would if they were unrestricted. Thus, firms do not have the option of shutting down, for shutting down entails investing a zero amount. When profits are negative for a firm at an ECW equilibrium, the losses must be paid for by citizens, according to their assigned shares of firm profits. In this case, the entitlement to a firm's profits becomes an obligation to cover the firm's losses.

To be slightly more precise, an *exactly-constrained Walrasian* (ECW) *equilibrium relative to a vector of sectoral investments* $\bar{I} = (\bar{I}_1, \ldots, \bar{I}_N)$ is a set of prices, an interest rate and an allocation such that:

(1) Each consumer-good firm j demands labor and supplies output to maximize the present value of profits over two periods at given prices, subject to its demanding the investment good exactly in amount $\bar{I}_j$; the investment-good firm simply demands labor and supplies the investment good to maximize profits at given prices (in particular, it receives no command from the government).
(2) Each citizen receives labor income and his share of (constrained) profits of each firm, and chooses consumption and savings to maximize his utility over both periods subject to his budget constraints (one for each period).
(3) All markets clear. (In particular, the supply of the investment good by firm 0 equals the total investment demanded by the consumer-good firms, and total citizens' savings equals the total cost of the investment good.)

If the government chooses to implement an investment vector which is very large compared to the unconstrained Walrasian investment allocation for the economy, there may well exist no ECW equilibrium relative to that investment vector. The reason: investment might be so high that, at any candidate vector of prices, the total profits of consumer-good firms are negative, and indeed so negative that some citizens face a negative net income (their wage income does not suffice to pay their share of corporate losses). Thus, there will exist some set of investment vectors that can be implemented as ECW equilibria for a given economic environment, and in general this set will be strictly smaller than the set of *feasible* investment vectors for the economic environment. A feasible investment vector is one which the economy is technologically capable of realizing. Indeed, we view the maximal feasible total level of investment as the amount of investment good that can be produced with the economy's entire supply of labor in the first period. (This assumes that citizens can survive with no consumption in the first period; otherwise, we must alter the maximum feasible amount of investment appropriately.) The maximal feasible level of investment can be divided among consumer-good firms arbitrarily (again, assuming there are no restrictions on the pattern of feasible consumption in the second period).

A second thought experiment relaxes the requirement that the firm invest *exactly* the amount commanded by the government, and replaces it with the requirement that the firm invest *at least* the amount commanded. Thus, each firm may elect to invest autonomously above the commanded amount, if that would increase profits at the given prices. We analogously define a *constrained Walrasian* (CW) *equilibrium relative to $\bar{I}$* as a set of prices and an allocation which satisfy (1)–(3) above, but with the relaxed restriction. There will be a set of investment vectors that can be implemented as constrained Walrasian equilibria. We are here interested in the aggregate level of investment in each sector (commanded plus autonomous investment). Note that every constrained Walrasian allocation is also an exactly-constrained Walrasian allocation. For if an aggregate investment vector $\bar{I}$ arises as a CW equilibrium, it also can be viewed as an ECW equilibrium, at the same prices, where the government commands firms to invest exactly at the levels of $\bar{I}$. The set of constrained Walrasian allocations is thus a proper sub-set of the set of exactly-constrained Walrasian allocations. The exactly-constrained Walrasian concept is interesting only if the government wants to limit investment in some firms to levels that are lower than their Walrasian levels, roughly speaking: for if it is concerned only to increase investment levels, it might as well set lower bounds only on the amount a firm must invest.

Although the set of investment vectors that can be implemented as constrained (or exactly-constrained) Walrasian equilibria is not as large as the set that could be implemented by a Stalinist system in which labor is directly allocated to the investment good industry, we take it to be a natural set of investment vectors to aim at implementing with market socialist techniques: for it relies upon the market to decentralize all resource allocation – not only the allocation and pattern of final consumption, but the allocation of labor to firms. In particular, as a consequence of the use of markets we have: any constrained (resp. exactly-constrained) Walrasian equilibrium relative to $\bar{I}$ is Pareto-efficient among the set of feasible allocations in which sectoral investments are greater than or equal to (resp. precisely equal to) $\bar{I}$.[5]

The command mechanism used here, however, is highly unrealistic, as in reality firms cannot be costlessly monitored, and it is hard to imagine that management of firms could be easily motivated to engage in production plans which entail losses. In particular, we shall assume throughout our discussion that incentives have been created that induce managers to maximize profits – such incentives would work counter to the implementation of CW (or ECW) allocations, and so some other mechanism must be used if we are to implement the CW allocations realistically.

In the next two sections, we propose alternative mechanisms which indeed can implement the set of allocations (and investment vectors) that can be theoretically reached as CW and ECW equilibria, but in ways that firms achieve the desired result by maximizing profits subject to no commands from the center.

4 A generalization of Lange's idea

Once it has a viable market, the state should have reliable leverage to influence economic processes. This includes, in the first place, a rational profit tax system for enterprises and an income tax system for the general population, financial controls, the state bank's regulation of money turnover as a single whole, and an active credit policy, including lending rates corresponding to actual economic conditions. (Mikhail S. Gorbachev[6])

Lange wrote that the state bank should generate the desired investment level in the economy by setting the interest rate at which firms can borrow. Since our planner desires to implement a vector of investment levels, her instrument will be a vector of N discounts (or surcharges) on the market interest rate: one at which each consumer-good firm can borrow to finance investment.

Suppose that the planner wishes to increase all investments of consumer-good firms above their unconstrained Walrasian levels. Let the Walrasian interest rate be r. Assuming that all other prices remain fixed at their Walrasian levels, the planner can increase the investments chosen by firms by posting interest rate discounts for them. This will increase the demand for investment. To generate the required savings from citizens to finance the increased demand for investment funds, the market interest rate must rise above r. But then the central bank will suffer a deficit at the end of the second period, for it collects interest at low rates from firms at that time, and must pay out interest at the higher market rate to citizens. The deficit must be covered by taxing citizens' incomes. We allow the planner to tax only corporation profits to cover the deficit.

With this motivation, we define a *Lange equilibrium with corporate taxation relative to a given vector of sectoral investments* $\bar{I}$ as a vector of prices and wages, a vector of N interest rate discounts, and a vector of tax rates[7] on the profits of the N consumer-good firms such that the following hold:

(1) Each consumer-good firm maximizes the present value of profits. It discounts its second-period profits by the interest rate appropriate for citizens (the "market rate"), since profit income is distributed to them; but it debits the cost of investment at the corporate interest rate it is charged. The investment-good firm simply maximizes period-one profits. All profits are sent to the center.

(2) The vector of investment levels (autonomously) chosen by firms is $\bar{I}$.

(3) The center disburses profits to citizens, according to their entitlements, after

levying taxation at the stated rates for each sector. If a citizen's net after-tax social dividend is negative, then he receives a tax bill from the government, instead of a positive dividend.

(4) All consumers choose consumption in each period and savings in the first period to maximize utility over both periods, subject to their budget constraints, which include wage income, social dividends, and interest from savings.

(5) All markets clear.

Figure 17.2 presents the pattern of money flows in the economy.

In a Lange equilibrium, the subsidy to firm j is the cost of its expenditure on investment times the interest discount that the firm enjoys: for this is precisely the deficit that the central bank sustains from financing the firm's investment expenditure with high-interest loans from citizens. Note that the tax levied on a firm's profits under this scheme may be greater than its profits. In this case, of course, the (negative) after-tax profits are charged to citizens according to their shares. Or, if the planner wishes to discourage investment by a particular firm, that firm will face an interest rate surcharge.

We define a Lange equilibrium as *pro-investment* if all firms receive (nonnegative) interest rate discounts (not surcharges). Our first theorem states: (A) in the simple socialist case, the set of CW allocations is exactly the set of pro-investment Lange equilibria; and (B) in the simple socialist case, the set of ECW allocations is exactly the set of Lange equilibria. Thus, in the simple socialist case the Lange model provides a *decentralized, non-command mechanism by which everything can be implemented that can be implemented using the command structure of the previous section.*[8] In particular, all firm managers are instructed, in the Lange model, to maximize profits facing prices and effective interest rates.[9]

In the general case (i.e., when the profit shares differ across firms as well as across citizens), the Lange model is *more powerful* than the exactly-constrained Walrasian model: the set of allocations that can be implemented with the former strictly includes the set that can be implemented with the latter.

We envisage the mechanism working as follows. The center announces the N interest rate discounts from the market rate for the firms in the various sectors, and the after-tax net dividends to consumers; all prices adjust until markets clear. Unlike Lange, we provide no tâtonnement story for convergence to equilibrium. Our view that the market "finds" the Lange equilibrium is as justified as the standard view that the unregulated market finds the Walrasian equilibrium.

It is worthwhile to examine the special case of Lange equilibrium in which the corporate profits' tax rates are constrained to be less than one. This, in particular, will guarantee that citizens always receive nonnegative social dividends. We call such an equilibrium a *limited-taxation Lange equilibrium relative to $\bar{I}$* to distinguish it from the general case when corporate tax rates can be greater than one. In the simple socialist case we have (Theorem 4.2): the set of allocations (and investment vectors) that can be implemented as limited-taxation Lange equilib-

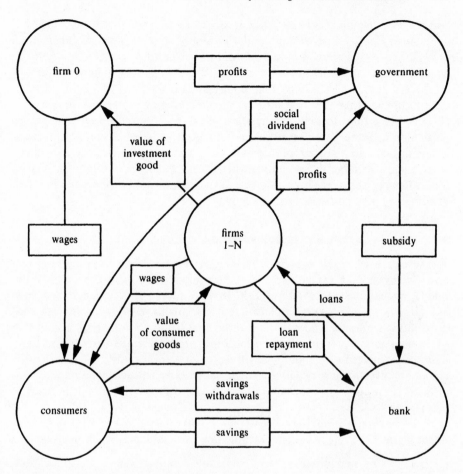

Figure 17.2   Money flows in the Lange model

ria is precisely the set of exactly-constrained Walrasian allocations in which total consumer-good firms' profits are nonnegative; and the set of allocations that can be implemented as limited-taxation pro-investment Lange equilibria is precisely the set of constrained Walrasian allocations in which total consumer-good firms' profits are nonnegative.

In any market socialist model, there will be opportunities for arbitrage, or black markets, for the government is interfering with the market mechanism. In the Lange model, the black market would be a capital market among consumer-good firms: firms that can borrow at a low interest rate could profit by lending to firms that can borrow only at a higher rate. This must be monitored by the center. There may also be opportunities for arbitrage between citizens who want to borrow (rather than save) but can do so only at the market rate, and firms that can borrow (and therefore lend) at low rates. In particular, firms might be tempted to lend to their workers under mutually advantageous arrangements. We initially suggested that the shares of total profits distributed to households be viewed as a supplement to wage income. We have now seen, however, that if the government wishes to implement an investment vector at which total profits of firms are less than the total subsidy, then the aforementioned shares become citizens' obligations to finance corporate subsidies from their wage income. In particular, a vector of large sectoral investments may be implementable only by assigning large shares of corporate profits (i.e., shares of after-tax corporate debt) to citizens with large labor endowments. More generally, the point is that a political party's proposal for a schedule of shares may not be independent of the investment plan it proposes to implement.

5   Direct provision of investment by the state

We next take what seems to be a more direct approach to implementing the center's investment targets. In the Lange model, the center acts only by interfering with the market interest rate. In the model to be described now, it acts as a large economic agent, purchasing the investment good on the market and distributing it, *gratis*, to consumer-good firms. It finances the purchase of the investment good by levying taxes on corporate profits. Firms are free to purchase more of the investment good if they must to maximize profits; they know the amount of investment they will receive from the state. This scheme is reminiscent of Brus' (1972, Ch. 5) proposal of "a planned economy with a built-in market mechanism."

To be precise, a *direct investment equilibrium relative to $\bar{I}$* is a set of prices, wages, an interest rate, a set of corporate tax rates, and an allocation at which:

(1) Every firm maximizes profits, choosing labor demands, outputs, and autonomous investment levels, knowing that it will receive the prescribed amount of investment, $\bar{I}_j$, from the state.
(2) All profits are distributed, net of corporation taxes, to citizens. Each citizen maximizes utility over two periods, subject to his budget constraints.
(3) Total taxes collected exactly finance the investment good purchased by the state.
(4) All markets clear.

We again specialize the direct investment concept to *limited-taxation direct investment equilibrium*, in which we restrict corporate tax rates to be between zero and one.

The first theorem is quite analogous to our result in section 4: in the simple socialist case, the set of direct-investment allocations is equal to the set of constrained Walrasian allocations, and the set of limited-taxation direct investment allocations is equal to the set of constrained Walrasian allocations in which total profits of consumer-good firms are nonnegative.

We conclude our analysis of the Lange and direct investment models by comparing the set of allocations that can be implemented with each of them. Theorem 5.2 states that: (A) in general, the set of allocations that can be implemented as limited-taxation pro-investment Lange equilibria is a proper sub-set of the set of limited-taxation direct investment equilibria. Thus, the direct investment mechanism is in principle more powerful than the Lange mechanism, as long as the center wants to encourage (rather than discourage) investment.[10] (If it wants to discourage some investment levels, then it will set an interest rate surcharge for some firms; the direct investment model is useless if discouragement is desired.) (B) However, the increased power of the direct investment mechanism *vis-à-vis* the Lange mechanism vanishes *in the simple socialist case*, for in that case we have that *the sets of limited-taxation Lange allocations and limited-taxation direct investment allocations are identical.*

We do not conclude that, in practice, these two implementation mechanisms – Lange and direct investment – would be equivalent in the simple socialist case. For they may well differ in certain aspects that we have ignored at the level of abstraction of our analysis. For instance, we have assumed that the center has available all the data describing the economic environment, and hence can calculate exactly the values of the instruments, such as interest rates, required to implement the desired investment vector. In reality, the center has only econometric and survey data. Suppose it announces the "wrong" vector of interest rate discounts, in the Lange model. It watches the markets, and adjusts the discounts as it sees what actually happens. This is relatively easy, and we can imagine that the economy will end up at some Lange equilibrium reasonably close to the one the center was aiming at, assuming its original information on demand functions and technologies was reasonably good. But in the direct investment model, the center commits itself to make certain purchases of the investment good, and to certain deliveries to firms. It may be much harder to adjust these obligations.

We may summarize the practical conclusion of sections 3, 4, and 5 as follows: in the simple socialist case, any allocation that can be implemented by the interventionist techniques of the command-market or direct investment mechanisms can also be implemented by the informationally superior, less interventionist Lange mechanism.

6   The sales-tax model

As in the Lange model, the government objective is to implement exactly a given strictly positive vector $\bar{I} = (\bar{I}_1, \ldots, \bar{I}_N)$ of sectoral investment. Again as in the Lange model, the firms follow price signals. But now the government instruments are taxes on sales, i.e., the prices faced by the firm differ from those faced by consumers. Because the present instrument requires the government to collect taxes (from citizens) instead of giving subsidies (to firms), running the scheme now generates a surplus instead of a deficit. Balancing the budget now requires the transfer of funds to the citizens, instead of from them. Balancing the budget does not therefore conflict with the need to keep the wealth of citizens positive.

The previous existence difficulties associated with this conflict thus do not appear here. Actually, existence of equilibrium can now be proved given an arbitrary rule for transferring the government surplus to citizens.

Another difference from the Lange model is that now all firms face the same input prices. This implies productive efficiency: contrary to the Lange and direct investment models, in a sales-tax equilibrium it is not possible to increase the output of all consumer goods by a mere reallocation of inputs.

We view the government as choosing $2N$ *ad valorem* tax rates, one for each consumer good in each period. This introduces a discrepancy between the price received by the producer and the price paid by the consumer (the latter being equal to the former multiplied by one plus the tax rate). Thus, the description of an equilibrium may specify the $2N$ producer prices and either the $2N$ tax rates or, equivalently, the $2N$ prices faced by consumers. We choose the second convention. The complete description of a *sales-tax equilibrium relative to the vector of sectoral investments $\bar{I}$ and to a given rule of (lump-sum) transfer of the government surplus* is given by (a) wage rates for the first and second periods, (b) a price for the investment good, interpreted as both the price received by the firm that produces it and the price paid by the firms that use it as an input, (c) first- and second-period producer prices for the N goods sold to consumers, (d) first- and second-period consumer prices for the same goods, and (e) an allocation such that:

(1) the profit-maximizing supply of the investment good (given the investment-good price and the wage) equals the sum of the components of $\bar{I}$

(2) the profit-maximizing demand for the investment good by each consumer-good firm (given the wage rates, the price of the investment good and the two-period prices of the consumer good faced by the firm) equals the relevant component of the vector $\bar{I}$

(3) the wealth of each citizen, which she takes as given, equals the value of her labor endowments, plus her profit income (evaluated at the prices faced by firms), plus her share in the government surplus as determined by the given transfer rule

(4) the two-period consumption of each citizen maximizes her utility subject to the constraint that the value of her two-period consumption, evaluated at consumer prices, does not exceed her wealth.

We adopt the following strategy for tackling the existence issue (Theorem 6.1). Set the first-period wage equal to one (i.e., first-period labor is used as numéraire), and set the price of the investment good at the level that induces its producer to supply exactly the required amount (namely, the sum of the components in the vector $\bar{I}$). The choice of first-period supplies of consumer goods is basically unrestricted: any positive amounts that use up the labor resource left after producing the investment good will do. After choosing these supplies, set the first-period producer prices at the level that induces the supply of precisely these quantities. Now we impose an assumption guaranteeing that the marginal rate of input substitution goes to zero with the amount of labor input used: a fixed-point argument guarantees that, under this assumption, an allocation of the second-period labor resource exists that equalizes the marginal rates of input substitution across firms when each firm is using the amount of investment good in $\bar{I}$. Because the price of the investment good is already given, this common marginal rate yields the appropriate second-period wage. By setting output prices equal to marginal costs we complete the description of the quantities supplied and producer prices. We are left with the description of consumer prices and quantities.

To this end, choose an arbitrary number α not lower than the value of the two-period output of consumer goods evaluated at the just specified producer prices. A second fixed-point argument shows the existence of a two-period vector of consumer prices that (a) clears the markets and (b) puts the aggregate value of the two-period output of consumer goods at precisely α dollars.

Intuitively, the center now has $2N$ instruments, namely, the tax rates on each consumption good in periods one and two, whereas it has only N objectives, the investment levels in N sectors. This leaves N degrees of freedom. The center may, in particular, induce any allocation among the N sectors using the amount of first-period labor left after producing the prescribed quantity of the investment good, using up $N - 1$ degrees of freedom. Moreover, it can, without affecting the amounts of each good produced, arbitrarily choose its total tax receipts. This suggests that a rich variety of allocations can be obtained as equilibria of the sales-tax model, for a given investment vector $\bar{I}$. There may, in particular, be large government surpluses which empower the given transfer rule with a significant distributional role. The sales-tax mechanism becomes particularly flexible if the transfer rule is not *a priori* given but can be chosen as a policy instrument.

Finally, we address the comparison of the direct investment and the sales-tax schemes. The comparison is not obvious because direct investment equilibria are second-best efficient under the sectoral investment constraints, but they typically display productive inefficiency (shifting both capital and labor among sectors could increase production). Sales-tax equilibria display productive efficiency and they distribute the produced amounts efficiently, but they are not second-best efficient relative to the sectoral investment constraints (shifting labor among sectors could yield a different output mix that could be distributed so as to Pareto-dominate the original allocation). But it turns out that the sales-tax mechanism is superior to the direct investment one in the following sense (Theorem 6.2): given a direct investment equilibrium, one can find a transfer rule with a sales-tax equilibrium that yields the same aggregate level of investment (i.e., the same sum of the components in $\bar{I}$) yet (weakly) Pareto-dominates the original direct investment equilibrium.

A sales-tax scheme may present serious political problems, especially when the mechanism involves large discrepancies between producer and consumer prices (i.e., large government surpluses). We conclude with a quotation from Lange (1938:96–97) on these difficulties:

There would be two sets of prices of consumers' goods. One would be the market prices at which the goods are sold to the consumers; the other, the accounting prices derived from the preference scale fixed by the Central Planning Board. The latter set of prices would be those on the basis of which the managers of production would make their decisions.

However, it does not seem very probable that such a system would be tolerated by the citizens of a socialist community. The dual system of prices of consumers' goods would reveal to the people that the bureaucrats in the Central Planning Board allocate the community's productive resources according to a preference scale different from that of the citizens.

We concur with this view, and believe that the direct investment or Lange mechanism may be politically more acceptable, at least domestically, in particular when financed by a corporation tax. It must be mentioned, however, that the use of interest rate or direct investment subsidies to firms producing internationally traded goods will draw accusations of unfair practices from governments of rival producers.

7   Conclusion

We have offered some preliminary, if lengthy, explorations on methods by which the center may implement a given target of sectoral investments in an economy where (a) firms maximize profits, (b) goods and labor are allocated through markets, and (c) profit shares are exogenously given. Two types of society are covered: first, a social democratic one, where firms are privately owned, profit shares simply reflect private property rights, and the state has an activist investment policy; second, a market socialist economy, where firms are publicly owned, managers are instructed to maximize profits, and profit shares are parameters, generated by a democratic process, for the distribution of the social surplus. We define the *simple socialist case* to be a socialist economy where profit shares do not vary across firms.

Our object is to study the range of investment vectors or allocations that can be achieved through the following instruments: (i) central commands to firms, (ii) interest rates faced by firms, as suggested by *Lange*; (iii) *direct investment* by the center; and (iv) *sales-tax* rates. The center must always balance its budget. We endow the center with the capability to tax profits as it sees fit for the amount needed to cover the cost of its investment program.

We consider command mechanisms, which share the feature of leaving to the market the allocation of labor and consumer goods while the center issues commands on investment. In the first one, called the *constrained Walrasian* mechanism, the center imposes a lower bound on the investment of each industry, but firms are free to invest more if they so wish. Thus, the mechanism is unable to force low levels of investment. In the second mechanism, called *exactly-constrained Walrasian*, the center commands exactly the investment level of the firm, and, hence, it can force both high and low investment levels. The *Lange* mechanism can in principle set interest rates for firms that are lower or higher than the market rate, and, as an effect, it may induce both high and low investment levels. We define the *pro-investment Lange* mechanism by requiring that the interest rates faced by firms do not exceed the market rate.

A first result is that, in the general case, *the Lange mechanism is more powerful than the exactly-constrained Walrasian mechanism*. (In a parallel manner, the pro-investment Lange mechanism is more powerful than the constrained Walrasian mechanism.) Thus, the indirect instruments of credit subsidy and profit taxation give the center more flexibility than direct commands on investment. The intuition is that the command method affects incomes only via investment, whereas the Lange mechanism has two tools: credit conditions, which affect both investment levels and incomes, and taxes, which are an independent instrument for income redistribution. This extra flexibility is, however, lost *in the simple socialist case*, where *the Lange mechanism is equivalent to the exactly-constrained one*. This is so because, in the simple socialist case, varying tax rates across firms has no effect on the tax bill of a consumer.

One should moreover note that these results are based on a strong form of taxation, because the center is able to tax profits at a rate exceeding 100 percent, in effect also taxing wage income. If this strong form of taxation is ruled out, and if attention is restricted to the *simple socialist case*, then the *Lange mechanism can achieve the same allocations that the exactly-constrained Walrasian mechanism can achieve with nonnegative aggregate profits* (and, in a parallel manner, the pro-investment Lange mechanism can achieve the same allocations that the constrained Walrasian can with nonnegative profits).

Next, we consider the direct investment mechanism. The center now distributes the investment good free of charge to firms, and does not restrict the autonomous investment of firms: it can induce high, but not low, investment levels. In particular, it may be unable to implement some low-investment states that could be reached either by exact constraints or by the Lange mechanism (via high effective interest rates). What about its power to encourage, rather than discourage, investment? The relevant comparison is between the pro-investment Lange mechanism and the direct investment mechanism, but with taxation limited to rates not exceeding 100 percent. This comparison gives sharp results: *the two mechanisms are equivalent in the simple socialist case, while in the general case the direct investment mechanism is, in principle, more powerful*.

Lastly, we consider the sales-tax mechanism, where the center may impose a divergence between the prices paid by consumers and those received by firms. It turns out that *the sales-tax mechanism can implement a large variety of allocations and investment vectors*, but it may require large price differences that are politically problematic. Thus, this scheme cannot easily be compared with the others.

While the direct investment mechanism often emerges here as not inferior to the Lange one, and sometimes superior to it, our abstractions may conceal some reasons favoring the interest rate-guided Lange approach. Two specific extensions of the analysis deserve study. First, the path-breaking work by Weitzman (1974) suggests that the superiority of price or quantity instruments under limited information may well depend on the curvature of the relevant functions. Second, if there are many firms in each industry, then sectoral investment targets may perhaps be implemented more simply via interest rates than by individual quantity signals. We conclude with an invitation to further research.

2*   The economic environment

There are $N + 1$ firms and two periods. Firm 0 produces an investment good in the first period. Firm j, for $j = 1, \ldots, N$, produces a consumption good in each period. In the first period, the production function of firm j is $f_j^1(L)$, for $j = 0, \ldots, N$, where L is labor; in the second period, the production functions are $f_j^2(I, L), j = 1, \ldots, N$ where I is the investment good. For $j = 0, \ldots, N$, we assume that the function f_j^1 is concave, strictly increasing, and differentiable on R_{++}, and satisfies $f_j^1(0) = 0$. For $j = 1 \ldots, N$, we assume that f_j^2 is concave, strictly increasing, and differentiable on R_{++}^2, and satisfies $f_j^2(0,0) = 0$.

There are M consumers. The utility function of consumer i is $u_i(x_1^1, \ldots, x_N^1, x_1^2, \ldots, x_N^2)$ where x_j^t is the consumption of good j in period t; the endowment of consumer i is a vector of labor inputs in the two periods, $(\bar{L}_i^1, \bar{L}_i^2)$ and a vector $(\theta_{i0}, \ldots, \theta_{iN})$ where θ_{ij} is i's share of firm j's profits. If our model is describing a social democracy,[11] then θ_{ij} has the usual interpretation as an ownership share. If we are describing a socialist economy, then we interpret the profits that i receives as a social dividend, to use Lange's phrase, in which case the vectors $\{\theta_i | i = 1, \ldots, M\}$ are chosen by the center. (According to Lange, θ_{ij} should be chosen to reflect need, perhaps in proportion to family size.) Note that consumers derive no utility from leisure; thus, consumer i always supplies his entire labor endowment.

We denote a *feasible allocation* as a tuple $(x^1, x^2, y^1, y^2, L^{1D}, L^{2D}, I)$ where $x^t \in R_+^{NM}$ for $t = 1, 2$, $y^1 = (y_0^1, y_1^1, \ldots, y_N^1) \in R_+^{N+1}$, $y^2 = (y_1^2, \ldots, y_N^2) \in R_+^N$, $L^{1D} = (L_0^{1D}, \ldots, L_N^{1D}) \in R_+^{N+1}$, $L^{2D} = (L_1^{2D}, \ldots, L_N^{2D}) \in R_+^N$, $I = (I_1, \ldots, I_N) \in R_+^N$, satisfying

$$\sum_{i=1}^{M} x_{ij}^t \leq y_j^t, \quad j = 1, \ldots, N; t = 1, 2,$$

$$\sum_{j=1}^{N} I_j \leq y_0^1,$$

$$f_j^1(L_j^{1D}) = y_j^1, \quad j = 0, \ldots, N,$$

$$f_j^2(I_j, L_j^{2D}) = y_j^2, \quad j = 1, \ldots, N,$$

$$\sum_{j=0}^{N} L_j^{1D} \leq \sum_{i=1}^{M} \bar{L}_i^1, \quad \text{and}$$

$$\sum_{j=1}^{N} L_j^{2D} \leq \sum_{i=1}^{M} \bar{L}_i^2.$$

Thus, x_{ij}^t is the consumption of good j by consumer i in period t; y_j^t is the production of firm j in period t; L_j^{tD} is the demand for labor by firm j in period t, etc. We will often denote vectors by deletion of a subscript: thus

$\theta_i = (\theta_{i0}, \ldots, \theta_{iN})$, $\bar{L}^1 = (\bar{L}^1_1, \ldots, \bar{L}^1_M)$, $x^1_i = (x^1_{i1}, \ldots, x^1_{iN})$, etc. Similarly, prices are denoted (p^1, p^2, w^1, w^2) where $p^1 = (p^1_0, p^1_1, \ldots, p^1_N) \in R^{N+1}_+$, $p^2 = (p^2_1, \ldots, p^2_N) \in R^N_+$, are goods' prices and $w^t \in R_+$, $t = 1, 2$, are wages. We write $p^1_{-0} = (p^1_1, \ldots, p^1_N)$, and $p_{-0} = (p^1_{-0}, p^2)$.

We will almost always take the Arrow–Debreu viewpoint and treat all trading decisions as made at the beginning of period 1, facing a vector of futures prices (p^1, p^2, w^1, w^2). Thus each consumer has one budget constraint over his "lifetime" and each firm maximizes the sum of profits over the two periods. The amounts that consumers save and firms borrow are therefore not explicitly shown, and the interest rate is hidden in the price vector.

3* Constrained Walrasian equilibrium: a command-market-thought experiment

Let $\bar{I} = (\bar{I}_1, \ldots, \bar{I}_N)$ be a given investment vector. Imagine the center commands firm j to invest precisely $\bar{I}_j$ ($j = 1, \ldots, N$); at an *exactly-constrained Walrasian* (ECW) *equilibrium relative to* $\bar{I}$, all markets clear, all consumers maximize utility, and all firms maximize profits subject to their investment constraints. Formally:

Definition 3.1
The price vector (p^1, p^2, w^1, w^2) and the allocation $(\bar{x}^1, \bar{x}^2, \bar{y}^1, \bar{y}^2, \bar{L}^{1D}, \bar{L}^{2D}, \bar{I})$ constitute an *ECW equilibrium relative to* $\bar{I}$ if:

(1) $(\bar{y}_0, \bar{L}^{1D})$, solves firm O's profit-maximization program:

$$\max \bar{p}^1_0 y^1_0 - \bar{w}^1 L^{1D}_0$$
$$\text{s.t.} \quad f^1_0 (L^{1D}_0) \geq y^1_0;$$

$(\bar{y}^1_j, \bar{y}^2_j, \bar{L}^{1D}_j, \bar{L}^{2D}_j)$ solves firms j's constrained profit-maximization program:

$$\max \bar{p}^1_j f^1_j (L^{1D}_j) - \bar{w}^1 L^{1D}_j + \bar{p}^2_j f^2_j (\bar{I}_j, L^{2D}_j) - \bar{w}^2 L^{2D}_j - \bar{p}^1_0 \bar{I}_j;$$

(2) $(\bar{x}^1_i, \bar{x}^2_i)$ solves consumer i's utility-maximization program:

$$\max u_i (x^1_i, x^2_i)$$
$$\text{s.t.} \quad \bar{p}^1_{-0} \cdot x^1_i + \bar{p}^2 \cdot x^2_i \leq \bar{w}^1 \bar{L}^1_i + \bar{w}^2 \bar{L}^2_i + \sum_{j=0}^N \theta_{ij} \pi_j,$$

where

$$\pi_0 = \bar{p}^1_0 \sum_{j=1}^N \bar{I}_j - \bar{w}^1 \bar{L}^{1D}_0 \text{ and, for } j = 1, \ldots, N,$$
$$\pi_j = \sum_{t=1}^2 (\bar{p}^t_j \bar{y}^t_j - \bar{w}^t \bar{L}^{tD}_j) - \bar{p}^1_0 \bar{I}_j;$$

(3) All markets clear; for example the market for investment goods clears,

$$\sum_{j=1}^N \bar{I}_j = \bar{y}^1_0.$$

In particular, consumers' wealths must be nonnegative at an ECW equilibrium, a substantive requirement, since it is possible that total profits are negative for some price vectors.

That an ECW equilibrium is Pareto-optimal subject to the constraint that the investment vector be precisely $(\bar{I}_1, \ldots, \bar{I}_N)$ follows from the usual proof of the "first welfare theorem."

Next, we define a constrained Walrasian (CW) equilibrium relative to $\bar{I}$ as a Walrasian equilibrium in which firm j $(j = 1, \ldots, N)$ is required to invest at least $\bar{I}_j$. Formally:

Definition 3.2

A *CW equilibrium relative to* $\bar{I}$ is a price vector $(\bar{p}^1, \bar{p}^2, \bar{w}^1, \bar{w}^2)$ and allocation $(\bar{x}^1, \bar{x}^2, \bar{y}^1, \bar{y}^2, \bar{L}^{1D}, \bar{L}^{2D}, \bar{R})$ such that

(1) Firm 0 maximizes profits at $(\bar{y}_0^1, \bar{L}_0^{1D})$; for $j = 1, \ldots, N$, $(\bar{L}_j^{1D}, \bar{L}_j^{2D}, \bar{R}_j)$ solves firm j's profit-maximization program:

$$\max \bar{p}_j^1 f_j^1 (L_j^{1D}) - \bar{w}^1 L_j^{1D} + \bar{p}_j^2 f_j^2 (R_j, L_j^{2D}) - \bar{w}^2 L_j^{2D} - \bar{p}_0^1 R_j$$

$$\text{s.t.} \quad R_j \geqq \bar{I}_j;$$

(2) All consumers maximize utility;
(3) All markets clear.

As above, the virtue of CW equilibria is that they are second-best Pareto-optimal, i.e., Pareto-optimal subject to the constraint that the vector of investments $\bar{R}$ is greater than or equal to $\bar{I}$.

4*   A generalization of Lange's idea

Our planner desires to implement a vector $\bar{I}$ of investment levels; her instrument will be a vector $(d_1, \ldots, d_N) \in R_+^N$, where d_j is the interest rate discount that firm j receives from the market rate; the financing scheme will be a vector $(\tau_1, \ldots, \tau_N) \in R_+^N$ of corporate tax rates. Recall from section 2 that firms must borrow to finance investment.

We write down the definition of Lange equilibrium using futures prices, where the interest rate discounts are not immediately evident:

Definition 4.1

A *Lange equilibrium relative to* $\bar{I} = (\bar{I}_1, \ldots, \bar{I}_N)$ is a vector of prices $(\bar{p}^1, \bar{p}^2, \bar{w}^1, \bar{w}^2)$, a vector $\lambda = (\lambda_1, \ldots, \lambda_N)$ in R_+^N, a vector of corporation profits' tax rates $(\tau_1, \ldots, \tau_N) \in R_+^N$ and an allocation $(\bar{x}^1, \bar{x}^2, \bar{y}^1, \bar{y}^2, \bar{L}^{1D}, \bar{L}^{2D}, \bar{I})$ such that:[12]

F1 $(\bar{x}_i^1, \bar{x}_i^2)$ solves:

$$\max u_i(x_i^1, x_i^2)$$

$$\text{s.t.} \quad \bar{p}_{-0}^1 \cdot x_i^1 + \bar{p}^2 \cdot x_i^2 \leqslant \bar{w}^1 \bar{L}_i^1 + \bar{w}^2 \bar{L}_i^2 + \theta_{i0} \bar{\pi}_0 + \sum_{j=1}^N (1 - \tau_j) \theta_{ij} \bar{\pi}_j$$

where $\bar{\pi}_j$ is the value of firm j's profits, given in F2a and F2b below:

F2a $(\bar{L}_0^{1D}, \bar{y}_0^1)$ solves:

$$\max \bar{p}_0^1 y_0 - \bar{w}^1 L_0^{1D}$$

s.t. $f_0(L_0^{1D}) \geqq y_0^1$;

F2b For $j = 1, \ldots, N$, $(\bar{L}_j^{1D}, \bar{y}_j^1, \bar{L}_j^{2D}, \bar{y}_j^2, \bar{I}_j)$ solves:

$$\max \bar{p}_j^1 y_j^1 - \bar{w}^1 L_j^{1D} + \bar{p}_j^2 y_j^2 - \bar{w}^2 L_j^{2D} - \lambda_j \bar{p}_0^1 I_j$$

s.t. $f_j^1(L_j^{1D}) \geqslant y_j^1$,

$f_j^2(I_j, L_j^{2D}) \geqslant y_j^2$;

F3 $\displaystyle\sum_{j=1}^{N} \tau_j \bar{\pi}_j = \sum_{j=1}^{N} (1 - \lambda_j) \bar{p}_0^1 \bar{I}_j$;

F4 $\displaystyle\bar{y}_0^1 = \sum_{j=1}^{N} \bar{I}_j$,

$\displaystyle\bar{y}_j^t = \sum_{i=1}^{M} \bar{x}_{ij}^t$, $j = 1, \ldots, N, t = 1, 2$,

$\displaystyle\sum_{j=0}^{N} \bar{L}_j^{tD} = \sum_i \bar{L}_i^t$, $t = 1, 2$.

Interpretation

$\lambda_j = \dfrac{1 + r_j}{1 + r_C}$, where r_j is the interest rate charged for loans to firm j, and r_C is the (market) interest rate faced by consumers. Thus λ_j acts as a discount on the price of the investment good (see F2b above), if the government subsidizes an industry, or a surcharge, if it wishes to depress investment in an industry. The expression on the r.h.s. of F3 is the total subsidy; F3 states that corporation taxes exactly cover the total subsidy.

Definition 4.2

A *pro-investment Lange equilibrium relative to the investment vector $\bar{I}$* is a Lange equilibrium in which, for $j = 1, \ldots, N$, $\lambda_j \leqslant 1$.

Define $\mathscr{A}^L$ to be the set of Lange equilibria relative to some investment vector, and $\mathscr{A}^{L[0,1]}$ to be the set of pro-investment Lange equilibria.

Theorem 4.1[13]

A. (*Simple socialist case*) If $\theta_{ij} = \theta_{ij'}$, for all $i = 1, \ldots, M$ and for all j, $j' = 1, \ldots, N$, then

$$\mathscr{A}^L = \mathscr{A}^{ECW} \quad \text{and} \quad \mathscr{A}^{L[0,1]} = \mathscr{A}^{CW}.$$

B. (*General case*) $\mathscr{A}^L \supset \mathscr{A}^{ECW}$, $\mathscr{A}^{L[0,1]} \supset \mathscr{A}^{CW}$, and the inclusions are strict.

We next introduce a second specialization of the definition of Lange equilibrium.

Definition 4.3
A *limited-taxation Lange equilibrium relative to* $\bar{I} = (\bar{I}_1, \ldots, \bar{I}_N)$ is a Lange equilibrium such that:

$$0 \leq \tau_j \leq 1, \quad \text{for all } j = 1, \ldots, N.$$

Similarly, a limited-taxation pro-investment Lange equilibrium is a limited-taxation equilibrium where for all j, $\lambda_j \leq 1$.

Let $\mathscr{A}^{LTL}$ be the set of allocations that arise as limited-taxation Lange equilibria, and $\mathscr{A}^{LTL[0,1]}$ be the allocations that arise as limited-taxation pro-investment Lange equilibria. Let $\mathscr{A}^{CW+}$ be the set of constrained Walrasian allocations where total profits in the consumer-good industries are nonnegative.

Theorem 4.2 (Simple socialist case)
If $\theta_{ij} = \theta_{ij'}$, for all $i = 1, \ldots, M$ and for all $j, j' = 1, \ldots, N$, then

$$\mathscr{A}^{LTL[0,1]} = \mathscr{A}^{CW+},$$

$$\mathscr{A}^{LTL} = \mathscr{A}^{ECW+}.$$

5*   Direct provision of investment by the state

Definition 5.1
A *direct investment* (DI) *equilibrium with corporate taxation relative to* $\bar{I}$ consists of prices $(\bar{p}^1, \bar{p}^2, \bar{w}^1, \bar{w}^2)$ an allocation $(\bar{x}^1, \bar{x}^2, \bar{y}^1, \bar{y}^2, \bar{L}^{1D}, \bar{L}^{2D}, \bar{M} + \bar{I})$, and tax rates $\tau = (\tau_1, \ldots, \tau_N) \in R_+^N$ on profits such that:

D1 $(\bar{y}_0, \bar{L}_0^{1D})$ solves firm 0's profit-maximization program:

$$\max \bar{p}_0^1 y_0^1 - \bar{w}^1 L_0^{1D}$$

$$\text{s.t. } f_0(L_0^1) \geq y_0^{1D};$$

$(\bar{y}_j^1, \bar{y}_j^2, \bar{L}_j^{1D}, \bar{L}_j^{2D})\bar{M}_j$ solves, for $j = 1, \ldots, N$,

$$\max \bar{p}_j^1 y_j^1 + \bar{p}_j^2 y_j^2 - \bar{w}^1 L_j^{1D} - \bar{w}^2 L_j^{2D} - \bar{p}_0 M_j$$

$$\text{s.t. } f_j^1(L_j^{1D}) \geq y_j^1,$$

$$f_j^2(\bar{I}_j + M_j, L_j^{2D}) \geq y_j^2,$$

$$M_j \geq 0;$$

D2 $(\bar{x}_i^1, \bar{x}_i^2)$ solves consumer i's utility-maximization program:

$$\max u_i(x_i^1 x_i^2)$$

$$\text{s.t. } \bar{p}_{-0}^1 \cdot x_i^1 + \bar{p}^2 \cdot x_i^2 \leq \bar{w}^1 \bar{L}_i^1 + \bar{w}^2 \bar{L}_i^2 + \theta_{i0}\pi_0 + \sum_{j=1}^{N} \theta_{ij}(1 - \tau_j)\pi_j,$$

where $\pi_j = \bar{p}_j^1 \bar{y}_j^1 + \bar{p}_j^2 \bar{y}_j^2 - \bar{w}^1 \bar{L}_j^{1D} - \bar{w}^2 \bar{L}_j^{2D} - \bar{p}_0^1 \bar{M}_j$ for $j = 1, \ldots, N$ and $\pi_0 = \bar{p}_0^1 \bar{y}_0^1 - \bar{w}^1 \bar{L}_0^{1D}$;

D3 $\displaystyle\sum_{j=1}^{N} \tau_j \pi_j = \bar{p}_0^1 \sum_{j=1}^{N} \bar{I}_j$ (the government's budget constraint);

D4 All markets clear; for instance, the market for investment goods clears,

$$\sum_{j=1}^{N} (\bar{M}_j + \bar{I}_j) = \bar{y}_0^1.$$

Note that all firms make nonnegative profits at a *DI* equilibrium.

As in section 4*, we define the following specialization of the above definition.

Definition 5.2

A *limited-taxation direct investment equilibrium relative to* $\bar{I}$ is a direct investment equilibrium such that, for all $j = 1, \ldots, N$, $0 \leqslant \tau_j \leqslant 1$.

Let $\mathscr{A}^{DI}$ be the set of direct investment allocations with corporate taxation relative to some $\bar{I}$. Let $\mathscr{A}^{LTDI}$ be the set of limited taxation *DI*-equilibrium allocations with corporate taxes.

Theorem 5.1 (Simple socialist case)

If for all $i = 1, \ldots, M$ *and* $j, j' = 1, \ldots, N$, $\theta_{ij} = \theta_{ij'}$ *then*

A. $\mathscr{A}^{CW} = \mathscr{A}^{DI}$.

B. $\mathscr{A}^{CW+} = \mathscr{A}^{LTDI}$.

Theorem 5.2

A. $\mathscr{A}^{LTL[0,1]} \subset \mathscr{A}^{LTDI}$. *In general the inclusion is strict.*[14]

B. *The simple socialist case, if for all* $i = 1, \ldots, M$ *and* $j, j' = 1, \ldots, N$, $\theta_{ij} = \theta_{ij'}$ *then* $\mathscr{A}^{LTL[0,1]} = \mathscr{A}^{LTDI} = \mathscr{A}^{CW+}$.

6* The sales-tax model

Assumption 6.1

The receipts T from taxes are returned to the consumers according to a given transfer rule $S : R \to R^M$ satisfying:

(a) for all $T \in R$, $\displaystyle\sum_{i=1}^{M} S_i(T) = T$;

(b) if $T \geqslant 0$, then $S_i(T) \geqslant 0$, $i = 1, \ldots, M$.

Remark 6.1

Assumption 6.1 is satisfied by the *proportional transfer rule* $S_i(T) = \sigma_i T$, for $(\sigma_1, \ldots, \sigma_M) \in R_+^M$ satisfying $\displaystyle\sum_{i=1}^{M} \sigma_i = 1$.

Remark 6.2

We interpret both T and $S_i(T)$ as measured in nominal terms, i.e., relative to an arbitrary unit of account. This allows the subsidy rule to be numéraire-dependent, although the proportional subsidy rate is not. Alternatively, one may avoid this feature by interpreting that both T and $S_i(T)$ are measured in real terms, i.e., in the units of a good selected as numéraire.

Remark 6.3

Sales receipts T could in principle be negative, i.e., the consumer purchases of some goods are subsidized by taxes on other goods and lump-sum taxes on consumers. Theorem 6.1 below will actually show the existence of an equilibrium with nonnegative T.

$$\text{Define:} \quad MRS_j(L_j) = \frac{(\partial f_j^2/\partial I_j)|(\bar{I}_j, L_j)}{(\partial f_j^2/\partial L_j^{2D})|(\bar{I}_j, L_j)}.$$

Assumption 6.2

For $j = 1, \ldots, N$, and $\bar{I}_j > 0$, $\lim_{\varepsilon \to 0} MRS_j(\varepsilon) = 0$.

Assumption 6.3

For $i = 1, \ldots, M$, $\bar{L}_i^1 > 0$, and u_i is strictly quasi-concave and strictly increasing.

Definition 6.1

Let $\bar{I} \gg 0$. A *second-period production equilibrium relative to* $\bar{I}$ is a vector $(\bar{w}^1, \bar{w}^2, \bar{p}_0^1, \bar{p}^2, \bar{L}^{2D}) \in R_+ \times R_+ \times R_+ \times R_+^N \times R_+^N$ satisfying

(i) $\displaystyle\sum_{j=1}^{N} \bar{I}_j$ solves $\max_y \bar{p}_0^1 y - \bar{w}^1 (f_0^1)^{-1}(y)$;

(ii) for $j = 1, \ldots, N$, $(\bar{I}_j, \bar{L}_j^{2D})$ solves $\max_{I_j, L_j} \bar{p}_j^2 f_j^2(I_j, L_j) - \bar{p}_0^1 I_j - \bar{w}^2 L_j^{2D}$;

(iii) $\displaystyle\sum_{j=1}^{N} \bar{L}_j^{2D} = \sum_{i=1}^{M} \bar{L}_i^2$.

Remark 6.4

If $(\bar{w}^1, \bar{w}^2, \bar{p}_0^1, \bar{p}^2, \bar{L}^{2D})$ is a second-period production equilibrium, then so is $(\lambda \bar{w}^1, \lambda \bar{w}^2, \lambda \bar{p}_0^1, \lambda \bar{p}^2, \bar{L}^{2D})$ for any $\lambda > 0$.

Lemma 6.1

Under Assumption 6.2, if $\bar{I} \gg 0$ and $\displaystyle\sum_{j=1}^{N} \bar{I}_j < f_0^1 \left(\sum_{i=1}^{M} \bar{L}_i^1 \right)$, then a second-period production equilibrium relative to $\bar{I}$ exists (with $\bar{w}^1 = 1$).

Proof (sketch)

Define, for $j = 1, \ldots, N$,

$$\phi_j : R_+ \to R_+ : \phi_j(L_j) = \begin{cases} 0 & \text{if } L_j = 0 \\ MRS_j(L_j) & \text{if } L_j > 0. \end{cases}$$

and

$$\beta_j(L) = (1/N) \sum_{i=1}^{N} \phi_i(L_i) - \phi_j(L_j), \quad j = 1, \dots, N;$$

Write $\hat{L} = \sum_{i=1}^{M} \bar{L}_i^2$. Define the $(N-1)$ dimensional simplex $\Delta_L = \left\{ L \in R_+^N \mid \sum_{j=1}^{N} L_j = \hat{L} \right\}$, and the continuous mapping $\Lambda : \Delta_L \to \Delta_L$,

$$\Lambda_j(L) = \frac{L_j + \hat{L} \max\{0, \beta_j(L)\}}{1 + \sum_{i=1}^{N} \max\{0, \beta_i(L)\}}.$$

A fixed point of Λ yields the desired second-period allocation of labor, see Ortuño-Ortin, Roemer and Silvestre (1991) for details.

Remark 6.5
Assumption 6.2 is indispensable for the validity of Lemma 6.1, see Example 3 in Ortuño-Ortin, Roemer and Silvestre (1991).

We view the government as choosing $2N$ tax rates $(\tau_1^1, \dots, \tau_N^1, \tau_1^2, \dots, \tau_N^2)$, where τ_j^t is the tax on good j at period t. Producer prices $p_{-0} = (p_1^1, \dots, p_N^1, p_1^2, \dots, p_N^2)$ are then related to consumer prices $\psi = (\psi_1^1, \dots, \psi_N^1, \psi_1^2, \dots, \psi_N^2)$ by the *sales-tax equalities*:

$$\psi_j^t = (1 + \tau_j^t)p_j^t,$$

or:

$$\tau_j^t = \frac{\psi_j^t - p_j^t}{p_j^t},$$

where τ_j^t can in principle range from -1 to $+\infty$.

Consumer i takes as given his wealth W_i and the consumer prices ψ. He chooses $x_i = (x_i^1, x_i^2) \in R_+^{2N}$ in order to maximize u_i on $\gamma(\psi, W_i) = \{x_i \in R_+^{2N} \mid \psi \cdot x_i \leqslant W_i\}$. This set is closed and convex, and it is nonempty for $W_i \geqslant 0$, but it fails to be compact when $\psi_j^t = 0$ for some t, j. Define:

$$k = 2 \sum_{j=1}^{N} \left[f_j^1\left(\sum_{i=1}^{M} \bar{L}_i^1\right) + f_j^2\left(f_0^1\left(\sum_{i=1}^{M} \bar{L}_i^1\right), \sum_{i=1}^{M} \bar{L}_i^2\right) \right],$$

$$K = \{(x_i^1, x_i^2) \in R_+^{2N} \mid x_{ij}^t \leqslant k \text{ for } j = 1, \dots, N \text{ and } t = 1, 2\},$$

and:

$$\bar{\gamma}(\psi, W_i) = \gamma(\psi, W_i) \cap K.$$

Define the functions:

$$\xi_i : R_{++}^{2N} \times R_+ \to R^{2N} : \xi_i(\psi, W_i) = \text{"the unique maximizer of } u_i \text{ on } \gamma(\psi, W_i)\text{,"}$$

and:

$$\xi_i : R_+^{2N} \times R_+ \to R^{2N} : \xi_i(\psi, W_i) = \text{``the unique maximizer of } u_i \text{ on } \bar{\gamma}(\psi, W_i).\text{''}$$

These functions are well defined, because they involve maximizing a continuous function on a compact set and because the uniqueness of the maximizer is guaranteed by strict quasi-concavity and strict monotonicity.

Write $\bar{p}_{-0} = (\bar{p}_1^1, \ldots, \bar{p}_N^1, \bar{p}_1^2, \ldots, \bar{p}_N^2)$ and $\bar{y}_{-0} = (\bar{y}_1^1, \ldots, \bar{y}_N^1, \bar{y}_1^2, \ldots, \bar{y}_N^2)$.

Definition 6.2

A sales-tax equilibrium relative to a (strictly positive) *vector of sectoral investments* $\bar{I} = (\bar{I}_1, \ldots, \bar{I}_n)$ *and to a transfer rule* $\bar{S}$ *is a vector* $(\bar{p}^1, \bar{p}^2, \bar{\psi}^1, \bar{\psi}^2, \bar{w}^1, \bar{w}^2, \bar{x}^1, \bar{x}^2, \bar{y}^1, \bar{y}^2, \bar{L}^{1D}, \bar{L}^{2D}) = (\bar{p}, \bar{\psi}, \bar{w}, \bar{x}, \bar{y}, \bar{L}) \in R^{2N+1} \times R^{2N} \times R^2 \times R^{2MN} \times R^{2N+1} \times R^{2N+1}$ *such that:*

(i) $(\bar{y}_0^1, \bar{L}_0^{1D})$ maximizes $\bar{p}_0^1 y - \bar{w}^1 L$ subject to $y = f_0^1(L)$;

(ii) for $j = 1, \ldots, N$, $(\bar{I}_j, \bar{L}_j^{1D}, \bar{L}_j^{2D})$ solves:

$$\max_{(I_j, L_j^{1D}, L_j^{2D})} \bar{p}_j^1 f_j^1(L_j^{1D}) - \bar{w}^1 L_j^{1D} + \bar{p}_j^2 f_j^2(I_j, L_j^{2D}) - \bar{w}^2 L_j^{2D} - \bar{p}_0^1 I_j;$$

(iii) for $j = 1, \ldots, N$, $\bar{y}_j^1 = f_j^1(\bar{L}_j^{1D})$ and $\bar{y}_j^2 = f_j^2(\bar{I}_j, \bar{L}_j^{2D})$;

(iv) $\bar{y}_0^1 = \sum_{j=1}^N \bar{I}_j$;

(v) $\bar{\psi} \gg 0$, and, for $i = 1, \ldots, M$, $\bar{x}_i = \xi_i(\bar{\psi}, \bar{W}_i)$, where

$$\bar{W}_i = \bar{w}^1 \bar{L}_i^1 + \bar{w}^2 \bar{L}_i^2 + \theta_{i0}(\bar{p}_0^1 \bar{y}_0^1 - \bar{w}^1 \bar{L}_0^1)$$

$$+ \sum_{j=1}^N \theta_{ij}(\bar{p}_j^1 \bar{y}_j^1 + \bar{p}_j^2 \bar{y}_j^2 - \bar{w}^1 \bar{L}_j^{1D} - \bar{w}^2 \bar{L}_j^{2D} - \bar{p}_0^1 \bar{I}_j)$$

$$+ S_i((\bar{\psi} - \bar{p}_{-0}) \cdot \bar{y}_{-0});$$

(vi) $\sum_{j=0}^N \bar{L}_j^{1D} = \sum_{i=1}^M \bar{L}_i^1$;

$$\sum_{j=1}^N \bar{L}_j^{2D} = \sum_{i=1}^M \bar{L}_i^2;$$

(vii) $\sum_{i=1}^M \bar{x}_{ij}^t = \bar{y}_j^t$; $j = 1, \ldots, N, t = 1, 2.$

Remark 6.6

Let S be proportional (see Remark 6.1 above), and assume that $(\bar{p}, \bar{\psi}, \bar{w}, \bar{x}, \bar{y}, \bar{L})$ is an equilibrium relative to $\bar{I}$ and that $\lambda \gg 0$. Then $(\lambda \bar{p}, \lambda \bar{\psi}, \lambda \bar{w}, \bar{x}, \bar{y}, \bar{L})$ is an equilibrium for $\bar{I}$. Of course, the same tax rates $\tau_j^t = (\bar{\psi}_j^t - \bar{p}_j^t)/\bar{p}_j^t$ apply to both equilibria. This is no longer true when S is numéraire-dependent, see Remark 6.2 above.

We now tackle the existence issue. Choose a positive second-period production equilibrium $(\bar{w}^1, \bar{w}^2, \bar{p}_0^1, \bar{p}^2, \bar{L}^{2D})$, which will be kept fixed in what follows

(Lemma 6.1 guarantees that this is possible). Write $\bar{y}_0^1 = \sum_{j=1}^{N} \bar{I}_j$ and $\bar{L}_0^{1D} = (f_0^1)^{-1}(\bar{y}_0^1)$. The choice of first-period magnitudes is basically unrestricted: let $(\bar{L}_1^{1D}, \ldots, \bar{L}_N^{1D})$ be *any* strictly positive vector satisfying

$$\sum_{j=1}^{N} \bar{L}_j^{1D} = \sum_{i=1}^{M} \bar{L}_i^1 - \bar{L}_0^{1D}.$$

For $j = 1, \ldots, N$, write $\bar{y}_j^1 = f_j^1(\bar{L}_j^{1D})$ and choose $\bar{p}_j^1$ so that $\bar{y}_j^1$ solves: $\max_y \bar{p}_j^1 y - (f_j^1)^{-1}(y)$. This choice is again possible by concavity. For future reference, we call a vector $(\bar{L}_1^{1D}, \ldots, \bar{L}_N^{1D}, \bar{p}_1^1, \ldots, \bar{p}_N^1)$ a *first-period production equilibrium* (we take $\bar{w}^1$ to be one). These choices of first- and second-period production equilibria define a vector $(\bar{p}, \bar{w}, \bar{y}, \bar{L})$, to be called a *production equilibrium* (relative to $\bar{I}$), which will be kept fixed in what follows. For $i = 1, \ldots, M$, define:

$$\tilde{W}_i(\psi) = \bar{w}^1 \bar{L}_i^1 + \bar{w}^2 \bar{L}_i^2 + \theta_{i0}(\bar{p}_0^1 \bar{y}_0^1 - \bar{w}^1 \bar{L}_0^{1D})$$
$$+ \sum_{j=1}^{N} \theta_{ij}(\bar{p}_j^1 \bar{y}_j^1 + \bar{p}_j^2 \bar{y}_j^2 - \bar{w}^1 \bar{L}_j^{1D} - \bar{w}^2 \bar{L}_j^{2D} - \bar{p}_0^1 \bar{I}_j)$$
$$+ S_i((\psi - \bar{p}_{-0}) \cdot \bar{y}_{-0}),$$
$$\tilde{\xi}_i(\psi) = \xi_i(\psi, \tilde{W}_i(\psi)) \in R^{2N},$$

and

$$\zeta(\psi) = \sum_{i=1}^{M} \tilde{\xi}_i(\psi) - \bar{y}_{-0} \in R^{2N}.$$

Lemma 6.2 (Walras' Law)
Under Assumptions 6.1 and 6.3, for all $\psi = (\psi^1, \psi^2) \in R^{2N}$, $\psi \cdot \zeta(\psi) = 0$.

Theorem 6.1
Under Assumptions 6.1–6.3, an equilibrium relative to $\bar{I}$ ($\bar{I} \gg 0$) and S exists.

Proof (sketch)
Take an arbitrary positive number α satisfying: $\alpha \geq \bar{p}_{-0} \cdot \bar{y}_{-0}$, and define the simplex $\Delta_\alpha = \{\psi \in R_+^{2N} | \psi \cdot \bar{y}_{-0} = \alpha\}$, which is homeomorphic to the standard $2N - 1$ dimensional simplex because $\bar{y}_j^t > 0$ ($j = 1, \ldots, N, t = 1, 2$). Define the continuous function: $\Psi : \Delta_\alpha \to \Delta_\alpha$,

$$\Psi_j^t(\psi) = \frac{\psi_j^t + (\alpha/\bar{y}_j^t) \max\{0, \zeta_j^t(\psi)\}}{1 + \sum_{i=1}^{N} \sum_{v=1}^{2} \max\{0, \zeta_i^v(\psi)\}}.$$

A fixed point of Ψ yields the desired consumer prices. See Ortuño-Ortin, Roemer and Silvestre (1991) for details.

The proof of Theorem 6.1 shows that for a $(\bar{w}, \bar{p}, \bar{y}, \bar{L}^D)$ satisfying the conditions of a production equilibria in both periods one can obtain a (at least one-dimensional) continuum of equilibria by varying the parameter α in the proof as long as $\alpha \geqq \bar{p}_{-0} \cdot \bar{y}_{-0}$. Our proof restricts α to be not lower than $\bar{p}_{-0} \cdot \bar{y}_{-0}$, thus ensuring that tax receipts are nonnegative and, hence, that the wealth of consumers is positive. If $\alpha < \bar{p}_{-0} \cdot \bar{y}_{-0}$, then an equilibrium with $\bar{y}_{-0} \cdot \psi = \alpha$ may or may not exist. It will not exist if the data of the economy are such that the wealth of a consumer becomes negative for negative and large (in absolute value) tax receipts.

Now we show that, given a direct investment equilibrium with aggregate level of investment K^* (i.e., $K^* = \Sigma \bar{I}_i + \Sigma \bar{M}_i$), there is a sales-tax equilibrium that yields the same aggregate investment K^* yet (weakly) Pareto-dominates the original direct investment equilibrium.

Theorem 6.2
Let $\bar{e} = (\bar{w}^1, 1, \bar{w}^2, \bar{p}^1, \bar{p}^2, \bar{x}^1, \bar{x}^2, \bar{y}^1, \bar{y}^2, \bar{L}^{1D}, \bar{L}^{2D}, \bar{I} + \bar{M})$ *be a direct investment equilibrium relative to* $\bar{I} \gg 0$. *Assume that the conditions of Theorem 6.1 are satisfied, and that*

$$\sum_{j=1}^{N} (\bar{I}_j + \bar{M}_j) < f_0^1(\bar{L}^1).$$

Then there exists a positive vector $\hat{I}$, *a proportional transfer rule* $\hat{S}$, $\hat{S}_i(T) = \hat{\sigma}_i T$, $i = 1, \ldots, M$, *and a sales-tax equilibrium* $\hat{e}$ *relative to* $\hat{I}$ *and* $\hat{S}$ *with associated consumption allocation* $\hat{x}$ *such that:*

(i) $\displaystyle \sum_{j=1}^{N} \hat{I}_j = \sum_{j=1}^{N} (\bar{I}_j + \bar{R}_j);$

(ii) $u_i(\hat{x}_i^1, \hat{x}_i^2) \geqq u_i(\bar{x}_i^1, \bar{x}_i^2)$.

Notes

1. For a good précis of the history of the concept, see W. Brus (1987). For discussions of the reforms in the Soviet Union, see Hewett (1988) and Aslund (1989).
2. Negative externalities associated with pollution, for instance; positive externalities associated with "endogenous growth," as in Romer (1986).
3. Another possibility occurs to us to explain Lange's insistence that the state set prices of investment goods. It would have been too radical, within the socialist community, to propose that the state set only the interest rates, and leave everything else to the market. Socialist parties, whom Lange presumably hoped to influence, would not have been content with so apparently minor an interventionist role.
4. We assume throughout that the center knows all the parameters of the economy; we are not concerned here with the implementation problem which must take into account incentive compatibility.
5. Although constrained Walrasian allocations are second-best Pareto-optimal as described, they are not generally technologically efficient. The given composition of output is efficiently distributed among citizens; labor is efficiently allocated among firms, given their levels of investment; but it is generally possible to find a reallocation

of investment among firms, and a reallocation of labor that would increase production of all outputs. Such reallocation of investment are, however, precluded given the government's investment objective.

6. In his speech after being sworn in to the Soviet presidency, as translated by Tass and reported in the *New York Times* of March 16, 1990.

7. Note that these tax rates may be greater than one.

8. Of course, Lange equilibria inherit the second-best Pareto-optimality of constrained Walrasian equilibria. Moreover, suppose the government wishes to implement only a given *aggregate* level of investment. It can accomplish this with just one interest rate discount for all firms. The resulting equilibrium will be technologically efficient, unlike constrained Walrasian equilibria. (It will still, however, be only second-best Pareto-optimal, as there will generally be reallocations of labor between the investment sector and the consumption sector that will produce a composition of output that can be distributed in a way to increase the utility of all citizens.) There is no natural way to implement a targetted aggregate level of investment in the command-market model of section 3. To whom would the center issue the command?

9. As we show in section 4*, the Lange model may also be interpreted atemporally, by using the device of futures' prices, in which case interest rates do not explicitly appear. In this version, it is as if the government refunds to the firm a portion of the cost of each unit of investment good the firm purchases. The price which the firm in sector j pays for the investment good is effectively discounted by the factor $\dfrac{1 + r_j}{1 + r_c}$, where r_j and r_c are the industry and market interest rates, respectively.

10. See, however, the caveat in n. 14 to Theorem 5.2 in section 5*.

11. We take a social democracy to be an economy with private ownership of firms in which the government is empowered to influence investment.

12. We assume that firm 0 is not taxed.

13. Proofs of all theorems are available in Ortuño-Ortin, Roemer and Silvestre (1991).

14. We show strict inclusion by providing an example where $N = 2$. Our example is not entirely satisfactory. It does, indeed, show the existence of an allocation that is implementable by direct investment but not by interest rates; however, the *investment vector* of the allocation is implementable in a Lange allocation. We have not found an example showing that the set of investment vectors implementable as Lange allocations is a proper sub-set of those implementable by direct investment. We have not searched in models with $N > 2$.

18 Capitalism and democracy: a summing up of the arguments

MARTIN L. WEITZMAN

1 Introduction

The possible connection between economic and political systems is one of the great issues of classical political economy. However, the subject is not much discussed by straight economists today, nor does it typically appear in contemporary economics courses.

This is too bad. The topic of "capitalism and democracy" is obviously of enormous general importance in its own right. Furthermore, the possible connections have lately become a more immediately operational issue. Without some sense of the logic behind possible relations between capitalism and democracy it is very difficult to understand many aspects of the economic "reforms" now taking place in formerly orthodox socialist countries. The connection between the economic and political spheres in the area of socialist reforms is usually of overpowering significance, typically overshadowing straight economic aspects of reform even for narrowly posed economic issues.

Advocates of free market economics, like Hayek and Friedman, have long perceived and articulated a link between capitalism and freedom or democracy. Now there is new evidence from the recent experiences of the former USSR, Eastern Europe, China, and other reforming socialist countries, and also from newly industrialized capitalist countries like Korea and Taiwan, hinting that capitalism and freedom or democracy tend to "go together."

In view of its importance, even for an understanding of straight economic issues, it is somewhat puzzling that mainstream economists have not devoted more professional research to the linkage problem. Perhaps one reason has to do with the technical difficulty of formalizing the ways capitalism and democracy might be connected. I feel that I know about this difficulty because for many years now I have tried formally to model the possible connection between capitalism and democracy – without notable success. In the course of this unsuccessful research program I have naturally read much of what has been written on this subject, especially by economists. And, just as naturally, I have been forced to consolidate and organize, in my own fashion, the major strands of arguments that have been made.

This chapter represents an attempt at summing up in a very succinct form what I view as the major arguments for a possible connection between capitalism and democracy. It makes no claim for originality, except possibly in organization and presentation. Nor do I make a serious effort to attribute original authorship to the various strands of argument, the subject being so loose as to make that a difficult historical task. The chapter may perhaps be helpful for pedagogical or other purposes where some concentrated statement might be useful.

2 Some definitions

The possible connection between capitalism and democracy represents a difficult area for analysis because the issues are not able to be cleanly and neatly stated as, by contrast, is the case for some problems in standard non-political economy. Right from the beginning there are serious problems of definition. Besides being difficult to define rigorously, the terms "socialism," "capitalism," "freedom," and "democracy" are frequently loaded with value judgments. A true believer in socialism or capitalism will typically build into the definition such good traits as freedom or democracy, essentially arguing that "real" socialism or capitalism must be good, while anything bad that is actually observed out there must represent an impure deviation.

There are many genuine definitional problems and ambiguities, but in order to move ahead to the main issues I want to wave aside distracting distinctions. Of course they can be contested, but for the purposes of this chapter I will use the following more or less standard definitions.

"Democracy" is a system equated with frequent, meaningful, competitive, free elections of major public officials. This is a traditional definition of democracy chosen, in part, because it comes with a semi-operational litmus test. The opposite pole is "dictatorship." It is fairly clear from this definition where to place Britain and the USA, on the one hand, and China and the USSR, on the other. Somewhat less clear is the standing of semi-authoritarian governments with a *de facto* but not *de jure* one-party system like, perhaps, Mexico. If forced to choose between the two extremes, my own tendency would be to classify everything that is not a fairly clear dictatorship as a form of democracy. This corresponds to a distinction sometimes made by political scientists between governments that are hard core dictatorships consistent with their own basic principles and governments that are, in principle, committed to genuinely free elections as a goal but for one reason or another are not actually holding free elections at the present time. My tendency is to classify as a democracy any government committed to the ideal of openly contested free elections. In any event, no definition is perfect and I will not get bogged down here in trying to find semantic niches for every in-between gray case.

It could legitimately be argued that universal suffrage is a relatively recent phenomenon, so that democracy in the sense of unrestricted voting rights has developed only in the twentieth century. Nevertheless, there are many cases where the basic idea of democracy has existed for a long time, except that the extent of the group enfranchised to vote was limited – e.g., to property owners, or free men, or citizens able to pass a literacy test, and so forth. With this modification of the scope of who is considered to be a voting citizen, the essential idea of democracy has a long historical continuity.

"Freedom" I would associate with meaningful civil liberties like freedom of speech, freedom of the press, freedom of assembly, etc. Now a truly magisterial treatment of this set of topics would perhaps attempt to explain the link between freedom and capitalism as well as that between democracy and capitalism. I find my present task daunting enough, however. For purposes of this chapter I am crudely lumping together "freedom" and "democracy" as if they always occur together. It will have to be the task of some other author of some other study at some other time to draw out the distinctions and connections between these two related topics. Perhaps because I am an economist and am impatient to get to what I see as the big issue, I attempt to aggregate the political side very roughly. So the question here concerns the possible connection between democracy-cum-liberty with capitalism.

About the definitions of capitalism and socialism I want both to be brief and to be expansive. On the brief side, by "socialism" I mean primarily public ownership of the means of production. I have in mind basically the communist, Marxist, centrally planned economies (CPEs) of the USSR, Eastern Europe, China, Cuba, North Korea, Vietnam, and so forth as they stood before 1989. The primary identifying characteristic is public ownership of the means of production. The capitalist economies are pretty much any alternative system with a strongly predominating component of private property embedded in a market system. Capitalism means primarily private ownership of the means of production. There may be some gray areas, but I think this short definition is sufficiently clear to place most countries. In my accounting a country like Sweden is clearly capitalist with some elements or overtones of socialist ideology. (Sweden has a high government expenditure relative to other capitalist countries, but (1) it is low relative to the true socialist countries, (2) most of the government budget represents transfer payments, (3) the fraction of state-owned enterprises is much lower than in the truly socialist economies.) The task of this chapter is to explore, after some further definitional excursions, why capitalism and democracy (or socialism and dictatorship) have some tendency to be correlated.

Having given short definitions of socialism and capitalism, I feel, as an economist who specializes in comparative systems, the need to expound on the differences at much greater length. In part this is because no single definition of capitalism or socialism is completely adequate, since they constitute two different systems or world views with clusters of correlated characteristics. The primary distinguishing characteristic of capitalism versus socialism for this chapter is taken to be private versus public ownership of the means of production. But instead of trying to make everything hinge on this one distinction, it seems more appropriate to develop as complete a description as possible of the whole syndrome. If this seems like a treatment at asymmetric levels of detail of the economic and political sides, I would plead that I am, after all, an economist. Perhaps it is only natural for an economist to make finer distinctions between capitalism and socialism than between democracy and dictatorship and to think that everyone else would think that this is the appropriate way to see things, too. In any event, I want to describe in some detail what I view as the major differences between the world views of capitalism and socialism. An understanding of these differences will be indispensable, I believe, in attempting to explain later the relation of the economic system to democracy. As usual, such descriptions represent my own highly stylized abstractions. These are my observations and classifications, not sharply verifiable truths.

3 Capitalism and socialism

Perhaps the most central differences between the philosophies of capitalism and socialism center on attitudes toward the basic triad of property, competition, and the invisible hand.

The philosophy of capitalism usually begins with an assignment of priority to the concept of private property. Typically, private property is viewed as a "natural right" – something normal, usual, promised to human beings, and predating governments or political ideologies. According to this philosophy, then, private property runs very deep in the fabric of the human species. Any society founded on non-private property constitutes an unnatural state because it is going against one of the most fundamental of human desires.

The second leg of the capitalist triad is the idea that competition and self-interest are a "natural propensity" of human beings. As Adam Smith put it, there is a "natural propensity to truck, barter, and trade." Human beings like to compete on the basis of self-interest – this is a deeply ingrained motive that is difficult to eradicate or replace.

The final leg of the capitalist triad is some form of "invisible hand" theorem, the idea that far from leading to chaos and anarchy as might be supposed, private property and free competition actually lead to good results and a good society, at least better than any conceivable alternative arrangements. The invisible hand idea has been cast in a rigorous form as the so-called fundamental welfare theorems of economics. This careful formulation represents a magnificent achievement, the "magna carta of economics" in Schumpeter's phrase. It forms the centerpiece of economics, a hard analytic core making that subject distinct from any other social science. But I do not think that the dazzling technical success of general equilibrium theory should blind us to the fact that there was initially and is now a more general notion of the invisible hand theorem. Even if there had been no Walras or no fixed-point theorem, or if the strict mathematical preconditions are not met, the basic idea of the invisible hand theorem – that private property and free competition lead to better results than the alternatives – would still remain an extremely powerful organizing principle of capitalist economic philosophy. Indeed, this is the way it is commonly understood by the average person who is not a professionally trained economist.

For me, the best way to describe socialism is by using the same organizational triad, to the basic questions of which it gives diametrically opposed answers.

A central ingredient of the socialist vision is the primacy of communal or social property. This is not to say that there is no place for private property in the socialist vision or among socialists. There is, but it is almost always a grudging, secondary, limited place. There is little enthusiasm for private property in the socialist world view, just as there is little enthusiasm for public property in the capitalist scheme of things. Instead of enthusiasm for an institution that is at the center of things, there is in both cases at best a tolerance that is bred of necessity. To the socialist, it is communal, group, or public property that is held to be natural, primeval, and inherent in arrangements of man the social animal.

The second leg of the socialist triad is the idea that cooperation and coordination are natural human instincts. Human beings want to cooperate with each other, need to cooperate with each other, and throughout history this has been the dominant instinct of all healthy societies.

Finally, socialists share the common vision of some form of "visible hand" theorem. This is the basic idea that institutions built upon communal property and social cooperation can form the preconditions of a good society, or at least can make a better world than the alternatives.

While I believe the clearest distinction between capitalist and socialist world views can be stated in terms of attitudes toward the above triad of beliefs, there are several other differences that it is important to mention. As usual, these differences are stated in terms of abstract ideal types, generalizations for which there may be many specific exceptions. And I do not make much attempt to sort out which beliefs define an ideology and which ones result from accepting it, confining myself to observations about raw correlations. In any case, these stereotypes represent my own opinion or formulation.

There is a sense in which capitalism is the less idealistic system, as it starts with the relatively cynical view that human beings must be taken for the highly imperfect material that they are and that the task of an economic society is to carry out damage control or to make the best of a given situation without expecting any fundamental changes in human nature. The typical capitalist mentality does not admit of any single "right answer" to basic questions of human existence or meaning. Pluralism, individualism, and private values are ends in themselves. Socialism, by comparison, typically has a more optimistic view of human potential and a more ambitious program for raising people to be closer to some standard of perfection. There is somewhat more of a sense that a right answer exists, that it can be knowable to a community or society, and that part of the right answer involves making people better citizens by raising them to be more selfless, more socially conscious, more helpful to others. On the nature–nurture debate, then, socialists stress the importance of environment, while capitalists tend on average to emphasize more the significance of the inherited situation.

There also tends to be a difference in attitudes toward equality. A person more inclined to accept capitalist ideology tends also to accept greater income or wealth inequality. The capitalist may not like inequality, but tends to think that it is not of such critical importance in the overall scheme of things, or else that it is a relatively small price to pay for the other good things capitalism offers. To the typical socialist, by comparison, some degree of equalitarianism is a relatively more important goal in itself, it is a big part of what socialism is about. Intelligent adherents on both sides recognize the trade offs between efficiency and equity (although they may not share the same estimate of the marginal rate of transformation), but put different weights on the outcomes.

There are differences also in what might be called sociological preferences. The capitalist tends to view ideal society as the more or less spontaneous outcome of free individual interactions. The socialist prototype entails more elements of a society viewed as a planned outcome of deliberate rational design. Each side fears and parodies the excesses of the other on this score.

Some additional differences in attitudes toward basic values are worth noting in the economic sphere.

While socialism is sympathetically inclined toward public ownership and is rather casual about contract law, capitalism favors private ownership with the sophisticated framework of legal contracts for classifying and resolving conflicts which that system implies.

Capitalism embraces the market, feels comfortable with it, is lost without it. Government regulation may be accepted as a necessary evil, but is almost always the object of scorn, is never desirable in itself. The typical socialist, by contrast, is suspicious of market processes and feels less bothered than the capitalist by non-market allocation systems like physical planning. The market may be needed under socialism, it may be tolerated, but it is rarely loved.

Socialism has a long tradition of tending to view the scarcity problem in a developed economy rather casually, as not being of the first magnitude. In a mature economy all basic needs can be met, ordinary people will be living as the very rich did in the past, and scarcity is not a fundamental issue. The real issue concerns making a better life, realizing higher goals, and so forth. There is thus a tendency in socialist thought to downplay the necessity of giving hard answers to the "what, how and for whom" questions persistently posed by capitalist-oriented economists. It is not that these questions should not be asked, or that there are no answers. Rather, it is more the idea that it is not that useful to spend an inordinate amount of time obsessively spelling out all the details for a truly socialist (or communist) economy, in which people are motivated by higher goals of the common good. In other words, for a true socialist the scarcity problem, while not invalid, has an archaic or quaint tone about it in reference to a developed socialist economy. By contrast, capitalism has an equally long tradition of seeing the scarcity problem as central almost always and everywhere. To the capitalist mentality there is something suspicious about an economic philosophy that cannot give, and does not revel in giving, a rock-hard answer to the "what, how, and for whom" question.

The capitalist world view sees individual initiative, entrepreneurship, and risk-taking as crucial elements in making an economy move forward. The socialist tends to view these concepts with suspicion, as being more of a cover-up for unequal wealth than a genuinely needed resource allocation mechanism. To the extent that they are needed in the socialist world, entrepreneurial functions are tolerated but never loved.

The capitalist ideology sees labor relations as essentially a sub-set of market relations. Of cource, labor is different from other commodities, but not enough so to warrant special treatment fundamentally different from the laws of supply and demand that rule other markets. The socialist, by contrast, assigns an absolutely unique place to labor. Labor has a special status that cannot be reduced to merely another monetary consideration. While the exact content of such feelings can differ among socialists, most feel to some degree that labor is the ultimate source of value, that labor should not be "exploited," and that labor should be assigned special rights at the workplace – all in excess of what the market would typically determine.

The proponent of the capitalist system offers no fundamental guarantee of employment or stability. While reformed capitalism may contain certain buffers or softeners, it does not promise economic security. Indeed, the essence of the capitalist system – and the promise of progress it delivers – involves some unemployment, some business failures, and a general climate of economic uncertainty. Socialism, on the other hand, is more committed to economic security – to nominally full employment and no abrupt enterprise "failures," as such.

So much for stereotypes about values and beliefs under capitalism and socialism. The above list could be supplemented, but the main themes have been covered.

4   Capitalism and democracy

The question I want to pose is why capitalism is correlated with democracy while socialism is correlated with dictatorship. The key word here is "correlated." No one is claiming a one to one relationship. The claim is that there exists a tendency that is reflected in a statistically significant correlation. In a truly complete treatment I would try to document this empirical generalization more carefully. Here, I merely point out that there have been serious attempts independently to quantify political and economic systems, and such studies typically show a statistically significant correlation between "freedom" and "capitalism." In any event, this rough empirical generalization is taken as a starting point.

The true believer in socialism will probably try to deny the correlation. He or she will point out exceptions, imperfect definitions, biases, ambiguities in formulation, and so forth. Sweden or Austria may be declared socialist, put forth as a counter-example, and made to bear an extremely heavy counter-weight. The rich historical experience of the USSR, all of Eastern Europe, China, Vietnam, Cuba, North Korea, and so forth will be downplayed because these countries, constituting over 35 percent of the world's population, are or were "not really socialist." The argument that they are (were) not really socialist in my opinion amounts to the argument that when a system is not nice it cannot be socialist because, by definition, socialism is a nice system. I think that an honest socialist has to take some responsibility for the experience of these countries and should attempt to answer honestly the question that has been posed. Why is it that economic systems oriented toward the capitalist pole described in the previous section have some tendency to be democratic on the political side, while there is some world-wide tendency for economic systems at the socialist extreme to be political dictatorships? I believe this to be a meaningful question, even if it is not likely to admit of an elegantly simple answer.

What follows is my own streamlined, very succinct version of what I consider to be the major strands of explanation for why there is a connection between capitalism and democracy. This not very original, highly compressed restatement is put forth in the hope that others may find it useful. In one form or another, some variant of these three arguments appears repeatedly in the literature but not always presented systematically. Of course categories are arbitrary to some degree, and what seems to be a natural or useful demarcation to one person may not to another.

4.1   Countervailing power

The essence of this argument is simple. The modern nation-state has enormous power and great resources potentially at its control. Any state or authority, it is asserted, has a natural tendency to expand its power if unchecked.

The capitalist economy, because of its high degree of decentralization, automatically builds in some countervailing power to check the encroachment of the state. There is not just one or a very small number of employers, financiers, or publishers. Instead there are lots of nooks and crannies in a capitalist economy where opponents of government policies can find jobs, locate a power base, finance operations, provide alternative viewpoints through privately-controlled media, and generally obtain economic resources to develop genuine political opposition.

Thus, according to this argument, a socialist economy is less likely to be able to check the encroachment of the state and, in so doing, effectively to defend democracy and freedom in the political arena.

4.2   Shared values, common culture, natural compatibility

This argument is complicated. The basic idea is that the essential philosophies of capitalism and democracy have so much in common that the human need for consistency consolidates them as one world view. Or, they may even represent alternative versions of the same world view. It might be possible in theory to subscribe to one philosophy without the other, but that is unlikely to happen in practice because it would be too jarring to human sensibilities, which crave consistency.

Historically, we have a very clear record of capitalism and democracy evolving together, at least in England. John Locke considered as natural rights: life, liberty, and property. Early voters were men of property. Jefferson changed Locke's "property" to "pursuit of happiness" in the Declaration of Independence, but the intended meaning was similar: to have the freely available possibility of owning property, which was Jefferson's ideal, was to have the freely available possibility of the means to pursue happiness.

Both capitalism and democracy share the common philosophy of free will of the individual, imperfectability of human beings, primacy of private values and property, the idea that no one can know "the right answer," the suspicion of – and consequent limited civil and economic power of – government or any other agglomeration of power. In this common philosophy, society is viewed as the spontaneous outcome of free individual interactions.

The underlying philosophy of socialism is based more on ideas of cooperation, social coordination, perfectability of human beings, primacy of social values and property, the possibility of a "right answer." Socialist society is idealized as the outcome of deliberate rational design.

There is therefore a natural overlap between (economic) capitalism and (political) democracy. Capitalism is a "marketplace of goods" and democracy is a "marketplace of ideas." Their underlying philosophies are similar and mutually reinforcing.

Under capitalism, and under democracy, the burden of proof is on society to say why something cannot be done by an individual. Under socialism, and under dictatorship, there is a greater burden of proof on the individual to show why he can do something in his individual interest.

Capitalism and democracy share a very important trait. Both elevate to great significance the idea of competition as a mechanism for uncovering good outcomes, since there is no single answer that in principle is knowable to a mandarin bureaucracy. In both systems, similar mechanisms, concepts, and legal frameworks are required for resolving the inevitable conflicts that arise in the political and economic arenas. In their attitudes toward competition, capitalism and democracy are so similar that they are practically two sides of the same coin. Since no one authority can know the right answer or the right product, or since there may be even no such thing, the primary task of government is to establish a consistent overall framework that will encourage healthy competition continually to bring forth those partially right answers appropriate to particular constellations of time and place, as they continually change.

Socialism is based more on notions of idealized cooperation. Conflict is viewed as avoidable and undesirable. Human beings can direct themselves in socially harmonious relations by committees or other collective forms. In a system based on the ideal of collective harmony, it seems natural that there is bound to be less perceived need to have formal guarantees for individual rights. Laissez-faire economic individualism is bound to be threatening to the philosophy of one-party politics. If individuals can know more about growing vegetables than the state, why not about foreign policy?

The "common culture" argument then comes down to the idea that it is difficult for people to adhere to economic and political philosophies that appear to contradict each other. There is a natural consistency between the political philosophy of democracy and the economic philosophy of capitalism, which, if it is long denied, causes tension that is eventually difficult to bear.

4.3   Overload

Democracy is an inherently inefficient, fragile collection of coalitions, unable to make and execute decisions as rapidly as dictatorships. It is difficult to imagine a representative, democratic parliament able to function effectively while thrashing out a huge multitude of central planning directives, each of which concerns in one way or another issues of income distribution, regional investment, and the like.

First of all there is a mechanical problem of democratically-elected legislators lacking the time, expertise, or patience to work out an effective central plan. Secondly, there being no single "popular will" to be discovered, there would be constant and probably irreconcilable arguments about what should be the national economic plan in a democratic state, with different constituencies arguing for a national plan favorable to their interests.

Thus, the overload argument boils down to the idea that a democratically-elected parliament cannot compose or execute a meaningful central plan, and hence the two are incompatible.

5   Conclusion

What is one to make of these "arguments"? As evidenced by my own inability to find enough consistency or tractibility to make a formal model of the connection between capitalism and democracy, I am uncomfortable with the incompleteness of the attempted categorization. On the other hand, the topic is important. Perhaps this attempt to set out the basic arguments may be found to have some use.

Bibliography

Abegglen, James and George Stalk, Jr., 1985. *Kaisha: The Japanese Corporation*, New York: Basic Books.

Akerlof, George, 1984. *An Economic Theorist's Book of Tales*, Cambridge: Cambridge University Press.

Akerlof, George and Janet Yellen, 1986. *Efficiency Wage Models of the Labor Market*, Cambridge: Cambridge University Press.

Alchian, Armen, 1984. "Specificity, specialization and coalitions," *Journal of Institutional and Theoretical Economics*: 34–39.

1987. "Property rights," in John Eatwell, Murray Millgate and P. Millgate (eds.), *The New Palgrave*, London: Macmillan: 1031–1034.

Alchian, Armen and Harold Demsetz, 1972a. "Production, information costs, and economic organization," *American Economic Review*, 62 (December): 777–795.

1972b. "The property rights paradigm," *Journal of Economic History*, 33: 16–27.

Aoki, Masahiko, 1984. *The Cooperative Game Theory of the Firm*, London: Oxford University Press.

1986. "Horizontal vs. vertical information structure of the firm," *American Economic Review*, 76: 971–83.

1987. *Information, Incentives and Bargaining in the Japanese Economy*, London: Cambridge University Press.

1990a. "Towards an economic theory of the Japanese firm," *Journal of Economic Literature*, 28: 1–27.

1990b. "The participatory generation of information rents and the theory of the firm," in Aoki *et al.* (1990): 26–52.

Aoki, Masahiko, Bo Gustafsson and Oliver E. Williamson, 1990. *The Firm as a Nexus of Treaties*, New York: Sage.

Armstrong, Peter, 1989. "Management, labour process and agency," *Work, Employment and Society*, 3 (September): 307–22.

Arrow, Kenneth J., 1963. *Social Choice and Individual Values*, 2nd edn, New York: John Wiley.

1982. "Risk perception in psychology and economics," *Economic Inquiry*, 20: 109.

1985. "The economics of agency," in J. W. Pratt and R. J. Zeckhauser (eds.), *Principals and Agents: The Structure of Business*, Cambridge, MA: Harvard University Press: 37–51.

1986. "Rationality of self and others in an economic system," *Journal of Business*, 59: 385–391.

Arrow, Kenneth J. and Gerard Debreu, 1954. "Existence of an equilibrium for a competitive economy," *Econometrica* (July): 265–90.

Arrow, Kenneth J. and Leonid Hurwicz, 1958. "On the stability of the competitive equilibrium, II," *Econometrica*, 26: 522–52.

Arrow, Kenneth J., H. D. Block and L. Hurwicz, 1959. "On the stability of competitive equilibrium," *Econometrica*, **27**: 89–109.

Ashby, R. W., 1963, *An Introduction to Cybernetics*, New York: Wiley.

Aslund, Anders, 1989. *Gorbachov's Struggle for Economic Reform*, London: Pinter.

Aston, T. H. and C. H. E. Philpin (eds.), 1985. *The Brenner Debate: Agrarian Class Structure and Economic Development in Pre-Industrial Europe*, Cambridge: Cambridge University Press.

Axelrod, Robert, 1984. *The Evolution of Cooperation*, New York: Basic Books.

Babbage, C., 1832. *On the Economics of Machines and Manufactures*, London: Charles Knight.

Bardhan, Pranab and John Roemer, 1992. "Market socialism: a case for rejuvenation," *Journal of Economic Perspectives*, **6**: 101–116.

Baron, James, 1988. "The employment relation as a social relation," *Journal of the Japanese and International Economies*, **2**: 492–525.

Barry, Brian, 1989. *Theories of Justice: A Treatise on Social Justice*, Berkeley: University of California Press.

Bartlett, Will and Milica Uvalic, 1986. "Labour managed firms, employee participation and profit-sharing: theoretical perspectives and European experience," *EUI Working Paper*, **86/236** and *Management Bibliographies and Reviews*, **12**(4).

Barzelay, M. and L. Thomas, 1986, "Is capitalism necessary? A critique of the neoclassical economics of organization," *Journal of Economic Behavior and Organization*, **7**: 225–233.

Battalio, R., J. Kagel and C. Kogut, 1987. "An experimental confirmation of the existence of Giffen goods," paper presented at the Joint Public Choice and Economic Science Association Meetings.

Becattini, G. (ed.), 1987. *Mercato e Forze Locali: il Distretto Industriale*, Bologna: Il Mulino.

Bellas, C., 1972. *Industrial Democracy and the Worker-Owned Firm*, New York: Praeger.

Benassy, Jean-Pascal, 1982. *The Economics of Market Disequilibrium*, Orlando, FL: Academic Press.

Benhabib, J. K. and R. H. Day, 1981. "Rational choice and erratic behavior," *Review of Economic Studies*, **158**: 459–71.

Ben-Ner, Avner, 1986. "Nonprofit organizations: Why do they exist in market economies?," in Susan Rose-Ackerman (ed.), *The Economics of Nonprofit Institutions: Studies in Structure and Policy*, Oxford: Oxford University Press: 94–113.

1987. "Producer cooperatives: Why do they exist in capitalist economies?," in W. Powell (ed.), *The Nonprofit Sector: A Research Handbook*, New Haven: Yale University Press.

1988a. "Comparative empirical observations on worker-owned and capitalist firms," *International Journal of Industrial Organization*, **6**: 1–31.

1988b. "The life cycle of worker-owned firms in market economies," *Journal of Economic Behavior and Organization*, **10**: 287–313.

Ben-Ner, Avner and Theresa Van Hoomissen, 1991. "Nonprofit organizations in the mixed economy: A demand and supply analysis," *Annals of Public and Cooperative Economics*, **62**(4).

Ben-Ner, Avner and Byoung Jun, 1991a. "Bargaining under asymmetric information: When do firms share information with unions, and how much?", University of Minnesota and Korea University, mimeo.

1991b. "Buy-out in a bargaining game with asymmetric information," University of Minnesota and Korea University, mimeo.

Ben-Ner, Avner and Egon Neuberger, 1990. "The feasibility of planned marker systems: The Yugoslav visible hand and negotiated planning," *Journal of Comparative Economics*, **14**: 768–790.

Ben-Porat, Yoram, 1980. "The F-connection: families, friends, and firms and the organization of exchange," *Population and Development Review*, **6** (March): 1–30.

Berger, Peter L., 1986. *The Capitalist Revolution*, New York: Basic Books.

Berle, Adolf and Gardiner Means, 1932. *The Modern Corporation and Private Property*, New York: Commerce Clearing House.

Berman, K. and M. Berman, 1989. "An empirical test of the theory of the labor-managed firm," *Journal of Comparative Economics*, **13**: 281–300.

Binmore, Ken, 1986. "Bargaining and coalitions," in Alvin Roth (ed.), *Game-Theoretic Approaches to Bargaining Theory*, Cambridge: Cambridge University Press.

Binmore, Ken, Ariel Rubinstein and Asher Wolinski, 1985. "The Nash bargaining solution in economic modelling," *Rand Journal of Economics*, **17**: 176–88.

Blasi, Joseph, 1988. *Employee Ownership: Revolution or Ripoff*, Cambridge, MA: Ballinger.

Blinder, Alan (ed.), 1990. *Paying for Productivity*, Washington DC: Brookings.

Bolt, James, 1983. "Job security: Its time has come," *Harvard Business Review* (November–December): 115–123.

Bonin, John P. and Louis Putterman, 1987. *Economics of Cooperation and the Labor-Managed Economy*, New York and London: Academic Publishers, Harwood.

Bonin, John P. and Alan Marcus, 1979. "Information, motivation, and control in decentralized planning: The case of discretionary managerial behavior," *Journal of Comparative Economics*, **3**: 235–253.

Bowles, Samuel, 1985. "The production process in a competitive economy: Walrasian, neo-Hobbesian, and Marxian models," *American Economic Review*, **75**(1) (March): 16–36.

1989a, "Capitalist technology: Endogenous claim enforcement and the choice of technique," University of Massachusetts, *Working Paper*.

1989b. "Social institutions and technical change," in M. Di Matteo, R. M. Goodwin, and A. Vercelli (eds.), *Technological and Social Factors in Long Term Fluctuations*, New York: Springer-Verlag.

1990. "Mandeville's mistake: The moral autonomy of the self-regulating market reconsidered," Amherst, mimeo.

Bowles, Samuel and Herbert Gintis, 1976. *Schooling in Capitalist America: Educational Reform and the Contradictions of Economic Life*, New York: Basic Books.

1982. "The welfare state and long-term economic growth: Marxian, neoclassical, and Keynesian approaches," *American Economic Review*, **72**(2) (May): 341–345.

1983. "The power of capital: on the inadequacy of the conception of the capitalist economy as 'private'," *Philosophical Forum*, **14**(3–4) (Spring–Summer): 225–245.

1986. *Democracy and Capitalism: Property, Community, and the Contradictions of Modern Social Thought*, New York: Basic Books.

1988. "Contested exchange: political economy and modern economic theory," *American Economic Review*, **78**: 145–150.

1990. "Contested exchange: New microfoundations of the political economy of capitalism," *Politics and Society*, **18**(2): 165–222.

1993. "An economic and political case for the democratic firm," in David Copp, Jean Hampton and John Roemer (eds.), *The Idea of Democracy*, Cambridge: Cambridge University Press.

Bradach, Jeffrey L. and Robert G. Eccles, 1989. "Price, authority, and trust: From ideal types to plural forms," *Annual Review of Sociology*, 15: 97–118.

Bradley, Keith and Alan Gelb, 1983. *Worker + Capitalism = The New Industrial Relations*, Cambridge, MA: MIT Press.

Braverman, Harry, 1974. *Labor and Monopoly Capital: The Degradation of Work in the Twentieth Century*, New York: Monthly Review Press.

Brenner, Robert, 1986. "The social basis of economic development," in Roemer (1986).

Brus, Wladimir, 1972. *The Market in a Socialist Economy*, London: Routledge & Kegan Paul.

1987. "Market socialism," in J. Eatwell, M. Milgate and P. Newman (eds.), *The Palgrave Dictionary of Economics*, London: Macmillan.

Brus, Wladimir and K. Laski, 1990. *From Marx to Market: Socialism in Search of an Economic System*, Oxford: Oxford University Press.

Brusco, S., 1982. "The Emilian model: Productive decentralization and social integration," *Cambridge Journal of Economics*, 6:167–184.

Buchanan, James M. 1975. *The Limits of Liberty*, Chicago: University of Chicago Press.

1977. *Freedom in Constitutional Contract*, College Station: Texas A&M University Press.

Buchanan, James M., Robert Tollison and Gordon Tullock, 1980. *Toward a Theory of the Rent-seeking Society*, College Station: Texas A&M University Press.

Business Week, 1989. "The Payoff from Teamwork" (July 10, 1989): 56–62.

Calsamiglia, Xavier, 1977. "Decentralized resource allocation and increasing returns," *Journal of Economic Theory*, 14: 263–283.

Calvo, Guillermo, 1979. "Quasi-Walrasian theories of unemployment," *American Economic Review*, 69(2) (May): 102–107.

Camacho, Antonio, 1970. "Externalities, optimality and informationally decentralized resource allocation processes," *International Economic Review*, 11: 318–327.

Coase, Ronald, 1932. "The nature of the firm," *Economica*, NS4 (November 1937).

1960. "The problem of social cost," *Journal of Law and Economics*, 3: 1–44.

Cohen, G. A., 1978. *Karl Marx's Theory of History: a Defence*, Oxford: Oxford University Press.

Commentary Symposium, 1978. "Capitalism, socialism, and democracy: A symposium," *Commentary*, 65(4) (April): 29–79.

Conn, David, 1978. "Economic theory and comparative economic systems: A partial literature survey," *Journal of Comparative Economics*, 2: 355–381.

1982. "Effort, efficiency, and incentives in economic organizations," *Journal of Comparative Economics*, 6: 223–234.

Cooper, Russell and Andrew John, 1988. "Coordinating coordination failures in Keynesian models," *Quarterly Journal of Economics*, 103(3) (August): 441–463.

Cremer, Jacques, 1990. "Common knowledge and the coordination of economic activities," in Aoki *et al.* (1990): 52–76.

Dahl, Robert A., 1957. "The concept of power," *Behavioral Science*, 2: 201–215.

1985. *Preface to the Theory of Economic Democracy*, Berkeley, CA: University of California Press.

Dahl, Robert and Charles Lindblom, 1953. *Politics, Economics and Welfare*, New York: Harper & Row.

Dasgupta, P. and P. David, 1988. "Priority, secrecy, patents and the socio-economics of science and technology," *Center for Economic Policy Research Publication*, 127, Stanford: Stanford University.

Davy, S. I., 1983. "Employee ownership: One road to productivity improvement," *Journal of Business Strategy*, **4**: 12–21.

Day, R. H. and W. Shafer, 1985. "Keynesian chaos," *Journal of Macroeconomics*, **7**: 277–295.

Debreu, Gerard, 1959. *Theory of Value*, New York: Wiley.

1974. "Excess demand functions," *Journal of Mathematical Economics*, **1**: 15–23.

Defourney, J., S. Estrin and D. C. Jones, 1985. "The effects of workers' participation on enterprise performance," *International Journal of Industrial Organization*, **3**: 197–217.

Demsetz, Harold, 1966. "Toward a theory of property rights," *American Economic Review*, **2**: 347–359.

Dickens, William, Larry Katz, Kevin Lang and Larry Summers, 1989. "Employee crime and the monitoring puzzle," *Journal of Labor Economics*, **7**: 331–347.

Dickson, T., H. V. McLachlan, P. Prior and K. Swales, 1988. "Big blue and the unions: IBM, individualism and trade union strategy," *Work, Employment and Society*, **2** (December): 506–20.

DiMaggio, Paul, 1988. "Interest and agency in institutional theory," in Lynne G. Zucker (ed.), *Institutional Patterns and Organizations: Culture and Environment*, Cambridge, MA: Ballinger: 3–21.

Di Matteo, M., R. M. Goodwin and A. Vercelli (eds.), 1989. *Technological and Social Factors in Long Term Fluctuations*, New York: Springer-Verlag.

Domar, Evsey, 1966. "The Soviet collective farm as a producer cooperative," *American Economic Review*, **56** (September): 743–757.

Dong, X.-Y. and Greg Dow, 1991. "Mutual monitoring in production teams: Theory and evidence from Chinese agriculture," *Research Paper*, **91–19**, Department of Economics, University of Alberta.

1993. "Monitoring costs in Chinese agricultural teams," *Journal of Political Economy*, forthcoming.

Dosi, G., 1988. "Sources, procedures and microeconomic effects of innovation," *Journal of Economic Literature*, **26** (September): 1120–1171.

Dow, Greg, 1986. "Control rights, competitive markets, and the labor management debate," *Journal of Comparative Economics*, **10**: 48–61.

1987. "The function of authority in transaction cost economics," *Journal of Economic Behavior and Organization*, **8**: 13–38.

1988a. "Information, production decisions, and intra-firm bargaining," *International Economic Review*, **29**: 57–79.

1988b. "The evolution of organizational form: Selection, efficiency, and the new institutional economics," *Economic Analysis and Workers' Management*, **22**: 139–167.

1989. "Knowledge is power: Informational precommitment in the capitalist firm," *European Journal of Political Economy*, **5**: 161–176.

1991. "Selling jobs: Moral hazard in capitalist and labor-managed firms," Department of Economics, University of Alberta, unpublished manuscript.

1992. "Democracy versus appropriability: Can labor-managed firms flourish in a capitalist world?", Chapter 11 in this volume.

1993a. "Why capital lures labor: A bargaining perspective." *American Economic Review*, forthcoming.

1993b. "The appropriability critique of transaction cost economics," in C. Pitelis (ed.), *Markets, Hierarchies and Transaction Costs: Critical Assessment*, Oxford: Basil

Blackwell, forthcoming.

Downs, Anthony, 1957. *An Economic Theory of Democracy*, New York: Harper & Row.

1989. *Labor Management, Contracts and Capital Markets*, New York: Basil Blackwell.

Drèze, Jacques, 1976. "Some theory of labor management and participation," *Econometrica*, **44**: 1125.

Edwards, P. K., 1990. "The politics of conflict and consent: How the labor contract really works," *Journal of Economic Behavior and Organization*, **13**: 41–61.

Edwards, Richard, 1979. *Contested Terrain: The Transformation of the Workplace in the Twentieth Century*, New York: Basic Books.

Elbaum, Bernard and Frank Wilkinson, 1979. "Industrial relations and uneven development: a comparative study of the American and the British steel industries," *Cambridge Journal of Economics*, **3**(3): 275–303.

Ellerman, David, 1986a. "Horizon problems and property rights in labor-managed firms," *Journal of Comparative Systems*, **10**: 62–78.

1986b. "Property appropriation and economic theory," in Philip Mirowski (ed.), *The Reconstruction of Economic Theory*, Boston: Kluwer-Nijhoff: 41–92.

Elster, Jon, 1984. *Ulysses and the Sirens*, Cambridge: Cambridge University Press.

1985. *The Multiple Self*, London: Cambridge University Press.

Elster, Jon and Karl Moene, 1989. "Introduction," in Jon Elster and Karl Moene (eds.), *Alternatives to Capitalism*, Cambridge: Cambridge University Press.

Estrin, Saul, 1983. *Self-management: Economic Theory and Yugoslav Practice*, Cambridge: Cambridge University Press.

Estrin, Saul and Derek Jones, 1988. "Do employee-owned firms invest less?", London School of Economics, mimeo.

Estrin, Saul and Ashok Kotwal, 1984. "The moral hazard of budget-breaking," *Rand Journal of Economics*, **15**: 578–581.

Estrin, Saul and J. Le Grand, 1989. *Market Socialism*, Oxford: Oxford University Press.

Estrin, Saul, Derek C. Jones and Jan Svejnar, 1987. "The productivity effects of worker participation: Producer cooperatives in Western economics," *Journal of Comparative Economics*, **11**: 40–61.

Eswaran, Mukesh and Ashok Kotwal, 1989. "Why are capitalists the bosses?", *Economic Journal*, **99**: 162–176.

Ettman, B. O., 1978. *Industrial Democracy: A Selected Bibliography*, MCB Publications, **11**, from the Institute of Business, Bradford.

Etzioni, Amitai, 1975. *A Comparative Analysis of Complex Organizations*, revised edn, New York: Free Press.

Fama, Eugene F., 1980. "Agency problems and the theory of the firm," *Journal of Political Economy*, **88**(2): 288–307.

Fehr, Ernst, 1988. *Economic Theory of Self-Management and Profit-Sharing*, in German, Frankfurt: Campus-Verlag.

1990. "Labor-managed and capitalist economics in the absence of entrance fees," *Discussion Paper*, University of Technology, Vienna.

1991. "Labor management," in E. Dulfer (ed.), *International Handbook of Co-operative Organizations*, Gottingen: Vandehoeck and Ruprecht.

Fehr, Ernst and Murat Sertel, 1991. "Two forms of workers' enterprises facing imperfect labor markets," *Discussion Paper*, University of Technology, Vienna.

Feldman, Allan, 1980. *Welfare Economics and Social Choice Theory*, Boston: Kluwer Nijhoff.

Fishburn, P., 1952. *Foundations of Expected Utility*, London: Reidel.

FitzRoy, Felix, 1980. "Notes on the political economy of a co-operative enterprise sector," in Felix FitzRoy, *The Political Economy of Co-operation and Participation: A Third Sector*, Oxford: Oxford University Press.

FitzRoy, Felix R. and Dennis C. Mueller, 1984. "Cooperation and conflict in contractual organization," *Quarterly Review of Economics and Business*, 24 (Winter): 24–49.

Foulkes, Fred, 1980. *Personnel Policies in Large Nonunion Companies*, Englewood Cliffs, NJ: Prentice-Hall.

Fox, Alan, 1974. *Beyond Contract: Work, Power, and Trust Relations*, London: Faber.

Freedom House, 1986. *Survey of Freedom*, London: Freedom House Publishers.

Frey, B., 1987. "On fairness of pricing," *Institute for Empirical Economic Research*, Kleinstrasse 15, CH-8008 Zurich, Switzerland.

Friedman, Milton, 1963. *Capitalism and Freedom*, Chicago: Phoenix Books.

Furubotn, E. G., 1979. "Decision making under labor management: The commitment mechanism reconsidered," *Zeitschrift für die gesamte Staatswissenschaft*, 135: 216.

   1980. "Tradable claims and self-financed investment in a capitalist labor managed firm," *Zeitschrift für die gesamte Staatswissenschaft*, 136: 630.

Furubotn, Eirik, and Svetozar Pejovich, 1970. "Property rights and the behavior of the firm in a socialist state: The example of Yugoslavia," *Zeitschrift für Nationalökonomie*, 30: 431–454.

Gambetta, Diego (ed.), 1988. *Trust: Making and Breaking Cooperative Relations*, Oxford: Blackwell.

Geanakoplos, J. and P. Milgrom, 1991. "A theory of hierarchies based on limited managerial attention," *Journal of the Japanese and International Economies*: 205–55.

Gerlach, Michael, 1987. "Business alliance and the strategy of the Japanese firm," *California Management Review*, 30 (Fall): 126–142.

Gintis, Herbert, 1972. "A radical analysis of welfare economics and individual development," *Quarterly Journal of Economics* (November): 572–599.

   1974. "Welfare criteria with endogenous preferences," *International Economic Review*, 15(2) (June): 415–429.

   1976. "The nature of the labor exchange and the theory of capitalist production," *Review of Radical Political Economics*, 8(2) (Summer): 36–54.

   1989a. "The power to switch: On the political economy of consumer sovereignty," in Samuel Bowles, Richard C. Edwards and William G. Shepherd (eds.), *Unconventional Wisdom: Essays in Honor of John Kenneth Galbraith*, New York: Houghton-Mifflin.

   1989b. "Financial markets and the political structure of the enterprises," *Journal of Economic Behavior and Organization*, 1: 311–322.

   1989c. "The principle of external accountability in financial markets," in Masahiko Aoki, Bo Gustafsson and Oliver Williamson (eds.), *The Firm as a Nexus of Treaties*, New York: Sage.

Gintis, Herbert and Tsuneo Ishikawa, 1987. "Wages, work discipline, and unemployment," *Journal of Japanese and International Economies*, 1: 195–228.

Goldberg, Victor, 1980. "Relational exchange: Economics and complex contracts," *American Behavioral Scientists*, 23(3) (January/February): 337–52.

Green, D. M. and J. A. Swets, 1974. *Signal Detection Theory and Psychophysics*, New York: Krieger.

Green, L. and H. Rachlin, 1972. "Commitment, choice, and self control," *Journal of the Experimental Analysis of Behavior*, 17: 15–22.

Grossman, Sanford J. and Oliver D. Hart, 1980. "Takeover bids, the free-rider problem and the theory of corporation," *Bell Journal of Economics*, **11**: 42–64.

1986. "The costs and benefits of ownership: A theory of vertical and lateral integration," *Journal of Political Economy*, **94**: 691–719.

Grout, Paul A., 1984. "Investment and wages in the absence of legally binding labour contracts," *Econometrica*, **52**: 449–460.

Groves, Theodore, 1973. "Incentives in teams," *Econometrica*, **41**: 617–633.

Groves, Theodore and J. Ledyard, 1977. "Optimal allocation of public goods: A solution to the 'free rider' problem," *Econometrica*, **45**: 783–811.

Gui, Benedetto, 1985. "Limits to external financing: A model and an application to labor-managed firms," in Derek C. Jones and Jan Svejnar (eds.), *Advances in the Economic Analysis of Participatory and Labor-Managed Firms, Vol. 1*, Greenwich, CT: JAI Press: 107–120.

Hansmann, Henry, 1988. "The ownership of the firm," *Journal of Law, Economics, and Organization*, **4**: 267–304.

1990a. "The viability of worker ownership," in Masahiko Aoki, Bo Gustafsson and Oliver Williamson (eds.), *The Firm as a Nexus of Treaties*, New York: Sage.

1990b. "When does worker ownership work? ESOPs, law firms, codetermination, and economic democracy," *Yale Law Journal*, **99**: 1749–1816.

Harsanyi, John C., 1977. *Rational Behavior and Bargaining Equilibrium in Games of Social Situations*, Cambridge: Cambridge University Press.

Hart, Oliver and John Moore, 1990. "Property rights and the nature of the firm," *Journal of Political Economy*, **98**(6) (December): 1119–1158.

Hayami, Yujiro and Vernon W. Ruttan, 1985. *Agricultural Development: An International Perspective*, Baltimore: Johns Hopkins University Press.

Hayek, Friedrich, 1945. "The use of knowledge in society," *American Economic Review*, **35**: 519–30.

1973–1979. *Law, Legislation, and Liberty*, 3 vols., Chicago: University of Chicago Press.

1978. *New Studies in Philososphy, Politics, Economics, and the History of Ideas*, Chicago: University of Chicago Press.

Hayek, Friedrich A. (ed.), 1935. *Collectivist Economic Planning: Critical Studies on the Possibilities of Socialism*, London: George Routledge.

Heiner, R. A., 1983. "The origin of predictable behavior," *American Economic Review*, **73**: 560–595.

1985a. "Origin of predictable behavior: Further modeling and applications," *American Economic Review*, **75**: 391–396.

1985b. "On reinterpreting the foundations of risk and utility theory," Princeton Institute for Advanced Study.

1985c. "Experimental economics: Comment," *American Economic Review*, **85**: 260–263.

1985d. "Rational expectations when agents imperfectly use information," *Journal of Post Keynesian Economics*, **8**: 2091–2207.

1985e. "Uncertainty, signal detection experiments, and modeling behavior," in R. Langlois (ed.), *Economics as a Process: Essays in the New Institutional Economics*, New York: Cambridge University Press.

1986. "Imperfect decisions and the law: On the evolution of legal precedent and rules," *Journal of Legal Studies*, **15**: 227–261.

1988a. "Imperfect decisions in organizations," *Journal of Economic Behavior and Organization*, **9**: 25–44.

1988b. "The necessity of imperfect decisions," *Journal of Economic Behavior and Organization*, **10**: 29–56.

1988c. "The necessity of delaying economic adjustment," *Journal of Economic Behavior and Organization*, **10**: 255–286.

1989a. "Origin of predictable dynamic behavior," *Journal of Economic Behavior and Organization*, **12**: 233–258.

1989b. "Imperfect decisions, evolutionary stability, and the origin of rules over flexible optimizing," in M. Commons and R. J. Herrnstein (eds.), *The Quantitative Analysis of Behavior*, New York: Lawrence Erlbaum.

Helper, Sue, 1990. "Supplier relations at a crossroads: Results of survey reseach in the US automobile industry," Case Western Reserve, mimeo.

Herrnstein, R. J., 1970. "On the law of effect," *Journal of the Experimental Analysis of Behavior*, **13**: 243–266.

Hernstein, R. J. and Heyman, G. M., 1979. "Is matching compatible with reinforcement maximization on concurrent variable interval, variable ratio?", *Journal of Experimental Analysis of Behavior*, **31**: 209–223.

Herrett, Edward, 1988. *Reforming the Soviet Economy*, Washington DC: Brooking.

Hill, P. M., M. McGrath and E. Reyes, 1981. *Cooperative Bibliography – an Annotated Guide to Works in English* on *Cooperatives and Cooperation*, University Centre for Cooperatives, Madison: University of Wisconsin.

Hill, Stephen, 1981. *Competition and Control at Work: The New Industrial Sociology*, Cambridge, MA: MIT Press.

Hodgson, Geoff M., 1988. *Economics and Institutions*, Oxford: Polity Press.

Holmstrom, Bengt, 1982. "Moral hazard in teams," *Bell Journal of Economics*, **13**: 324–340.

Houthakker, H. S. and L. S. Taylor, 1966. *Consumer Demand in the United States 1929–57: Analysis and Projections*, Cambridge, MA: Harvard University Press.

Huber, George and Reuben McDaniel, 1986. "The decision making paradigm of organizational design," *Management Science*, **3** (May): 622–642.

Hurwicz, Leonid, 1960. "Optimality and informational efficiency in resource allocation processes," in Kenneth J. Arrow, Samuel Karlin and Patrick Suppes (eds.), *Mathematical Methods in Social Sciences*, Stanford: Stanford University Press: 27–46.

1972a. "On informationally decentralized systems," in Roy Radner and N. McGuire (eds.), *Decision and Organization*, Amsterdam: North-Holland.

1972b. "Organizational structures for joint decision making: A designer's point of view," in M. Tuite, R. Chisholm and M. Radnor (eds.), *Interorganizational Decision Making*, Chicago: Aldine.

1975. "The design of mechanisms for resource allocation," in M. D. Intrilligator and D. A. Kendrick (eds.), *Frontiers of Quantitative Economics, II*, Amsterdam: North-Holland.

1987. "Inventing new institutions: The design perspective," *The American Journal of Agricultural Economics*, **69**:395–402.

1988. "On modeling institutions," paper presented at the American Economic Association Meetings in New York (December 30).

1989. "Mechanisms and institutions," in Takashi Shiraishi and Shigeto Tsuro (eds.), *Economic Institutions in a Dynamic Society: Search for a New Frontier*, London: Macmillan.

1992. "Toward a framework for analyzing institutions and institutional change," Chapter 4 in this volume.

Hurwicz, Leonid and Hans Weinberger, 1990. "A necessary condition for decentralizability and an application to intertemporal allocation," *Journal of Economic Theory*, 15(2): 313–345.

Ireland, Norman J. and Peter J. Law, 1982. *The Economics of Labour Managed Enterprises*, London: Croom Helm.

1988. "Management design under labor management," *Journal of Comparative Economics*, 12: 1–23.

Itoh, H., 1987. "Information processing capacity of the firm," *Journal of the Japanese and International Economies*, 1: 299–326.

Jensen, Michael, 1986. "Agency costs of free cash flow corporate finance, and tax covers," *American Economic Review*, 76: 323–329.

1987. "Chaos," *Scientific American*, 75: 168–176.

Jensen, Michael and William Meckling, 1976. "Theory of the firm: managerial behavior, agency costs, and ownership structure," *Journal of Financial Economics*, 3: 305–360.

1979. "Rights and production functions: An application to labor-managed firms and codetermination," *Journal of Business*, 52: 469–506.

Jones, Derek C. and Jan Svejnar, 1985a. *Advances in the Economic Analysis of Participatory and Labor-Managed Firms*, Greenwich, CT: JAI Press.

1985b. "Participation, profit sharing, worker ownership and efficiency in Italian producer cooperatives, *Economica*, 52: 449–465.

Jones, Derek C. and Jan Svejnar (eds.), 1987. *Advances in the Economic Analysis of Participatory and Labour Managed Firms*, vol. 3, Greenwich, CT and London: JAI Press.

1991. *Advances in the Economic Analysis of Participatory and Labour Managed Firms*, Greenwich, CT and London: JAI Press.

Jones, S. R. G., 1984. *The Economics of Conformism*, Oxford: Basil Blackwell.

Jun, B., 1989. "Non-cooperative bargaining and union formation," *Review of Economic Studies*, 56: 59–76.

Kaen, F. R. and Rosenman, R. E., 1986. "Predictable behavior in financial markets: Some evidence in support of Heiner's hypothesis," *American Economic Review*, 76: 212–220.

Kagel, J., H. Rechlin, L. Green, R. Battalio, R. Basemann and W. Klemm, 1978. "Experimental studies of consumer demand behavior using laboratory animals," *Economic Inquiry*, 13: 22–39.

Kahneman, D., J. L. Knetsch and R. Thaler, 1986. "Fairness as a constraint on profit seeking: Entitlements in the market," *American Economic Review*, 76: 728–741.

Kahneman, D., P. Slovic and A. Tversky, 1982. *Judgement Under Uncertainty: Heuristics and Biases*, Cambridge: Cambridge University Press.

Kant, I., 1985, *Critique of Practical Reason*, trans. L. Beck, New York: Macmillan.

Kanter, Rosabeth M., 1983. *The Change Masters*, New York: Simon & Schuster.

Keeton, W., 1980. *Biological Science*, 3rd edn, New York: Wiley.

Keynes, John Maynard, 1930. *A Treatise on Money*, vol. 1, London: Macmillan.

Klein, Benjamin R. and Keith Leffler, 1981. "The role of market forces in assuring contractual performance," *Journal of Political Economy*, 89 (August): 615–641.

Klein, Benjamin, R. Crawford and Armen Alchian, 1978. "Vertical integration, appropriable rents, and the competitive contracting process," *Journal of Law and Economics*, 21: 297–326.

Knetsch, J. L., R. Thaler and D. Kahneman, 1987. "Experimental tests of the endowment effect and the Coase theorem," Economics Department, Cornell University.

Knight, Frank, 1921. *Risk, Uncertainty and Profit*, New York: Houghton Mifflin.

Kochan, Thomas, Harry Katz and Nancy Mower, 1985. "Worker participation and American unions," in Thomas Kochan (ed.), *Challenges and Choices Facing American Labor*, Cambridge, MA: MIT Press.

Kochan, Thomas A., John Paul MacDuffie and Paul Osterman, 1988. "Employment security at DEC: Sustaining values and environmental change," *Human Resource Management*, **27**(2) (Summer): 121–144.

Koike, Kazuo, 1988. *Understanding Industrial Relations in Modern Japan*, New York: St Martin's Press.

Kornai, János, 1980. *Economics of Shortage*, New York: North-Holland.

1982. *Growth, Shortage, and Efficiency: A Macrodynamic Model of the Socialist Economy*, Berkeley: University of California Press.

1986. "Soft budget constraint." *Kyklos:* 3–30.

1988. "Individual freedom and reform of the socialist economy," *European Economic Review*, **32**(2/3): 233–267.

Kreps, David, 1990a. "Corporate culture in economic theory," in J. Alt and K. Shepsle (eds.), *Positive Perspectives on Political Economy*, Cambridge: Cambridge University Press.

1990b. *A Course in Microeconomic Theory*, New York: Harvester Wheatsheaf.

Krueger, Anne, 1974. "The political economy of the rent seeking society," *American Economic Review*, **64** (June): 291–303.

Kunreuther, H., 1978. *Disaster Insurance Protection*, New York: Wiley.

Lange, Oskar and F. M. Taylor, 1938. *On the Economic Theory of Socialism*, Minneapolis: University of Minnesota Press.

Langlois, Richard (ed.), 1986. *Economics as a Process: Essays in the New Institutional Economics*, New York: Cambridge University Press.

Lawler, Edward, 1986. *High Involvement Management*, San Francisco: Jossey Bass.

Lazear, Edward P., 1981. "Agency, earnings profiles, productivity, and hours' restrictions," *American Economic Review*, **71**(4) (September): 606–620.

Leijonhufvud, Axel, 1986. "Capitalism and the factory system," in Langlois (1986).

Leland, J., 1986. "Individual choice under uncertainty: Finite discriminatory ability and systematic deviations from 'strict' rationality," Ph.D. Dissertation, Economics Department, UCLA.

Lerner, Abba, 1972. "The economics and politics of consumer sovereignty," *American Economic Review*, **62**.

Levine, D. I., 1991a. "Cohesiveness, productivity, and wage dispersion," *Journal of Economic Behavior and Organization*, **15** (March): 237–255.

1991b. "Just cause employment policies in the presence of worker adverse selection," *Journal of Labor Economics*, **9**(3) (July): 294–305.

1992a. "Demand variability and work organisation," Chapter 10 in this volume.

1992b. "Public policy implications of imperfections in the market for worker participation," *Economic and Industrial Democracy*, **13** (2) (May): 183–206.

Levine, David I. and Douglas Kruse, 1991. "Employee involvement efforts: Incidence and effects," **OBIR-49**, Haas School of Business, University of California, Berkeley.

Levine, David I. and Richard J. Parkin, 1993. "Work organization, employment security and macroeconomic stability," *Journal of Economic Behavior and Organization*,

Levine, David I. and George Strauss, 1989. "Employee participation and involvement," in

Investing in People, Report for the Commission on Workforce Quality and Labor Market Efficiency, Background papers, vol. II, paper **35b**, US Department of Labor (September): 1893–1948.

Levine, David I. and Laura d'Andea Tyson, 1990. "Participation, productivity, and the firm's environment," in Blinder (ed.) (1990).

Levy, D., 1988. "Utility-enhancing consumption constraints," *Economics and Philosophy*, **4**: 69–88.

Li, T. and J. A. Yorke, 1975. "Period three implies chaos," *American Mathematical Monthly*, **82**: 985–992.

Lincoln, James and Arne Kalleberg, 1990. *Culture, Control and Commitment*, Cambridge: Cambridge University Press.

Lindblom, Charles E., 1972. *Politics and Markets*, New York: Basic Books.

Lindemann, Albert S., 1983. *A History of European Socialism*, New Haven: Yale University Press.

Lindkvist, Lars and Ann Westenholz (eds.), 1987. *Medarbetaragda foretag i Norden* (Worker Owned Enterprises in the Nordic Countries), Copenhagen: Nordisk Ministerra.

Littler, C. R., 1982. *The Development of the Labor Process in Capitalist Societies*, London: Heineman.

Lucas, R. E., Jr., 1986. "Adaptive behavior and economic theory," *Journal of Business*, **59**: 401–426.

Mackenzie, Kenneth D., 1986. "Virtual position and power," *Management Science*, **32** (May): 622–642.

MacLeod, W. Bentley, 1984. "A theory of cooperative teams," *CORE Discussion Paper*, **8441**, Université Catholique de Louvain.

  1987. "Behavior and the organization of the firm," *Journal of Comparative Economics*, **11**: 207–220.

MacLeod, W. Bentley and J. M. Malcomson, 1988. "Reputation and hierarchy in dynamic models of employment," *Journal of Political Economy*, **96**: 832–854.

Mailath, G. and A. Postelwaite, 1990. "The worker vs. the firm: Bargaining over a firm's value," *Review of Economic Studies*, **57**: 369–380.

Malone, Thomas, 1987. "Modelling coordination in organizations and markets," *Management Science*, **33** (October): 1317–1332.

Manne, Henry G., 1965. "Mergers and the market for corporate control," *Journal for Political Economy*, **73**: 110–120.

Manning, Alan, 1981. "An asymmetrical information approach to the comparative analysis of participatory and capitalist firms," *Oxford Economic Papers*, **41**: 312–326.

  1989. "An symmetric information approach to the comparative analysis of participatory and capitalist firms," *Oxford Economic Papers*, **41**: 312–326.

Manz, Charles C. and Dennis Gioia, 1983. "The interrelationship of power and control," *Human Relations*, **5**: 459–476.

Marglin, Stephen, 1974. "What do bosses do?", *Review of Radical Political Economics*, **6** (1974): 60–112.

  1979. "Catching flies with honey: An inquiry into management initiatives to humanize work," *Economic Analysis and Workers' Management*, **13**: 473–495.

  1984. *Growth Distribution and Prices*, Cambridge, MA: Harvard University Press.

Marschak, Jacob and Roy Radner, 1972. *The Economic Theory of Teams*, New Haven: Yale University Press.

Marsden, P., 1986. *The End of Economic Man*, Brighton: Wheatsheaf.

Marx, Karl, 1967. *Capital: A Critique of Political Economy*, trans. Samuel Moore and Edward Aveling, ed. Frederick Engels, vol. 1, *The Process of Capitalist Production*, New York: International Publishers.

Maskin, Eric, 1988. "Nash equilibrium and welfare optimality," *Working Paper*, Cambridge, MA: MIT Press.

Masten, S., 1988. "A legal basis for the firm," *Journal of Law, Economics, and Organization*, 4: 181–198.

Mathewson, Stanley, 1931. *Restriction of Output Among Unorganized Workers*, New York, Viking Press.

Matthews, R.C.O. (ed.), 1985. *Economy and Democracy*, New York: St Martin's Press.

Maurice, M., F. Sellier and J. Silvestre, 1984. "The search for a societal effect in the production of company hierarchy: A comparison of France and Germany," in Osterman (1984).

Mazer, J. and A. Logue, 1978. "Choiced in a 'self-control paradigm': Effects of a fading procedure," *Journal of the Experimental Analysis of Behavior*, 30: 11–17.

McCall, J., 1965. "The economics of information and optimal stopping rules," *Journal of Business*, 38: 300–317.

Meade, James, 1972a. "The theory of labor-managed firms and of profit sharing, *Economic Journal*, 82 (Supp.): 402–428.

1972b. "The adjustment processes of labor co-operatives with constant returns to scale and perfect competition," *Economic Journal*, 82: 402–428.

1979. "The adjustment processes of labour co-operatives with constant returns to scale and perfect competition," *Economic Journal*, 89: 781–788.

1986a. *Alternative Systems of Business Organization and of Workers' Renumeration*, London: Allen & Unwin.

1986b. *Different Forms of Share Economy*, London: Public Policy Centre.

1989. *Agathotopia – The Economics of Partnership*, Aberdeen: Aberdeen University Press.

Meurs, Mieke, 1989. "Incentives, effort, and distribution in a socialist firm," *Working Paper*, 146, Department of Economics, American University.

Meyer, M., 1991. "Learning from coarse information: Biased contests and career profiles," *Review of Economic Studies*, 58: 15–41.

Milgrom, Paul and John Roberts, 1990a. "Bargaining costs, influence costs, and the organization of economic activity," in J. E. Alt and K. A. Sheple (eds.), *Perspectives on Positive Political Economy*, Cambridge: Cambridge University Press.

1990b. "The economics of modern manufacturing: Technology, strategy, and organization," *American Economic Review*, 80: 511–528.

Mill, John Stuart, 1958. *Considerations On Representative Government*, New York: Bobbs-Merrill.

Miller, D., 1990. *Market, State, and Community: Theoretical Foundations of Market Socialism*, Oxford: Oxford University Press.

Miller, Jeffrey and Peter Murrell, 1981. "Limitations on the use of information-revealing schemes in economic organizations," *Journal of Comparative Economics*, 5: 251–271.

Mintzkerg, Henry, 1979. *The Structure of Organization: A Synthesis of the Results*, Englewood Cliffs, NJ: Prentice-Hall.

Moene, Karl Ove, 1988. "Unions' threats and wage determination," *Economic Journal*, 98.

1989. "Strong unions or worker control?", in Jon Elster and Karl Moene (eds.), *Alternatives to Capitalism*, Cambridge: Cambridge University Press.

Moene, Karl Ove and Michael Wallerstein, 1993. "Collective bargaining versus workers' ownership." *Journal of Comparative Economics*, forthcoming.

Morishima, Michio, 1982. *Why Has Japan "Succeeded"? Western Technology and the Japanese Ethos*, Cambridge: Cambridge University Press.

Moulin, Hervé and Bezalel Peleg, 1982. "Cores of effectivity functions and implementation theory," *Journal of Mathematical Economics*, 10 (June): 115–145.

Mount, Kenneth and Stanley Reiter, 1974. "The informational size of message spaces," *Journal of Economic Theory*, 8: 161–192.

Murrell, Peter, 1984. "Incentives and income under market socialism," *Journal of Comparative Economics*, 8: 261–276.

Nano, George, 1988. Presentation before the Labor Center Reporter Editorial Group, Berkeley CA (September 12).

Nelson, Richard and Sidney Winter, 1982. *An Evolutionary Theory of Economic Change*, Cambridge, MA: Harvard University Press.

North, Douglass, C., 1981. *Structure and Change in Economic History*, New York: Norton.

1990a. "Institutions and economic growth: An historical introduction," in Vernon Ruttan (ed.), *Agriculture, Environment, and Health Institutional Innovation for Sustainable Development into the Twentieth Century*, Minneapolis: University of Minnesota.

1990b. *Institutions, Institutional Change and Economic Performance*, Cambridge: Cambridge University Press.

North, Douglass C. and Robert Thomas, 1972. *The Rise of the Western World: A New Economic History*, Cambridge: Cambridge University Press.

Nove, Alec, 1983. *The Economics of Feasible Socialism*, London: Allen & Unwin.

Nozick, Robert, 1974. *Anarchy, State, and Utopia*, New York: Basic Books.

Nuti, D. Mario, 1987a. "The share economy: Plausibility and viability of Weitzman's model," in Stefan Hedlund (ed.), *Incentives and Economic Systems*, London: Croom Helm: 267–290.

1987b. "Co-determination, profit-sharing and full employment," in Jones and Svejnar (eds.) (1987).

1987c. "Profit-sharing and employment: Claims and overclaims," *Industrial Relations*, 26(1) (Winter): 18–29.

1989. "The new Soviet cooperatives: advances and limitations," *Economic and Industrial Democracy*, 10: 311–327.

1991a. *On traditional cooperatives and James Meade's labour capital discriminating partnerships*, in Jones and Svejnar (eds.) (1991): 1–26.

1991b. "Limiti e potenziale dell'impresa cooperativa" (Limits and potential of the cooperative enterprise). Conference on "Cooperativa e impresa," *Associazione Generale Cooperative Italiane AGCI* (April).

Nutzinger, Hans G., 1982. "The economics of property rights – A new paradigm in social science?", in W. Stegmuller, W. Balzer and W. Spohm (eds.), *Philosophy of Economics*, Berlin: Springer-Verlag: 169–190.

Ognedal, Tone, 1990. "Unstable Ownership," paper presented at the SCASSS Uppsala Conference (18–21 June).

Okun, Arthur, 1975. *Equality and Efficiency: The Big Trade-Off*, Washington DC: Brookings.

Olson, Mancur, 1965. *The Logic of Collective Action*, Cambridge, MA: Harvard University Press.

Ortuño-Ortin, Ignacio, John Roemer and Joachim Silvestre, 1991. "Investment planning in market socialism: The proofs," Department of Economics, University of California, Davis, *Working Paper*, **356**.

Osterman, Paul, 1984. *Internal Labor Markets*, Cambridge, MA: MIT Press.

Ouchi, William, 1981. *Theory Z*, Avon, NY: Addison-Wesley.

Pagano, Ugo, 1985. *Work and Welfare in Economic Theory*, Oxford: Basil Blackwell.

1991a. "Property rights, asset specificity, and the division of labour under alternative capitalist relations," *Cambridge Journal of Economics*, **15**(3):315–342.

1991b. "Braverman," in P. Arestis and M. C. Sawyer, *Biographical Dictionary of Dissenting Economists*, Cheltenham: Edward Elgar.

1991c. "Organizational equilibria and institutional stability," *Economic Notes*, **20**(2): 189–228.

1992a. "Property rights equilibria and institutional stability," Chapter 6 in this volume.

1992b. "Authority, co-ordination and disequilibrium: an explanation of the co-existence of markets and firms," *Change Structural and Economic Dynamics* **3**(1): 53–77.

Pejovich, Svetozar, 1969. "The firm, monetary policy and property rights in a planned-economy," *Western Economic Journal*, **42**: 277–281.

Pfeffer, Jeffrey, 1981. *Power in Organizations*, Marshfield, MA: Pitman.

Piore, Michael and Charles E. Sabel, 1984. *The Second Industrial Divide*, New York: Basic Books.

Prasnikar, Janez and Jan Svejnar, 1991. "Workers' participation in management versus social ownership and government policies: Yugoslav lessons for transforming socialist economies," paper prepared for "Perspectives on Market Socialism" Conference, Berkeley, California (May).

Przeworski, Adam and John Sprague, 1986. *Paper Stones: A History of Electoral Socialism*, Chicago: University of Chicago Press.

Purcell, John, 1979. "A strategy for management control in industrial relations," in John Purcell, *The Control of Work*, London: Macmillan.

Putterman, Louis, 1982. "Some behavioral perspectives on the dominance of hierarchal over democratic forms of enterprise," *Journal of Economic Behavior and Organization*, **3**: 139–160.

1984. "On some recent explanations of why capital hires labor," *Economic Inquiry*, **22**: 171–187.

1986. *The Economic Nature of the Firm, A Reader*, Cambridge: Cambridge University Press.

1988a. "The firm as association versus the firm as commodity: Efficiency, rights, and ownership," *Economics and Philosophy*, **4**: 243–266.

1988b. "Marx and disequilibrium: Comment," *Economics and Philosophy*, **4**: 333–336.

1990. *Division of Labor and Welfare: An Introduction to Economic Systems*, Oxford: Oxford University Press.

Ramey, Garey and Valerie Ramey, 1990. "Are economic fluctuations costly?", UCSD, mimeo.

Rawls, John, 1971. *A Theory of Justice*, Cambridge, MA: Harvard University Press.

Rebitzer, James, 1987. "Unemployment, long term employment relations, and productivity growth," *Review of Economics and Statistics*, **69**(4) (November): 624–635.

Rebitzer, James and Lowell Taylor, 1988. "A model of dual labor markets when product demand is uncertain," University of Texas, Austin (July) mimeo.

Reiter, Stanley and Jonathan Hughes, 1981. "A preface on modeling the regulated U.S. economy," *Hofstra Law Review*, **9**.

Robbins, Lionel C., 1963. "Freedom and order," in Lionel C. Robbins, *Politics and Economics: Papers in Political Economy*, New York: St Martin's Press.

Robertson, Dennis H., 1930. *Control of Industry*, London: Nisbet & Co.

Romer, John, 1979. "Divide and conquer: Micro foundations of the Marxian theory of discrimination," *Bell Journal of Economics*, **10** (Autumn): 695–705.

1988a. *Free to Lose: An Introduction to Marxist Economic Philosophy*, London: Radius.

1988b. "Incentives and agency in socialist economies," xerox.

1990. "Incentives and agency in socialist economies," *Working Paper* **339**, Department of Economics, University of California.

Roemer, John (ed.), 1986. *Analytical Marxism*, Cambridge: Cambridge University Press.

Roemer, Thomas and Howard Rosenthal, 1979. "Bureaucrats versus voters: On the political economy of resource allocation by direct democracy," *Quarterly Journal of Economics*,**93**.

Roethlisberger, F. J. and W. J. Dickson, 1939. *Management and the Worker*, Cambridge, MA: Harvard University Press.

Romer, P., 1986. "Increasing returns and long run growth," *Journal of Political Economy*, **94**: 1002–1037.

Rosner, Menachem and Louis Putterman, 1991. "Factors behind the supply and demand for nonalienating work, and some international illustrations," *Journal of Economic Studies*, **18**(1): 18–41.

Ross, D., 1983. *The Right and the Good*, London: Oxford University Press.

Ross, Stephen, 1973. "The economic theory of agency: The principal's problem," *American Economic Review*, **63**: 134–139.

Rowthorn, Bob., 1988. "Solidaristic corporatism and labour process performance," in *Economics and Institutions: Proceedings of the International School of Economic Research*, Siena.

Rubinstein, Ariel, 1982. "Perfect equilibrium in a bargaining model," *Econometrica*, **50**:98–109.

Ryan, Paul, 1984. "Job training, employment practices, and the large enterprise: The case of costly transferable skills," in Osterman (1984).

Sacks, Stephen R., 1977. "Transfer prices in decentralized self-managed enterprises," *Journal of Comparative Economics*, **1**: 183–193.

Samuelson, Paul, 1952. "Wages and interest: A modern dissection of Marxian economics," *American Economic Review*, **47**.

Schelling, T., 1984., *Choice and Consequences*, Cambridge, MA: Harvard University Press.

Schlicht, Ekkehart, 1979. "The transition to labor management as a Gestalt shift," *Gestalt Theory*, **1**: 54–67.

Schlicht, Ekkehart and C. C. von Weiszäcker, 1977. "Risk financing in labour managed economies: The commitment problem," *Zeitschrift für Gesamte Staatwissenschaft*, **133**:33–66.

Schotter, Andrew, 1981. *The Economic Theory of Social Institutions*, Cambridge: Cambridge University Press.

Schumpeter, Joseph A., 1911/1942. *Capitalism, Socialism, and Democracy*, New York: Harper & Row.

Sen, Amartya, 1966. "Labor allocation in a cooperative enterprise," *Review of Economic Studies*, **33**: 361–371.

1967. "Isolation, assurance, and the social rate of discount," *Quarterly Journal of Economics*, **81**: 112–124.

1971. *Collective Choice and Social Welfare*, Amsterdam: North-Holland.

1977. "Rational fools: A critique of the behavioral foundations of economic theory," *Philosophy and Public Affairs*, **6** (Summer): 317–44.

Sertel, Murat R. 1982a. *Workers and Incentives*, New York: North-Holland.

1982b. "A rehabilitation of the labor-managed firm," in Murat Sertel (ed.), *Workers and Incentives*, Amsterdam: North-Holland.

1987. "Workers' enterprises are not perverse," *European Economic Review*, **31**: 1619–1625.

Shannon, C. and W. Weaver, 1963. *The Mathematical Theory of Communication*, Urbana: University of Illinois Press.

Shapiro, Carl and Joseph E. Stiglitz, 1984. "Unemployment as a worker discipline device," *American Economic Review*, **74**(3) (June): 433–444.

Shapiro, S. P., 1987. "The social control of impersonal trust," *American Journal of Sociology*, **16** (Winter): 623–658.

Shapley, L. S., 1953. "A value for n-person games," in L. S. Shapley, *Contributions to the Theory of Games*, Princeton: Princeton University Press.

Shavell, Steven, 1979. "Sharing and incentives in the principal and agent relationship," *Bell Journal of Economics*, **10**(1) (Spring): 55–73.

Simon, Herbert, 1951. "A formal theory of the employment relationship," *Econometrica*, **19**: 293–305.

1955. "A behavioral theory of rational choice," *Quarterly Journal of Economics*, **69**: 99–118.

Slovic, P. and Lichtenstein, S., 1983. "Preference reversals: A broader perspective," *American Economic Review*, **73**: 596–605.

Smith, V. L., 1985. "Experimental economics: Reply," *American Economic Review*, **75**: 264–268.

1986. "Experimental methods in the political economy of exchange," *Science*, **234**: 167–173.

Smith, V. L., G. L. Suchanek and A. W. Williams, 1988. "Bubbles, crashes, and endogenous expectations in experimental spot asset markets," *Econometrica*, **56**.

Solidarity, 1981. *Program*, accepted by the Congress of Delegates, Gdansk (October 7).

Solow, Robert, 1980. "On theories of unemployment," *American Economic Review*, **70**(1) (March): 1–11.

Sonnenschein, Hugo, 1973a. "Do Walras' identity and continuity characterize the class of community excess demand functions?", *Journal of Economic Theory*, **6**: 345–354.

1973b. "The utility hypothesis and market demand theory," *Western Economic Journal*, **11**: 404–410.

Stigler, G. J., 1981. "The economics of information," *Journal of Political Economy*, **89**.

Stiglitz, Joseph E., 1974. "Incentives and risk sharing in sharecropping," *Review of Economic Studies*, **41**: 219–256.

1985. "Credit markets and the control of capital," *Journal of Money, Credit and Banking*, **17**.

1987. "The causes and consequences of the dependence of quality on price," *Journal of Economic Literature*, **25** (March): 1–48.

Stiglitz, Joseph E. and Andrew Weiss, 1981. "Credit rationing in markets with imperfect information," *American Economic Review*, **71** (June): 393–411.

Strotz, R., 1956. "Myopia and dynamic consistency," *Review of Economic Studies*, **23**.

Sutton, J., 1986. "Non-cooperative bargaining theory: An introduction," *Review of Economic Studies*, **53**: 709–724.

Tannenbaum, Arnold, 1976. *Control in Organizations*, San Francisco: Jossey Bass.

Taylor, Barbara, 1983. *Eve and the New Jerusalem: Socialism and Feminism in the Nineteenth Century*, New York: Pantheon.

Taylor, Michael, 1987. *The Possibility of Cooperation*, Cambridge: Cambridge University Press.

Telser, Lester G., 1980. "A theory of self-enforcing agreements," *Journal of Business*, **41** (January): 27–4.

Thaler, Richard, 1990. "Saving, fungibility, and mental accounts," *Journal of Economic Perspectives*, **4**(1) (Winter): 193–205.

Thaler, Richard and S. Sheffrin, 1981. "A theory of consumer habits," *Journal of Political Economy*, **89**: 392–412.

Thomas, H. and C. Logan, 1982. *Mondragon: An Economic Analysis*, London: Allen & Unwin.

Thompson, P., 1983. *The Nature of Work: An Introduction to Debates on the Labour Process*, London: Macmillan.

Tirole, Jean, 1986. "Hierarchies and bureaucracies: On the role of collusion in organizations," *Journal of Law, Economics and Organization*, **2**: 181–214.

1988. "The multicontract organization," *Canadian Journal of Economics*, **21** (August): 459–475.

de Tocqueville, Alexis, 1969. *Democracy in America*, New York: Doubleday.

Tversky, A. and D. Kahneman, 1974. "The framing of decisions and the psychology of choice," *Science*, **185**: 1124–1128.

1986. "Rational choice and the framing of decisions," *Journal of Business*, **59**: 251–281.

Usher, Dan, 1981. *The Economic Prerequisite to Democracy*, New York: Columbia University Press.

Uvalic, Milica, 1991a. *The PEPPER Report* (Promotion of Employees' Participation in Profits and Enterprise Results), Brussels: DG-V EEC.

1991b. *Investment and Property Rights in Yugoslavia*, Cambridge: Cambridge University Press.

Vanek, Jaroslav, 1965. "Workers' profit participation, unemployment and the Keynesian equilibrium," *Weltwirtschaftliches Archiv*, **94**(2): 206–214.

1970. *The General Theory of Labor-Managed Market Economies*, Ithaca: Cornell University Press.

[1972] 1977. "The macroeconomic theory and policy of an open worker-managed economy" [1972], in Jaroslav Vanek, *The Labor-Managed Firm*, Ithaca: Cornell University Press: 239–255.

1977. "The basic theory of financing participatory firms," in Jaroslav Vanek, *The Labor Managed Economy: Essays by Jaroslav Vanek*, Ithaca: Cornell University Press: 186–198.

Vaughn, W. and R. J. Herrnstein, 1987. "Stability melioration, and natural selection," in L. Green and J. Kagel (eds.), *Advances in Behavioral Economics*, vol. 1, Norwood, NJ: Ablex Publishers.

Wachtel, Howard, 1973. *Workers' Management and Workers' Wages in Yugoslavia*, Ithaca: Cornell University Press.

Wallerstein, Michael, 1989. "Union organization in advanced industrial democracies," *American Political Science Review*, **83**: 481–501.

Walras, Leon, 1957. *Elements of Pure Economics*, London: George Allen & Unwin.

Ward, Benjamin N., 1958. "The firm in Illyria: Market syndicalism," *American Economic Review*, **48**(4) (December): 566–589.

1967, *The Socialist Economy: A Study of Organization Alternatives*, New York: Random House.

Weiner, Myron, 1987. "Empirical democratic theory," in Myron Weiner and E. Ozbudun (eds.), *Competitive Elections in Developing Countries*, Durham: Duke University Press.

Weitzman, Martin L., 1974. "Prices vs. quantities," *Review of Economic Studies*, **41**: 477–491.

1984. *The Share Economy*, Cambridge, MA: Harvard University Press.

1989. "A theory of wage dispersion and job market segmentation," *Quarterly Journal of Economics*, **104**(1) (February): 121–138.

Weitzman, Martin L. and Douglas L. Kruse, 1990. "Profit sharing and productivity," in Alan S. Blinder (ed.), *Evidence*: 95–141.

Whyte, William F. and Kathleen K. Whyte, 1988. *Making Mondragon: The Growth and Dynamics of the Worker Cooperative Complex*, Ithaca: ILR Press, Cornell University.

Wiener, Hans and Robert Oakeshott, 1987. *Worker-Owners: Mondragon Revisited*, London: Anglo-German Foundation for the Study of Industrial Society.

Williams, A. W., 1987. "The formation of price forecasts in experimental markets," *Journal of Money, Credit and Banking*, **19**: 1–18.

Williamson, Oliver E., 1975. *Markets and Hierarchies: Analysis and Anti-Trust Implications*, New York: Free Press.

1979. "Transactions-cost economics: The governance of contractual relations," *Journal of Law and Economics*, **22**: 233–61.

1980. "The organization of work: A comparative institutional assessment," *Journal of Economic Behavior and Organization*, **1**: 5–38.

1985. *The Economic Institutions of Capitalism: Firms, Markets, Relational Contracting*, New York: Free Press.

1987. "Transaction cost economics: The comparative contracting perspective," *Journal of Economic Behavior and Organization*, **8**: 617–625.

1988. "Internal economic organization," in O. Williamson, S.-E. Sjostrand and J. Johanson, *Perspectives on the Economics of Organization* (Crafoord Lectures, 1), Institute of Economic Research, Lund University: 9–48.

1990. "The firm as a nexus of treaties: An introduction," in Masahiko Aoki, Bo Gustafsson and Olive Williamson (eds.), *The Firm as a Nexus of Treaties*, London: Sage.

Author Index

Subject Index